# English Learners
# *in* STEM Subjects

## TRANSFORMING CLASSROOMS,
## SCHOOLS, *and* LIVES

David Francis and Amy Stephens, *Editors*

Committee on Supporting English Learners in STEM Subjects

Board on Science Education

Board on Children, Youth, and Families

Division of Behavioral and Social Sciences and Education

A Consensus Study Report of
*The National Academies of*
SCIENCES · ENGINEERING · MEDICINE

THE NATIONAL ACADEMIES PRESS
*Washington, DC*
**www.nap.edu**

THE NATIONAL ACADEMIES PRESS 500 Fifth Street, NW Washington, DC 20001

This activity was supported by a contract between the National Academy of Sciences and the National Science Foundation (#10003038). Any opinions, findings, conclusions, or recommendations expressed in this publication do not necessarily reflect the views of any organization or agency that provided support for the project.

International Standard Book Number-13: 978-0-309-47908-0
International Standard Book Number-10: 0-309-47908-8
Digital Object Identifier: https://doi.org/10.17226/25182
Library of Congress Control Number: 2018964628

Additional copies of this publication are available for sale from the National Academies Press, 500 Fifth Street, NW, Keck 360, Washington, DC 20001; (800) 624-6242 or (202) 334-3313; http://www.nap.edu.

Suggested citation: National Academies of Sciences, Engineering, and Medicine. (2018). *English Learners in STEM Subjects: Transforming Classrooms, Schools, and Lives*. Washington, DC: The National Academies Press. doi: https://doi.org/10.17226/25182.

*The National Academies of*
# SCIENCES · ENGINEERING · MEDICINE

The **National Academy of Sciences** was established in 1863 by an Act of Congress, signed by President Lincoln, as a private, nongovernmental institution to advise the nation on issues related to science and technology. Members are elected by their peers for outstanding contributions to research. Dr. Marcia McNutt is president.

The **National Academy of Engineering** was established in 1964 under the charter of the National Academy of Sciences to bring the practices of engineering to advising the nation. Members are elected by their peers for extraordinary contributions to engineering. Dr. C. D. Mote, Jr., is president.

The **National Academy of Medicine** (formerly the Institute of Medicine) was established in 1970 under the charter of the National Academy of Sciences to advise the nation on medical and health issues. Members are elected by their peers for distinguished contributions to medicine and health. Dr. Victor J. Dzau is president.

The three Academies work together as the **National Academies of Sciences, Engineering, and Medicine** to provide independent, objective analysis and advice to the nation and conduct other activities to solve complex problems and inform public policy decisions. The National Academies also encourage education and research, recognize outstanding contributions to knowledge, and increase public understanding in matters of science, engineering, and medicine.

Learn more about the National Academies of Sciences, Engineering, and Medicine at **www.nationalacademies.org**.

*The National Academies of*
# SCIENCES · ENGINEERING · MEDICINE

**Consensus Study Reports** published by the National Academies of Sciences, Engineering, and Medicine document the evidence-based consensus on the study's statement of task by an authoring committee of experts. Reports typically include findings, conclusions, and recommendations based on information gathered by the committee and the committee's deliberations. Each report has been subjected to a rigorous and independent peer-review process and it represents the position of the National Academies on the statement of task.

**Proceedings** published by the National Academies of Sciences, Engineering, and Medicine chronicle the presentations and discussions at a workshop, symposium, or other event convened by the National Academies. The statements and opinions contained in proceedings are those of the participants and are not endorsed by other participants, the planning committee, or the National Academies.

For information about other products and activities of the National Academies, please visit www.nationalacademies.org/about/whatwedo.

*v*

# Preface

English learners (ELs) comprise a diverse and multitalented pool of learners that is persistently increasing, both in absolute size and as a percentage of the U.S. school population. ELs span more than 350 language groups, represent diversity in cultural groups, and reach the full range of social classes within U.S. society. Such diversity is at once a strength of the EL population and a complication to finding simple solutions to improving science, technology, engineering, and mathematics (STEM) outcomes for the group writ large. Long-held accounting practices in education and U.S. policy complicate the development of a clear picture of the educational attainment of ELs. Thus, high school graduation rates, college going, and career choices among ELs are misestimated in many official statistics and reports because of the failure to consider those English-proficient students who began school as ELs.

These facts notwithstanding, ELs are underrepresented in STEM fields in college as well as in the workforce. These lower participation rates are made more troublesome by the ever-increasing demand for workers and professionals in STEM fields and by the disproportionate economic value that these jobs bring to society and, as a result, to the individuals employed in STEM fields. In general, jobs in STEM fields have higher earning potential than non-STEM jobs, and the number of jobs in STEM have outpaced all other fields since 1990. Opening avenues to success in STEM for the nation's ELs offers a path to improved earning potential, income security, and economic opportunity for these students and their families. At least as important, increasing the diversity of the STEM workforce confers benefits to the society as a whole, not only due to the improved economic circumstances for a substantial segment of society, but also because diversity in the STEM workforce will bring new ideas and new solutions to STEM challenges. Organizing schools and preparing teachers so that all students can reach their full potential in STEM has the potential to transform the lives of individual students, as well as the lives of the teachers, the schools, and society as a whole.

In the report that follows, the committee attempts to determine what can be learned from the research literature to help guide improvements in the educational system, through improved assessments and assessment practices; reporting and classification; improved instruction that recognizes the central role that content area instruction plays in children's language development and content area achievement; leveraging connections to home, culture, and school; better preparation of teachers and administrators; and the establishment of federal, state, and local policies that will build and sustain capacity of school systems to allow all ELs to reach their full potential as STEM learners.

The report is essentially organized into three sections. The first set of chapters were provided by the committee in an effort to detail the essential background that readers must understand to benefit from the reviews of the literature in the subsequent chapters and the resultant conclusions and recommendations that follow from the committee's deliberations. The committee found throughout its conversations that we shared a patchwork of common understanding about ELs as a population, about the schools and programs that serve these students, about the roles of standards in each of the STEM disciplines, and about the symbiotic central importance of language to the development of content area proficiency and of active engagement in content area learning to the development of language. I believe that it is fair to say that each of us had some understanding of portions of the overlapping patchwork, but none of us had as firm an understanding of the entire patchwork at the outset as we do today. Our objective in providing the early framing chapters was to detail, as best as possible, the essential background knowledge that guided our organization of the literature, and our thinking regarding the pieces and how they fit together. These chapters provide the *givens* that defined the starting point for the committee, and that we felt must be understood by the reader as the essential context for the chapters that detail our reviews, conclusions, and recommendations.

Throughout its work, the committee kept its focus on the students, teachers, administrators, parents, families, communities, policy makers, and researchers, as well as the specific roles that each plays in the STEM attainment of ELs and the challenges that each faces in effectively fulfilling its role. Our perspective is very much an educational systems perspective, but our focus in individual chapters was necessarily on specific components of the system. I hope that this systems perspective comes through in the individual chapters albeit in a more limited scope. This perspective is critical to real, substantial, and sustainable improvement. Focusing singularly on assessment, on instruction, on home-school connections, or on teacher preparation will not achieve what is possible through orchestrated, persistent, system-wide efforts. Coordinated effort is more difficult to achieve than concentrated effort by a single individual or type of individual, but ultimately more effective and more sustainable. I hope that each of the groups mentioned above finds specific, actionable steps that it can take to improve STEM outcomes for ELs. More importantly I hope that this report will motivate members of each of these groups to work together to create focused, system-wide effort toward the goal of allowing each child who enters a U.S. school as an EL to reach her or his full potential in STEM and proficiency in English.

This report has been a labor of love for each of the committee members. To a person, the committee worked exceptionally hard to complete its work and produce this consensus report. Each individual's commitment to working as a part of the team to develop a shared understanding of the students, the teachers, the homes and families, and the components of the educational system and what can be done to improve ELs' STEM outcomes was remarkable. The committee was beyond fortunate to have Dr. Amy Stephens as the study director. Her steady hand, expert knowledge of the content and process, personal support of each of the committee members, and shear perseverance and hard work down the stretch made the impossible not only possible, but also enjoyable. I cannot thank her enough.

In closing, I hope that readers will find much value in this consensus committee report of the National Academies and that individuals will be personally motivated to do their part in contributing to improved STEM education for ELs. While many questions remain unanswered by the current research literature, the report outlines what can be done now and what steps can be taken to guide future steps through research.

David Francis, *Chair*
Committee on Supporting English Learners in STEM Subjects

# Acknowledgments

This Consensus Study Report represents the work of many individuals, especially those who served on the committee and participated in the committee's open sessions. The first thanks are to the committee members for their deep knowledge and contributions to the study.

This report was made possible by the important contributions of the National Science Foundation. We particularly thank Julio Lopez-Ferrao, program director in the Division of Research on Learning in Formal and Informal Settings (EHR/DRL), who advocated for this study.

The committee benefited from presentations by, and discussions with, the many individuals who participated in our fact-finding meetings. We thank Julie Bianchini, University of California, Santa Barbara; Rebecca Callahan, The University of Texas at Austin; Sylvia Celedón-Pattichis, University of New Mexico; Daryl Greenfield, University of Miami; Tom Humphries, University of California, San Diego; Kara Jackson, University of Washington; Bill McCallum, University of Arizona; Kylie Peppler, Indiana University, Bloomington; Nancy Songer, Drexel University; Julie Sugarman, Migration Policy Institute; Ruby Takanishi, New America; Karen Thompson, Oregon State University; Sara Tolbert, University of Arizona; Sultan Turkan, Educational Testing Service; Claudio Vargas, coordinator of science programs K–12 in California's Oakland Unified School District; Mark Warschauer, University of California, Irvine; and Amelia Wenk Gotwals, Michigan State University.

This Consensus Study Report has been reviewed in draft form by individuals chosen for their diverse perspectives and technical expertise. The purpose of this independent review is to provide candid and critical comments that will assist the National Academies of Sciences, Engineering, and Medicine in making its published report as sound as possible and to ensure that it meets institutional standards for objectivity, evidence, and responsiveness to the study charge. The review comments and draft manuscript remain confidential to protect the integrity of the deliberative process. We thank the following individuals for their review of this report: Diane L. August, Center for English Language Learners, American Institutes for Research; Filiberto Barajas-López, Mathematics Education, University of Washington; George C. Bunch, Education Department, University of California, Santa Cruz; Ester de Jong, School of Teaching and Learning, University of Florida; Richard P. Duran, Graduate School of Education, University of California, Santa Barbara; Kara Jackson, College of Education, University of Washington; Robert Linquanti, California Comprehensive Center, WestEd; Luciana C. Oliveira, Department of Teaching and Learning, University of Miami; Maria Chiara Simani, California Science Project, Department of Physics and Astronomy, University of California, Riverside; and Karen Thompson, College of Education, Oregon State University.

Although the reviewers listed above provided many constructive comments and suggestions, they were not asked to endorse the content of the report nor did they see the final draft of the report before its release. The review of this report was overseen by Donna Christian, senior fellow, Center for Applied Linguistics and Douglas S. Massey, Department of Sociology, Princeton University. They were responsible for making certain that an independent examination of this report was carried out in accordance with the standards of the National Academies and that all review comments were carefully considered. Responsibility for the final content of this report rests entirely with the authoring committee and the National Academies.

Thanks are also due to the project staff: Amy Stephens of the Board on Science Education (BOSE) directed the study. Tiffany Taylor helped with drafting and editing parts of the report (transitioning from a Christine Mirzayan science and technology policy fellow to a research associate during this project). Kenne Dibner, program officer with BOSE, and Suzanne Le Menestrel, senior program officer with the Board on Children, Youth, and Families, were instrumental in thinking through committee dynamics during meetings and about engaging key stakeholder groups. Margaret Kelly managed the study's logistical and administrative needs, and Leticia Garcilazo Green stepped in at the end to help with study completion. Heidi Schweingruber, director of BOSE, provided thoughtful advice and helpful suggestions throughout the entire process.

Staff of the Division of Behavioral and Social Sciences and Education also provided help: Paula Whitacre edited and substantially improved the readability of the report; Kirsten Sampson Snyder expertly guided the report through the review process, and Yvonne Wise masterfully guided the report through production.

# Contents

# Summary

nglish learners (ELs) bring a wealth of resources to science, technology, engineering, and mathematics (STEM) learning, including knowledge and interest in STEM-related content that is born out of their experiences in their homes and communities, home languages, variation in discourse practices, and, in some cases, experiences with schooling in other countries. ELs are those students ages 3 through 21, enrolled in an elementary or secondary school, not born in the United States or whose native language is a language other than English, and whose proficiency in speaking, reading, writing, or understanding the English language may be sufficient to deny the individual the ability to successfully achieve in classrooms where the language of instruction is English. The diversity of ELs includes heterogeneity in cultures, languages, and experiences that may have an impact on these students' education (including the contexts that expose them to risk factors that may have negative impacts). Federal, state, and local policies can either facilitate ELs' opportunities in STEM or constrain teaching and learning in ways that are detrimental. This report addresses the factors that affect ELs' access and opportunity to rigorous, grade-appropriate STEM learning.

The National Science Foundation commissioned the National Academies of Sciences, Engineering, and Medicine to examine the research on ELs' learning, teaching, and assessment in STEM subjects, including the role of language in learning STEM, successful programs for ELs or interventions both within the United States and abroad, and the learning needs of preservice and in-service STEM teachers with respect to ELs in PreK–12. The committee was asked to consider the complex social and academic use of language delineated in the new mathematics and science standards, the diversity of the population of ELs, and the integration of English as a second language instruction with core instructional programs in STEM. The committee was also asked to consider all children and youth who are learning and speaking a language other than English at home (often referred to as dual- or multi-language learners) and give particular attention to students who have limited English skills and may have been formally identified as such by the school or district.[1] What follows are some core findings discussed within the different chapters of the report.

## CORE FINDINGS

### Educational Context

Inconsistencies in the classification of ELs is an undercurrent that has substantial implications for understanding ELs' performance in STEM, given that it affects everything from policy to research to instruction. The practice of excluding recently English-proficient ELs from the EL accountability group leads to overestimation of academic achievement gaps in STEM between ELs and non-ELs, and consequently to misperceptions of ELs' STEM proficiency and ineffective policy responses. Moreover, some schools operate under the incorrect assumption that English proficiency is a prerequisite to meaningfully engage with STEM learning. However, the research suggests that a shift is needed by recognizing the assets that ELs bring to the classroom and understanding that some deficits in student performance arise from lack of access and not from limited ability, language proficiency, or cultural differences.

### STEM Learning and English Language Development

ELs develop STEM knowledge and language proficiency when they are engaged in meaningful interaction in the classroom that includes participation in the kinds of activities in which STEM experts and professionals regularly engage. Whereas there is no language without content, there is some content that is less dependent on language. STEM subjects afford opportunities for alternate routes to knowledge acquisition (i.e., experimentation, demonstration of phenomena, and demonstration of practices) through which students can gain a sense of STEM content without resorting predominantly to language to access meaning—it is through this experience that language is also learned. The committee acknowledges that just as language develops, students develop increasingly sophisticated understandings

---

[1]The full statement of task appears in Box 1-1 in Chapter 1.

of core disciplinary ideas; as such, engaging ELs early in their education when their peers are also gaining exposure to STEM content is important.

## Effective Instructional Strategies and Teacher Education

A review of the evidence on instructional strategies suggests that teachers of ELs who effectively engage with these students are more likely to understand that language is learned through meaningful and active engagement by ELs with language in the context of authentic STEM activities and practices. They encourage ELs to draw on their full range of linguistic and communicative competencies and resources while guiding them toward a focus on STEM meaning-making. Effective teachers of ELs also engage in experiences that foster self-reflection about their assumptions regarding diverse students' and families' engagement with STEM and STEM education. However, although the committee identified many instructional strategies that show great promise for ELs in building disciplinary content knowledge, access to practices, and language proficiency, less effective instructional strategies are still used. This may be related in part to the evidence showing that STEM teachers are not adequately prepared to provide robust learning opportunities that foster simultaneous content knowledge and language development in their classrooms.

## The Role of Families and Communities

Children are members of families and larger social communities that help to shape their knowledge and interest in school and in STEM. Families and communities are resources that can bolster schools' efforts to engage ELs in STEM learning. Effective family and community engagement models for ELs in STEM recognize and make connections to families' and communities' cultural and linguistic practices as they relate to STEM topics. Such models can help teachers and schools shift to an asset orientation toward ELs' STEM learning, can increase the engagement of families of ELs in other school-based activities, and can improve ELs' motivation in their STEM learning.

## Assessment

The committee identified several challenges in EL testing practice and policy to include the fact that language is the means through which tests are administered, limiting the extent to which appropriate generalization can be made about ELs' academic achievement based on test scores alone. With respect to classroom formative and summative assessments, the research is nascent with respect to ELs, limiting the understanding of linguistically diverse groups and classrooms. Overall, it is imperative that ELs be included during large-scale and classroom-level test development and teacher preparation/professional learning to better reflect the heterogeneity of EL populations, leading to fair, valid, and reliable assessment measures.

## Building Capacity to Transform STEM Learning

Policies at the federal, state, and local levels can either facilitate ELs' opportunities in STEM or constrain teaching and learning in ways that are detrimental to ELs' access to and success in STEM learning. School districts demonstrating success with teaching ELs in STEM have leaders who attend to system coherence and do so by designing and implementing organizational structures that enable the integration of language and content within and between levels (i.e., state, district, school) and components of the system (e.g., instruction, curriculum, assessment, professional development, policies for categorization of ELs). Integration of STEM learning and English language learning is possible but may require adjustment to the allocation of fiscal and human resources. Some systems that have succeeded in supporting ELs in STEM have demonstrated flexibility in allocating and aligning fiscal and human resources in service of their desired objectives.

## RECOMMENDATIONS

Following its analysis of the available information, the committee reached consensus on a set of conclusions and recommendations. The conclusions and recommendations, as well as a research agenda, to identify gaps in the current research are discussed in Chapter 9. The full set of recommendations are included in the summary below.

RECOMMENDATION 1: Evaluate current policies, approaches, and resources that have the potential to negatively affect English learners' (ELs') access to science, technology, engineering, and mathematics (STEM) learning opportunities, including classification and reclassification, course-taking, classroom instruction, program models offered, professional development, staffing, and fiscal resources, etc.

- Federal agencies should evaluate the ways in which funds are allocated for research and development that would enhance teaching and learning in STEM for ELs, including efforts that foster pipeline and training programs to increase the number of teachers qualified to teach STEM to ELs.
- States should evaluate their definition of EL including proper specification of entrance and exit procedures and criteria for districts.

Districts should examine the policies and procedures that are in place for consistently implementing these state procedures/criteria for classifying/reclassifying ELs.

- States should evaluate policies associated with the timing of large-scale state assessments and waivers for assessment (i.e., waivers for science assessment), frameworks for teacher certification, and the distribution of financial and human resources.
- District leaders and school personnel should examine (a) the program models and placement of ELs in STEM courses with particular attention to grade bands as well as issues associated with overrepresentation of ELs in remedial courses, (b) preparation of STEM teachers with attention to schools with large EL populations, (c) the opportunities for teacher collaboration and professional development, and (d) the distribution of financial and human resources.
- Schools should evaluate ELs' success in STEM classes, the quality of STEM classroom instruction and the positioning of ELs in the classroom, the qualifications of teachers hired, the professional development opportunities offered to teachers, and the resources (e.g., time and space) allocated to STEM learning.

RECOMMENDATION 2: Develop a high-quality framework to identify and remove barriers to English learners' (ELs') participation in rigorous science, technology, engineering, and mathematics (STEM) learning opportunities.

- District and school leaders should identify and enact norms of shared responsibility for success of ELs in STEM both within the district central office and within schools, developed by teams of district and school leaders associated with STEM and English language development/English as a second language education.
- States should take an active role in collecting and sharing resources across schools and districts.
- Leaders in states, districts, and schools should continuously evaluate, monitor, and refine policies to ensure that ELs' STEM learning outcomes are comparable to their never-EL peers.

RECOMMENDATION 3: Equip teachers and teacher candidates with the requisite tools and preparation to effectively engage and positively position English learners (ELs) in science, technology, engineering, and mathematics (STEM) content learning.

- Preservice teacher education programs should require courses that include learning research-based practices on how to best support ELs in learning STEM subjects.
- Preservice teacher education programs and providers of in-service professional development should provide opportunities to engage in field experiences that include ELs in both classroom settings and informal learning environments.
- English as a second language teacher education programs and providers of in-service professional development should design programs that include collaboration with teachers of STEM content to support ELs' grade-appropriate content and language learning in STEM.
- Teacher educators and professionals involved in pre- and in-service teacher learning should develop resources for teachers, teacher educators, and school and district leaders that illustrate productive, research-based instructional practices for supporting ELs in STEM learning.
- Preservice teacher education and teacher credentialing programs should take account of teacher knowledge of large-scale STEM assessment interpretation, classroom summative task design, and formative assessment practices with ELs.

RECOMMENDATION 4: Develop high-quality science, technology, engineering, and mathematics (STEM) curricular materials and integrate formative assessment into classroom practice to both facilitate and assess English learners' (ELs') progress through the curriculum.

- Curriculum developers, educators, and EL researchers should work together to develop curricular materials and resources that consider the diversity of ELs' needs as the materials are being developed and throughout the design process.
- EL researchers, curriculum developers, assessment professionals, teacher educators, professional learning providers, and teachers should work collaboratively to strengthen teachers' formative assessment skills to improve STEM instruction and promote ELs' learning.

RECOMMENDATION 5: Encourage and facilitate engagement with stakeholders in English learners' (ELs') local environment to support science, technology, engineering, and mathematics (STEM) learning.

- Schools and districts should reach out to families and caregivers to help them understand the available instructional programs in

STEM and the different academic and occupational opportunities related to STEM, including what resources might be available in the community.

- Schools and districts should collaborate with community organizations and form external partnerships with organizations that focus on informal STEM learning to make an active effort to directly engage ELs and their caregivers in STEM-related learning activities in an effort to understand their EL families' and communities' assets and needs.

RECOMMENDATION 6: Design comprehensive and cohesive science, technology, engineering, and mathematics (STEM) assessment systems that consider English learners (ELs) and the impact of those assessments on STEM academic achievement for all students.

- Developers of large-scale STEM assessments need to develop and use population sampling frameworks that better reflect the heterogeneity of EL populations to ensure the proper inclusion of statistically representative samples of ELs in the process of test development according to sociodemographic variables including language proficiency, first language, geographical distribution, and socioeconomic status.
- Decision makers, researchers, funding agencies, and professionals in the relevant fields need to develop standards on the numbers and characteristics of students that need to be documented and reported in projects and contracts involving EL STEM assessment.

RECOMMENDATION 7: Review existing assessment accommodation policies and develop accessibility resources.

- States, districts, and schools need to review their existing policies regarding the use of accommodations during accountability assessments to ensure that English learners (ELs) are afforded access to those linguistic accommodations that best meet their needs during instruction as well as during assessment.
- States, districts, and schools should also examine their implementation of accommodations to ensure that accommodations are implemented with high fidelity for all ELs, take steps to improve implementation when high fidelity is not realized, and improve poor implementation when it is present.
- States and districts involved in developing new computer-administered assessments or revising existing computer-administered

assessments, should develop those assessments to incorporate accessibility resources rather than rely on accommodations.

- States involved in the development of new science, technology, engineering, and mathematics assessments should apply universal design principles in the initial development and consider ELs from the beginning.

# 1

# Introduction

The imperative that all students, including English learners (ELs), achieve high academic standards and have opportunities to participate in science, technology, engineering, and mathematics (STEM) learning has become even more urgent and complex given shifts in science and math standards. As a group, these students are underrepresented in STEM fields in college and in the workforce at a time when the demand for workers and professionals in STEM fields is unmet and increasing. Jobs in STEM have outpaced all other fields since 1990 (Pew Research Center, 2018), and although the number of underrepresented minorities in STEM fields has also increased over this period, they still represent a diminishing proportion of the STEM workforce. According to Funk and Parker (Pew Research Center, 2018), Hispanics comprise 16 percent of the U.S. workforce, but only 7 percent of the STEM workforce. These data do not speak directly to the underrepresentation of ELs in STEM fields because EL status during K–12 schooling cannot be inferred from ethnicity, and because ELs come from many ethnic segments of society. Nonetheless, reduced participation and success in STEM coursework in high school and college among ELs lend support to such an inference based on workforce participation data. At the same time, jobs in STEM fields have higher earning potential than non-STEM jobs. Opening avenues to success in STEM for the nation's ELs offers a path to improved earning potential, income security, and economic opportunity for these students and their families. At least as important, increasing the diversity of the STEM workforce confers benefits to society as a whole, not simply due to the improved economic circumstances for a substantial segment of society, but also because diversity in the STEM workforce will bring new ideas and new solutions to STEM challenges. Organizing schools and preparing teachers so that all students can reach their full potential in STEM has the potential to transform the lives of individual students, as well as the lives of the teachers, the schools, and society as a whole.

The term *EL* used throughout the report is consistent with the federal definition:[1] a student who is ages 3 through 21, enrolled in an elementary or secondary school, not born in the United States or whose native language is a language other than English, and whose proficiency in speaking, reading, writing, or understanding the English language may be sufficient to deny the individual the ability to successfully achieve in classrooms where the language of instruction is English. These students are instructed under a variety of different program models (including English as a second language [ESL] approaches as well as bilingual approaches) intended to support both language and content learning (U.S. Department of Education, 2012).

Supporting ELs to develop disciplinary content and language simultaneously has been a focus of educational policies throughout this century (e.g., the Civil Rights Act of 1964, the Bilingual Education Act enacted in 1968, the Equal Educational Opportunity Act of 1974, and the No Child Left Behind Act of 2002). This evolution in federal policy reflects modern understandings of the intricate interplay between language and content, specifically the fundamental role that language plays in academic proficiency, and the reciprocal role that content learning plays in language development (Lee, 2018). Language and content are learned in tandem, not separately or sequentially. At its core, this realization makes clear that language proficiency is not a prerequisite for content instruction, but an outcome of effective content instruction. Moreover, the direction of this relationship (i.e., that language proficiency standards align to content standards and not the other way around) suggests that the language to be learned needs to focus on the important STEM content and what is known about how children learn STEM content. As content standards are continuously evolving, English language proficiency (ELP) standards must also change and evolve (Lee, 2018).

The National Science Foundation requested the Board on Science Education of the National Academies of Sciences, Engineering, and Medicine to examine the state of the research on ELs' learning, teaching, and assessment in STEM subjects, including the role of language in learning STEM, with respect to ELs in PreK–12.

---

[1]According to Section 9101(25) of the Elementary and Secondary Education Act (ESEA) of 1965.

## EVOLUTION OF RESEARCH ON LANGUAGE
## AND STEM LEARNING

College- and career-ready standards present both opportunities and challenges for ELs, necessitating that educators at multiple levels of the education system develop new areas of expertise. Historically, within the classroom, STEM content learning has been considered the province of STEM content educators, while language learning has been considered the province of language educators. Current understanding of the co-development of language and content necessitates that educators of STEM content are familiar with the nature of language, language learning, and exemplary STEM instruction that includes attention to language. To achieve this objective, educators of STEM content must learn to interrogate their preconceived notions and tacit assumptions about language, starting with the most fundamental, though rarely discussed, question, "What is language?" In the same way, language educators will need to become familiar with the nature of STEM content areas. To use science as an example, language educators should ask the question, "What is science?" They will need to understand how STEM subjects are conceptualized in modern standards, such as how science is conceptualized in the *Next Generation Science Standards* (NGSS Lead States, 2013), as these standards reflect the field's most current conceptualization. In the case of mathematics, language educators and math educators who work with ELs will need to know how research has answered the questions, "What is mathematics proficiency? How do students learn mathematics through using language?"

Appreciation of the role of language in content learning has developed over time with historical roots dating back to the last quarter of the previous century. To understand current research and practice in STEM teaching and in the education of ELs requires working knowledge of some of the more salient elements of that history. In this section, we provide a brief overview of the historical developments behind current thinking about the intersection of language development, STEM learning, and STEM education of ELs. This overview is not exhaustive, but provides an essential, albeit brief, historical context for the current charge and report.

### Research on Language Among English Learners

As ELs increased in numbers and became a focus of attention in K–12 classrooms, the first response was to prepare ESL teachers who would teach English to ELs in separate classrooms and then send them to "content" classrooms once they had developed sufficient proficiency. An early response of the field of TESOL (Teachers of English to Speakers of Other Languages) to the challenge of ELs keeping up with grade-level learning in K–12 contexts was the emergence of "content-based language teaching" (Mohan, 1986; Short, 1993; Snow, Met, and Genesee, 1989). This approach recognized that children best learn language if it is taught in meaningful contexts of use, and that for children in school, the meaningful contexts are the subject areas. This idea was further supported by the work of Cummins (1981); in particular, he made a distinction between informal conversational language and more formal academic language in his research on children developing bilingual competence at school. This distinction generated controversy from the beginning (see Cummins, 2000, for discussion), but has nonetheless proved valuable in drawing attention to the many ways that individuals use and understand language in education, as well as more generally. Nevertheless, as "content-based language teaching" developed, it was unclear how the relationship between "content learning" and "language learning" was to be articulated.

During the same time period, research was increasingly pointing to the need for explicit attention to language itself as part of the second-language learning process in school contexts, as exposure to the language alone did not lead to development of proficiency (see Lightbown and Spada, 2013; Spada and Tomita, 2010, for reviews). Whereas initially this research primarily studied the ways teachers helped ELs use English with greater accuracy by providing feedback on errors, subsequently the main focus of research on English development has changed in recognition that learners inevitably make errors as they expand their meaning-making repertoires (Valdés, 2005).

One issue in research on ELs is the use of the construct *academic language*.[2] Introduced by Cummins through his notion of CALP (cognitive academic language proficiency), this term has been widely employed since the 1980s to describe the language children are exposed to and that they may need to develop to succeed in schools. The term has been critiqued as presenting a "symbolic language border" (Valdés, 2016, p. 330) that can be detrimental if ELs are seen to bring only limited language resources to STEM education, but we use it in this report to describe the range of *registers* used in STEM learning. *Register* refers to the variation in language choices that people make in engaging in a range of activities throughout the day. Chapter 3 develops this definition, illustrating how the *content* to be learned, the kinds of *interactions* students are expected to engage in, and the linguistic and nonlinguistic *modalities* they use for meaning-making shape the language choices they make. Understanding academic language as part of a set of *registers* positions it as more than just disciplinary vocabulary that can tend to be the focus, and enables the recognition of

---

[2]For example, the *Promising Futures* report (NASEM, 2017), like many current reports on ELs, refers to *academic language*.

and research on sentence and discourse dimensions of language that make broader and often discipline-specific demands on students in the classroom (e.g., Bailey, 2010; Bailey et al., 2007; Bunch, 2014; Chamot and O'Malley, 1994; Gibbons, 2002; Schleppegrell, 2004, 2007; Zwiers, 2007).

## Mathematics Learning with English Learners

Research on mathematics learning with ELs over the past 30 to 40 years shows movement toward new ways of conceptualizing the meaning of "mathematics language," the definitions of mathematics activity, and a focus on resources rather than obstacles. Early studies of bilingual mathematics learners failed to include bilingualism as a resource, framing the "problem" as one entirely owing to linguistic challenges: solving word problems, understanding individual vocabulary terms, or translating from English to mathematics symbols (Cocking and Mestre, 1988; Cuevas, 1984; Spanos and Crandall, 1990). Later studies developed a broader view of mathematics activity, examining not only responses to arithmetic computation, reasoning, and problem solving, but also the strategies children used to solve arithmetic word problems (Secada, 1991), and student conceptions of two-digit quantities (Fuson et al., 1997).

Since these early studies focused on carrying out arithmetic computation and solving word problems, conclusions were limited to these two mathematics topics. It was not possible to generalize from studies on arithmetic computation and algebra word problems to other topics in mathematics, such as geometry, measurement, probability, or proportional reasoning. Following the failure of an emphasis on only procedural skills, research has focused on approaches that include the other strands of mathematics proficiency, especially conceptual understanding and reasoning, as well as mathematics discourse (Cobb, Wood, and Yackel, 1993; Forman, 1996; Lampert, 1990; Moschkovich, 2007) (see Chapter 3). Additional research has begun to explore how students use and connect their linguistic and cultural resources to the learning of mathematics (Barajas-López and Aguirre, 2015; Domínguez, 2011).

## Science Learning with English Learners

The general direction of early research on science learning with ELs did not attend to the practical need for all students to meet the full range of science standards or abilities while also developing English proficiency. In the 1990s, studies of disciplinary practices in science education emerged from the scholarship of science studies—the empirical study of science communities. Sociology and anthropology of science identified the important ways that science is constructed through discourse and social practices (Kelly and

Chen, 1999; Latour, 1987; McGinn and Roth, 1999). Much of the early literature on effective science instruction with ELs focused on engaging ELs in hands-on activities to make science concrete and experiential while reducing language load. In addition, discrete science process skills (e.g., hypothesizing, observing, inferring, predicting) were perceived as compatible with language functions (e.g., describing, summarizing, reporting). Focusing on the social and discourse practices of science education began to situate instances of talk and action around meaning-making in ongoing social and cultural practices of the specified classroom, laboratory group, museum, or other educational setting.

Lemke's *Talking Science* (1990) was a seminal work in science education. This study of primarily teacher-led discourse practices identified the important ways that the thematic content of scientific knowledge was instantiated in secondary science classrooms. Through detailed linguistic analysis of discourse processes, Lemke identified the many ways that science can be obscure, difficult, and alienating to students. This study opened up the field to take a closer look at the various discourse processes and practices of science.

Studies of discourse in science education have identified ways that student interests, narratives, and personal and cultural worlds contribute to how they are positioned and how they come to see themselves as science learners (Brown, 2006; Varelas et al., 2008; Varelas, Kane, and Wylie, 2012). Given the variation in students' home culture and language practices, educators have sought to understand how students' cultural knowledge, affiliations, and identities are constructed within the context of science learning (Bang, 2015; Bang et al., 2013; Hudicourt-Barnes, 2003; Warren et al., 2001).

## CHARGE TO THE COMMITTEE

The Board on Science Education of the National Academies of Sciences, Engineering, and Medicine, in collaboration with the Board on Children, Youth, and Families, convened an expert committee to synthesize the existing evidence base on supporting EL students in STEM subjects from PreK–12 and provide guidance on how to improve learning outcomes in STEM for these students (see Box 1-1). The study explored both the research evidence and successful programs/interventions to identify promising practices for supporting ELs in STEM. It considered the needs of STEM teachers with respect to instruction and issues related to the valid and reliable assessment of ELs.

**BOX 1-1**
**Statement of Task**

The committee will examine research on supporting ELs PreK–12 in learning, teaching, and assessment in STEM subjects, including the role of language in learning STEM; successful programs or interventions both within the United States and abroad, and the learning needs of both preservice and in-service STEM teachers with respect to ELs. The committee will consider the complex social and academic use of language delineated in the new math and science standards, the diversity of the population of ELs (e.g., age, language proficiency, country of origin, culture and community, SES, disability status), and the integration of English as a second language instruction with core instructional programs in STEM. In the context of the study, the committee will consider all children and youth who are learning and speaking a language other than English at home (often referred to as dual- or multi-language learners) and give particular attention to students who have limited English skills (often referred to as English language learners) and who may have been formally identified as such by the school or district. The committee will address the following questions:

- Based on research-informed and field-tested models, strategies, and approaches, what are promising approaches to support ELs (including students with disabilities) in learning STEM? Given the diversity within the ELs population, what has worked, for whom, and under what conditions? What can be learned from these models and what additional research is needed to understand what makes them effective? What commonly used approaches may be less effective?
- What is the role of teachers in supporting the success of ELs in STEM? What is known about the biases teachers may bring to their work with EL students and how can these be effectively addressed? What kinds of curriculum, professional development experiences, and assessment are needed in order for STEM teachers to improve their support for ELs in STEM?
- How can assessments in STEM (both formative and summative) be designed to reflect the new content standards and to be appropriate for EL students? What assessment accommodations might need to be considered?
- How do policies and practices at the national, state, and local level constrain or facilitate efforts to better support ELs in STEM (including policies related to identification of students)? What kinds of changes in policy and practice are needed?
- What are the gaps in the current research base and what are the key directions for research, both short term and long term?

## STUDY APPROACH

The committee met five times over an 11-month period in 2017 and 2018 to gather information and explore the range of issues associated with ELs and their STEM learning opportunities. During this time, the committee reviewed the published literature pertaining to its charge and had opportunities to engage with many experts. Additionally, the committee commissioned five papers during the information-gathering phase of the process.

### Study Process

The committee spent a great deal of time discussing the charge and the best ways to respond to it. Evidence was gathered from presentations and a review of the existing literature over the past 10 to 15 years (see Box 1-2

---

**BOX 1-2**
**National Academies of Sciences, Engineering, and Medicine Reports on English Learners**

Previous consensus studies and other activities by the National Academies of Sciences, Engineering, and Medicine have addressed similar issues since 1997 when the first report was released on this topic (see *Improving Schooling for Language Minority Children: A Research Agenda* [Institute of Medicine and National Research Council, 1997]), sparking a significant shift in both the amount and type of research focused on ELs. In 2000, *Testing English Language Learners in U.S. Schools* (National Research Council, 2000) acknowledged the need for information about individual students' progress and needs for accountability data for schools, districts, and states. Building from these reports, emphasis was placed on ensuring access to special and gifted education programs (see *Minority Students in Special and Gifted Education* [National Research Council, 2002a]) and issues pertaining to closing the achievement gap (see *Language Diversity, School Learning, and Closing Achievement Gaps: A Workshop Summary* [National Research Council, 2010]). The most recent of these reports was released in 2017, titled *Promoting the Educational Success of Children and Youth Learning English: Promising Futures*. This report examined the evidence based on research relevant to the development of dual language learners/ELs birth to age 21 that could inform policies and practices that could lead to better educational outcomes. The release of the *Promising Futures* report was timely for the committee, as there was predictable overlap in the literatures reviewed by the two committees to address their respective charges. Wherever our review of the literature and conclusions were in agreement with the prior report, we refer readers to the earlier report, rather than repeat those findings and conclusions.

for the National Academies reports related to this topic). The committee searched for information on ELs' learning outcomes associated with different policies at the state and district levels, program models, instructional strategies employed across the various STEM content areas, and the professional development of teachers. The committee also reviewed the literature on assessment, including formative and summative assessment. For each of these areas, careful consideration was given to the strength of the evidence (described below) as well as across the various grade bands. During the review, it was clear that there is an imbalance in the research for different disciplinary content areas. That is, there is more information for science and mathematics with relatively sparse information available for technology and engineering. Therefore, the committee acknowledges that science and mathematics are necessarily overrepresented throughout the report.

As the committee reviewed the evidence on teachers, it was clear that a closer look at classroom factors was important, including teachers' perceptions and knowledge of ELs' abilities and of their families. As such, the committee also reviewed literature on school, family, and community interactions as related to STEM broadly and specific to ELs. When examining the outcomes specific to ELs and the various subpopulations (described below) in STEM learning, the committee recognized that there are limitations in the literature as to how ELs are characterized. Whereas some studies noted the different subpopulations included, others did not. Moreover, it was not always clear how reclassified ELs were included in the analyses, if at all. As such, the committee was unable to address fully one of the questions embedded in Question 1 of the charge: "What has worked, for whom, and under which conditions?" The committee synthesized the available evidence and came to consensus on recommendations that we believe should apply to ELs broadly; however, we acknowledge that it is still important to consider the learner and the context of the learning environment. The committee also gave careful consideration to research conducted outside of the United States. Although some literature is included, constraints of time prevented an exhaustive review of literature outside of the United States.

Over the course of this study, members of the committee benefited from discussion and presentations by the many individuals who participated in our three fact-finding meetings. At the first meeting, the committee heard presentations on ways in which to consider progress with respect to reclassification and learning progressions, as well as on new frames for thinking about mathematics and science learning given the Common Core Mathematics and Next Generation Science Standards.

During the second meeting, the presentations centered on the research examining factors associated with equitable educational contexts. In particular, the presentations focused on ELs' access to STEM courses and course-taking patterns in high school, the preparation of science educators by describing the Secondary Science Teaching with English Language and Literacy Acquisition (SSTELLA) project, and the research on attending to teachers' views of their ELs' capabilities through professional learning experiences. Additional presentations looked at state and district policies and the implementation of equitable educational opportunities, such as immigration trends and educational impacts, funding patterns associated with federal accountability, and a district-level perspective on ways to build capacity for teachers to provide rigorous science learning opportunities to their students, including ELs. Also during the second meeting, the committee considered issues centered on technology, computational thinking, and digital media through presentations that discussed technology-based programs designed to improve learning outcomes and broaden participation among ELs while also addressing the limited evidence base on technology and ELs.

Acknowledging that the committee had less expertise in the PreK space, at the third and final fact-finding meeting, the committee was briefed on three areas of emerging research on science education with ELs in PreK to include curricular development, home-to-school connections, and assessment of student science ability.

The committee commissioned five papers to provide more in-depth analysis on key issues.[3] Rebecca Callahan (The University of Texas at Austin) authored a paper on K–12 ELs' science and mathematics education with a focus on curricular equity, including issues centered on access to rigorous STEM learning opportunities. Julie Bianchini (University of California, Santa Barbara) provided a comprehensive overview of teachers' knowledge and beliefs about ELs and their impact on STEM learning. Through their discussions, the committee recognized the growing role of ESL teachers in the classroom and commissioned Sultan Turkan (Educational Testing Service) to provide an overview of the changing role of ESL teachers in K–12, the nature of collaboration with science and mathematics content teachers, and the preparation that is needed. The committee acknowledged some lack in expertise on secondary science education and early mathematics education for ELs; as such, they commissioned papers on these topics from Sara Tolbert (University of Arizona) and Sylvia Celedón-Pattichis (University of New Mexico), respectively.

In reviewing the evidence, many different types of studies were included: qualitative case studies, ethnographic and field studies, interview studies, and a few large-scale studies. The committee recognized that the literature consisted predominantly of studies that were more descriptive in nature with few studies that could describe causal effects (as characterized in the National Research Council [2002b] *Scientific Research in Education*

---

[3]Commissioned papers are available at http://www.nas.edu/ELinSTEM [October 2018].

report). As appropriate, throughout the report, the evidence is qualified to articulate the type of research being reviewed and its strength. The committee was also careful to qualify and temper the conclusions and subsequent recommendations that could be made based on the type of evidence and its strength.

### Defining English Learner Populations and Contexts

As part of the deliberation process, the committee acknowledged that many other terms exist to characterize the population, for example, dual language learners, multi-language learners, and emergent bilinguals (see National Academies of Sciences, Engineering, and Medicine, 2017). However, as stated at the opening of the chapter, the committee adopted the use of the term "English learner" to define the population—it was described as such in the charge and is consistent with federal definitions. As described in more detail in Chapter 2, the committee examined the literature broadly and considered all program models—those associated with either ESL or bilingual approaches. The report focuses exclusively on the context of learning STEM content and language development, making some generalizations that are unique to this context and transcending the different approaches. When necessary, the report distinguishes between the different program models.

As part of the charge, the committee was asked to consider the disability status of ELs. The *Promising Futures* report (Chapter 10) provided an in-depth discussion of the impact of disability status for ELs in many areas, including identification, testing and the need for accommodations, and classroom-based interventions. The current committee acknowledged the limited evidence with respect to STEM learning and ELs with disabilities and, when appropriate, discussed issues specific to the charge (see Chapters 7 and 8).

In considering the heterogeneity of ELs, the committee grappled with how to describe the various subpopulations. Of note, the committee recognized that a major segment of the population has been designated by an evolving sequence of labels, such as Hispanic,[4] Latino/a,[5] Latin@,[6] and

---

[4] "Hispanic" has been generally abandoned, in part because of its literal emphasis on the Spanish language and culture, in favor of the more functional pan-ethnic identifier.

[5] "Latino/a" is typically used to describe individuals in the United States who are descendants of, or direct immigrants from, Latin America.

[6] "Latin@" appears to have been introduced as a typographic contraction of "Latino/a." It further avoids the preferential ordering, "o" before "a," or the reverse.

Latinx.[7] The committee was faced with the need to make a decision as to how to describe this particular population and the implications our choice might have for individual readers and groups who identify more strongly with one or another label, who may feel disenfranchised by the choice of other labels, as well as for the implications that our choice(s) could have for how to describe the many varied EL subpopulations. However, we could find no such label that serves both to identify the members to the broader society and speaks to the identity of each of the individual members. We were unable to reach a consensus on a single best term to use for this specific subpopulation of the nation's diverse society. As such, as appropriate, the committee uses the nomenclature from the studies described throughout the report and recognizes that this leads to inconsistencies in reporting.

The committee also examined the evidence related to newcomers—those who come to school without prior knowledge of English (see Chapter 2). The evidence for this particular population is relatively limited. The committee views newcomers as students who can interact with children who speak English and can participate and contribute within authentic STEM learning contexts. Given this, the discussion and recommendations throughout the report apply to all ELs, including newcomers, acknowledging that the opportunities for language development need to be calibrated to their newcomer status.

Another subpopulation of ELs that has received increasing attention are those labeled as long-term ELs (LTELs). LTELs are those who generally have been educated in U.S. schools for 6 years or more and yet have not met reclassification criteria for their state and still receive bilingual education or ESL services (Batalova, Fix, and Murray, 2007; Menken and Kleyn, 2010; Solis and Bunch, 2016). Although the designation of LTELs was intended to draw awareness to a particular group of students to improve educational outcomes, the designation has been associated with a more deficit view of ELs (Kibler, Walqui, and Bunch, 2015; Thompson, 2015). As will be described in Chapter 2, reclassification is a challenging issue and can lead to negative outcomes (Robinson-Cimpian, Thompson, and Umansky, 2016). These outcomes are not only illustrated in measures of academic achievement or attrition for school, but also extend to the perception of how these students are viewed as well as how they view themselves (Flores, Kleyn, and Menken, 2015). It is important to note that even within this designation, there is still variability in language proficiency and STEM-related academic

---

[7]The term "Latinx" was introduced, with the "x" avoiding the inherent binary nature of the a/o form inherent in Spanish. The committee gave significant consideration to using Latinx, but ultimately failed to reach a consensus on adopting this usage throughout the report, perhaps reflecting the lack of consensus within the community of individuals who identify with any of the terms Hispanic, Latino/a, Latin@, and Latinx.

achievement (Thompson, 2015). The issue of classification and reclassification and the implications for placement and achievement in STEM subjects is a major theme discussed throughout the report.

## AN ASSET-ORIENTED VIEW OF ENGLISH LEARNERS

This report presents substantial evidence that with appropriate curricular and instructional support, ELs can participate, contribute, and succeed in STEM classrooms. ELs bring *multicompetence* to the STEM classroom, with broader aspects of language knowledge and cultural knowledge than monolingual ("monocompetent") speakers (Cook, 1991, 2003). ELs are actually engaged in a more challenging task than other students, as they are developing bilingual competence at the same time they are learning school subjects, something other students are not expected to do. Their language proficiency in both languages will continue to develop with their exposure to and participation in communicative, meaningful activities, using the language(s) they are developing (Hall, Cheng, and Carlson, 2006). For that reason, in the literature, the label "English learner" is being rejected in favor of referring to these students as *emergent bilinguals* (Garcia, Kleifgen, and Falchi, 2008). Seeing them as students who are developing a greater capacity for using language is one way of recognizing the strengths they bring and the contributions they can make in STEM classrooms.

In addition, ELs bring new perspectives and resources to the classroom through their participation and sharing of experience that can benefit their peers. In the contexts of STEM classrooms, ELs' cultural diversity represents opportunities for sharing new ideas and new ways of thinking about STEM (Lee and Fradd, 1998; see Leverage Multiple Meaning-Making Resources in Chapter 4). These contributions have the potential to add new dimensions to the ways STEM topics are addressed through instruction. In addition, students who have had STEM instruction in other countries may also bring important proficiency in content, or may have alternative ways of doing STEM work that other students could learn from (Khisty and Chval, 2002).

This report takes an asset-oriented view of ELs that sees them as competent learners who are doing more than the typical student by developing as bilinguals at the same time they are learning school subjects. It recognizes that ELs, coming from other cultural backgrounds, bring perspectives that can inform and strengthen STEM learning for all (see Chapter 4). The report also views the linguistic knowledge ELs are developing as a set of repertoires (*registers*; see Chapter 3) that they are learning to draw on, with language as a resource for learning. Language and content are not learned separately, as there is no "content-less" language nor "language-free" content by and large (see Chapter 3). This means that the language

ELs develop will vary with the opportunities they have to participate in STEM learning. We report on research demonstrating that ELs are able to participate in STEM learning even with low English proficiency when they are challenged through instruction that respects them and what they have to offer (see the section on positioning in Chapter 4). Such instruction recognizes that opportunities to build from the language they already speak, and opportunities to draw on their full range of resources for meaning-making (everyday language, gesture, drawing, etc.), are important ways learners draw on their full range of multicompetences (see Wei, 2011).

To leverage the full potential of these opportunities, the committee provides guidance on ways in which to build capacity within the system (Chapter 8). The United Nations Development Programme (2009) defines capacity building as "the process through which individuals, organizations, and societies obtain, strengthen, and maintain the capabilities to set and achieve their own development objectives over time" (p. 5). Central to such capacity building is transformation, or the changing of mindsets and attitudes, which is generated and sustained over time (United Nations Development Programme, 2009). As such, the committee views capacity building as more than the allocation of resources and engagement in improvement efforts; it also requires the questioning of broader policies and practices and concerted efforts to shift them.

## REPORT ORGANIZATION

This report examines the research on ELs including their heterogeneity and the implications that this heterogeneity has for their learning opportunities in STEM subjects. Chapters 2 and 3 provide the foundation upon which the subsequent chapters build. These chapters provide the guiding framework for the report, the essential background on ELs, the role of language in content learning, and the importance of standards in shaping education; in essence the various premises that the committee understands as given. These chapters provide readers with the background through which the committee understood its charge and reviewed the literature. Chapter 2 describes the heterogeneity among ELs and their educational experiences through different program models that affect ELs' access to STEM courses. Chapter 3 extends this discussion by articulating the inextricable relationship between language development and STEM learning, describes the vision for STEM classrooms, and discusses the important role of content area standards in education as they relate to this study.

Chapter 4 examines the evidence related to instructional strategies and curriculum, identifying instructional strategies that are most promising. It also considers the teacher as a key player in creating a classroom environment that leverages ELs' assets by considering the positioning of ELs in the classroom and how the teacher's perceptions are influential. Building from what teachers do in the classroom, Chapter 5 explores how teachers and schools can partner with ELs' families and communities to create a more cohesive approach that optimizes opportunities in STEM, whereas Chapter 6 discusses the necessary preparation that teachers must make when engaging ELs in STEM learning. It describes the themes that are important for ensuring that preservice and in-service teachers are equipped with the requisite skills and knowledge to ensure that ELs receive the rigorous STEM learning opportunities that they deserve.

Chapter 7 discusses assessment, including large-scale assessment, as well as classroom-level formative and summative assessment. The report brings all of the preceding pieces together in Chapter 8, examining the roles of policies and educational systems and describing approaches for designing educational systems that build capacity at local, state, and national levels. Finally, Chapter 9 presents our conclusions and recommendations and identifies key questions warranting future research.

## REFERENCES

Bailey, A.L. (2010). Implications for assessment and instruction. In M. Shatz and L. Wilkinson (Eds.), *The Education of English Language Learners: Research to Practice* (pp. 222–247). New York: Guilford Press.

Bailey, A.L., Butler, F.A., Stevens, R., and Lord, C. (2007). Further specifying the language demands of school. In A.L. Bailey (Ed.), *The Language Demands of School: Putting Academic English to the Test* (pp. 103–156). New Haven, CT: Yale University Press.

Bang, M. (2015). Culture, learning, and development about the natural world: Advances facilitated by situative perspectives. *Educational Psychologist, 50*(3), 220–233.

Bang, M., Warren, B., Rosebery, A.S., and Medin, D. (2013). Desettling expectations in science education. *Human Development, 55*(5-6), 302–318.

Barajas-López, F., and Aguirre, J.M. (2015). Fostering English language learner perseverance in mathematical problem-solving in high school. In L. de Oliveira, A. Bright, and H. Hansen-Thomas (Eds.), *Common Core State Standards in Mathematics for English Language Learners: High School* (pp. 123–137). New York: TESOL International Press.

Batalova, J., Fix, M., and Murray, J. (2007). *Measure of Change: The Demography and Literacy of Adolescent English Learners: A Report to the Carnegie Corporation of New York*. Washington, DC: Migration Policy Institute.

Brown, B.A. (2006). "It isn't no slang that can be said about this stuff": Language, identity, and appropriating science discourse. *Journal of Research in Science Teaching, 43*(1), 96–126.

Bunch, G.C. (2014). The language of ideas and the language of display: Reconceptualizing "academic language" in linguistically diverse classrooms. *International Multilingual Research Journal, 8*(1), 70–86.

Chamot, A., and O'Malley, J. (1994). *The CALLA Handbook: Implementing the Cognitive Academic Language Learning Approach*. Reading, MA: Addison-Wesley.

Cobb, P., Wood, T., and Yackel, E. (1993). Discourse, mathematical thinking, and classroom practice. In E.A. Forman, N. Minick, and C.A. Stone (Eds.), *Contexts for Learning: Sociocultural Dynamics in Children's Development* (pp. 91–119). New York: Oxford University Press.

Cocking, R.R., and Mestre, J.P. (1988). *The Psychology of Education and Instruction. Linguistic and Cultural Influences on Learning Mathematics.* Hillsdale, NJ: Lawrence Erlbaum Associates.

Cook, V.J. (1991). The poverty-of-the-stimulus argument and multicompetence. *Interlanguage Studies Bulletin (Utrecht), 7*(2), 103–117.

Cook, V.J. (2003). *Effects of the L2 on the L1.* Clevedon, UK: Multilingual Matters.

Cuevas, G.J. (1984). Mathematics learning in English as second language. *Journal for Research in Mathematics Education, 15*(2), 134–144. doi:10.2307/748889.

Cummins, J. (1981). The role of primary language development in promoting education success for language minority students. In California State Department of Education (Ed.), *Schooling and Language Minority Students: A Theoretical Rationale* (pp. 3–29). Los Angeles: California State University.

Cummins, J. (2000). *Language, Power and Pedagogy: Bilingual Children in the Crossfire.* Clevedon, UK: Multilingual Matters.

Domínguez, H. (2011). Using what matters to students in bilingual mathematics problems. *Educational Studies in Mathematics, 76,* 305–328.

Flores, N., Kleyn, T., and Menken, K. (2015). Looking holistically in a climate of partiality: Identities of students labeled long-term English language learners. *Journal of Language, Identity, and Education, 14,* 113–132.

Forman, E. (1996). Learning mathematics as participation in classroom practice: Implications of sociocultural theory for educational reform. In L. Steffe, P. Nesher, P. Cobb, G. Goldin, and B. Greer (Eds.), *Theories of Mathematical Learning* (pp. 115–130). Mahwah, NJ: Lawrence Erlbaum Associates.

Fuson, K.C., Wearne, D., Hiebert, J.C., Murray, H.G., Human, P.G., Olivier, A.I., Carpenter, T.P., and Fennema, E. (1997). Children's conceptual structures for multidigit numbers and methods of multidigit addition and subtraction. *Journal for Research in Mathematics Education, 28*(2), 130–162.

García, O., Kleifgen, J.A., and Falchi, L. (2008). *From English Language Learners to Emergent Bilinguals* (Research Review No. 1). New York: Teachers College Press.

Gibbons, P. (2002). *Scaffolding Language, Scaffolding Learning: Teaching Second Language Learners in the Mainstream Classroom.* Portsmouth, NH: Heinemann.

Hall, J.K., Cheng, A., and Carlson, M.T. (2006). Reconceptualizing multicompetence as a theory of language knowledge. *Applied Linguistics, 27*(2), 220–240.

Hudicourt-Barnes, J. (2003). The use of argumentation in Haitian Creole science classrooms. *Harvard Educational Review, 70*(1), 73–93.

Institute of Medicine and National Research Council. (1997). *Improving Schooling for Language Minority Children: A Research Agenda.* Washington, DC: National Academy Press.

Kelly, G.J., and Chen, C. (1999). The sound of music: Constructing science as sociocultural practices through oral and written discourse. *Journal of Research in Science Teaching, 36*(8), 883–915.

Khisty, L.L., and Chval, K.B. (2002). Pedagogic discourse and equity in mathematics: When teachers' talk matters. *Mathematics Education Research Journal, 14*(3), 154–168.

Kibler, A.K., Walqui, A., and Bunch, G.C. (2015). Transformational opportunities: Language and literacy instruction for English language learners in the common core era in the United States. *TESOL Journal, 6*(1), 9–35.

Lampert, M. (1990). When the problem is not the question and the solution is not the answer: Mathematical knowing and teaching. *American Educational Research Journal, 27*(1), 29–63.

Latour, B. (1987). *Science in Action: How to Follow Scientists and Engineers through Society.* Milton Keynes, UK: Open University Press.

Lee, O. (2018). English language proficiency standards aligned with content standards. *Educational Researcher.* Available: http://journals.sagepub.com/doi/abs/10.3102/0013189X18763775 [June 2018].

Lee, O., and Fradd, S.H. (1998). Science for all, including students from non-English-language backgrounds. *Educational Researcher, 27*(4), 12–21.

Lemke, J.L. (1990). *Talking Science: Language, Learning and Values.* Norwood, NJ: Ablex.

Lightbown, P.M., and Spada, N. (2013). *Oxford Handbooks for Language Teachers: How Languages Are Learned.* Oxford, UK: Oxford University Press.

McGinn M.K., and Roth, W.-M. (1999). Preparing students for competent scientific practice: Implications of recent research in science and technology studies. *Educational Researcher, 28*(3), 14–24.

Menken, K., and Kleyn, T. (2010). The long-term impact of subtractive schooling in the educational experiences of secondary English language learners. *International Journal of Bilingual Education and Bilingualism, 13*(4), 399–417.

Mohan, B.A. (1986). *Language and Content* (vol. 5288). Reading, MA: Addison Wesley.

Moschkovich, J.N. (2007). Examining mathematical discourse practices. *For the Learning of Mathematics, 27*(1), 24–30.

NASEM (National Academies of Sciences, Engineering, and Medicine). (2017). *Promoting the Educational Success of Children and Youth Learning English: Promising Futures.* Washington, DC: The National Academies Press.

National Research Council. (2000). *Testing English Language Learners in U.S. Schools: Report and Workshop Summary.* Washington, DC: National Academy Press.

National Research Council. (2002a). *Minority Students in Special and Gifted Education.* Washington, DC: National Academy Press.

National Research Council. (2002b). *Scientific Research in Education.* Washington, DC: National Academy Press.

National Research Council. (2010). *Language Diversity, School Learning, and Closing Achievement Gaps: A Workshop Summary.* Washington, DC: The National Academies Press.

NGSS Lead States. (2013). *Next Generation Science Standards: For States, By States.* Washington, DC: The National Academies Press.

Pew Research Center. (2018). *Women and Men in STEM Often at Odds Over Workplace Equity.* Available: http://assets.pewresearch.org/wp-content/uploads/sites/3/2018/01/09142305/PS_2018.01.09_STEM_FINAL.pdf [September 2018].

Robinson-Cimpian, J.P., Thompson, K.D., and Umansky, I.M. (2016). Research and policy considerations for English learner equity. *Policy Insights from the Behavioral and Brain Sciences, 3*(1), 129–137.

Schleppegrell, M.J. (2004). *The Language of Schooling: A Functional Linguistics Perspective.* New York: Routledge.

Schleppegrell, M.J. (2007). The linguistic challenges of mathematics teaching and learning: A research review. *Reading & Writing Quarterly, 23*(2), 139–159.

Secada, W.G. (1991). Degree of bilingualism and arithmetic problem solving in Hispanic first graders. *The Elementary School Journal, 92*(2), 213–231.

Short, D.J. (1993). Assessing integrated language and content instruction. *TESOL Quarterly, 27*(4), 627–656.

Snow, M.A., Met, M., and Genesee, F. (1989). A conceptual framework for the integration of language and content in second/foreign language instruction. *TESOL Quarterly, 23*(2), 201–217.

Solís, J., and Bunch, G.C. (2016). Responsive approaches for teaching English learners in secondary science classrooms. In E.G. Lyon, S. Tolbert, J. Solís, P. Stoddart, G.C. Bunch (Authors), *Secondary Science Teaching for English Learners: Developing Supportive and Responsive Learning Contexts for Sense-Making and Language Development* (pp. 21–50). Lanham, MD: Rowman & Littlefield.

Spada, N., and Tomita, Y. (2010). Interactions between type of instruction and type of language feature: A meta-analysis. *Language Learning, 60*(2), 263–308.

Spanos, G., and Crandall, J. (1990). Language and problem solving: Some examples from math and science. In A.M. Padilla, H.H. Fairchild, and C.M. Valadez (Eds.), *Bilingual Education: Issues and Strategies* (pp. 157–170). Newbury Park, CA: SAGE.

Thompson, K.D. (2015). Questioning the long-term English learner label: How categorization can blind us to students' abilities. *Teachers College Record, 117*(12), 1–50.

United Nations Development Programme. (2009). *Capacity Development: A UNDP Primer.* New York: Author.

U.S. Department of Education, Office of Planning, Evaluation and Policy Development, and Policy and Program Studies Service. (2012). *Language Instruction Educational Programs (LIEPs): A Review of the Foundational Literature.* Washington, DC: Author. Available: https://www2.ed.gov/rschstat/eval/title-iii/language-instruction-ed-programs-report.pdf [August 2018].

Valdés, G. (2005). Bilingualism, heritage language learners, and SLA research: Opportunities lost or seized? *The Modern Language Journal, 89*(3), 410–426.

Valdés, G. (2016). Entry visa denied: The construction of symbolic language borders in educational settings. In O. Garcia, N. Flores, and M. Spotti (Eds.), *The Oxford Handbook of Language in Society* (pp. 321–348). New York: Oxford University Press.

Varelas, M., Kane, J.M., and Wylie, C.D. (2012). Young black children and science: Chronotopes of narratives around their science journals. *Journal of Research in Science Teaching, 49*(5), 568–596.

Varelas, M., Pappas, C.C., Kane, J.M., Arsenault, A., Hankes, J., and Cowan, B.M. (2008). Urban primary-grade children think and talk science: Curricular and instructional practices that nurture participation and argumentation. *Science Education, 92*(1), 65–95.

Warren, B., Ballenger, C., Ogonowski, M., Rosebery, A.S., and Hudicourt-Barnes, J. (2001). Re-thinking diversity in learning science: The logic of everyday sense-making. *Journal of Research on Science Teaching, 38*(5), 529–552.

Wei, L. (2011). Multilinguality, multimodality, and multicompetence: Code- and mode-switching by minority ethnic children in complementary schools. *The Modern Language Journal, 95*(3), 370–384.

Zwiers, J. (2007). Teacher practices and perspectives for developing academic language. *International Journal of Applied Linguistics, 17*(1), 93–116.

# 2

# Factors Shaping English Learners' Access to STEM Education in U.S. Schools

English learners (ELs) in U.S. schools vary in many ways, in their home languages and the cultures they represent, their proficiency in their home language, the age at which they enter school and their prior schooling in other contexts, and their language abilities and prior knowledge about science, technology, engineering, and mathematics (STEM) subjects. The variability within the EL population was articulated by the National Academies of Sciences, Engineering, and Medicine report *Promoting the Educational Success of Children and Youth Learning English: Promising Futures* (hereafter referred to as *Promising Futures*) (NASEM, 2017):

> ELs vary in their home language, language abilities, age, race/ethnicity, immigration circumstances, generational status in the United States, geographic distribution, academic achievement, parental characteristics and socioeconomic resources, disability status, and other demographic attributes (Capps, 2015; Fry, 2007). Thus, while on average, ELs have a number of unique characteristics that distinguish them from the general population of non-ELs (Capps, 2015; Fry, 2007), broad comparisons of ELs with non-ELs mask significant heterogeneity within both groups. (pp. 63–64)

Of greatest importance, in relation to placement for STEM learning, is their prior knowledge about STEM subjects, but children are not typically assessed for their content knowledge when entering U.S. schools. Instead, their identification and course placement, at least at the secondary level, is typically determined by their level of English proficiency. As this report further describes in this chapter and throughout the report, the English proficiency of any person is multifaceted. ELs typically have varying levels of proficiency, both across modes of language use (reading, writing, speaking, listening) and across domains of knowledge, according to opportunities they have had to learn and use language. In addition, the experiences of ELs entering U.S. schools in kindergarten are different from those of ELs entering U.S. schools in late elementary through high school, as older children have greater levels of cognitive development and may have formal knowledge of STEM subjects developed in other contexts. Additionally, some older students may not be orally proficient in English, but may have English reading and writing skills based on prior educational experiences in English in their home countries, which facilitates their pathway to English proficiency and STEM learning in English. On the other hand, some ELs may come to U.S. schools in the secondary years without knowledge of English. They may also have experienced interrupted schooling or significant trauma that prevented them from developing literacy in their primary language or formal knowledge in STEM subjects. This report outlines ways that STEM programs can be designed to offer access to STEM learning opportunities for this range of ELs.

Below we discuss key issues that currently shape the extent to which STEM learning opportunities are accessible to ELs, including (1) the heterogeneity of ELs; (2) the program models through which ELs gain access to STEM subjects; (3) the processes of classification and reclassification of ELs that shape their access to STEM learning; (4) the academic achievement gap; and (5) the particular issues that affect placement of ELs in STEM courses at the secondary level.[1]

## HETEROGENEITY OF ENGLISH LEARNERS

ELs constitute a sizable and fast-growing segment of the student population in the United States. In 2002–2003, 8.7 percent of the enrollment in public schools—about 4.1 million students—was classified as ELs (Kena et al., 2015); in 2014–2015, this percentage rose to 9.4 percent—about 4.6 million students (McFarland et al., 2017). Whereas eight states have EL enrollments of 10 percent of students or more in their public schools, EL enrollment is also growing in most states. For example, the number of states with 6 to 10 percent of students classified as ELs increased from 14 in 2010–2011 (Kena et al., 2015) to 18 in 2014–2015 (McFarland et al., 2017). While in 2013, there was a growth of 7 percent in the general student population over 10

---

[1]This chapter includes content from a paper commissioned by the committee titled *K–12 English Learners' Science and Math Education: A Question of Curricular Equity* (Callahan, 2018).

years, the growth in the EL student population was 60 percent (Grantmakers for Education, 2013). Similar figures for the past decade are reported by other sources (see Durán, 2008; National Clearinghouse for English Language Acquisition and Language Instruction Educational Programs, 2011; for information on available EL data resources, see Sugarman, 2018). Box 2-1 presents additional discussion of the complexity of EL heterogeneity.

---

**BOX 2-1**
**Unpacking the Complexity of the Heterogeneity**
**of English Learner (EL) Students**

Effectively addressing heterogeneity is critical to properly supporting ELs to have access to STEM subjects through placement, instruction, and assessment. This heterogeneity has two facets. The first concerns the wide linguistic diversity and complex geographical distribution of ELs. There are nearly 5 million students classified as ELs in K–12 public schools (and many others who have gained proficiency in English)—about 10 percent of the student enrollment (U.S. Department of Education, 2018). Altogether, these students are native users of a total of 150 languages. The most common is Spanish (more than 77%), followed far behind by Arabic (2.4%), Chinese (2.1%), Vietnamese (1.7%), and other languages spoken by less than one-tenth of 1 percent of ELs each. However, there are seven states (Alaska, Hawaii, Maine, Montana, North Dakota, South Dakota, and Vermont) in which the most frequently native language among ELs is a language other than Spanish (Batalova and McHugh, 2010). Although about two-thirds of the total enrollment of ELs in the country is concentrated in eight states (California, Colorado, Florida, Illinois, New York, North Carolina, Texas, and Washington), there are states with high and rapidly increasing percentages of ELs, as is the case of Nevada, with 17 percent of its students classified as ELs (Ruiz-Soto, Hooker, and Batalova, 2015). Due to this heterogeneity, each state has a unique set of challenges to overcome to properly support EL students.

The second aspect of heterogeneity concerns the fact that English proficiency has multiple forms and is shaped by cultural experience. Against common intuition, the majority of ELs in the country are U.S. born (Zong and Batalova, 2015). Their diversity originates not only from their multiple cultural heritages, but also from their wide variety of schooling histories and, therefore, the different kinds of support they have received to both develop English as a second language and to continue developing their first language. As a result of this variety, each EL student has a unique set of linguistic skills. For example, two ELs who are in the same classroom and are native users of the same language may differ considerably in their skills across the four language modalities (listening, speaking, reading, and writing) in each of their two languages. Even if both are fluent in conversation in their first language, their reading and writing skills in the first language may vary considerably if one has a history of instruction in that language and the other does not. Clearly, broad categories of English proficiency do not provide the kind of information on English proficiency that is needed to make sound decisions for ELs.

*continued*

---

**BOX 2-1 Continued**

Legislation, policies, programs, and instructional and assessment strategies are limited in their effectiveness to serve ELs when this tremendous heterogeneity is not recognized. For example, testing all ELs in their first language could be more harmful than beneficial for those who have received limited formal instruction (and, therefore, have developed limited reading and writing skills) in that language (Solano-Flores and Hakuta, 2017). Particularly concerning is the fact that this failure to address heterogeneity may lead educators and schools to overestimate proficiency in the first language and to underestimate English proficiency.

Decisions concerning instruction and assessment need to be made based on recognizing the tremendous heterogeneity of EL populations if their access to STEM content is to be effectively supported. Proper strategies in instruction and assessment include (1) making decisions based on detailed information on proficiency in the four language modalities of English, beyond the simple use of broad classification categories; (2) using multiple sources of information (in addition to scores on English proficiency tests) in judging students' English proficiency; (3) looking for approaches that are sensitive to each student's needs; (4) avoiding making assumptions about the proficiency of students in English or in their native language; and (5) encouraging educators to develop a good sense of each of their ELs' strengths in English, based on continuously interacting with them.

---

### Long-Term ELs

The majority of the U.S. EL population across all ages between 5 and 17 is born in the United States and typically has at least one immigrant parent; however, in the secondary grades there are almost equivalent levels of U.S.-born and foreign-born ELs as compared to elementary settings that are predominantly U.S. born (NASEM, 2017, pp. 73–74). Often referred to as "long-term ELs" or "LTELs," many of these students have been receiving English language development/English as a second language (ELD/ESL) services in U.S. schools for at least 6 years and yet have not met reclassification criteria for their state (Batalova, Fix, and Murray, 2007; Menken and Kleyn, 2010; Solis and Bunch, 2016). This group has attracted increased attention as they represent a sizable portion of the EL population (Menken, 2013). Some states are beginning to provide a designation for these students; however, there may not be consistency across states in defining this particular subpopulation of ELs (Olsen, 2010). The lack of a consistent definition makes it difficult to interpret and draw conclusions with respect to how these students are performing in STEM subjects.

The research has shown that there is a plateauing of English proficiency for LTELs from middle to high school and that this may be related to the academic tracking of ELs that occurs in these grades (NASEM, 2017). Although the intention of tracking may be to advance LTELs to be classified as English proficient, they are often assigned to low-level academic classes (described in more detail later). The continued placement of these students in ESL courses, as this chapter will detail, often prevents them from accessing STEM education and the opportunities STEM offers for language development (Callahan, Wilkinson, and Muller, 2010).

## Newcomers

Few studies provide research evidence related to newcomers, those foreign-born ELs and their families who have recently arrived in the United States (U.S. Department of Education, 2016). Heterogeneity within this group of students compares to the heterogeneity within the U.S.-born EL population and is driven by many of the same factors, as well as factors unique to this subgroup. These students may have experienced interrupted or limited formal education and often exhibit low levels of English language proficiency and academic achievement compared with their peers (NASEM, 2017). The initial difficulties newcomers experience may be linked to having to adjust to a new language and culture while developing literacy as well as oral and academic proficiency in English in a relatively brief period of time (Menken, 2013). Newcomers often receive specialized ESL instruction that socializes them into the new school practices they encounter and provides opportunities for language development calibrated to their newcomer status. However, even newcomers can interact with children who speak English and participate and contribute in authentic STEM learning contexts. As newcomers begin to use language to learn and interact socially, their interaction with peers and adults in authentic learning contexts leads to continued control of English (Solano-Flores, 2008).

## Linguistic Heterogeneity

If teachers get information about the ELs in their classrooms, the students' English proficiency may be reported at particular levels of proficiency in *listening, reading* (language comprehension), *speaking,* and *writing* (language production), or they may receive an overall proficiency level. However, research has suggested that formal, largely summative, large-scale language assessments may be a problematic way to measure language proficiency (Cumming, 2008; Valdés, Capitelli, and Alvarez, 2011; Valdés, Poza, and Brooks, 2014; see Box 2-2), missing much of the communicative aspects of authentic classroom interaction during instruction (Bailey and Durán, in press). ELs vary in their control of these different skills and this can interact with their prior schooling (Solano-Flores, 2008). Box 2-2 illustrates the ways in which ELs can vary along the various dimensions of English proficiency measured. Given this variability in the EL population, it is important for educators to find out what learners know about STEM subjects from their previous schooling and experiences, and to connect with and build on prior learning in their first languages. As stated in previous reports, ELs can develop fluency in language and the language of STEM subjects over several years of engagement and participation in grade-appropriate activities (NASEM, 2017).

Although the process of language learning is similar for all students, ELs experience different overall trajectories in their learning of language and STEM content related to their ages and levels of English proficiency, prior knowledge, and community context (Solano-Flores, 2008). As described above, older children who can read and write in their first language may

---

**BOX 2-2**
**Using Linguagrams to Understand the Heterogeneity**
**of English Learners (ELs) in the Classroom**

Linguagrams are conceptual tools created with the intent to support teachers to reason about the linguistic heterogeneity of EL students in their classrooms (Solano-Flores, 2016). A linguagram consists of a symmetric bar graph that represents an individual's proficiency in English and in their first language in each of the four language modalities—listening, speaking, reading, and writing—on a scale that ranges from 0 (total lack of proficiency) to 100 (full proficiency).

The figure below shows the linguagrams of three hypothetical EL students who are in the same classroom and are native speakers of the same language. Different personal experiences (e.g., family, community, friends) and different schooling histories produce different sets of opportunities to become proficient in listening (L), speaking (S), reading (R), and writing (W) in each language. The three cases shown are among the many possible combinations of levels of proficiency that different ELs may have in their two languages.

To reason about the linguistic diversity in their classrooms, teachers can be asked to construct linguagrams of each of their EL students using information from multiple sources, in addition to test scores. Examples of these sources are observations of the students interacting with other ELs or with never-EL students, teachers' informal interactions with the students, students' participation in class, examination of students' written work, and conversations with the students' parents (e.g., to know the students' schooling history).

Linguagrams are not a formal assessment instrument, but a tool to support have an advantage over younger children who have yet to develop literacy in any language. Younger children may need additional support when learning language and STEM content (see Chapter 4). With respect to community context, children who live in more linguistically homogeneous communities are well positioned to draw on their first-language proficiency as an asset in STEM learning, making bilingual education and/or strategic use of the first language in the classroom an important part of their learning contexts. For ELs who live in more linguistically diverse communities, attention to and participation in a range of oral and written languages and registers at school (see Chapter 3) can be a part of their STEM learning experiences (for review, see U.S. Department of Education, 2012). For all ELs, opportunities to participate in authentic STEM practices, with attention to language use in meaningful ways, are crucial to enabling these learners to bring their full range of knowledge and resources to learning and to realize their full potential as STEM learners (see Chapter 4).

teachers to realize that (1) little information is typically available about their EL students' proficiency in English or in their first language; (2) although useful, information from tests of language proficiency does not have the level of detail needed to know exactly how to support ELs in the classroom; (3) a great deal of the information needed to develop a good sense of the linguistic proficiency of ELs needs to be obtained through socially interacting with them; (4) each EL has a unique pattern of language dominance; and (5) language proficiency varies considerably across contexts (e.g., in class, during a mathematics conversation, or in informal situations).

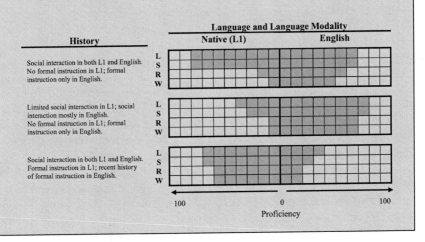

## PROGRAM MODELS FOR ENGLISH LEARNERS

Federal legislation over the past 20 years has called for English instruction for ELs that enables them to succeed in learning across school subjects. The No Child Left Behind (NCLB) Act of 2001 mandated that states "establish standards and objectives for raising the level of English proficiency . . . that are *aligned* [emphasis added] with achievement of the challenging State academic content and student academic achievement standards" (U.S. Department of Education, 2001, pp. 270–271). Even though the U.S. Department of Education has allowed flexibility on federal accountability provisions, it has still required that each state "adopt English language proficiency (ELP) standards that *correspond* [emphasis added] to its college- and career-ready standards" (U.S. Department of Education, 2012, p. 1). Although subsequent legislation has used slightly different terminology, the mandate has remained the same: ELP standards must describe how ELs will use language to master content. This series of federal legislation communicates a clear message that the aims of content learning and language learning are closely tied to each other and are best addressed in parallel or in conjunction, rather than separately or sequentially (Lee, 2018). In other words, ELP is not a prerequisite for ELs' inclusion in content instruction.

Prior to 2000, much of the research on ELs was focused on the language *of* instruction—the use of primary language in instruction (Francis, Lesaux, and August, 2006): that is, that research was preoccupied with the question of *which* language to use when instructing non-native speakers of the societal language. Although current research focuses more closely on the language *in* instruction, regardless of whether that language is the home language or English, the language models under which a student has learned represent an important dimension of the heterogeneity of schooling experiences. In other words, whereas current research focuses more on the quality of the language used in instruction than on the choice of whether to deliver instruction in the children's home language or the societal language, this choice of the language *of* instruction marks an important dimension along with ELs educational experiences differ. Moreover, the variety of program models and variability in the quality of instruction under all program models complicates the process of drawing inferences from the literature on effective practices.

Program models can first be distinguished by their use of students' primary language in instruction. Table 2-1 highlights several types of primary language development programs, summarizing each program and illustrating many of the key features (NASEM, 2017). These programs, whether it be an ESL or bilingual program model, differ in their emphasis on the primary language. For example, in transitional programs (see TBE in table), the primary language is viewed as a bridge to support instruc-

**TABLE 2-1** Language Instruction Educational Program Models for Teaching English Learners (ELs) in PreK–12

| Model | Description | Format |
|---|---|---|
| English as a Second Language (ESL)[a] | • ELs provided with explicit language instruction to develop language proficiency.<br>• Teachers do not need to be fluent in ELs' home language.<br>• Language and content goals are not integrated. | • Students may have a dedicated class in school day or may receive pull-out ESL instruction.<br>• Not specific to grade levels. |
| Content-Based ESL | • ELs provided with language instructions that uses content as a medium for building language skills.<br>• Teachers do not need to be fluent in ELs' home language.<br>• Language and content goals are integrated. | • Students may have a dedicated class in school day or may receive pull-out ESL instruction.<br>• Not specific to grade levels. |
| Sheltered Instruction (SI) | • Instruction for ELs focuses on teaching academic content rather than English itself.<br>• Teachers do not need to be fluent in ELs' home language.<br>• Language and content goals are integrated. | • Generally used in EL-only classrooms designed specifically for ELs.<br>• Not specific to grade levels. |
| Transitional Bilingual Education (TBE)[b] | • ELs begin in elementary receiving instruction in home language and transition to English; may exit as late as Grade 5.<br>• Teachers need to be fluent in ELs' home language.<br>• Language and content goals may be integrated. | • Balance between home language and English. The division of instruction across languages varies across instructional time and content areas from program to program.<br>• Typically, elementary only. |

*continued*

**TABLE 2-1** Continued

| Model | Description | Format |
|---|---|---|
| Developmental Bilingual Education (DBE)[c] | • Students predominantly from one primary language group serving different kinds of language learners.<br>• Teachers need to be fluent in ELs' home language.<br>• Language and content goals may be integrated.<br>• Students' home language is a cognitive resource to be developed and maintained for academic proficiency. | • Typically begin in elementary grades and stay enrolled until end of elementary school. |
| Two-Way Dual Language Immersion[d] | • Students are ELs and English-proficient students (approx. 50-50 mix).<br>• Teachers need to be fluent in ELs' home language.<br>• Language and content goals may be integrated.<br>• Objective is to develop bilingual proficiency and bilingual academic competence in both ELs and non-ELs. | • Programs may balance languages by dividing instructional time according to content area, class period, instructor, week, or unit.<br>• Although typically elementary only, programs can extend through high school. |
| Newcomer | • ELs who are recent immigrants and new to formal education settings Provided with both language and content instruction.<br>• Teachers do not need to be fluent in ELs' home language.<br>• Language and content goals are not integrated. | • Receive specialized schooling, ranging from half-day, in-school program full-time, or self-contained school. |

[a]Alternative Names: English Language Development (ELD), English for Speakers of Other Language (ESOL).

[b]Alternative Name: Early-Exit Bilingual Education.

[c]Alternative Names: One-Way Dual Language Program; Late Exit Bilingual; Maintenance Bilingual.

[d]Alternative Names: Dual Immersion (DI); Dual Language; Two-Way Immersion (TWI).

SOURCES: Adapted from NASEM (2017, Table 7-1) and U.S. Department of Education (2012, Exhibits 3 and 4).

tion until students can function independently in English-only instruction. Transitional programs differ from one another not only in the timing of the transition to English but also in the extent to which primary language is used in content and literacy instruction. Developmental bilingual programs and maintenance programs view primary language as a cognitive resource to develop and/or maintain throughout the child's time in the program. This development typically occurs in literacy instruction and occasionally in content area instruction. Dual-language programs (see Two-Way Dual Language Immersion in table) differ in that by design they include never-ELs who seek to become proficient in a language other than English (U.S. Department of Education, 2012). This type of program offers content instruction in all subject areas in and across both languages of instruction.

Program labels mask the heterogeneity in instructional settings, in the extent of English and primary language in instruction, the areas of instruction in which the two languages might be used, and the quality of the instruction. Moreover, program labels imply an approach to instruction that may not extend to content area instruction. One cannot assume that bilingual instruction extends to instruction in STEM, nor can one assume that ELs are receiving STEM instruction, regardless of the program label. These circumstances mean that ELs may have little access to grade-appropriate STEM content and will continue to fall behind in their STEM development as the challenges of STEM learning increase at every grade level.

These trends have historical roots in federal policy. For example, the Bilingual Education Act of 1968 framed bilingual instruction as a means to English proficiency rather than as support for continued subject area learning as students learn English (Evans and Hornberger, 2005; Ruiz, 1984). Given that the underlying goal of this policy was to move students to English-only instruction as quickly as possible, bilingual programs have not always provided support for ELs' continued development of grade-level content knowledge (García, 2009; Ramírez et al., 1991). Even when bilingual programs are offered, the provision of primary language support for STEM learning is uneven, as some programs are designed such that students engage in language arts instruction in their primary language, but mathematics and science instruction is offered only in English (Boals, 2001). It is important to note that research on program models has tended to focus on student performance in reading and mathematics and has concentrated in the elementary grades, suggesting a need for further research. This focus is not surprising given that federal policy has not legislated assessment of student outcomes in science until recently, and even now science is assessed in a limited number of grades in comparison to reading and mathematics. This general lack of focus on STEM outcomes beyond mathematics until recently and these sources of variation that exist even within programs of the same type are important for the reader to keep in mind in the discussions about supporting teachers, structuring classrooms, and setting policies in later chapters. The first of these had led to a paucity of focused research on STEM instruction for ELs whereas the latter complicates the formation of easy generalizations from the research that does exist.

In all programs serving ELs, special attention to their ELD is crucial and required by law. Program models differ in how ELD support is provided. In some settings, ELs are pulled out of general education classrooms to receive ELD support, which precludes them from accessing the content in general education classrooms. As currently operationalized in many U.S. schools, ELD is often not organized in a way that enables ELs to maintain and develop age-appropriate knowledge of STEM subjects (Saunders, Goldenberg, and Marcelletti, 2013). When ELs are integrated into content classes, teachers, both those who teach ELD and those who teach content, are not typically prepared to support ELs' simultaneous development of language and STEM content knowledge (Bunch, Aguirre, and Téllez, 2009). Classrooms that provide sheltered approaches often provide highly simplified content that seldom satisfies grade-level STEM content expectations (Dabach, 2014; Saunders, Goldenberg, and Marceletti, 2013). Later chapters in this report will describe how such support for ELs can be provided in STEM classrooms and how ELD and STEM can be integrated.

Research demonstrates that primary language instruction during the elementary grades facilitates greater academic achievement in language arts and mathematics for ELs than English-medium instructional programs (Steele et al., 2017; Valentino and Reardon, 2015). This trend is likely related to the fact that ELs' early access to academic content is notably higher in instructional programs that use the primary language (Calderón, Slavin, and Sánchez, 2011), and that the language of instruction is an indicator of ELs' academic content access and exposure (Baker, 2011; García, 2009; National Research Council, 1997).

Moreover, continuing to develop ELs' content knowledge through bilingual support clearly shapes students' long-term academic trajectories (Steele et al., 2017; Valentino and Reardon, 2015). In a lottery study using seven cohorts of students who applied at a PreK or kindergarten immersion program, Steele et al. (2017) found that there was a 6 percentage point reduction in the probability of being classified as an EL in 5th grade and a 14 point reduction in 6th grade; however, the effects on mathematics and science learning were less evident. Valentino and Reardon (2015) examined four different instructional program models—Transitional Bilingual (TB), English Immersion (EI), Developmental Bilingual (DB), and Dual Immersion (DI)—and ELs' academic outcomes in English language arts and mathematics. They found that in 2nd grade, mathematics scores of ELs enrolled in all program models were significantly higher than the state average, with those enrolled in DB and TB classrooms even higher, respectively.

However, by 7th grade, the rate of growth was slowest for DB classrooms, about average for EI and DI programs, and those in TB programs were higher than the state average (Valentino and Reardon, 2015). At the same time, Umansky (2016) used a regression discontinuity design to assess the impact of program model by comparing students classified as EL and students with similar language skills who just missed being classified as EL. Umansky (2016) found a negative effect of EL classification on content area outcomes where students were enrolled in EI programs that was not present for students enrolled in bilingual instruction. Regardless of any conclusions about specific program models, what is clear from this research is that, even very early on, the language of instruction shapes ELs' content area access and academic trajectories.

The advantages of bilingual and primary language instruction identified above are not automatically obtained, nor are bilingual programs the norm in the United States. Whereas quality bilingual instructional programs could be more widespread than they are, the diversity of languages spoken by U.S. school children, the dearth of qualified bilingual educators, and the sparse representation of some languages in some locales (McFarland et al., 2017) make instruction in the primary language not always feasible. These factors necessitate that *all* schools be prepared to provide high-quality instruction to ELs, regardless of the choice of language program model within that school, including the implementation of effective programs within that school.

## ENGLISH LEARNER CLASSIFICATION STATUS AND STEM ACCESS

The classification of students as EL is complex and varies considerably across states, and even across districts within states (Cimpian, Thompson, and Makowski, 2017). Initial EL classification is determined by a student's level of ELP as demonstrated by standardized assessment results (discussed in more detail in Chapters 7 and 8). Although in many states, the state ELP assessment is the sole criterion for classification and reclassification as English proficient, or a student's readiness to exit EL status and related programs and services, other criteria include (1) academic achievement measured by standardized test scores and/or grades in English language arts and/or mathematics, (2) teacher evaluation, and (3) in some cases, parent consultation and/or approval. The inclusion of the second indicator, which requires that ELs perform at grade level in school subjects before being reclassified, varies across states and districts within states, and is used in some states with large EL populations. While including proficiency in content achievement as a criterion for language proficiency appears reasonable, the fact that many students who are non-ELs are not proficient in content achievement raises questions about content achievement as a criterion for English proficiency. Most importantly, tying reclassification to content achievement often delays reclassification and precludes ELs from being enrolled in STEM courses. In this sense, EL status penalizes students by preventing them from having access to academically rigorous curricula, in spite of research indicating that access to academic content is associated with ELs' achievement, as it is for non-ELs (Oakes, 2005). Moreover, given that students continuously enter and exit EL status (Hopkins et al., 2013), it is challenging to develop complete understandings of how ELs fare in schools and classrooms, and the extent to which both ELs and reclassified ELs have access to rigorous STEM content.

Reclassification is a challenging issue, as both too-early reclassification and too-late reclassification have negative outcomes for ELs (Robinson-Cimpian, Thompson, and Umansky, 2016). Slama's (2014) longitudinal analyses found that ELs who were reclassified early in elementary school (Grades K–2) struggled later on, with nearly one-quarter being retained a year. Slama and colleagues (2015) illustrated how early reclassification among ELs in English-only contexts is not only associated with retention, but also with attrition from the K–12 education system entirely. For ELs, as for all young children, language development continues in the early elementary grades as they continue developing literacy skills, so ensuring that EL supports are reduced at the appropriate time is an important issue. Although early reclassification may appear to indicate success, long-term consequences with respect to retention and attrition matter more in the long run (Thompson, 2015b). Most ELs continue to benefit from language support even after they demonstrate conversational fluency and ability to participate fully with the curriculum in the earliest grades (Saunders, Goldenberg, and Marceletti, 2013).

On the other hand, keeping ELs in specialized language programs can prevent them from having access to STEM learning opportunities. Reclassification by the end of the elementary grades, for example, is important for facilitating ELs' access to advanced STEM courses in high school. In a longitudinal analysis of student-level data from the Los Angeles Unified School District, the largest EL-enrolling school district in the nation, Thompson (2017a) found that the vast majority of ELs demonstrated English language proficiency within 4–7 years. However, her analyses also indicated that if a student missed the late elementary reclassification window, the likelihood of ever reclassifying dropped significantly. In fact, a full 25 percent of ELs remained classified after 9 years in the school system (Thompson, 2017a).

Thompson (2015b) also showed how missing the reclassification window can result in long-term EL status and continued placement in EL-isolated programs that provide limited access to grade-level curriculum. Specifically, Thompson (2017b) showed how external, organizational constraints prevent long-term EL students from advancing in mathematics. However, barriers to EL students extend beyond access to courses. Callahan and Humphries (2016) further showed how EL students experience lower returns on advanced mathematics course-taking relative to both other immigrants and native-born, native-English speakers. Even when EL students manage to complete honors-level advanced mathematics, calculus or beyond, they fail to receive the same boost in 4-year college-going experienced by all other student groups. These effects are present even after controlling for student performance in advanced mathematics courses. Accuracy in reclassification is especially important because the retention of students in EL status longer than necessary also results in stigmatizing, negative educational experiences (Estrada and Wang, 2013; Thompson, 2015a) and can be academically and linguistically detrimental to students (Calderón and Minaya-Rowe, 2011; Menken and Kleyn, 2009; Olsen, 2010). In a recent qualitative case study of three students who were labeled long-term ELs, Thompson (2015a) demonstrated the stigmatizing, limiting aura associated with this status, as well as how the students experience its accompanying constraints to their academic identities. Often, long-term ELs internalize the negative social and academic perceptions that have come to characterize EL-focused courses and programs (Dabach, 2015). These negative perceptions are fueled in part by the inaccurate reporting of student achievement among students who enter school as ELs that results from the routine exclusion of reclassified ELs when reporting on EL achievement (Saunders and Marcelletti, 2013).

## FACTORS AND CHALLENGES ASSOCIATED WITH "ACHIEVEMENT GAP" METRICS

The EL subgroup is unlike other accountability subgroups under Title I in that the EL designation is dynamic—a student's classification as EL changes as the student becomes proficient in English. Importantly, as children become proficient in English, they are reclassified and no longer count in the category of EL. This dynamism in EL classification leads to overestimation of achievement gaps between ELs and never-ELs (Saunders and Marcalletti, 2013), overestimation of ELs in special education (Umansky, Thompson, and Diaz, 2017), and underestimation of EL graduation rates (Thompson et al., 2017). In fact, Saunders and Marcalletti (2013) have termed the achievement gap "The Gap That Can't Go Away," because as ELs gain proficiency in English, they are also increasingly likely to demonstrate proficiency in content area achievement, but are now counted among the non-EL category for accountability purposes, creating an achievement gap that must persist.

The best indicators of this achievement gap are provided by the National Assessment of Educational Progress (NAEP)—a national assessment that has been administered to representative samples of students at Grades 4, 8, and 12 from all states since 1969. The performance of ELs on this assessment has been substantially lower than that of their non-EL counterparts. This trend has not changed substantially since 1996, when NAEP started collecting data for ELs. According to data from 2015, the mathematics performance of ELs was, on average, 25 points lower than that of non-ELs at Grade 4—a gap that is not different from the gap observed in 1996. For Grade 8, while the gap narrowed from 46 points in 1996 to 41 points in 2013, and to 38 points in 2015, these data show a clear increase in the mathematics achievement gap with grade level. For Grade 12, in 2015, the gap was also 38 points different, but the percentage of students "below basic" was higher for ELs than non-ELs than in Grade 8 (for both mathematics and science) (McFarland et al., 2017).

These trends indicate an increase in the achievement gap between EL and non-ELs as they progress across grades in school. However, as described above, this difference could be exacerbated by the exclusion of English-proficient ELs from the EL group. A recent analysis by Kieffer and Thompson (2018) attempted to address this issue. They found that the mathematics performance of students designated as multilingual (defined as the primary home language or languages other than English) was improved as compared to current ELs (defined as those not yet proficient in English in the year of assessment). Including potentially English-proficient ELs in the EL (multilingual) group showed a reduction in the achievement gap. Given these confounding factors, it is difficult to make simple interpretations of the change in the magnitude of the EL—non-EL academic achievement gap between Grades 4 and 8.

Bailey, Maher, and Wilkinson (2018) also reported increases in the achievement gap with grade level for NAEP science assessment scores, and even larger discrepancies between EL and non-ELs than those reported for mathematics: The science performance of ELs in 2015, on average, was 37 points lower than that of non-ELs at Grade 4 and 47 points lower at Grades 8 and 12. Consistent with these trends, data from a longitudinal study with ELs grouped according to different levels of English proficiency at the time they entered kindergarten show that, at Grade 8, reading, mathematics, and science scale scores decline as the level of English proficiency declines (Mulligan, Halle, and Kinukawa, 2012).

Not surprisingly, these trends are reflected in high dropout rates among ELs. About 90 percent of native English users between the ages of 18 and 24 years who are not enrolled in high school have completed high school or earned a GED (Callahan, 2013). In contrast, only 69 percent of ELs within the same age not enrolled in high school have completed high school or earned a GED. In general, at Grade 10, ELs are twice as likely as their never-EL peers to drop out (Callahan, 2013).

Several important factors may contribute to these achievement gaps, although their influence is subject to debate. On one hand, the most important and obvious set of factors concern the intrinsic challenges that stem from learning and being assessed in a second language and from developing academic language (see Schleppegrell, 2004). Whereas experts question the soundness of assessing students in a language that they are still developing (Hakuta, Butler, and Witt, 2000; Moore and Redd, 2002), this notion is not reflected in assessment legislation and policy, which persistently appear to be driven by the implicit assumption that a few years of schooling in English paves the way for ELs to meet the linguistic demands inherent to benefitting from instruction. On the other hand, based on the notion that "what gets measured gets done," some argue that including ELs and other minority subgroups in large-scale assessment programs is a way of ensuring that these groups are properly served, as there is no evidence that ELs' educational outcomes were better when ELs were excluded from assessment and accountability (Abedi, 2010).

There is consensus among specialists that linguistic demands in both science and mathematics content can be substantial, and learning in these content areas is associated in part with meeting these linguistic expectations and discourse practices (for science, see Snow, 2010). In the case of mathematics, these understandings run counter to prior assumptions that mathematics learning did not rely heavily on linguistic demands. These linguistic demands concern not only vocabulary, but also discursive forms, ways of constructing arguments, and sophisticated conventions of socialization through language. From a broader perspective, learning science and mathematics entails learning to interpret and to represent knowledge through multiple semiotic modalities (e.g., textual, symbolic, and visual forms of representation) according to conventions that are mediated by cultural experience (Avalos, Medina, and Secada, 2018; Lemke, 1998). These multimodal representations may help to mitigate some of the linguistic demands. This notion holds not only for content learned or taught, but also for the tests that assess that content, as test items have formatting and linguistic features not frequent in other forms of text and may be unfamiliar to many ELs (Bailey and Butler, 2004; Solano-Flores, 2016).

A second set of factors concerns the effectiveness of the support ELs receive. There is a serious lack of educators with formal training in the teaching of ELs (Darling-Hammond and Berry, 2006; Santos, Darling-Hammond, and Cheuk, 2012) and the resource educators who may be in charge of supporting ELs may not have the formal qualifications needed. In addition, the support received by ELs may emphasize English skills over academic content (see Chapter 4 for more information).

A third set of factors concerns social disadvantage, which is reflected by indicators such as household income, parents' education, and opportunity to learn. Compared to their never-EL peers, ELs are more likely to live in households with an income below the poverty line. Also, ELs are less likely than their never-EL counterparts to have a parent with a college degree and more likely than their never-EL counterparts to attend low socioeconomic status (SES) schools with poorly qualified or unexperienced teachers (see EPE Research Center, 2009). It is worth noting that high-quality dual language education programs may moderate the effects of SES and poverty (Collier and Thomas, 2017; García, 2009) on EL outcomes as well as capitalizing on the resources that families bring to schools (Yosso, 2005).

It is not reasonable to expect that students perform well on tests on content that they are not taught (see Porter, 2002). Thus, opportunity to learn through exposure to content is especially important in interpreting EL performance. There is evidence of correlation between measures of mathematics achievement and measures of class-level opportunity to learn that comprise indicators such as whether topics are covered in class, the time allocated to cover those topics, the kind of emphasis those topics are given in the curriculum, and the effectiveness with which teachers support students to learn them (Herman, Klein, and Abedi, 2000).

## ENGLISH LEARNER PLACEMENT IN STEM COURSEWORK

As articulated in the previous section, achievement gaps between ELs and never-ELs increase from elementary school to secondary school (Kena et al., 2016), and ELs are graduating from high school at lower rates than other traditionally underrepresented groups such as never-EL Latino students, African American students, or low-income students. Research across a variety of state contexts has shown that ELs are often systematically excluded from rigorous or advanced coursework in science due to scheduling constraints as well the misconception that they must be proficient in English before they can be successful in content area classes (Callahan, 2017; Gándara and Hopkins, 2010). This exclusion has had severe consequences on educational opportunities for ELs (Combs, Iddings, and Moll, 2014). ELs fare far better in terms of both content and language measures as well as requirements for graduation and college admissions when they have opportunities to learn rigorous academic content, such as that found in advanced secondary science courses (Callahan, 2005, 2017).

Students' course placement has long been used by researchers as a metric of content area access and exposure for students, especially at the secondary level. The sequential nature of mathematics course-taking makes it a de facto gate-keeper to more rigorous mathematics and science courses (Gamoran, 2010; Lucas, 1999; Lucas and Berends, 2002; Oakes, 2005). For example, 8th-grade placement in Algebra I (Gamoran and Hannigan, 2000; Stevenson, Schiller, and Schneider, 1994) indicates access to rigorous mathematics content, and Algebra II has been identified as a core indicator of preparation for higher education at the national level (Adelman, 2006). In a study using the nationally representative High School Longitudinal Study (HSLS:2009) data, Schneider and Saw (2016) found course-taking to be a stronger predictor of college-going than individual students' concrete knowledge of college itself, improving the likelihood of college-going for academically marginalized youth.

Yet the availability of rigorous STEM courses varies by school and community. Using the Education Longitudinal Study of 2002 (ELS:2002) data, Riegle-Crumb and Grodsky (2010) found that low-income Latino and African American students enrolled in segregated schools[2] struggled the most to reach the highest levels of mathematics course-taking. In an investigation of access to advanced mathematics courses within the context of the New Latino Diaspora,[3] Dondero and Muller (2012) found evidence of greater Latino-white disparities in mathematics course-taking when taking into account school composition, quality, and resources. Others have found that only one in three students graduate in high EL-density schools (Silver, Saunders, and Zarate, 2008), and that second-generation ELs experience a more concentrated negative estimated effect of ESL placement on their mathematics and science course-taking than their foreign-born peers (Callahan et al., 2009).

More recent data from the HSLS:2009 high school transcript study[4] demonstrated students' course-taking patterns after the onset of the national accountability movement initiated with NCLB. Once again, disparities in course-taking emerge by student linguistic status. The data showed that ELs were overrepresented in lower-level mathematics courses compared to other bilinguals and native English speakers. Initially, twice the share of high school ELs fail to complete any mathematics classes during high school relative to their native English-speaking peers (4.8% compared to 2.4%). And, at the tail of the distribution, fewer than 5 percent of ELs complete advanced mathematics coursework, after calculus, compared to 18 percent of other bilinguals and 10 percent of native English speakers. These disparities in the highest levels of mathematics course-taking remain, even

---

[2]Segregated schools are defined as schools with a higher share of students from traditionally underrepresented backgrounds: that is, the percentage of the student body that is either African American or Hispanic.

[3]The New Latino Diaspora: Research in this area examines the relatively recent (past 20 years) movement of new immigrants and Latinos into the Midwest and the U.S. Southeast. For more information on this topic, see writings on the New Latino Diaspora (Lowenhaupt, 2016).

[4]The EL population is defined in the HSLS as EL students who take ESL coursework during high school. In accordance with National Center for Education Statistics restricted use guidelines, all sample sizes are rounded to the nearest 50.

after the implementation of a national accountability movement intended to improve student success.

With respect to science course-taking, the story is more complex; unlike mathematics, science course-taking is neither linear nor hierarchical. Again using the HSLS:2009 dataset, the data indicate that ELs are more likely not to take any science course, and complete higher shares of lower-level, noncollege preparatory sciences (e.g., integrated and earth science) than other bilinguals or native English speakers. In addition, while one-half of ELs (50.4%) complete chemistry, a fairly standard requirement for 4-year college-going, the chemistry completion rates of other bilinguals and native English speakers are nearly 20 percentage points higher (72.4% and 70.4%, respectively). Likewise, while nearly 12 percent of ELs take honors-level science courses during high school, that number is far lower than the 20 percent of native English speakers and nearly 30 percent of other bilinguals who do so.

It is important to keep in mind that the data from these studies merely present descriptive statistics; these analyses do not account for English proficiency, time in U.S. schools, or any of the myriad issues that shape both EL status and students' overall course-taking. Nonetheless, they point to disparities in ELs' access to STEM coursework, a trend that has persisted for decades (Hopstock and Stephenson, 2003). For example, Callahan (2005) examined ELs' English proficiency against their course placement and found that whereas course-taking demonstrated a strong positive association with high school credit completion, overall GPA, and mathematics test scores, students' level of English proficiency was associated only with reading and language arts test scores.

Even in courses designed specifically to meet ELs' needs, research shows that they often cover less content, and do so at a slower pace compared to general education classes (Ek, 2009; Estrada and Wang, 2013; Harklau, 1994). Estrada and Wang's (2013) analyses specifically characterized courses designed for ELs as following a slower pace and engaging students in less depth and rigor of content. Moreover, they showed that the vast majority of ELs who are placed in general education mathematics courses performed poorly and thus had to repeat them. In some cases, these trends in poor performance are related to disparities in curricular resources and access to highly qualified teachers in schools serving ELs (Umansky, 2016). As such, although course-taking is an important marker of EL access to STEM content, research has demonstrated a persistent, negative relationship between EL status and mathematics and science course-taking. Moreover, mere placement in STEM courses does not mean that ELs are afforded equitable access to rigorous STEM content.

## SUMMARY

Throughout this chapter, many of the factors that have been suggested to impact an understanding of ELs and their access to rigorous STEM content were addressed. ELs come to U.S. schools having varying levels of proficiency, both in their home language and in English, across the modes of language use (listening, speaking, reading, and writing) and having varying prior experience with STEM learning. This heterogeneity is further compounded by heterogeneity in the age at which they enter school, as foreign-born ELs may have no formal school experience prior to arrival in the United States. They may also have experienced interrupted schooling, or significant trauma that prevented school attendance or did not allow for literacy in their primary language to be attained. Added to this heterogeneity in the population, there are a variety of program models used in the United States—ESL or bilingual approaches—that differ in their emphasis on language development and STEM content learning. These approaches have implications for ELs' acquisition of English proficiency, their reclassification to English-proficient, and can further impact their access to STEM courses and rigorous content. At the same time, these factors simply define the starting point for examining the research to determine how the educational experiences of ELs can be transformed to create more optimal STEM learning for this large, growing, and diverse subset of U.S. students.

## REFERENCES

Abedi, J. (2010). *Performance Assessments for English Language Learners.* Stanford, CA: Stanford University, Stanford Center for Opportunity Policy in Education.

Adelman, C. (2006). *The Toolbox Revisited—Paths to Degree Completion from High School through College.* Washington, DC: U.S. Department of Education.

Avalos, M.A., Medina, E., and Secada, W.G. (2018). Reading mathematics problems: Exploring how language counts for middle school students with varying mathematics proficiency. In A. Bailey, C. Maher, and L. Wilkinson (Eds.), *Language, Literacy and Learning in the STEM Disciplines: How Language Counts for English Learners* (pp. 55–78). New York: Routledge.

Bailey, A., Maher, C., and Wilkinson, L. (Eds.). (2018). *Language, Literacy and Learning in the STEM Disciplines: How Language Counts for English Learners.* New York: Routledge.

Bailey, A.L., and Butler, F.A. (2004). Ethical considerations in the assessment of the language and content knowledge of U.S. school-age English learners. *Language Assessment Quarterly, 1*(2-3), 177–193.

Bailey, A.L. and Durán, R. (in press). Language in practice: A mediator of valid interpretations of information generated by classroom assessments among linguistically and culturally diverse students. In S.M. Brookhart and J.H. McMillan (Eds.), *Classroom Assessment and Educational Measurement.* NCME Book Series. Philadelphia: National Council on Measurement.

Baker, C. (2011). *Foundations of Bilingual Education and Bilingualism* (5th ed., vol. 79). Bristol, UK: Multilingual Matters.

Batalova, J., and McHugh, M. (2010). *Top Languages Spoken by English Language Learners Nationally and by State.* Washington, DC: Migration Policy Institute. Available: http://migrationpolicy.org/programs/ell-information-center [August 2018].

Batalova, J., Fix, M., and Murray, J. (2007). *Measure of Change: The Demography and Literacy of Adolescent English Learners: A Report to the Carnegie Corporation of New York.* Washington, DC: Migration Policy Institute.

Boals, T. (2001). Ensuring academic success: The real issue in educating English language learners. *Mid-Western Educational Researcher, 14*(4), 3–8.

Bunch, G.C., Aguirre, J.M., and Téllez, K. (2009). Beyond the scores: Using candidate responses on high stakes performance assessment to inform teacher preparation for English learners. *Issues in Teacher Education, 18*(1), 103–128.

Calderón, M.E., and Minaya-Rowe, L. (2011). *Preventing Long-Term ELs: Transforming Schools to Meet Core Standards.* Thousand Oaks, CA: Corwin Press.

Calderón, M.E., Slavin, R.E., and Sánchez, M. (2011). Effective instruction for English learners. *The Future of Children, 21*(1), 103–127.

Callahan, R.M. (2005). Tracking and high school English learners: Limiting opportunity to learn. *American Educational Research Journal, 42*(2), 305–328.

Callahan, R.M. (2013). The academic achievement of immigrant adolescents: Exploration of school factors from sociological and educational perspectives. In M. Gowda and A. Khanderia (Eds.), *Educational Achievement: Teaching Strategies, Psychological Factors and Economic Impact* (pp. 53–74). New York: Nova Science.

Callahan, R.M. (2017). *Equity and Access: High School EL Students' STEM Course-taking.* Presentation to the Committee on Supporting English Learners in STEM Subjects, Washington, DC, July 26. Available: http://www.nas.edu/ELinSTEM [October 2018].

Callahan, R.M. (2018). *K–12 English Learners' Science and Math Education: A Question of Curricular Equity.* Washington, DC: The National Academies Press. Available: http://www.nas.edu/ELinSTEM [October 2018].

Callahan, R.M., and Humphries, M. (2016). Undermatched? School-based linguistic status, college going, and the immigrant advantage. *American Educational Research Journal, 53*(2), 263–295.

Callahan, R.M., Wilkinson, L., Muller, C., and Frisco, M.L. (2009). ESL placement and schools: Effects on immigrant achievement. *Educational Policy, 23*(2), 355–384.

Callahan, R.M., Wilkinson, L., and Muller, C. (2010). Academic achievement and course taking among language minority youth in U.S. schools: Effects of ESL placement. *Educational Evaluation and Policy Analysis, 32*(1), 84–117.

Capps, R. (2015). *Trends in Immigration and Migration of English and Dual Language Learners.* Presentation to the National Research Council Committee on Fostering School Success for English Learners, Washington, DC, May 28. Available: http://www.nationalacademies.org/hmd/~/media/Files/Activity%20Files/Children/DualLanguageLearners/2015-MAY-28/1Capps%20Randy.pdf [August 2018].

Cimpian, J.R., Thompson, K.D., and Makowski, M.B. (2017). Evaluating English learner reclassification policy effects across districts. *American Educational Research Journal, 54*(1, Suppl.), 255S–278S.

Collier, V.P., and Thomas, W.P. (2017). Validating the power of bilingual schooling: Thirty-two years of large-scale longitudinal research. *Annual Review of Applied Linguistics, 37*, 1–15.

Combs, M.C., Iddings, A.C.D.S., and Moll, L.C. (2014). 21st century linguistic apartheid: English language learners in Arizona public schools. In P. Orelus (Ed.), *Affirming Language Diversity in Schools and Society* (pp. 41–52). New York: Routledge.

Cumming, A. (2008). Assessing oral and literate abilities. In E. Shohamy and N. Hornberger (Eds.), *Encyclopedia of Language and Education: Language Testing and Assessment* (pp. 3–18). New York: Springer.

Dabach, D.B. (2014). "I am not a shelter!" Stigma and social boundaries in teachers' accounts of students' experience in separate "sheltered" English learner classrooms. *Journal of Education for Students Placed at Risk, 19*(4), 98–124.

Dabach, D.B. (2015). Teacher placement into immigrant English learner classrooms: Limiting access in comprehensive high schools. *American Educational Research Journal, 52*(2), 243–274.

Darling-Hammond, L., and Berry, B. (2006). Highly qualified teachers for all. *Educational Leadership, 64*(3), 14–20.

Dondero, M., and Muller, C. (2012). School stratification in new and established Latino destinations. *Social Forces, 91*(2), 477–502.

Durán, R.P. (2008). Assessing English-language learners' achievement. *Review of Research in Education, 32*(1), 292–327.

Ek, L.D. (2009). Language and literacy in the Pentecostal church and the public high school: A case study of a Mexican ESL student. *The High School Journal, 92*(2), 1–13.

EPE Research Center. (2009). *Quality Counts 2009: Portrait of a Population.* Bethesda, MD: Editorial Projects in Education.

Estrada, P., and Wang, H. (2013). *Reclassifying and Not Reclassifying English Learners to Fluent English Proficient, Year 1 Findings: Factors Impeding and Facilitating Reclassification and Access to the Core.* Paper presented at the American Educational Research Association, San Francisco, CA, April 27–May 1. Available: https://eric.ed.gov/?id=ED550098 [June 2018].

Evans, B.A., and Hornberger, N.H. (2005). No Child Left Behind: Repealing and unpeeling federal language education policy in the United States. *Language Policy, 4*(1), 87–106.

Francis, D.J., Lesaux, N., and August, D. (2006). Language of instruction. In D. August and T. Shanahan (Eds.), *Developing Literacy in Second-Language Learners* (pp. 365–413). Mahwah, NJ: Lawrence Erlbaum Associates.

Fry, R. (2007). *How Far Behind in Math and Reading Are English Language Learners?* Washington, DC: Pew Hispanic Center.

Gamoran, A. (2010). Tracking and inequality: New directions for research and practice. In *The Routledge International Handbook of the Sociology of Education* (pp. 213–228). Madison: University of Wisconsin, Wisconsin Center for Education Research.

Gamoran, A., and Hannigan, E.C. (2000). Algebra for everyone? Benefits of college-preparatory mathematics for students with diverse abilities in early secondary school. *Educational Evaluation and Policy Analysis, 22*(3), 241–254.

Gándara, P., and Hopkins, M. (Eds.). (2010). *Forbidden Language: English Learners and Restrictive Language Policies.* New York: Teachers College Press.

García, O. (2009). *Bilingual Education in the 21st Century: A Global Perspective.* Malden, MA: Wiley-Blackwell.

Grantmakers for Education. (2013). *Educating English Language Learners: Grantmaking Strategies for Closing America's Other Achievement Gap.* Available: https://edfunders. org/sites/default/files/Educating%20English%20Language%20Learners_April%202013. pdf [June 2018].

Hakuta, K., Butler, Y.G., and Witt, D. (2000). *How Long Does It Take English Learners to Attain Proficiency?* Santa Barbara: University of California Linguistic Minority Research Institute.

Harklau, L. (1994). ESL versus mainstream classes: Contrasting L2 learning environments. *TESOL Quarterly, 28*(2), 241–272.

Herman, J.L., Klein, D.C.D., and Abedi, J. (2000). Assessing students' opportunity to learn: Teacher and student perspectives. *Educational Measurement: Issues and Practice, 19*(4), 16–24.

Hopkins, M., Thompson, K.D., Linquanti, R., Hakuta, K., and August, D. (2013). Fully accounting for English learner performance: A key issue in ESEA reauthorization. *Educational Researcher, 42*(2), 101–108.

Hopstock, P.J., and Stephenson, T.G. (2003). *Descriptive Study of Services to LEP Students and LEP Students with Disabilities: Special Topic Report #1 Native Languages of LEP Students.* Washington, DC: U.S. Department of Education, Office of English Language Acquisition.

Kena, G., Musu-Gillette, L., Robinson, J., Wang, X., Rathbun, A., Zhang, J., Wilkinson-Flicker, S., Barmer, A., and Dunlop Velez, E. (2015). *The Condition of Education 2015* (NCES 2015-144). Washington, DC: U.S. Department of Education, National Center for Education Statistics. Available: https://nces.ed.gov/pubs2015/2015144.pdf [June 2018].

Kena, G., Hussar, W., McFarland, J., de Brey, C., Musu-Gillette, L., Wang, X., Zhang, J., Rathbun, A., Wilkinson-Flicker, S., Diliberti, M., Barmer, A., Bullock Mann, F., and Dunlop Velez, E. (2016). *The Condition of Education 2016* (NCES 2017-144). Washington, DC: U.S. Department of Education, National Center for Education Statistics. Available: https://files.eric.ed.gov/fulltext/ED565888.pdf [June 2018].

Kieffer, M.J., and Thompson, K.D. (2018). Hidden progress of multilingual students on NAEP. *Educational Researcher.* doi: 10.3102/0013189X18777740.

Lee, O. (2018). English language proficiency standards aligned with content standards. *Educational Researcher.* Available: http://journals.sagepub.com/doi/abs/10.3102/0013189X18763775 [June 2018].

Lemke, J.L. (1998). Multiplying meaning: Visual and verbal semiotics in scientific text. In J.R. Martin and R. Veel (Eds.), *Reading Science: Critical and Functional Perspectives on Discourses of Science* (pp. 87–113). New York: Routledge.

Lowenhaupt, R. (2016). Immigrant acculturation in suburban schools serving the new Latino diaspora. *Journal of Education, 16*(3), 348–365.

Lucas, S.R. (1999). *Tracking Inequality: Stratification and Mobility in American High Schools.* New York: Teachers College Press.

Lucas, S.R., and Berends, M. (2002). Sociodemographic diversity, correlated achievement, and de facto tracking. *Sociology of Education, 75*(4), 328–348.

McFarland, J., Hussar, B., de Brey, C., Snyder, T., Wang, X., Wilkinson-Flicker, S., Gebrekristos, S., Zhang, J., Rathbun, A., Barmer, A., Bullock Mann, F., and Hinz, S. (2017). *The Condition of Education 2017* (NCES 2017-144). Washington, DC: U.S. Department of Education, National Center for Education Statistics. Available: https://nces.ed.gov/pubsearch/pubsinfo.asp?pubid=2017144 [June 2018].

Menken, K. (2013). Emergent bilingual students in secondary school: Along the academic language and literacy continuum. *Language Teaching, 46*(4), 438–476.

Menken, K., and Kleyn, T. (2009). The difficult road for long-term English learners. *Educational Leadership, 66*(7). Available: http://www.ascd.org/publications/educational_leadership/apr09/vol66/num07/The_Difficult_Road_for_Long-Term_English_Learners.aspx [June 2018].

Menken, K., and Kleyn, T. (2010). The long-term impact of subtractive schooling in the educational experiences of secondary English language learners. *International Journal of Bilingual Education and Bilingualism, 13*(4), 399–417.

Moore, K.A., and Redd, Z. (2002). *Children in Poverty: Trends, Consequences, and Policy Options* (Research Brief No. 2002-54). Washington, DC: Child Trends.

Mulligan, K., Halle, T., and Kinukawa, A. (2012). *Reading, Mathematics, and Science Achievement of Language-Minority Students in Grade 8* (NCES 2015-144). Washington, DC: U.S. Department of Education, National Center for Education Statistics. Available: https://nces.ed.gov/pubs2012/2012028.pdf [November 2017].

NASEM. (National Academies of Sciences, Engineering, and Medicine). (2017). *Promoting the Educational Success of Children and Youth Learning English: Promising Futures.* Washington, DC: The National Academies Press.

National Clearinghouse for English Language Acquisition and Language Instruction Educational Programs. (2011). *The Growing Number of English Learner Students.* Washington, DC: Author. Available: http://www.ncela.gwu.edu/files/ uploads/9/growingLEP_0809.pdf [June 2018].

National Research Council. (1997). *Improving Schooling for Language Minority Children: A Research Agenda.* Washington, DC: National Academy Press.

Oakes, J. (2005). *Keeping Track: How Schools Structure Inequality.* New Haven, CT: Yale University Press.

Olsen, L. (2010). *Reparable Harm: Fulfilling the Unkept Promise of Educational Opportunity for California's Long Term English Learners.* Long Beach: Californians Together.

Porter, A. (2002). Measuring the content of instruction: Uses in research and practice. *Educational Researcher, 31*(7), 3–14.

Ramírez, J., Pasta, D., Yuen, S., Ramey, D., and Billings, D. (1991). *Final Report: Longitudinal Study of Structured English Immersion Strategy, Early-Exit and Late-Exit Bilingual Education Programs for Language-Minority Children.* San Mateo, CA: Aguirre International. Available: https://files.eric.ed.gov/fulltext/ED330216.pdf [June 2018].

Riegle-Crumb, C., and Grodsky, E. (2010). Racial-ethnic differences at the intersection of math course-taking and achievement. *Sociology of Education, 83*(3), 248–270.

Robinson-Cimpian, J.P., Thompson, K.D., and Umansky, I.M. (2016). Research and policy considerations for English learner equity. *Policy Insights from the Behavioral and Brain Sciences, 3*(1), 129–137.

Ruiz, R. (1984). Orientations in language planning. *NABE: The Journal for the National Association of Bilingual Education, 8*(2), 15–34.

Ruiz-Soto, A.G., Hooker, S., and Batalova, J. (2015). *States and Districts with the Highest Number and Share of English Language Learners.* Washington, DC: Migration Policy Institute. Available: http://www.migrationpolicy.org/ellinfo [September 2018].

Santos, M., Darling-Hammond, L., and Cheuk, T. (2012). *Teacher Development to Support English Language Learners in the Context of Common Core State Standards.* Stanford, CA: Stanford University, Understanding Language. Available: https://ca01000043.schoolwires.net/cms/lib08/CA01000043/Centricity/Domain/173/TeacherPDforELLsCCSS_Santos_Darling-Hammond_Cheuk.pdf [November 2017].

Saunders, W.M., and Marcelletti, D.J. (2013). The gap that can't go away: The catch-22 of reclassification in monitoring the progress of English learners. *Educational Evaluation and Policy Analysis, 35*(2), 139–156.

Saunders, W., Goldenberg, C., and Marcelletti, D. (2013). English language development: Guidelines for instruction. *American Educator*, 13–25. Available: https://www.aft.org/sites/default/files/periodicals/Saunders_Goldenberg_Marcelletti.pdf [June 2018].

Schleppegrell, M.J. (2004). *The Language of Schooling: A Functional Linguistics Perspective.* Mahwah, NJ: Lawrence Erlbaum Associates.

Schneider, B., and Saw, G. (2016). Racial and ethnic gaps in postsecondary aspirations and enrollment. *RSF: The Russell Sage Foundation Journal of the Social Sciences, 2*(5), 58–82.

Silver, D., Saunders, M., and Zarate, M.E. (2008). *What Factors Predict High School Graduation in the Los Angeles Unified School District.* Santa Barbara: California Dropout Research Project.

Slama, R.B. (2014). Investigating whether and when English learners are reclassified into mainstream classrooms in the United States: A discrete-time survival analysis. *American Educational Research Journal, 51*(2), 220–252.

Slama, R.B., Haynes, E.F., Sacks, L., Lee, D.H., and August, D. (2015). *Massachusetts English Language Learners' Profiles and Progress: A Report for the Massachusetts Department of Elementary and Secondary Education.* Washington, DC: American Institute for Research.

Snow, C. (2010). Academic language and the challenge of reading and learning about science. *Science, 328*(5977), 450–452.

Solano-Flores, G. (2008). Who is given tests in what language by whom, when, and where? The need for probabilistic views of language in the testing of English language learners. *Educational Researcher, 37*(4), 189–199.

Solano-Flores, G. (2016). *Assessing English Language Learners: Theory and Practice.* New York: Routledge.

Solano-Flores, G., and Hakuta, K. (2017). *Assessing Students in Their Home Language.* Stanford University, Understanding Language. Available: https://stanford.app.box.com/s/uvwlgjbmeeuokts6c2wnibucms4up9c2 [August 2018].

Solís, J., and Bunch, G.C. (2016). Responsive approaches for teaching English learners in secondary science classrooms. In E.G. Lyon, S. Tolbert, J. Solís, P. Stoddart, G.C. Bunch (Authors), *Secondary Science Teaching for English Learners: Developing Supportive and Responsive Learning Contexts for Sense-Making and Language Development* (pp. 21–50). Lanham, MD: Rowman & Littlefield.

Steele, J.L., Slater, R.O., Zamarro, G., Miller, T., Li, J., Burkhauser, S., and Bacon, M. (2017). Effects of dual-language immersion programs on student achievement: Evidence from lottery data. *American Educational Research Journal, 54*(1_suppl), 282S–306S.

Stevenson, D.L., Schiller, K.S., and Schneider, B. (1994). Sequences of opportunities for learning. *Sociology of Education, 67*(3), 184–198.

Sugarman, J. (2018). *A Guide to Finding and Understanding English Learner Data.* Washington, DC: Migration Policy Institute. Available: https://www.migrationpolicy.org/research/guide-finding-understanding-english-learner-data [August 2018].

Thompson, K.D. (2015a). English learners' time to reclassification: An analysis. *Educational Policy, 31*(3), 330–363.

Thompson, K.D. (2015b). Questioning the long-term English learner label: How categorization can blind us to students' abilities. *Teachers College Record, 117*(12).

Thompson, K.D. (2017a). English learners' time to reclassification: An analysis. *Educational Policy, 31*(3), 330–363.

Thompson, K.D. (2017b). What blocks the gate? Exploring current and former English learners' math course-taking in secondary school. *American Educational Research Journal, 54*(4), 757–798.

Thompson, K.D., Rew, J., Martinez, M.I., and Clinton, C. (2017). *Understanding Student Outcomes by Using the "Ever English Learner" Category.* Available: https://ies.ed.gov/blogs/research/post/understanding-outcomes-for-english-learners-the-importance-of-the-ever-learner-category [July 2018].

U.S. Department of Education. (2001). *No Child Left Behind.* Available: https://www2.ed.gov/policy/elsec/leg/esea02/107-110.pdf [June 2018].

U.S. Department of Education. (2012). *Elementary and Secondary Education Act.* Available: https://www2.ed.gov/about/overview/budget/budget12/justifications/a-eseaoverview.pdf [June 2018].

U.S. Department of Education, Institute of Education Sciences, National Center for Education Statistics. (2018). *English Language Learners in Public Schools.* Available: https://nces.ed.gov/programs/coe/indicator_cgf.asp [August 2018].

U.S. Department of Education, Office of English Language Acquisition. (2016). *Newcomer Tool Kit*. Washington, DC: Author. Available: https://www2.ed.gov/about/offices/list/oela/newcomers-toolkit/ncomertoolkit.pdf [September 2018].

U.S. Department of Education, Office of Planning, Evaluation and Policy Development, and Policy and Program Studies Service. (2012). *Language Instruction Educational Programs (LIEPs): A Review of the Foundational Literature*. Washington, DC: Author. Available: https://www2.ed.gov/rschstat/eval/title-iii/language-instruction-ed-programs-report.pdf [August 2018].

Umansky, I.M. (2016). To be or not to be EL: An examination of the impact of classifying students as English learners. *Educational Evaluation and Policy Analysis, 38*(4), 714–737.

Umansky, I.M., Thompson, K.D., and Diaz, G. (2017). Using an ever-English learner framework to examine disproportionality in special education. *Exceptional Children, 84*(1), 79–96.

Valdés, G., Capitelli, S., and Alvarez, L. (2011). Realistic expectations: English language learners and the acquisition of "academic" English. In J.A. Banks (Ed.), *Latino Children Learning English: Steps in the Journey* (pp. 15–42). New York: Teachers College Press.

Valdés, G., Poza, L., and Brooks, M. (2014). Educating students who do not speak the societal language: The social construction of language learner categories. *Profession*. Available: https://profession.mla.hcommons.org/2014/10/09/educating-students-who-do-not-speak-the-societal-language/ [September 2018].

Valentino, R.A., and Reardon, S.F. (2015). Effectiveness of four instructional programs designed to serve English learners: Variation by ethnicity and initial English proficiency. *Educational Evaluation and Policy Analysis, 37*(4), 612–637.

Yosso, T. (2005). Whose culture has capital? A critical race theory discussion of community cultural wealth. *Race, Ethnicity, and Education, 8*, 69–91.

Zong, J., and Batalova, J. (2015). *The Limited English Proficient Population in the United States*. Washington, DC: Migration Policy Institute. Available: http://www.migrationpolicy.org/article/limited-english-proficient-population-united-states#Age,%20Race,%20and%20Ethnicity [August 2018].

# 3

# Relationship Between Language and STEM Learning for English Learners

E nglish learners (ELs) develop science, technology, engineering, and
mathematics (STEM) knowledge and language proficiency when they
are engaged in meaningful interaction in the classroom and participate in the kinds of activities in which STEM experts and professionals
regularly engage. This chapter provides the committee's consensus views of
the inextricable relationship between language and content. It begins with
the committee's stance on language in the STEM subjects and articulates the
ways in which ELs can be afforded opportunities in the STEM classroom
to draw on language and other meaning-making resources while engaging
in disciplinary content. The committee then describes the current view of
the STEM subjects in PreK–12 and concludes with a vision of STEM education for ELs.

## THE ROLE OF LANGUAGE AND CULTURE IN STEM LEARNING

All children grow up in communities that use language to engage in
cultural practices that have developed historically and are shaped in ongoing ways to achieve the goals and values of the communities (Nasir et al.,
2014). Each community has particular ways of conceptualizing, representing, evaluating, and engaging with the world, and initially children are
socialized into the language and ways of being in their families and local
communities (Gutiérrez and Rogoff, 2003). Over time, however, each person becomes a member of a larger set of communities and engages in new
cultural practices that are sometimes complementary but may sometimes

conflict with the practices of their home communities (Moje, 2000). For most children, these new communities include both in-school and out-of-school affiliations through which they engage in new cultural practices (Nasir et al., 2014).

Any particular student coming from a home community into a school context may present herself or himself in a variety of ways, including ways that may or may not be consistent with stereotypes of the home communities or different cultural groups. Expecting individuals to act or think in particular ways because of their group memberships limits those individuals' opportunities to learn and constrains their opportunity to thrive in educational settings. Schools are enriched through the diverse experiences and perspectives of children and families from different cultural communities, and ELs simultaneously bring unique experiences as individuals and as knowledgeable members of the communities to which they belong (Gutiérrez and Rogoff, 2003; Moll et al., 1991; see Chapter 5 for a deeper discussion of the role of families, communities, and cultural contexts). All of these experiences, individual and collective, can provide resources for learning STEM (Ishimaru, Barajas-López, and Bang, 2015; Nasir et al., 2014).

Once they enter preschool, children encounter communities of academic disciplines, and they leverage their existing linguistic and cultural resources as they begin to engage in this context. The STEM disciplines constitute communities in which language and other ways of making sense of the world have evolved to enable participants to accomplish their functional goals. STEM subjects offer the potential for membership in the communities of mathematicians, scientists, engineers, and other technical experts—communities with their own ways of conceptualizing, representing, evaluating, and engaging with the world. In turn, STEM students from a wide range of backgrounds bring the potential to contribute to shaping STEM fields in critical ways that transform and remake focal topics, practices, and contributions (Vossoughi, Hooper, and Escudé, 2016).

Language is simultaneously a cognitive ability and a cultural resource that children first learn to draw on in their homes and communities. As they interact with caregivers in the early years, the language they develop enables them to participate in the community's cultural practices and learn its ways of being, as well as to organize and make sense of their complex worlds. For example, children begin to learn about cause and effect in everyday contexts as they experience and talk about conditions, purposes, and reasons (e.g., Painter, 1999). Their understanding of cause and effect develops along with the language through which causal relationships are expressed (e.g., through language such as *if you see a snake, don't touch it because it may be dangerous*). Through many such interactions, they learn both the language and values of their culture and are introduced to concepts relevant for later STEM learning. For some children, this development occurs in more than one language.

When children enter school, they begin to use language in new ways and encounter new cultural practices through talk, text, and other systems for sharing meaning (e.g., gesture, visual display) and making sense of the world (Schleppegrell, 2004). These new ways of using language can build upon and enhance children's experiences, as well as encourage new ideas and knowledge. Across school subjects, as children learn new concepts, they also learn new *discourse* patterns, new ways of using language to interact with all of their meaning-making resources to share their perspectives as they engage with the concepts. In other words, language development and concept development occur simultaneously; in humans, language development and concept development are inextricable (National Research Council, 2000). As learners add concepts and language, adding new concepts through language becomes progressively easier as the linguistic skills and abilities of the learner increase. The learner possesses a broader and deeper foundation upon which to layer new concepts and language. Concept development is made more challenging for ELs to the extent that educators rely exclusively on the English language to develop concepts and may not recognize the added challenge of learning new concepts in a language that one is also learning (Coady, Harper, and de Jong, 2016; de Araujo, 2017).

To learn STEM subjects, students will learn the requisite new patterns of language and expression only through opportunity for and engagement in STEM disciplinary practices. The developmental pathways available to individual learners in STEM classrooms are influenced by the opportunities they are offered to participate in the practices and discourses of STEM fields. As described throughout Chapter 4, participation in these practices and discourses increases learners' capacities to generalize and express abstract ideas, develop disciplinary habits of mind and dispositions, and achieve success in STEM learning. Learning STEM subjects requires support for learning to use the discourse patterns through which the knowledge in each subject area is presented and engaged with. All children require such support, including those learning in their mother tongues or first language (also referred to as L1). For ELs, success often hinges on engaging in classroom and out-of-school experiences that encourage them to draw on the languages and multicompetences they already control and to connect new concepts with the knowledge they bring from their homes and communities (Moll et al., 1991). When allowed to interact in varied ways to build from what they already know and to develop new technical knowledge at school, ELs can learn STEM content and practices while simultaneously building their proficiency in English beyond STEM.

## LANGUAGE AS MEANING-MAKING

Language is experienced as sounds and wordings (words/phrases), but the primary *function* of language is to make sense of the world and share meanings with others. The use of language is to "make meanings" that fulfill goals in the social contexts where people interact (Schleppegrell, 2004). The meanings vary not only according to what is being done (the "content"), but also according to with whom the interactions take place (e.g., how many people are present, the status of the relationships, the roles taken on in the discourse, etc.) And it is not just in language that people interact. Along with language, nonlinguistic modalities—including gesture, visual displays (e.g., symbols, diagrams, graphs, tables), and other multimodal representations (e.g., in everyday life, maps, emojis, pictures, etc.; in STEM subjects, artifacts of engineering design, computational modeling, etc.)—offer different affordances and limitations, potentials, and constraints for meaning-making (Bezemer and Kress, 2008).

It is important to recognize that the content taught in STEM subjects is not separable from the language through which the content is presented (Schleppegrell, 2007). There is no language-free content; language use always presents some content, and most representations of content require some language use, even with multimodal resources for meaning-making. This understanding of language means that to learn the language of STEM subjects, students must participate in STEM contexts and activities. For ELs, this means that they must be encouraged to draw on all of their multicompetencies, which include all of their languages and their different varieties, as well as gesture, drawing, and other modalities for meaning-making.

Language is used in different ways depending on what is being done—making different language choices in doing mathematics than in doing science, for example—and who is being spoken to (e.g., a friend or family member versus a stranger) and the mode of communication (e.g., talking on the phone or writing a letter) (Schleppegrell, 2004, 2007). Linguists use the term *register* to refer to this kind of variation in the ways that meaning-making resources are drawn upon. *Register* refers to the different ways people draw on linguistic and nonlinguistic resources as they engage in different kinds of activities, with different kinds of people, through different modes of communication. It is a concept articulated by linguist Michael Halliday[1] in describing features of the language of mathematics (1978) and science

---

[1]Halliday (1978, 2014) and Halliday and Martin (1993) developed systemic functional linguistics (SFL), a theory of language that relates language choices to features of social contexts. SFL offers a *functional grammar* that can be used to describe and analyze the meanings that are expressed in different registers, helping show how linguistic choices vary across fields of study and in different tasks and contexts within the same field of study. There have been others who have conceptualized and studied registers (see Ferguson, 1994).

(1993) and has been a key linguistic construct for exploring variation in meaning in context in all subjects. Students use multiple registers as they engage in classroom activities in the same ways they use multiple registers as they engage in activities outside of school. Figure 3-1 shows how three aspects of a context, the *content* being engaged with, the *relationships* being enacted, and the *modalities* available to draw on, shape the actual language and meanings being presented.

It is perhaps most obvious that language varies according to *content*. Different words are used in mathematics than in science. But consider how different *modalities* present and enact meaning; for example, by writing rather than speaking, and how different wordings depending on the *relationship* of the speakers, for example, whether speaking one-on-one or with a small group. The registers used respond to the contexts participated in, so shaping contexts to enable students to expand their linguistic repertoires is an important goal of instruction in all subjects; adding new registers and developing existing registers is a main goal of schooling. The notion of register helps point out how teachers can engage learners in activities that build from everyday ways of interacting toward more formal ways of presenting disciplinary meanings, as well as how learners can unpack disciplinary meanings into language that connects with the language and meanings they bring to the classroom. The notion of register also helps teachers recognize students' subject-matter understandings even as their proficiency

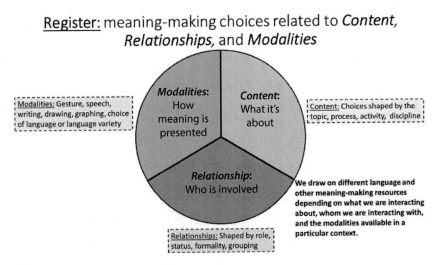

**Register:** meaning-making choices related to *Content, Relationships,* and *Modalities*

Modalities: Gesture, speech, writing, drawing, graphing, choice of language or language variety

**Modalities:** How meaning is presented

**Content:** What it's about

Content: Choices shaped by the topic, process, activity, discipline

**Relationship:** Who is involved

We draw on different language and other meaning-making resources depending on what we are interacting about, whom we are interacting with, and the modalities available in a particular context.

Relationships: Shaped by role, status, formality, grouping

**FIGURE 3-1** A perspective on language as variation in *Register*.
SOURCE: Based on concepts proposed by Halliday (1978).

in English is still developing. Within the same classroom, different activities offer learners different affordances for drawing on language and the multicompetencies they already are comfortable with and for learning new ways of making meaning that are subject-specific.

"Content" can be held constant as students who are learning English engage with the same concept in different ways across a set of activities designed to involve them in sense-making as they learn STEM subjects. ELs who are less proficient in English may be most confident in participating when encouraged to use a range of modalities and work in a small group setting with peers, while those with greater proficiency may participate in imperfect but comprehensible English and interact in whole class settings. While different participation structures present different challenges and affordances to particular students, language will develop as students have multiple opportunities to engage with the same content and concepts over a unit of study (Haynes and Zacarian, 2010). The particular ways to talk and write (discourse patterns) about the content will not be the same across the unit. Introducing and working with a concept initially, students may use everyday language and informal vocabulary and sentence structure. As they become more familiar with the technical aspects of the STEM concepts they are learning and the STEM practices they are engaging in, they move toward more disciplinary ways of talking about what they are learning, using technical language, sentence structure, and arguments more typical of written or formal discourse. This is how students develop new academic registers at the same time they learn new concepts, and teachers' awareness of the affordances of this register development over time can enable them to challenge ELs (Gibbons, 2015).

For example, in a unit of instruction about division with fractions, the activities that 5th-grade students can engage in move from hands-on interaction to reporting on the interaction and then writing about what was learned. In moving across these different activities, students work in different participation structures and use different modalities, even while the underlying "content," understanding and using the concept of division by a fraction in a word problem involving the *measurement* meaning of division (not the *partitive* meaning used in "fair share" problems), remains the same. Table 3-1 illustrates the variation in *register* that results as the children work to make sense of, represent, and discuss multiple solutions to a problem. It presents hypothetical responses that could occur with any group of children as they engage in different participation structures across an activity sequence:

> Sophia wants to make peach tarts for her friends. She needs two-thirds of a peach for each tart and she has 10 peaches. What is the greatest number of tarts that she can make with 10 peaches?

**TABLE 3-1** Shifting Registers in Mathematics Activities While Holding Content Constant

| Context | Context 1 | Context 2 | Context 3 | Context 4 |
|---|---|---|---|---|
| Modalities | <u>Spoken</u> by a small group of students <u>with accompanying</u> action or gesture | <u>Spoken</u> by a student about the action, <u>after</u> the event | <u>Written</u> by a student | <u>Written</u> using equations in the textbook |
| | **S1:** Mark it like this <br> **S2:** No, try this way <br> **S1:** Ok, count those . . . 30 <br> **S2:** the tarts all need 2; 30 divided by 2 <br> **S1:** 15 | **S1:** We drew the 10 peaches and then cut each 1 into 3 parts. Then we counted all the parts. So it was 30 parts, and each tart had to have 2 parts, so we divided 30 by 2 and got 15. | When you want to find how many thirds there are, you can divide each peach into 3. When you count how many thirds, you get 30. Since each tart needs two thirds, you can divide 30 by 2 and get 15. That means that Sophia can make 15 tarts. | To divide a whole number by a fraction, multiply the whole number by the reciprocal of the fraction. $10 \div (2/3)$ <br> $\quad = 10 * (3/2)$ <br> $\quad = (10*3)/2)$ <br> $\quad = 15$ |
| Relationship | Peer-to-peer, face-to-face interaction | Reporting on behalf of a small group | Individual written production for the teacher | Author writing for a remote audience of learners |
| Content | Solving a fractions division problem | Solving a fractions division problem | Solving a fractions division problem | Solving a fractions division problem |

In **Context 1**, the children first interact in a small group using manipulatives that represent the peaches to explore this problem. In this context, while the "content" is about the problem, their relationship is that of small group interaction, and the modalities they use to make meaning involve talk, gestures, and perhaps drawings. Their language includes commands to each other to act, sentence fragments, and words like *this* and *those* that are meaningful only because of the shared context and the objects or manipulatives. This language and interaction is functional for finding and discussing solutions in a small group.

In **Context 2**, when a student has to tell the class what the group did, although the "content" is still about the word problem and the meaning of division by a fraction, the relationship is now one student talking to the whole class about something that the others have not experienced. This change in context leads to different language choices. Instead of *those,* the student says *the 10 peaches,* as the shift in context requires the speaker to make explicit referents that could be pointed at when the group was interacting with the manipulatives. Instead of commands to act, the student uses past tense to say what the group did, and sequencing terms (*then*) to order the procedures they engaged in, and conjunctions (*so*) to draw conclusions.

In **Context 3,** the students work individually to write about their solutions, discuss which solution may be general, and finally settle on a general statement. The language choices are different as the students discuss multiple solutions and write a general statement about how to find the answer. The audience is now distant, so everything that could be left implicit, known from the context, in Context 1, has to be made explicit. When the goal is to share a generalized description of the experience, instead of *what we did,* the writer would describe what a generalized *you* can do to make sense of and solve the problem, using simple present tense to present timeless generalizations. Words like *since* and phrases such as *that means* help the writers construct a cohesive description of what they did to solve the problem and words like *because* would be part of an explanation or justification for why they did what they did and why it works.

These students are shifting registers, drawing on language and other meaning-making resources in different ways as they engage with the same content and present it to audiences with which they have different relationships. A textbook, as in **Context 4,** represents yet another register with which students must engage; this register presents a mathematical generalization about the meaning of division by fractions in a sentence that distills several concepts into technical language accompanied by an equation in mathematical symbolic language. To understand this technical language, teacher and students are likely to engage in further talk and interaction that "unpacks" the technicality and uses more everyday register features to help learners see meaning in what is represented through mathematical symbols. Through opportunities to engage with language in all these different forms of interactions, none of which is inherently "better" or "more appropriate" than any others in the abstract, learners are enabled to move between the language(s) and registers they bring to the classroom and the new registers they are learning to engage with as they participate in STEM learning. With textbooks, through which students are exposed to the written language of the disciplines, stylistic differences in language are also well-documented (e.g., Bailey et al., 2007).

This understanding of language suggests important implications for providing instruction and supports that will engage and challenge ELs and enable their success in learning STEM content, concepts, and practices. In Chapter 4, the committee reports on what is known about how best to support high-quality instruction for ELs; with more evidence in science and mathematics than in technology and engineering. This understanding of language is also fundamental to preparing teachers to create learning environments and design STEM instruction that is effective with diverse learners, including ELs. Chapter 6 reports on research that shows how teachers' knowledge about language and STEM can be developed in preservice and in-service contexts. It is the committee's stance that through participation in such STEM learning contexts that engage all learners in using all of their meaning-making capacities, ELs will develop English language proficiency along with subject area knowledge, understanding, and practices.

## CURRENT CONTEXT OF STEM PREK–12 EDUCATION FOR ENGLISH LEARNERS

In this section, the committee describes contemporary views of STEM education with ELs that provide important background for understanding the current literature; specific instructional strategies and the research associated with these views are discussed in Chapter 4. Due to the imbalance of research in these disciplinary content areas, we acknowledge that science and mathematics are necessarily overrepresented.

### Science and Science Education

Based on extensive research on how children learn science in school (National Research Council, 2006, 2007) and in informal settings (National Research Council, 2009), the National Research Council (2012) report *A Framework for K–12 Science Education: Practices, Crosscutting Concepts, and Core Ideas* (hereafter referred to as the Framework) captures contemporary knowledge of what counts as science and engineering and provides a broad set of expectations for K–12 students (see Box 3-1).

### Science and Language Instructional Shifts with English Learners

Recent years have witnessed parallel shifts toward promoting the social and sense-making nature of both science learning and second language development. In science education, whereas traditional views focused on individual learners' mastery of discrete elements of science content, contemporary views emphasize that students engage in science and engineering practices (e.g., developing models, arguing from evidence, constructing explanations) to make sense of the world around them (National Research Council, 2012). Because this approach to science learning involves using

**BOX 3-1**
**The *Framework*: Science and Language**
**with English Learners (ELs)**

The new vision of science education expects students to engage in science and engineering as scientists and engineers carry out their work. In the science classroom, students make sense of phenomena or design solutions to problems by engaging in three-dimensional learning. In doing so, they build their science understanding with more sophistication over the course of instruction. The *Framework* recommends organizing science learning around three dimensions: scientific and engineering practices, crosscutting concepts, and disciplinary core ideas.

The first dimension of scientific and engineering practices include the following:

1. Ask questions (for science) and define problems (for engineering)
2. Develop and use models
3. Plan and carry out investigations
4. Analyze and interpret data
5. Use mathematics and computational thinking
6. Construct explanations (for science) and design solutions (for engineering)
7. Engage in argument from evidence
8. Obtain, evaluate, and communicate information

The second dimension of crosscutting concepts, which unify the study of science and engineering through their common application across fields include patterns; cause and effect; scale, proportion, and quantity; systems and system models; energy and matter; structure and function; and stability and change. The third dimension includes disciplinary core ideas in four areas: physical sciences; life sciences; earth and space sciences; and engineering, technology, and applications of science. The Next Generation Science Standards, written as performance expectations, blend these three dimensions to express what students should be able to do at the end of a grade band or grade level.

The work by Lee, Valdés, and Llosa (2015–2019) illustrates how science and language instruction mutually support each other with all students, and with ELs in particular. A unit of science instruction starts with an anchoring phenomenon that students select with the guidance of their teacher (e.g., "Our school, home, and community make large amounts of garbage, which all goes to a landfill"). From this anchoring phenomenon, students generate the driving question of the unit ("What happens to our garbage?"). Over the course of the unit, students ask a series of subquestions ("What is that smell?") that helps answer the driving question. To answer each subquestion, students engage in three-dimensional learning. They engage in a relevant science and engineering practice (develop a model) to describe their understanding of a disciplinary core idea (smell is a gas that is made of particles) and a crosscutting concept (particles are too small to see in terms of scale). This new understanding, in turn, generates a new subquestion (what causes smell from the garbage? what happens to the weight of the garbage when some materials seem to have vanished?) toward answering the driving question.

As lessons fit together coherently and build on each other over the course of instruction, students develop deeper and more sophisticated understanding of science to make sense of the anchoring phenomenon for the unit of science instruction. As ELs develop deeper and more sophisticated science understanding over time, their language use becomes more sophisticated. To communicate the sophistication of their ideas, ELs use modalities more strategically (e.g., they may use dots to represent particles of smell, arrows to represent movement of smell particles, and different shapes or colors to distinguish between smell particles and air particles that are intermingled) and more specialized registers (e.g., they progress from "it stinks" to "smell is a gas made of particles too small to see that are moving freely in space and reaching my nose").

The specialized register allows ELs to be more precise as their science understanding becomes more sophisticated (Quinn, Lee, and Valdés, 2012). Precision goes beyond science vocabulary (e.g., "particles") and privileges disciplinary meaning by focusing on how ELs use language to engage in science and engineering practices. For example, in constructing a scientific explanation of how smell travels across the room, ELs can communicate precise disciplinary meaning about the scale at which gas particles can be observed ("too small to see") and the movement of the particles ("move freely around in space") with less sophisticated language. As ELs use language in a variety of settings—individually, in pairs, small-groups, and whole-class settings—they learn to adapt their language to meet the communicative demands of different interactions ("check this out" in one-to-one interaction when there is a shared frame of reference, "the food materials are decomposing and producing smell" in one-to-many interaction when language needs to be explicit). Overall, the science classroom presents a rich science learning environment that also promotes language learning for all students, including ELs, who benefit from sustained opportunities to *use language to do science*.

The science classroom may be particularly beneficial to ELs when their contributions are valued for the merit of their ideas regardless of social status or linguistic accuracy. They communicate their ideas using a wide range of semiotic resources, including home languages, linguistic and nonlinguistic modalities of science disciplines, and registers starting from everyday to specialized language to meet the communicative demands of different types of interactions in the science classroom (Grapin, 2018; Lee, Grapin, and Haas, 2018). Language is a product of doing science, not a precursor or prerequisite for doing science and ELs need ample opportunities to do science.

SOURCE: Adapted from National Research Council (2012).

and applying knowledge for a particular purpose, it has been referred to as *knowledge-in-use* (e.g., Harris et al., 2016). In second-language development, whereas earlier theories saw it as the accumulation of discrete elements of vocabulary (lexicon) and grammar (syntax) to be internalized by learners, more recent thinking has taken a sociocultural turn, viewing language as a set of dynamic meaning-making practices learned through participation in social contexts (Beckner et al., 2009; Larsen-Freeman, 1997, 2007; Valdés, 2015; Zuengler and Miller, 2006). Because this approach to language learning involves using language for a particular purpose, it has been referred to as *language-in-use* (e.g., Lee, Quinn, and Valdés, 2013). Knowledge-in-use in science education and language-in-use in second-language development complement each other, such that science instructional shifts promote language learning with ELs, while language instructional shifts promote science learning with ELs. Recognizing science and language instructional shifts as mutually supportive can lead to better and more coherent instructional approaches that promote both science and language learning with all students, especially ELs (see the example in Box 3-1 and more details in Chapter 4).

### Language, Discourse, and Practices in Science

The importance of discourse processes in science education builds from longstanding research examining the multiple ways language supports the creation of knowledge. In particular, sociocultural approaches brought more focused attention to the role of cultural tools such as language in mediating the processes of individual learning and cultural production and change (Nasir et al., 2014). This perspective offers an important opportunity to see how scientific knowledge accrues and changes over time as well as how knowledge is created and negotiated through social engagement and discussion in classroom settings. As will be further articulated in the Mathematical Practices section below, classroom activities should be constructed to be developmentally appropriate approximations of scientific practices, as described in Box 3-1.

Research on science practices often focuses on the establishment and evaluation of knowledge claims. These epistemic practices are central to learning the disciplinary knowledge and ways of being for various science fields. Kelly (2008) defined epistemic practices as "specific ways members of a community propose, justify, evaluate, and legitimize knowledge claims" (p. 99). Such practices vary across disciplinary communities, ways of knowing, and power dynamics that also operate in the presentation of cultures (Knorr-Cetina, 1999; Watson-Verran and Turnbull, 1995). Those epistemic practices leading to generalized knowledge claims about nature tend to be legitimized in disciplinary communities in science and engineering (Kelly,

2016). Chinn, Buckland, and Samarapungavan (2011), drawing on work in the philosophy of science, suggested five focal areas: (1) epistemic aims and values, (2) structure of knowledge and other epistemic achievements, (3) sources of justification of knowledge, (4) epistemic virtues and vices, and (5) reliable and unreliable processes for achieving epistemic aims. These epistemic practices of science have been examined in a number of studies. For example, Manz (2012) examined how uses of epistemic practices supported students' use of modeling of a local ecosystem adjacent to their school.

Studies of student uses of knowledge in problem solving also entail engagement in scientific practices. This focus on everyday knowledge construction practices forms students' practical epistemology[2] that can serve to help make sense of phenomena, to develop conceptual knowledge, and to learn about the nature of science (Sandoval, 2005; Wickman, 2004; see Chapter 4 for a deeper discussion on phenomena and place-based learning). In each of these cases, examining student engagement in epistemic or scientific practices relies on a methodological focus on discourse processes because the ways that communities affiliate, build knowledge, and construct social practices are constructed in and through discourse (Berland et al., 2016; Jiménez-Aleixandre, 2014; Kelly and Licona, 2018; Östman and Wickman, 2014; Pluta, Chinn, and Duncan, 2011; Sandoval, 2014).

Working in groups engages students in discourse through which they both construct knowledge and enact relationships, highlighting the social nature of science learning. By focusing on the ways that knowledge was constructed, negotiated, and valued, a number of studies identified key aspects of discourse for productive educational aims (Duschl, 2008; Herrenkohl and Cornelius, 2013). For example, the interaction of the interpersonal and cognitive was made evident in Bianchini's (1999) study of student groupwork. This study showed how students' perceived status influenced participation and science learning. A number of studies illustrated how access to scientific knowledge was negotiated through discourse processes and tied to the ongoing social practices and norms of the classrooms (Alozie, Moje, and Krajcik, 2010; Barton and Tan, 2009; Oliveira, 2010).

An important development in the study of classroom discourse emerged from a focus on teachers' and students' uses of evidence. The alignment of evidence in disciplinary-specific and genre-specific forms of language has entered studies of science education as argumentation (Duschl and Osborne, 2002). Studies of argumentation have explored different contexts, have drawn from multiple argumentation analytics for analysis, and

---

[2]Epistemology deals with questions about what knowledge is and how knowledge is developed. Practical epistemology is "the epistemological ideas that students apply to their own scientific knowledge building through inquiry" (Sandoval, 2005).

have focused on different dimensions of science from conceptual learning to socioscientific issue (Berland and Reiser, 2011; Bricker and Bell, 2008; Cavagnetto, 2010; Evagorou, Jiménez-Aleixandre, and Osborne, 2012; Sadler, 2009; Sampson and Clark, 2008). Argumentation has been applied across multiple science subject areas (Herrenkohl and Cornelius, 2013) and entered into teacher education to prepare teachers to orchestrate uses of evidence among students (Elby and Hammer, 2010; Sadler, 2006; Zembal-Saul, 2009).

## Technology and Technology Education

Education related to technology—the T in STEM—is interpreted in a variety of ways (National Academy of Engineering and National Research Council, 2014, pp. 17–18). One interpretation focuses on technological literacy, which is defined as the "ability to use, manage, assess, and understand technology" (International Technology Education Association, 2000, p. 242), and traditionally, career and technical education (CTE) programs of study have emphasized technological literacy as a goal (Asunda, 2012). A second interpretation focuses on educational, or instructional, technology as a central tool for teaching and learning (language and content) both in and out of the classroom. Some influential educational technologies to date are personal computers (as well as laptops, tablet computers, and smartphones), the Internet (including online resources and educational software), and cloud computing. A third interpretation focuses on the tools used by practitioners of science, mathematics, engineering, and beyond. These tools include computers, software, sensors, and other data collection instruments. For all interpretations, there is limited research on technology and technology education with respect to ELs; nevertheless, we highlight what is known from the existing literature.

Within K–12, the goal of technology education is to prepare students to make well-informed decisions about matters that influence technology or are influenced by technology (National Academy of Engineering and National Research Council, 2002). Typically, aspects of technology education are incorporated into multiple disciplines (e.g., mathematics aligned to the Common Core State Standards, science and engineering aligned to the Next Generation Science Standards [NGSS], and computer science aligned to the Computer Science Teachers Association [CSTA] standards), but many states have also developed separate technology education standards. Yet, no explicit recommendations for supporting linguistically diverse students in meeting these standards have been outlined.

Research describing teachers' conceptualization of the role of technology in teaching and learning highlights that the primary goal is for students to become skillful communicators of the language learned rather than simply learners of the language, maximizing student autonomy and empowerment in the classroom (Garrett, 2009; Warschauer and Meskill, 2000). For example, students were found to write more via computer compared to when given pen and paper, and computer-based collaborative activities encouraged more attentiveness to listening, speaking, reading, and writing (Warschauer and Meskill, 2000). Moreover, these activities help students integrate language and culture, which led students to converse in English in more meaningful ways (Garrett, 2009; Warschauer and Meskill, 2000). These findings have implications for how technology could support ELs in engaging in meaningful discourse beyond learning a language.

Likewise, educational technologies have also been shown to benefit ELs in learning science content (Ryoo and Bedell, 2017; Zheng et al., 2014). In a year-long, quasi-experimental study involving linguistically diverse 5th-grade students, laptop use was found to be correlated with higher science scores for ELs on the California Standards Test compared to their counterparts in the control group (Zheng et al., 2014). In a mixed-methods study approach, Ryoo and Bedell (2017) investigated the impact of interactive visualizations on 7th-grade students' coherent understanding of complex life science core ideas. These visualization technologies were embedded in Web-based inquiry instruction in science, and EL and non-EL students were randomly assigned to either a static or dynamic visualization condition. Compared to the students in the static group, ELs and non-ELs within the dynamic visualization group engaged in more discourse and used both text and visual representations to make sense of the scientific phenomena. Additionally, these students more successfully evaluated the range of ideas presented in order to develop coherent scientific explanations based on evidence from the visualizations. These findings suggest that dynamic visualization technology can support the development of coherent scientific understanding for all students, including ELs (Ryoo and Bedell, 2017).

Related to the third interpretation, computational thinking is becoming increasingly essential for all students to become STEM professionals or participants in an information society. The STEM Education Act of 2015 that was recently signed into law states that "the term 'STEM education' means education in the subjects of science, technology, engineering, and mathematics, including computer science."[3] Thus, the definition of STEM education has been formally expanded to include computer science.

There has been an emergence of the importance of adding computational thinking to "every child's analytical ability as a vital ingredient of science, technology, engineering, and mathematics (STEM) learning" (Grover and Pea, 2013, p. 38). Computational thinking, according to Wing (2006), "involves solving problems, designing systems, and understanding human

_____

[3]See https://www.congress.gov/bill/114th-congress/house-bill/1020/text [June 2018].

behavior, by drawing on the concepts fundamental to computer science" (p. 33) and involves key aspects, such as abstraction, pattern generalization, representational competence, modularization, algorithmic notions of flow of control, and conditional logic (Grover and Pea, 2013).

Despite the growing emphasis on computational thinking in STEM education, incorporating computational thinking in the school curriculum faces challenges. One major challenge involves lack of an agreement on what constitutes computational thinking (National Research Council, 2010, pp. vii–viii). One approach emphasizes computer literacy, which generally involves using tools to create newsletters, Web pages, or multimedia presentations. A second approach emphasizes computer science by teaching students about programming in particular languages as a way to process, analyze, and interpret information with an emphasis on key computer science concepts such as abstraction, modularization, loops, and conditionals. A third approach emphasizes programming applications, such as games, robots, and simulations, often with an emphasis on students' participation and identity in authentic communities and practices. A fourth approach emphasizes learning to think computationally[4] as a fundamental analytical skill that everyone, not just computer scientists, can use to help solve problems, design systems, and understand human behavior. This approach mirrors the growing recognition that computational thinking (and not just computation) has begun to influence and shape thinking in STEM disciplines and beyond (Weintrop et al., 2016). Few studies have examined instructional materials that enable teachers of STEM subjects to support ELs in developing computational thinking.

### Engineering and Engineering Education

Engineering is a relatively recent addition to K–12 education (Carr, Bennett, and Strobel, 2012). It traces some of its beginnings to CTE programs and technology education programs at the middle and high school levels, which traditionally involved a trade or job skills program, but over the past decade, have adopted a more academic program of study (Park, Pearson, and Richardson, 2017). Over time, individual states introduced engineering in their CTE or science standards and some, such as Massachusetts, expanded to include engineering at the elementary level as well (Massachusetts Department of Education, 2001). Such state-level efforts, coupled with a series of influential reports produced by the National Academy of Engineering (National Academy of Engineering, 2010; National Academy of Engineering and National Research Council, 2002, 2009,

---

[4]To formulate a problem and express its solution(s) in a way that a computer can effectively carry out.

2014) propelled the idea that engineering should be included in K–12 education. In 2012, the *Framework* (National Research Council, 2012) and the resulting NGSS articulated a new vision for three-dimensional learning by blending disciplinary core ideas, crosscutting concepts, and science and engineering practices that encompass both engineering and science.

The inclusion of engineering in these documents was pivotal for efforts to integrate engineering into K–12 settings. Many more schools and teachers across the country have begun to consider how to implement engineering in their classrooms. The introduction of a new discipline in classrooms offers a number of exciting opportunities with respect to ELs.

Engineering design and analysis offer unique opportunities for ELs. Most age-appropriate engineering for elementary and middle school students focuses on producing a material product. As they do so, students explore different materials and their properties and consider which ones are important to the functioning of their design. For example, creating a materials table, such as the one shown in Figure 3-2, not only stores such information, but also introduces students to a variety of descriptive properties to consider as they communicate. As students construct and manipulate materials and design solutions, they can show their understandings with concrete models. Designs are tangible, possibilities and ideas demonstrated, and the performance of a design against a set of evaluative criteria observed. This materiality can invite participation of students with varying degrees of English proficiency—they can show what they know.

Authentic engineering tasks are open-ended, permitting multiple solutions. Thus, students can draw upon their own funds of knowledge (see Positioning of ELs in the Classroom in Chapter 4) and creativity as they generate possible designs. As they engage in such meaningful, relevant, purposeful activity, they naturally use different registers to describe their unique ideas and convince others to consider their approaches. The use of language is tied to and often follows from experiences with concrete materials, models, and designs—there is an interplay of concepts, words, language, and experiences (Yocom de Romero, Slater, and DeCristofano, 2006).

As students engage with a real problem, they build identity with the discipline and begin to consider it as a possible future (Kelly, Cunningham, and Ricketts, 2017). Thus, engaging in the language-rich tasks of engineering design and analysis provides opportunities to use language in science, mathematics, and engineering, while building students' confidence through the development of their academic identities.

Because the discipline is new at the precollege level, research studies of K–12 engineering education are nascent. Although some studies of classroom engineering include students from culturally, linguistically, racially, ethnically, and economically diverse backgrounds (Cunningham

**FIGURE 3-2** Example of a materials table.
SOURCE: Reprinted by permission of the publisher. From C.M. Cunningham and the Museum of Science, Boston, *Engineering in Elementary STEM Education: Curriculum Design, Instruction, Learning, and Assessment.* New York: Teachers College Press. Copyright © 2018 by Christine M. Cunningham and the Museum of Science, Boston. All rights reserved.

and Kelly, 2017; Hertel, Cunningham, and Kelly, 2017; Kelly et al., 2017; Silk, Schunn, and Cary, 2009; Wendell, Wright, and Paugh, 2017), to date no studies of K–12 classroom engineering specifically focus on ELs.

## Mathematics and Mathematics Education

The mathematics education community presents a contemporary view of mathematics instruction based on decades of research on mathematical proficiency and beliefs, and more recent research on mathematical practices, mathematical discourse, and the role of language in learning and teaching mathematics. Research focusing on language and mathematical discussions blossomed in the past 30 years (i.e., since Pimm, 1987), and research specifically on ELs has started to appear in the past 20 years (i.e., since Khisty, 1995). A view of academic literacy in mathematics (Moschkovich, 2015a) that balances the three components—mathematics proficiency, practices, and discourse—is especially crucial for supporting ELs (Moschkovich, 2015a). These three aspects of mathematics instruction are based on mathematics education research and are evident in reforms initiated by the National Council of Teachers of Mathematics (NCTM) in the 1990s. They are also evident in the report *Adding It Up* (National Research Council, 2001) and are reflected in the Common Core State Standards (CCSS) for Mathematics:

1. Make sense of problems and persevere in solving them
2. Construct viable arguments and critique the reasoning of others
3. Reason abstractly and quantitatively
4. Model with mathematics
5. Attend to precision
6. Use appropriate tools strategically
7. Look for ad make sure of structure
8. Look for and express regularity in repeated reasoning[5]

## Mathematical Proficiency

A current description of mathematical proficiency (National Research Council, 2001) shows five intertwined strands, meant to portray the successful mathematics learner:

1. conceptual understanding, or comprehension of mathematical concepts, operations, and relations;
2. procedural fluency, or skill in carrying out procedures flexibly, accurately, efficiently, and appropriately;
3. strategic competence, or competence in formulating, representing, and solving mathematical problems (novel problems, not routine exercises);
4. adaptive reasoning, or logical thought, reflection, explanation, and justification; and
5. productive disposition, a habitual inclination to see mathematics as sensible, useful, and worthwhile, coupled with a belief in diligence and one's own efficacy.

Procedural fluency refers to computational fluency, strategic competence to problem-solving skills, and adaptive reasoning to justification

---

[5]See http://www.corestandards.org/Math/Practice [September 2018].

and proof. Moreover, the second part of productive disposition (belief in diligence and one's own efficacy) anticipates current ideas around *growth mindset*.[6] This view of mathematical proficiency has important implications for instruction. In particular, all strands of proficiency, not just procedural fluency, are developed through access to effective instruction, materials, and interactions. If students are excluded from instructional interactions designed to foster conceptual understanding, strategic competence, adaptive reasoning, and productive disposition, their opportunity to develop proficiency will be limited to procedural fluency.

For example, if teachers want their ELs to learn whole number multiplication, either as grade-level instruction in the early grades or as remediation in later grades, this does not mean their instruction should be focused principally or primarily on memorizing multiplication facts. Such a narrow focus includes only procedural fluency while disregarding the other four components of mathematical proficiency. In particular, this narrow focus leaves out conceptual understanding, which supports accurate recall. Based on research on how to best teach multiplication for student understanding, as ELs learn whole number multiplication, instruction balances a focus on procedural fluency or drill with support for conceptual understanding by asking students to represent, apply, and connect the meaning of multiplication to other important mathematical ideas. This balance can be accomplished, for example, by representing multiplication using arrays and area models, solving multidigit multiplication exercises by grouping and regrouping and making a connection to the distributive property, or solving multiplication word problems.

It is crucial that teachers who work with ELs develop a contemporary view of what conceptual understanding is and how to teach mathematics for understanding. Conceptual understanding is fundamentally about the meanings that learners construct for mathematical solutions: knowing the meaning of a result (i.e., what the number, solution, or result represents), knowing why a procedure works, or explaining why a particular result is the right answer. Another central aspect of conceptual understanding involves connecting representations (e.g., words, drawings, symbols, diagrams, tables, graphs, equation, etc.), procedures, and concepts (Hiebert and Carpenter, 1992).

Reasoning, logical thought, explanation, and justification are closely related to conceptual understanding. Student reasoning is evidence of conceptual understanding when a student explains why a particular result is the right answer or justifies a conclusion. For example, multiplication involves many subtle issues: If multiplication of whole numbers is repeated addition,

---

[6]Research by Carol Dweck defines *growth mindset* as the understanding that abilities and intelligence can be developed (Blackwell, Trzesniewski, and Dweck, 2007).

why is it commutative? If multiplying by 10 puts a 0 on the right, why doesn't this work for decimal numbers? Why doesn't multiplying always make a number larger? Why is a negative times a negative positive? Why do we invert and multiply when dividing by a fraction? Using multiple representations, explaining the meaning of what they are doing when they perform a calculation, and justifying why they chose a particular operation to solve a word problem are all evidence of students' conceptual under-standing. Typically, making sense of a problem (a mathematical practice discussed below) includes creating meaning by connecting representations, one procedure to other procedures, and/or a procedure to a concept.

Teachers who develop a contemporary view of mathematics instruction that does not rigidly prescribe the sequence of mathematical topics are better positioned to provide challenging grade-level instruction to ELs. An important result from research on mathematical proficiency is that students profit from exposure to advanced competencies as they build proficiency in less advanced competencies. For example, students who are still developing proficiency with whole number multiplication are not precluded from participating in instruction that supports algebraic thinking; proficiency with the first is not a rigid prerequisite for exposure to and progress toward proficiency in the second. Instruction that supports early algebraic thinking can be provided in the early grades or in parallel with instruction focusing on whole number operations (Carpenter et al., 1999).

Lastly, teachers who develop a broader view of the role of communication are better positioned to work with ELs in mathematics; for these teachers, English proficiency is not seen as a prerequisite for doing more complex mathematics, because conceptual understanding and communication are closely related. Communicating about mathematics is important because it supports conceptual understanding. The more opportunities a learner has to make connections among multiple representations, the more opportunities that learner has to develop conceptual understanding (Grapin, 2018; Lemke, 1990). However, not all kinds of communication will support conceptual understanding in mathematics. Classroom communication that engages students in evidence-based arguments by focusing on explanations, arguments, and justifications builds conceptual understanding (Moschkovich, 2010) whereas communication limited to just procedures or calculation may be inadequate. Communication that includes multiple modes (e.g., talking, listening, writing, drawing, etc.) is also essential, because making connections among multiple ways of representing mathematical concepts is central to developing conceptual understanding in mathematics (Dominguez, 2005; Sorto and Bower, 2017).

In summary, this view of mathematical proficiency has important implications for instruction for ELs. If, for example, ELs are building proficiency in procedural skills for whole number multiplication, instruction that balances a focus on procedural fluency or drill approaches to multiplication facts with the other four strands of mathematical proficiency will help students understand, represent, apply, and connect multiplication to other important mathematical ideas.

## Mathematical Practices

The five strands of mathematical proficiency, described above, provide a cognitive account of mathematical activity focused on knowledge and beliefs. From a contemporary sociocultural perspective, mathematics students are not only acquiring mathematical knowledge, but also learning to participate in valued mathematical practices (Moschkovich, 2004, 2007, 2013). In 1992, Schoenfeld described mathematical practices as being acquired through enculturation and socialization, entry into the mathematical community, legitimate peripheral participation (Lave and Wenger, 1991), and interaction with others: "If we are to understand how people develop their mathematical perspectives, we must look at the issue in terms of the mathematical communities in which the students live and the practices that underlie those communities. The role of interaction with others will be central in understanding learning. . . (p. 363)."[7]

Work in mathematics education in the past 20 years has assumed that mathematics instruction in schools should parallel, at least in some ways, the practices of mathematicians (e.g., Cobb, Wood, and Yackel, 1993; Lampert, 1990; Schoenfeld, 1992). These proposals emphasize classroom activities that are developmentally appropriate approximations of academic mathematical practices. This view of students as mathematicians expects student activities to approximate at least some aspects of a mathematician's practices, such as making generalizations or conjectures and subjecting them to review and refutation by a (classroom) community. Students are expected to explore the nature of mathematical objects, make and test conjectures, and construct arguments, and instruction is expected to emphasize abstracting and generalizing as central mathematical practices. Bringing the practices of mathematicians into the classroom creates a common set of practices that parallel academic mathematical practices. Students are expected to make conjectures, agree or disagree with the conjectures made by their peers or the teacher, and engage in public discussion and evaluation of claims and arguments made by others. This approach is intended to give students access to academic mathematical practices, such as the construction and presentation of mathematical proofs or arguments.

From a contemporary research perspective, mathematical practices

---

[7]A new series of books published by the National Council of Teachers of Mathematics focuses on access and equity. See https://www.nctm.org/Publications/Books [August 2018].

are cognitive, in that they involve mathematical thinking and reasoning as described in the five strands of mathematical proficiency. They are social, cultural, and discursive, because they arise from communities, mark membership in communities, and involve discourse. They are also semiotic, because they involve such semiotic systems as signs, tools, and their meanings.

Academic mathematical practices can be understood in general as using language and other symbols systems to think, talk, and participate in the practices that are the objective of school learning. There is no single set of mathematical practices or one mathematical community (see Moschkovich, 2002). Mathematical activity can involve different communities (e.g., mathematicians, teachers, or students) and different genres (e.g., explanations, proofs, or presentations). Practices vary across communities of research mathematicians, traditional classrooms, and reformed classrooms. However, across these various communities and genres, there are common practices that can be labeled as academic mathematical practices (see CCSS mathematical practices listed above).

## Mathematical Discourse

The sociocultural framing of mathematical practices described above has implications for connecting practices to discourse. Discourse is central to participation in many mathematical practices, as meanings are situated and constructed while participating in mathematical practices.

Work on the language of disciplines (e.g., Bailey et al., 2007; Pimm, 1987; Schleppegrell, 2007) provides a complex view of mathematical language not only as specialized vocabulary—new words and new meanings for familiar words—but also as extended discourse that includes other symbolic systems as well as artifacts (Moschkovich, 2002), syntax and organization (Crowhurst, 1994), the mathematics register (Halliday, 1978), and discourse practices (Moschkovich, 2002, 2007). Mathematical discourse refers to the *communicative competence* necessary and sufficient for competent participation in mathematical practices (Moschkovich, 2007).

Mathematical discourse is not principally about formal or technical vocabulary (Moschkovich, 2002, 2007). Textbook definitions and formal ways of talking are only one aspect of school mathematical discourse. In classrooms, students use multiple resources, including everyday registers and experiences, to make sense of mathematics. It is not always possible or constructive to tell whether a student's competence in communicating mathematically originates in their everyday or school experiences. It is thus important to avoid construing everyday and academic registers as opposites (Moschkovich, 2010). Box 3-2 provides a discussion of recent research with ELs on language practices during mathematical activity.

Mathematical discourse as described here is complex. As a contrast, a simplified view would be that it lies primarily in individual word meaning, an assumption that could have dire consequences for ELs, as they are likely to use imperfect language to describe their mathematical thinking. For example, one interpretation of CCSS Mathematical Practice Standard 6 "attending to precision" is that precision lies in using two different words for the set of symbols "x + 3" and "x + 3 = 10." By focusing on precision at the individual word meaning level, the first is an "expression" while the second is an "equation." However, the mathematical practice of attending to precision should not be interpreted as using the perfect word. Attending to precision can also refer to deciding when and what kind of precision is necessary during a computation, including when an exact answer is or is not necessary, a mathematical practice that does not require a precise word. Attending to precision is also involved in making precise claims, a practice that is not at the word level but at the discourse level. For example, contrast the claim "Multiplication makes bigger," which is not precise, with the claim "Multiplication makes the result bigger than the original number when the original number is positive and you multiply by a positive number greater than 1." When contrasting the two claims, precision does not lie in the individual words nor are the words used in the second claim more precise or formal mathematical words. Rather, the precision lies in specifying when the claim is true. In a classroom, a teacher's response to the first claim focusing on precision at the word level might be to ask a student to use a more formal word for "bigger." In contrast, a teacher focusing on precision at a discourse level would ask, "When does multiplication make a result bigger?"

## NEW OPPORTUNITIES FOR EL STEM LEARNING

Educational standards shape the educational system, students' experience within education, and the research that is conducted in education. New standards such as those put forth in the states' College and Career Readiness Standards set new high standards, while new instructional frameworks in science (National Research Council, 2012) and mathematics (National Governors Association Center for Best Practices and Council of Chief State School Officers, 2010) promote linguistically rich teaching and a focus on disciplinary practices. This report references these and other sets of standards and frameworks, but such reference does not constrain or limit the report's relevance to other sets of standards or instructional frameworks. This report is agnostic with respect to specific sets of standards except to say that expectations for what all students should know and be able to do are delineated in states' educational standards, and that high standards are the foundation for high achievement expectations for all students. We will have occasion to point out specific aspects of standards that have the

**BOX 3-2**
**Language-Switching, Code-Switching, and Translanguaging**

English learners (ELs), even as they are learning English, can participate in discussions where they grapple with important mathematical content (see Moschkovich [1999] and Khisty [1995] for examples of lessons where ELs participate in mathematical discussions). Research and findings on two common practices, language-switching during computation and code-switching during discussions, are described next.

One common practice among bilingual mathematics learners is switching languages during arithmetic computation. Adult and adolescent bilinguals sometimes switch languages when carrying out arithmetic computations and adult bilinguals may have a preferred language for carrying out arithmetic computation, usually the language of arithmetic instruction. Language-switching can be swift, highly automatic, and facilitate rather than inhibit solving word problems in the language of instruction, provided the student's proficiency in the language of instruction is sufficient for understanding the text of a word problem. These findings suggest that classroom instruction allow bilingual/multilingual students to choose the language they prefer for arithmetic computation and support all students in learning to read and understand the text of word problems in the language of instruction.

Another common practice among bilinguals is switching languages during a sentence or conversation, called "code-switching" or "translanguaging." Code-switching is typically defined as inserting words and phrases from one language into discourse in another language, and typically calls on theories of dual competence (having two separate languages that are working together). Translanguaging refers to using all of one's meaning-making resources (from different languages and varieties of language), and seeing them as one meaning-making system (see Hawkins and Mori, 2018; for implications for the science classroom, see Poza, 2018).

In mathematics classrooms, the language children choose principally depends on the language ability and choice of the person addressing them. After the age of 5, young bilinguals tend to "speak as they are spoken to" (Zentella, 1981). If Spanish-English bilinguals are addressed in English, they reply in English; if they are addressed in Spanish, they reply in Spanish; and if they are addressing a bilingual speaker, they may code-switch. When they are supported in making meaning through whatever meaning-making resources they have available to make their meaning known, they often "translanguage," speaking with the resources from both languages as they try to make themselves understood.

A common misunderstanding is that code-switching is somehow a sign of deficiency in one or the other language, but even fluent speakers of both languages engage in this complex process (Valdés-Fallis, 1978), depending on the interlocutor, domain, topic, role, and function. Choosing and mixing two codes also involves a speaker's cultural identities. Bilingual speakers have been documented using their two languages as resources for mathematical and science discussions, for example, giving an explanation in one language and then repeating the explanation in another language (Moschkovich, 2002; Zahner and Moschkovich, 2011) or to support participation in mathematical practices (Moschkovish, 2015b).

SOURCE: Based on Healy and Fernandes (2014).

potential to promote academic success for ELs; such is the case with recent developments in mathematics and science to which the research community quickly responded (Lee, Quinn, and Valdés, 2013; Moschkovich, 2012).

In fact, the most recent standards and frameworks have articulated language demands that comprise considerable potential for literacy development (Kibler, Walqui, and Bunch, 2015) if ELs are granted full curricular access. To fully realize this potential, and for the new standards and frameworks to ensure equity, considerable efforts must be made to improve upon teachers' professional development for EL students (National Research Council, 2012; Quinn, Lee, and Valdés, 2012). In addition, if ELs are to truly access rich academic content, assessments must be developed alongside the new frameworks and standards (Bunch, Walqui, and Pearson, 2014).

## SUMMARY

Learning STEM subjects involves extending students' meaning-making potential through language. To engage effectively with disciplinary learning, students expand their repertoires of language skills developed during the early years of schooling and learn to recognize how language is used to make meaning, discuss ideas, present knowledge, construe value, and create specialized texts across disciplines. This expansion of students' language repertoires is observed in the science, mathematics, and engineering classroom as ELs use language purposefully in the service of "doing" and communicating ideas about science, engineering, and mathematics. Just as each discipline requires that students engage with a specialized body of knowledge and practices, each also requires that students engage with the specialized language through which the knowledge and practices are presented. And because practices vary across disciplines, these practices are best learned and taught within each discipline.

STEM subjects are best learned with the help of teachers who can support ELs in engaging in the disciplinary practices through which both disciplinary concepts and disciplinary language are developed simultaneously. Supporting language development across STEM disciplines requires that teachers develop both disciplinary concepts and practices, as well as knowledge about language and registers relevant to the discipline. This knowledge has been characterized in various ways: as *literacy pedagogical content knowledge* (Love, 2010), *pedagogical language knowledge* (Bunch, 2013; Galguera, 2011), or *disciplinary linguistic knowledge* (Turkan et al., 2014). Bunch (2013), for example, argued that teachers need "knowledge of language directly related to disciplinary teaching and learning and situated in the particular (and multiple) contexts in which teaching and learning take place" (p. 307). Teachers also need to effectively use their own language during content instruction. That is, they can be intentional in their *linguistic pedagogies* such as crafting STEM explanations in ways that make content most accessible to ELs without reducing the level of complexity of the content (Bailey and Heritage, 2017).

## REFERENCES

Alozie, N.M., Moje, E.B., and Krajcik, J.S. (2010). An analysis of the supports and constraints for scientific discussion in high school project-based science. *Science Education, 94*(3), 395–427.

Asunda, P. (2012). Standards for technological literacy and STEM education delivery through career and technical education programs. *Journal of Technology Education, 23(2),* 44–60.

Bailey, A.L., Butler, F.A., Stevens, R., and Lord, C. (2007). Further specifying the language demands of school. In A.L. Bailey (Ed.), *The Language Demands of School: Putting Academic English to the Test* (pp. 103–156). New Haven, CT: Yale University Press.

Bailey, A.L., and Heritage, M. (2017). Imperatives for teacher education: Findings from studies of effective teaching for English language learners. In M. Peters, B. Cowie, and I. Menter (Eds.), *A Companion to Research in Teacher Education.* (pp. 697–712). Berlin, Germany: Springer.

Barton, A.C., and Tan, E. (2009). Funds of knowledge and discourses and hybrid space. *Journal of Research in Science Teaching, 46*(1), 50–73.

Beckner, C., Blythe, R., Bybee, J., Christiansen, M., Croft, W., Ellis, N.C., Holland, J., Ke, J., Larsen-Freeman, D., and Schoenemann, T. (2009). Language is a complex adaptive system: Position paper. *Language Learning, 59*(1), 1–26. doi:10.1111/j.1467-9922.2009.00533.x.

Berland, L.K., and Reiser, B.J. (2011). Classroom communities' adaptations of the practice of scientific argumentation. *Science Education, 95*(2), 191–216.

Berland, L.K., Schwarz, C.V., Krist, C., Kenyon, L., Lo, A.S., and Reiser, B.J. (2016). Epistemologies in practice: Making scientific practices meaningful for students. *Journal of Research in Science Teaching, 53*(7), 1082–1112.

Bezemer, J., and Kress, G. (2008). Writing in multimodal texts: A social semiotic account of designs for learning. *Written Communication, 25*(2), 166–195.

Bianchini, J.A. (1999). From here to equity: The influence of status on student access to and understanding of science. *Science Education, 83*(5), 577–601.

Blackwell, L.S., Trzesniewski, K.H., and Dweck, C.S. (2007). Implicit theories of intelligence predict achievement across an adolescent transition: A longitudinal study and an intervention. *Child Development, 78*(1), 246–263.

Bricker, L.A., and Bell, P. (2008). Conceptualizations of argumentation from science studies and the learning sciences and their implications for the practices of science education. *Science Education, 92*(3), 473–493.

Bunch, G.C. (2013). Pedagogical language knowledge: Preparing mainstream teachers for English learners in the new standards era. *Review of Research in Education, 37*(1), 298–341.

Bunch, G.C., Walqui, A., and Pearson, P.D. (2014). Complex text and new common standards in the United States: Pedagogical implications for English learners. *TESOL Quarterly, 48*(3), 533–559.

Carpenter, T.P., Fennema, E., Franke, M.L., Levi, L., and Empson, S.B. (1999). *Children's Mathematics: Cognitively Guided Instruction.* Portsmouth, NH: Heinemann.

Carr, R.L., Bennett, L.D., and Strobel, J. (2012). Engineering in the K–12 STEM standards of the 50 U.S. states: An analysis of presence and extent. *Journal of Engineering Education, 101*(3), 539–564.

Cavagnetto, A.R. (2010). Argument to foster scientific literacy: A review of argument interventions in K–12 science contexts. *Review of Educational Research, 80*(3), 336–371.

Chinn, C.A., Buckland, L.A., and Samarapungavan, A. (2011). Expanding the dimensions of epistemic cognition: Arguments from philosophy and psychology. *Educational Psychologist, 46*(3), 141–167.

Coady, M.R., Harper, C., and de Jong, E. J. (2016). Aiming for equity: Preparing mainstream teachers for inclusion or inclusive classrooms? *TESOL Quarterly, 50*(2), 340–356. doi:10.1002/tesq.223.

Cobb, P., Wood, T., and Yackel, E. (1993). Discourse, mathematical thinking, and classroom practice. In E.A. Forman, N. Minick, and C.A. Stone (Eds.), *Context for Learning: Sociocultural Dynamics in Children's Development* (pp. 91–119). New York: Oxford University Press.

Crowhurst, M. (1994). *Language and Learning Across the Curriculum.* Scarborough, Ontario: Allyn and Bacon.

Cunningham, C.M., and Kelly, G.K. (2017). Framing engineering practices in elementary school classrooms. *International Journal of Engineering Education, 33*(1B), 295–307.

de Araujo, Z. (2017). Connections between secondary mathematics teachers' beliefs and their selection of tasks for English language learners. *Curriculum Inquiry, 47*(4), 363–389. doi:10.1080/03626784.2017.1368351.

Dominguez, H. (2005). Articulation and gesticulation of mathematical knowledge during problem solving. *Bilingual Research Journal, 29*(2), 269–293.

Duschl, R.A. (2008). Science education in three-part harmony: Balancing conceptual, epistemic, and social learning goals. *Review of Research in Education, 32*, 268–291.

Duschl, R.A., and Osborne, J. (2002). Supporting and promoting argumentation discourse in science education. *Studies in Science Education, 38*(1), 39–72.

Elby, A., and Hammer, D. (2010). Epistemological resources and framing: A cognitive framework for helping teachers interpret and respond to their students' epistemologies. In L.D. Bendixen and F.C. Feucht (Eds.), *Personal Epistemology in the Classroom: Theory, Research, and Implications for Practice* (pp. 409–434). Cambridge: Cambridge University Press.

Evagorou, M., Jiménez-Aleixandre, M.P., and Osborne, J. (2012). 'Should we kill the grey squirrels?' A study exploring students' justifications and decision-making. *International Journal of Science Education, 34*(3), 401–428.

Ferguson, C.A. (1994). Dialect, register, and genre: Working assumptions about conventionalization. In D. Biber and E. Finegan (Eds.), *Sociolinguistic Perspectives on Register* (pp. 15–30). New York: Oxford University Press.

Galguera, T. (2011). Participant structures as professional learning tasks and the development of pedagogical language knowledge among preservice teachers. *Teacher Education Quarterly, 38*(1), 85–106.

Garrett, N. (2009). Technology in the service of language learning: Trends and issues. *The Modern Language Journal, 23*, 697–718.

Gibbons, P. (2015). *Scaffolding Language, Scaffolding Learning: Teaching English Language Learners in the Mainstream Classroom* (2nd ed.). Portsmouth, NH: Heinemann.

Grapin, S.E. (2018). Multimodality in the new content standards era: Implications for English learners. *TESOL Quarterly.* Available: https://onlinelibrary.wiley.com/doi/abs/10.1002/tesq.443?af=R [June 2018].

Grover, S., and Pea, R. (2013). Computational thinking in K–12: A review of the state of the field. *Educational Researcher, 42*(1), 38–43.

Gutiérrez, K.D., and Rogoff, B. (2003). Cultural ways of learning: Individual traits or repertoires of practice. *Educational Researcher, 32*(5), 19–25.

Halliday, M.A.K. (1978). Sociolinguistic aspects of mathematical education. In *The Social Interpretation of Language and Meaning* (pp. 194–204). London, UK: University Park Press.

Halliday, M.A.K. (2014). *Halliday's Introduction to Functional Grammar* (4th ed.). New York: Routledge.

Halliday, M.A.K., and Martin, J.R. (1993). *Writing Science: Literacy and Discursive Power*. Pittsburgh, PA: University of Pittsburgh Press.

Harris, C.J., Krajcik, J.S., Pellegrino, J.W., and McElhaney, K.W. (2016). *Constructing Assessment Tasks That Blend Disciplinary Core Ideas, Crosscutting Concepts, and Science Practice for Classroom Formative Applications*. Menlo Park, CA: SRI International.

Hawkins, M.R., and Mori, J. (2018). Special issue on 'trans' perspectives. *Applied Linguistics*, 39(1).

Haynes, J., and Zacarian, D. (2010). *Teaching English Language Learners Across the Content Areas*. Alexandria, VA: ACSD.

Healy, L., and Fernandes, S.H.A.A. (2014). Blind students, special needs, and mathematics learning. In S. Lerman (Ed.), *Encyclopedia of Mathematics Education* (pp. 61–63). Dordrecht: Springer.

Herrenkohl, L.R., and Cornelius, L. (2013). Investigating elementary students' scientific and historical argumentation. *Journal of the Learning Sciences*, 22(3), 413–461.

Hertel, J.D., Cunningham, C.M., and Kelly, G.K. (2017). The roles of engineering notebooks in shaping elementary engineering student discourse and practice. *International Journal of Science Education*, 39(9), 1194–1217. doi:10.1080/09500693.2017.1317864.

Hiebert, J., and Carpenter, T.P. (1992). Learning and teaching with understanding. In D.A. Grouws (Ed.), *Handbook of Research on Mathematics Teaching and Learning: A Project of the National Council of Teachers of Mathematics* (pp. 65–97). New York: Macmillan.

International Technology Education Association. (2000). *Standards for Technological Literacy: Content for the Study of Technology*. Reston, VA: Author. Available: https://www. iteea.org/42511.aspx [August 2018].

Ishimaru, A., Barajas-López, F., and Bang, M. (2015). Centering family knowledge to develop children's empowered mathematics identifies. *Journal of Family Diversity in Education*, 1(4), 1–22.

Jiménez-Aleixandre, M.P. (2014). Determinism and underdetermination in genetics: Implications for students' engagement in argumentation and epistemic practices. *Science & Education*, 23(2), 465–484.

Kelly, G.J. (2008). Inquiry, activity, and epistemic practice. In R. Duschl and R. Grandy (Eds.), *Teaching Scientific Inquiry: Recommendations for Research and Implementation* (pp. 99–117, 288–291). Rotterdam, The Netherlands: Sense.

Kelly, G.J. (2016). Methodological considerations for the study of epistemic cognition in practice. In J.A. Greene, W.A. Sandoval, and I. Braten (Eds.), *Handbook of Epistemic Cognition* (pp. 393–408). New York: Routledge.

Kelly, G.J., and Licona, P. (2018). Epistemic practices and science education. In M.R. Matthews (Ed.), *History, Philosophy, and Science Teaching: New Perspectives* (pp. 139–165). Springer International.

Kelly, G.J., Cunningham, C.M., and Ricketts, A. (2017). Engaging in identity work through engineering practices in elementary classrooms. *Linguistics & Education*, 39, 48–59. doi:10.1016/j.linged.2017.05.003.

Khisty, L.L. (1995). Making inequality: Issues of language and meanings in mathematics teaching with Hispanic students. In W.G. Secada, E. Fennema, and L.B. Adajian (Eds.), *New Directions for Equity in Mathematics Education* (pp. 279–297). New York: Cambridge University Press.

Kibler, A.K., Walqui, A., and Bunch, G.C. (2015). Transformational opportunities: Language and literacy instruction for English language learners in the common core era in the United States. *TESOL Journal, 6*(1), 9–35.

Knorr-Cetina, K. (1999). *Epistemic Cultures: How the Sciences Make Knowledge.* Cambridge, MA: Harvard University Press.

Lampert, M. (1990). When the problem is not the question and the solution is not the answer: Mathematical knowing and teaching. *American Educational Research Journal, 27*(1), 29–63.

Larsen-Freeman, D. (1997). Chaos/complexity science and second language acquisition. *Applied Linguistics, 18*(2), 141–165. doi:10.1093/applin/18.2.141.

Larsen-Freeman, D. (2007). Reflecting on the cognitive-social debate in second language acquisition. *The Modern Language Journal, 7*(S1), 773–787.

Lave, J., and Wenger, E. (1991). *Situated Learning: Legitimate Peripheral Participation.* Cambridge, UK: Cambridge University Press.

Lee, O., Quinn, H., and Valdés, G. (2013). Science and language for English language learners in relation to Next Generation Science Standards and with implications for Common Core State Standards for English language arts and mathematics. *Educational Researcher, 42*(4), 223–233.

Lee, O., Valdés, G., and Llosa, L. (2015–2019). *Development of Language-Focused Three-Dimensional Science Instructional Materials to Support English Language Learners in Fifth Grade.* Alexandria, VA: National Science Foundation, Discovery Research K–12.

Lee, O., Grapin, S., and Haas, A. (2018). How science instructional shifts and language instructional shifts support each other for English learners: Talk in the science classroom. In A. Bailey, C. Maher, and L. Wilkinson (Eds.), *Language, Literacy and Learning in the STEM Disciplines: How Language Counts for English Learners* (pp. 35–52). New York: Routledge.

Lemke, J.L. (1990). *Talking Science: Language, Learning and Values.* Norwood, NJ: Ablex.

Love, K. (2010). Literacy pedagogical content knowledge in the secondary curriculum. *Pedagogies: An International Journal, 5*(4), 338–355.

Manz, E. (2012). Understanding the co-development of modeling practice and ecological knowledge. *Science Education, 96*(6), 1071–1105.

Massachusetts Department of Education. (2001, May). *Massachusetts Science and Technology/Engineering Framework.* Available: http://www.doe.mass.edu/frameworks/scitech/2001/ [July 2018].

Moje, E.B. (2000). "To be part of the story": The literacy practices of "gangsta" adolescents. *Teachers College Record, 102*(3), 652–690.

Moll, L.C., Amani, C., Neff, D., and Gonzalez, N. (1991). Funds of knowledge for teaching: Using a quantitative approach to connect homes and classrooms. *Theory into Practice, XXXI*(2), 132–141.

Moschkovich, J.N. (1999). Supporting the participation of English language learners in mathematical discussions. *For the Learning of Mathematics, 19*(1), 11–19.

Moschkovich, J.N. (2002). A situated and sociocultural perspective on bilingual mathematics learners. *Mathematical Thinking and Learning, 4*(2–3), 189–212.

Moschkovich, J.N. (2004). Appropriating mathematical practices: A case study of learning to use and explore functions through interaction with a tutor. *Educational Studies in Mathematics, 5*(1/3), 49–80.

Moschkovich, J.N. (2007). Examining mathematical discourse practices. *For the Learning of Mathematics, 27*(1), 24–30.

Moschkovich, J.N. (2010). Language(s) and learning mathematics: Resources, challenges, and issues for research. In J.N. Moschkovich (Ed.), *Language and Mathematics Education: Multiple Perspectives and Directions for Research* (pp. 1–28). Charlotte, NC: Information Age.

Moschkovich, J.N. (2012). How equity concerns lead to attention to mathematical discourse. In B. Herbel-Eisenmann, J. Choppin, D. Wagner, and D. Pimm (Eds.), *Equity in Discourse for Mathematics Education: Theories, Practices, and Policies*. New York: Springer.

Moschkovich, J.N. (2013). Issues regarding the concept of mathematical practices. In Y. Li and J.N. Moschkovich, (Eds.), *Proficiency and Beliefs in Learning and Teaching Mathematics: Learning from Alan Schoenfeld and Günter Toerner* (pp. 257–275). Rotterdam, The Netherlands: Sense.

Moschkovich, J.N. (2015a). Academic literacy in mathematics for English Learners. *Journal of Mathematical Behavior, 40*(Pt. A), 43–62.

Moschkovich, J.N. (2015b). Scaffolding mathematical practices. *ZDM, The International Journal on Mathematics Education, 47*(7), 1067–1078.

Nasir, N.S., Rosebery, A.S., Warren, B., and Lee, C.D. (2014). Learning as a cultural process: Achieving equity through diversity. In *The Cambridge Handbook of the Learning Sciences* (2nd ed., pp. 686–706). New York: Cambridge University Press.

National Academy of Engineering. (2010). *Standards for K–12 Engineering Education?* Washington, DC: The National Academies Press.

National Academy of Engineering and National Research Council. (2002). *Technically Speaking: Why All Americans Need to Know More About Technology*. Washington, DC: National Academy Press.

National Academy of Engineering and National Research Council. (2009). *Engineering in K–12 Education*. Washington, DC: The National Academies Press.

National Academy of Engineering and National Research Council. (2014). *STEM Integration in K–12 Education: Status, Prospects, and an Agenda for Research*. Washington, DC: The National Academies Press.

National Governors Association, Center for Best Practices, and Council of Chief State School Officers. (2010). *Reaching Higher: The Common Core State Standards Validation Committee*. Available: http://www.corestandards.org/assets/CommonCoreReport_6.10.pdf [September 2018].

National Research Council. (2000). *How People Learn: Brain, Mind, Experience, and School: Expanded Edition*. Washington, DC: National Academy Press.

National Research Council. (2001). *Adding It Up: Helping Children Learn Mathematics*. Washington, DC: National Academy Press.

National Research Council. (2006). *America's Lab Report: Investigations in High School Science*. Washington, DC: The National Academies Press.

National Research Council. (2007). *Taking Science to School: Learning and Teaching Science in Grades K–8*. Washington, DC: The National Academies Press.

National Research Council. (2009). *Learning Science in Informal Environments: People, Places, and Pursuits*. Washington, DC: The National Academies Press.

National Research Council. (2010). *Report of a Workshop on the Scope and Nature of Computational Thinking*. Washington, DC: The National Academies Press.

National Research Council. (2012). *A Framework for K–12 Science Education: Practices, Crosscutting Concepts, and Core Ideas*. Washington, DC: The National Academies Press.

Oliveira, A.W. (2010). Improving teacher questioning in science inquiry discussion through professional development. *Journal of Research in Science Teaching, 47*(4), 422–453.

Östman, L., and Wickman, P.-O. (2014). A pragmatic approach on epistemology, teaching, and learning. *Science Education, 98*(3), 375–382.

Painter, C. (1999). *Learning through Language in Early Childhood*. London, UK: Cassell.

Park, T., Pearson, D., and Richardson, G.B. (2017). Curriculum integration: Helping career and technical education students truly develop college and career readiness. *Peabody Journal of Education, 92(2),* 192–208.

Pimm, D. (1987). *Speaking Mathematically: Communication in Mathematics Classrooms.* London, UK: Routledge.

Pluta, W.J., Chinn, C.A., and Duncan, R.G. (2011). Learners' epistemic criteria for good scientific models. *Journal of Research in Science Teaching, 48(5),* 486–511.

Poza, L.E. (2018). The language of ciencia: Translanguaging and learning in a bilingual science classroom. *International Journal of Bilingual Education and Bilingualism, 21(1),* 1–19.

Quinn, H., Lee, O., and Valdés, G. (2012). *Language Demands and Opportunities in Relation to Next Generation Science Standards for English Language Learners: What Teachers Need to Know.* Stanford, CA: Stanford University, Understanding Language. Available: http://ell.stanford.edu/sites/default/files/pdf/academic-papers/03-Quinn%20Lee%20Valdes%20Language%20and%20Opportunities%20in%20Science%20FINAL.pdf [June 2018].

Ryoo, K., and Bedell, K. (2017). The effects of visualizations on linguistically diverse students' understanding of energy and matter in life science. *Journal of Research in Science Teaching, 54(10),* 1274–1301.

Sadler, T.D. (2006). Promoting discourse and argumentation in science teacher education. *Journal of Science Teacher Education, 17(4),* 323–346.

Sadler, T.D. (2009). Situated learning in science education: socio-scientific issues as contexts for practice. *Studies in Science Education, 45(1),* 1–42.

Sampson, V., and Clark, D. (2008). Assessment of the ways students generate arguments in science education: Current perspectives and recommendations for future directions. *Science Education, 92(3),* 447–472.

Sandoval, W. (2005). Understanding students' practical epistemologies and their influence. *Science Education, 89,* 634–656.

Sandoval, W. (2014). Conjecture mapping: An approach to systematic educational design research. *Journal of the Learning Sciences, 23(1),* 18–36.

Schleppegrell, M.J. (2004). *The Language of Schooling: A Functional Linguistics Perspective.* Mahwah, NJ: Lawrence Erlbaum Associates.

Schleppegrell, M.J. (2007). The linguistic challenges of mathematics teaching and learning: A research review. *Reading & Writing Quarterly, 23(2),* 139–159.

Schoenfeld, A.H. (1992). Learning to think mathematically: Problem solving, metacognition, and sense making in mathematics. In D.A. Grouws (Ed.), *NCTM Handbook of Research on Mathematics Teaching and Learning* (pp. 334–370). New York: Macmillan. Available: http://hplengr.engr.wisc.edu/Math_Schoenfeld.pdf [June 2018].

Silk, E.M., Schunn, C.D., and Cary, M.S. (2009). The impact of an engineering design curriculum on science reasoning in an urban setting. *Journal of Science Education and Technology, 18(3),* 209–223.

Sorto, M.A., and Bower, R.S.G. (2017). Quality of instruction in linguistically diverse classrooms: It matters! In A. Fernandes, S. Crespo, and M. Civil (Eds.), *Access and Equity: Promoting High Quality Mathematics in Grades 6–8* (pp. 27–40). Reston, VA: National Council of Teachers of Mathematics.

Turkan, C., de Oliveira, C., Lee, O., and Phelps, G. (2014). Proposing a knowledge base for teaching academic content to English language learners: Disciplinary linguistic knowledge. *Teachers College Record, 116(3).*

Valdés, G. (2015). Latin@s and the intergenerational continuity of Spanish: The challenges of curricularizing language. *International Multilingual Research Journal, 9(4),* 253–273.

Valdés-Fallis, G. (1978). Code switching and the classroom teacher. *Language in Education: Theory and Practice* (vol. 4). Wellington, VA: Center for Applied Linguistics.

Vossoughi, S., Hooper, P., and Escudé, M. (2016). Making through the lens of culture and power: Towards transformative visions for educational equity. *Harvard Educational Review, 86*(2), 206–232.

Warschauer, M., and Meskill, C. (2000). Technology and second language learning. In J. Rosenthal (Ed.), *Handbook of Undergraduate Second Language Education* (pp. 303–318). Mahwah, NJ: Lawrence Erlbaum Associates.

Watson-Verran, H., and Turnbull, D. (1995). Science and other indigenous knowledge systems. In S. Jasanoff, G.E. Markle, J.C. Peterson, and T. Pinch (Eds.), *Handbook of Science and Technology Studies* (pp. 115–139). Thousand Oaks, CA: SAGE.

Weintrop, D., Beheshti, E., Horn, M., Orton, K., Jona, K., Trouille, L., and Wilensky, U. (2016). Defining computational thinking for mathematics and science classrooms. *Journal of Science Education and Technology, 25*(1), 127–147.

Wendell, K.B., Wright, C.G., and Paugh, P. (2017). Reflective decision-making in elementary students' engineering design. *Journal of Engineering Education, 106*(3), 356–397.

Wickman, P.-O. (2004). The practical epistemologies of the classroom: A study of laboratory work. *Science Education, 88*(3), 325–344.

Wing, J.M. (2006). Computational thinking. *Communications of the ACM, 49*(3), 33–35.

Yocom de Romero, N., Slater, P., and DeCristofano, C. (2006). Design challenges are "ELL-ementary." *Science & Children*, 34–37.

Zahner, W., and Moschkovich, J.N. (2011). Bilingual students using two languages during peer mathematics discussions: What does it mean? In K. Tellez, J. Moschkovich, and M. Civil (Eds.), *Latinos/as and Mathematics Education: Research on Learning and Teaching in Classrooms and Communities* (pp. 37–62). Charlotte, NC: Information Age.

Zembal-Saul, C. (2009). Learning to teach elementary school science as argument. *Science Education, 93*(4), 687–719.

Zentella, A.C. (1981). Tá bien, You could answer me en cualquier idioma: Puerto Rican code switching in bilingual classrooms. In R. Durán (Ed.), *Latino Language and Communicative Behavior* (pp. 109–130), Norwood, NJ: Ablex.

Zheng, B., Warschauer, M., Hwang, J.K., and Collins, P. (2014). Laptop use, interactive science software, and science learning among at-risk students. *Journal of Science Education and Technology, 23*(4), 591–603.

Zuengler, J., and Miller, E. (2006). Cognitive and sociocultural perspectives: Two parallel SLA worlds? *TESOL Quarterly, 40*(1), 35–58.

# 4

# Effective Instructional Strategies for STEM Learning and Language Development in English Learners

Participation in science, technology, engineering, and mathematics (STEM) disciplines offers unique learning opportunities for English learners (ELs). However, as described in Chapter 2, historically ELs have not been given access to grade-level, content-rich, language-rich STEM learning opportunities due to the misconception that a certain level of English proficiency is a prerequisite for participation in STEM learning (Callahan, 2005). Chapter 3 establishes that ELs develop STEM knowledge and language proficiency when they are engaged in meaningful interaction in the context of shared experience in the classroom. Teachers are crucial to creating classroom environments that can leverage the assets that ELs bring to STEM learning.

Building from these foundational chapters, the committee reviewed the extant literature on the classroom structures and instructional strategies for ELs in STEM learning.[1] It should be noted that although there has been an increase in research with ELs in STEM subjects, there are few large-scale systematic studies to demonstrate widespread effectiveness of particular strategies and approaches (see National Research Council, 1992, for similar issues related to bilingual education). Moreover, the committee found limited evidence that could provide strong links to students' outcomes of

---

[1]This chapter includes content drawn from papers commissioned by the committee titled *Teachers' Knowledge and Beliefs about English Learners and Their Impact on STEM Learning* by Julie Bianchini (2018), *Mathematics Education and Young Dual Language Learners* by Sylvia Celedón-Pattichis (2018), *Secondary Science Education for English Learners* by Sara Tolbert (2018), and *The Role of the ESL Teacher in Relation to Content Teachers* by Sultan Turkan (2018).

specific practices to engage ELs at different proficiency levels and from different backgrounds. Given the limited causal evidence, the committee drew upon the available descriptive evidence and case examples to look for emerging themes suggestive of promising strategies and approaches.

This chapter is organized to first give an overview of classroom culture—describing some of the views that teachers of STEM have about ELs, the way ELs are positioned in the STEM classroom, and the value of teachers engaging with ELs' families. It is then followed by a brief discussion of the changing role of the English as a second language (ESL) teacher in the STEM classroom. The committee then identifies promising instructional strategies for enriching STEM learning and language development and concludes with a brief discussion of curriculum.

## CLASSROOM CULTURE

Teachers must "purposefully enact opportunities for the development of language and literacy in and through teaching . . . core curricular content, understandings, and activities" if they are to interest, engage, and challenge their EL students (Bunch, 2013, p. 298). Their efforts to construct safe classroom communities and effectively implement instructional strategies have been found to impact both ELs' views of themselves as learners and their math and science achievement (Carlone, Haun-Frank, and Webb, 2011; Lewis et al., 2012; Llosa et al., 2016). Given that "teachers are both on the front line and responsible for the bottom line" in providing ELs with the knowledge, practices, and habits of mind needed to excel in and affiliate with STEM disciplines, it is important to understand teachers' views and experiences (Gándara, Maxwell-Jolly, and Driscoll, 2005, p. 2).

### Teachers' Knowledge and Beliefs about ELs' Learning in STEM

Researchers have examined a wide range of teachers' knowledge and beliefs about the resources, interests, and strengths of their ELs both within and across studies. Overall, it is clear that there is substantial variability in the views teachers of ELs in STEM subjects hold, including asset-based and deficit-based orientations toward ELs. Table 4-1 provides an overview of some of the beliefs that teachers of STEM content have regarding ELs and their potential for STEM learning.

Research has documented that, although some practicing and preservice teachers conceive of language as integral to the nature of mathematics or science (Bunch, Aguirre, and Téllez, 2009; Swanson, Bianchini, and Lee, 2014), other teachers may fail to see language as integral to the nature, concepts, and practices of mathematics (Bunch, Aguirre, and Téllez, 2009; McLeman and Fernandes, 2012). For example, McLeman and Fernandes

**TABLE 4-1** Summary of the General Views Teachers Have about English Learners' (ELs') Science, Technology, Engineering, and Mathematics (STEM) Capabilities

| Teachers who hold asset views typically: | Teachers who hold deficit views typically: |
| --- | --- |
| Hold high expectations for EL's success | Hold low expectations for ELs' success |
| View ELs as *willing* and *able* to learn both STEM content and English—as eager and capable learners | View ELs as homogeneously low in language proficiency in STEM—conflating English language proficiency with STEM content understanding |
| Recognize ELs as a diverse, rather than homogeneous, group—background, interests, and/or English proficiency level | Hold stereotypes of ELs grounded in their first language, ethnicity, and/or country of origin |
| Believe that ELs bring valuable knowledge and experiences to STEM classrooms that should be elicited and built on | Believe that ELs lack relevant prior knowledge, experiences, and/or language |
| View ELs as entitled to rich learning opportunities (and) adequate scaffolds and supports | See ELs as unable or unwilling to communicate with teachers and/or with their non-EL peers |
| Assume ELs enrich the classroom for all students | Assume ELs are motivated and hardworking rather than intelligent |
| Engage ELs in disciplinary meaning-making | Engage ELs in low-level cognitive demand tasks |
| Believe ELs have access to different yet important cultural knowledge that is dependent upon their experiences in and out of school | Believe ELs have access to the same cultural knowledge as non-EL students |
| See ELs as potential future scientists and mathematicians | See ELs as having limited future vocations or professions |
| Believe that ELs require similar time as non-EL peers to have their needs met | Believe that ELs require more time to have their needs met than their non-EL peers |
| Believe that ELs are constrained by institutional and economic forces and experience fundamental inequities in their lives that teachers and schools could help to address | Believe that ELs experience fundamental inequities in their lives that teachers and schools should not be expected to address |

SOURCE: Developed and adapted from commissioned paper *Teachers' Knowledge and Beliefs about English Learners and Their Impact on STEM Learning* by Julie Bianchini (2018). Available: http://www.nas.edu/ELinSTEM [October 2018].

(2012) found that the majority of the 330 preservice K–12 teachers from 12 different states they surveyed thought mathematics was ideal for beginning ELs to transition into learning English; at the same time, preservice teachers most likely viewed mathematics as "devoid of language" and purely symbolic in nature. However, the majority of preservice teachers who intended to teach high school mathematics and who had exposure to learning a second language themselves provided responses aligned with research on the complex nature of language and discourse in mathematics.

For those teachers who accept the need to integrate content and language, additional struggles are identified (Coady, Harper, and de Jong, 2016; de Araujo, 2017; Gándara, Maxwell-Jolly, and Driscoll, 2005). Coady, Harper, and de Jong (2016) found that while their two elementary teacher participants had been trained in and recognized the need to integrate content and language learning, they continued to value content learning over language learning (for an example, see Box 4-1). As such, in their teaching of mathematics, both relied on mere exposure to English and Euro-American cultural experiences rather than explicit instruction in linguistic and cultural norms to meet the needs of their EL students. On the other hand, de Araujo and colleagues (de Araujo, 2017; de Araujo, Smith, and Sakow, 2016; de Araujo et al., 2015) found that secondary math teachers constrained ELs' opportunities to use mathematics concepts or practices because the teachers prioritized their support of students' language for students labeled ELs. Additional examples of perceived challenges in integrating language and content include struggles to find enough time both to teach ELs subject matter and develop English proficiency and to address the needs of both ELs and other students (Gándara, Maxwell-Jolly, and Driscoll, 2005); difficulties in differentiating misunderstandings grounded in content versus those grounded in language (Roberts et al., 2017); and failures to consistently use ESL strategies to promote English language development in STEM lessons (Lee et al., 2009).

Some teachers appear to ignore the value of student talk, equate discourse with vocabulary, work with ELs in isolation rather than as part of the whole class, or fail to adequately support groupwork (Chval and Pinnow, 2010). Others, however, believe that a welcoming and safe classroom community is needed if ELs are to participate and learn (Chval and Chavez, 2011; Deaton, Deaton, and Koballa, 2014; Harper and de Jong, 2009) and understand the importance of engaging ELs in STEM disciplinary talk and practices (Bunch, Aguirre, and Téllez, 2009; Johnson, Bolshakova, and Waldron, 2016; Pettit, 2013).

---

**BOX 4-1**
**Mismatch Between Teachers' Beliefs and**
**Practices in Science Classrooms**

If the expectation is for all students, including English learners, to learn science, teachers need to develop learning environments and instructional strategies that acknowledge the cultural and linguistic resources that students bring to the science classroom, not only the challenges that their students face in engaging in science inquiry. This is not easy work.

Patchen and Cox-Petersen (2008) found that two elementary teacher participants, well known for their efforts to create constructivist science classrooms, were not always able to translate their beliefs into practice. Both teachers valued students' cultures, experiences, and languages, seeing them as integral to good instruction. Both thought it important to encourage student participation, and they worked to establish relationships with their students, provide a safe classroom environment, encourage native language use, and implement groupwork. Both thought it important to elicit and build on student experiences and understanding as well. However, although the teachers assessed their students' understanding, they fell short of building it: They rarely extended students' contributions in any substantive way beyond merely repeating what they said, and regularly used their own examples or analogies rather than their students to do the work of knowledge transference. Further, although both teachers used a variety of teaching methods, including visuals, hands-on activities, cooperative learning, and experiments, they avoided implementing inquiry and used direct instruction to scaffold academic material. As a result of this mismatch between beliefs and practices, students did not have opportunities to actively construct their own science understanding or participate in disciplinary practices.

SOURCE: Developed and adapted from commissioned paper *Teachers' Knowledge and Beliefs about English Learners and Their Impact on STEM Learning* by Julie Bianchini (2018). Available: http://www.nas.edu/ELinSTEM [October 2018].

---

## Positioning of ELs in the Classroom

In order to engage ELs in challenging STEM instruction, it is important to create a climate that positions them as capable participants with rights and duties in classroom social interactions. Positioning theory[2] addresses the psychology of interactions through microanalysis of the role of rights and duties (Harré et al., 2009). Pinnow and Chval (2015) reported on the ways ELs can be positioned inequitably in peer-to-peer and whole-class dis-

---

[2]In positioning theory, interactions are composed of *positions, storylines,* and *speech acts.* Among the triad of positions, storylines, and speech acts, *positions* in classrooms are social in that they can be viewed as the rights and duties that participants are required to carry out in social interactions.

cussions, making it more difficult for them to gain access to academic debate and discussion. In that case, the inequitable positioning constrains ELs' access to learning opportunities necessary for developing both advanced STEM learning and English language proficiency. Research examining classroom interactions emphasizes the teacher's role in promoting EL academic success and participation (Iddings, 2005; Verplaetse, 2000; Yoon, 2008). If teachers position ELs as students with deficits who consistently need assistance, this will shape ELs' positioning in peer-to-peer interactions (Cohen and Lotan, 1995, 1997, 2014; Pinnow and Chval, 2015).

ELs may be silent during classroom activities. Yoon (2008) argued that "the main reason for [ELs'] anxiety, silence, and different positioning has much to do with being outsiders in the regular classroom context" (p. 498). Pappamihiel (2002) noted that student silence is often the result of unfair or inequitable positioning in content classrooms that can subsequently reduce student opportunities to engage in meaningful learning opportunities. Hansen-Thomas (2009) compared how three 6th-grade mathematics teachers used language to draw ELs into content-focused classroom participation and found that in classes where teachers regularly elicited language from ELs, these students were successful on academic assessments, whereas students in other classes were not.

Teachers play a key role in partnering students so that ELs have regular opportunities to share their ideas and are then positioned as competent classroom community members (Yoon, 2008; see Box 4-2), thus placing them on a trajectory toward greater competence and participation (Empson, 2003; Turner et al., 2009). Chval and colleagues (2018) present examples from Courtney, a 3rd-grade teacher, and Sara, a 5th-grade teacher, whose practices they researched (see, e.g., Khisty and Chval [2002] and Chval, Pinnow, and Thomas [2015]) to illustrate teaching practices that have facilitated equitable partnerships for ELs in mathematics classrooms. These teachers (1) established environments in which students respected one another and valued partnerships, (2) used criteria for partner selection, (3) identified subtle cues that indicate inequitable partnership patterns, and (4) used strategies to intervene when necessary. Razfar, Khisty, and Chval (2011) reported on a 5th-grade teacher documented to be highly effective in working with ELs: "Overall, through her instruction, she creates an activity system that repositions students as agents of knowledge construction who collectively move toward a common goal using multiple mediational and semiotic tools. Through this activity system, her students not only develop mathematically but also appropriate complex writing practices in English" (p. 196). Chapter 5 provides a deeper discussion of the ways in which teachers position the families' culture in classrooms.

---

**BOX 4-2**
**Positioning in the Kindergarten Mathematics**
**Discourse Community**

Positioning English learners as competent problem solvers means that teachers believe in students' capabilities to show their peers how they solve word problems, even in early childhood contexts such as kindergarten classrooms. In this example, teachers used strategic open- and close-ended questioning coupled with positioning to support students' participation in a Mathematics Discourse Community—conceptualized as the ways of being, doing, thinking, and speaking as they manifest in teachers' and students' interactions in the mathematics classroom. Teachers invited students to share their mathematical thinking whereby even the shyest students at beginning stages of English language development in an English as a second language classroom shifted from problem solvers to problem posers from beginning to end of the kindergarten year (Turner et al., 2009).

In the Center for the Mathematics Education of Latinos/as (CEMELA) Kindergarten Study funded by the National Science Foundation, teachers were observed positioning students as competent when asking the students to listen (i.e., "Fold your hands and let's listen to Amalia") and called on students to show their work on the board (i.e., "Show us"). These teacher actions were coupled with support of students as they explained their mathematical thinking to others in the class. Another way they positioned students as problem posers was having students write their own word problems and then ask other students to solve them.

SOURCE: Developed and adapted from commissioned paper *Mathematics Education and Young Dual Language Learners* by Sylvia Celedón-Pattichis (2018). Available: http://www. nas.edu/ELinSTEM [October 2018].

---

## Teachers' Value of Family-Community Engagement

It is essential to acknowledge that all children, irrespective of their home culture and first language, arrive at school with rich knowledge and skills that have great potential as resources for STEM learning. However, the teachers who instruct students who are "minoritized" according to their social class and cultural and linguistic backgrounds need support to recognize, leverage, and use these as potential instructional resources (Rosebery and Warren, 2008). When teachers better understand their students and their families, they can then recognize students' multiple ways of doing and demonstrating knowledge or understanding of mathematics and science content available in different contexts (Civil, 2012).

There is a need for teachers (and other school personnel) to gain a better understanding of their students' and their families' backgrounds and experiences (see Chapters 5 and 6). This can help teachers see that STEM learning is not culture-free and can open up paths to teaching innovations that build on students' experiences. One approach to teachers learning from families is work using the concept of Funds of Knowledge. As Moll and colleagues (1992) wrote, "We use the term 'funds of knowledge' to refer to these historically accumulated and culturally developed bodies of knowledge and skills essential for household or individual functioning and well-being" (p. 133). Chapter 5 provides a more in-depth discussion of the interactions between the teacher, school, family, and community that are important for ELs' success in STEM learning.

## INTERACTIONS BETWEEN STEM CONTENT TEACHERS AND ESL TEACHERS

ESL teachers play significant roles in various ESL education programs at elementary and secondary levels. At elementary schools, some of the program models in which teachers of ELs play significant roles include pull-out, push-in, or inclusion models, and team teaching (Becker, 2001). At the secondary level, sheltered content classes are common (Faltis, 1993) to meet ELs' language needs in content classrooms. (However, as noted in Chapter 2, sheltered classes often have more simplified disciplinary content.)

The challenges in collaboration between the STEM content teachers and ESL teachers are evident in research (Arkoudis, 2000, 2003; Tan, 2011). Tan (2011) showed how teachers in a STEM content-based language teaching environment viewed their roles as content teachers only and did not assume any language-related responsibilities nor did they approach collaboration positively. This kind of negative stance is a great challenge for collaboration. Further, Arkoudis (2000, 2003) showed in ethnographic work on ESL teachers' roles in relation to the mainstream science teacher that the participating ESL teacher had less authority and agency over the lesson planning process. Arkoudis (2006) reported that the epistemological authority and power that the science teacher holds over the ESL teacher is directly linked to the institutional hierarchy within the education system.

Moreover, in the kind of content-based language teaching that has until recently been most common, ESL teachers are asked to develop "content objectives" and "language objectives." MacDonald, Miller, and Lord (2017, p. 183) provided examples of typical "language objectives":

- Students will compare landforms using descriptive language.
- Students will describe the molecular changes that occurred using the past tense '-ed' form.

As the authors point out, goals like these, based on the assumption that language learning will be supported by focusing on grammatical forms (past tense) or only on a particular function out of context ("compare"....) lose sight of the larger goals of the instructional work, such as a focus on concepts and student participation in practices. Approaches that are currently being promoted for work with ELs in STEM classrooms instead focus on objectives that are relevant to deep STEM learning focused on disciplinary concepts and practices. For the same instructional focus, MacDonald and colleagues (2017, p. 184) presented these revised objectives:

- Students will collaboratively develop a model that explains and predicts patterns in the changes to the land caused by wind and rain.
- Students will collaboratively construct an explanation of the effect of thermal energy on molecular movement.

Objectives such as these focus the instruction on the science to be learned and embed attention to the functional use of language. As students *explain* and *predict* in developing a model and constructing an explanation, the teacher can support these discursive goals that develop students' language at the same times the students learn science. Goals like these, recognizing the functional use of language in learning, align with the focus of science educators on disciplinary concepts and practices and offer new opportunities for collaboration between ESL and content teachers of STEM, where the role of the ESL teacher is to identify how a strategic focus on language can support the content teacher in reaching the content learning goals with ELs. As these objectives illustrate, classroom interaction with peers and engagement in meaningful activities is central to this view of STEM instruction.

## PROMISING INSTRUCTIONAL STRATEGIES TO SUPPORT STEM CONTENT AND LANGUAGE DEVELOPMENT

The *Promising Futures* report (National Academies of Sciences, Engineering, and Medicine, 2017) set the stage for this report by highlighting the diversity of ELs in terms of their cultures, languages, and experiences that may have an impact on their education. The 2017 report concluded that many schools were not prepared to provide adequate instruction to ELs in acquiring English proficiency while ensuring academic success. The committee of that report identified several promising and effective strategies for ELs in PreK–12. In the early grades, the strategies include (1) provide explicit instruction in literacy components; (2) develop academic language during content area instruction; (3) provide visual and verbal supports to make core content comprehensible; (4) encourage peer-assistant learning opportunities; (5) capitalize on students' home language, knowledge, and cultural assets; (6) screen for language and literacy challenges and monitor progress; and (7) provide small-group support in literacy and English language development for ELs who need additional support.

When moving into the middle and high school grades, the strategies are similar, such as capitalizing on a student's home language, knowledge, and cultural assets and providing collaborative, peer-group learning communities to support and extend teacher-led instruction. However, the *Promising Futures* report also highlights the need to support comprehension and writing related to core content and to develop academic English as part of subject-matter learning. Overall, the majority of the practices focus on promoting literacy development.

Building from these strategies, the present committee examined the literature more specific to STEM learning. As described in Chapter 2, ELs have had a history of limited access to STEM instruction and with a favoring to develop English proficiency; this stemmed from a narrow view that for participation in STEM subjects, ELs first needed to have proficiency in the disciplinary talk—the words, vocabulary, or definitions. However, it is now better understood that ELs benefit when they are engaged in meaningful classroom activities that enable interaction with others during STEM meaning-making.

ELs benefit when the classroom offers opportunities to build on their home languages and everyday registers, drawing on the full range of meaning-making resources they bring and move back and forth between more informal and formal registers. In addition, they benefit when their teachers are able to raise their awareness of the language of instruction and how it works in learning and teaching STEM. This chapter offers a review of research on instructional strategies in mathematics and science classrooms that have shown promise for supporting ELs through opportunities to engage in disciplinary practices, interact in meaningful and varied ways that draw on their language and other meaning-making resources, and attend to language and its meanings as they do disciplinary work. Given all of this, the five promising instructional strategies discussed include

1. Engage Students in Disciplinary Practices
2. Engage Students in Productive Discourse and Interactions with Others
3. Utilize and Encourage Students to Use Multiple Registers and Multiple Modalities
4. Leverage Multiple Meaning-Making Resources
5. Provide Some Explicit Focus on How Language Functions in the Discipline

## Engage Students in Disciplinary Practices

As students engage in STEM disciplinary practices, they communicate their ideas with peers and the teacher and co-construct disciplinary meaning in the STEM classroom community. Language is a product of interaction and learning, not a precursor or prerequisite. Gibbons (2006) called for EL learning in authentic curriculum contexts that engage learners in tasks that are intellectually challenging and that call for interaction with others in contexts of high support. When students engage in highly demanding disciplinary practices, they grapple with the ideas, concepts, and practices of the discipline, transform what they learn into a different form or present it to a different audience, and move between concrete and abstract knowledge. They engage in substantive conversation about what they are learning, make connections between the spoken and written practices and meaningful artifacts of the discipline, and problematize knowledge and question accepted wisdom (Gibbons, 2007).

STEM subjects often involve authentic engagement with material supports and central ideas. Work with artifacts can be extended into opportunities for generalizing and reasoning about concepts, using language, and other meaning-making resources. Focusing on a topic over a sustained period of instruction, learners have opportunities to engage in experiences about the new topic, and then reflect on and consolidate that learning through talk or written work. This exposes them to different registers and modes of communication and enables them to draw on multiple meaning-making resources (as articulated in Chapter 3).

## Science Practices

Science is the practice of making and testing evidence-based conjectures about the world. In the science classroom, students engage in science as scientists do as they try to make sense of phenomena (see Box 4-3 for an illustration of this process as ELs engage in a science lesson focused on antibiotic resistance of MRSA). According to *A Framework for K–12 Science Education*, phenomena or problems are central to science and science learning, as "the goal of science is to develop a set of coherent and mutually consistent theoretical descriptions of the world that can provide explanations over a wide range of phenomena" (National Research Council, 2012, p. 48). In elementary and secondary grades, local phenomena promote ELs' access to science and inclusion in the science classroom by engaging all students, including ELs, to use their everyday experience and everyday language from their homes and communities (Lee and Miller, 2016; Lee et al., in press; Lyon et al., 2016; Tolbert, 2016). Once students identify a compelling phenomenon that offers access to science and inclusion in the

**BOX 4-3**
**Engaging English Learners (ELs) in Science Learning**

In one example of a lesson that incorporates the Secondary Science Teaching with English Language and Literacy Acquisition (SSTELLA) framework, ELs (along with non-ELs) learn core ideas about natural selection through studying the antibiotic resistance of MRSA (Lyon, 2016). The multiday lesson is designed with attention to the Next Generation Science Standards (NGSS) HS-LS4-2, Biological Evolution: Unity and Diversity, whereby the performance expectation is that students will be able to use evidence to explain how evolution results from population growth, differential reproductive success, competition, and heritable genetic variation. The lesson also addresses WIDA[a] English language proficiency standards (Standard 4, Grades 9–12), Common Core State Standards (CCSS) for Literacy in Social Sciences, Sciences, and Technical Subjects (Writing 2: Grades 9–10), and productive and receptive language functions as outlined in the Framework for English Language Proficiency Development Standards corresponding to the CCSS and NGSS (Council of the Chief State School Officers, 2012).

During the lesson series, students construct an explanatory model that draws on the theory of natural selection to describe a real-world problem, the antibiotic resistance of MRSA. The overarching objective is that students will "explain how the species Staphylococcus aureus changed so that over 60 percent are methicillin resistant" (Lyon, 2016, p. 40). Essential to this framing context is the elicitation of students' own experiences with relatives or friends in hospitals. After sharing their own experiences in hospitals (e.g., experiencing an injury, the birth of a relative, visiting hospitalized friends and relatives, etc.), they respond to the question, "Do you think someone could be harmed from bacteria while staying in a local hospital?" (Lyon, 2016, p. 36). After discussing this question with a partner and then as a whole class, students watch a brief YouTube clip from a local news report about "superbugs." The reporter asks, "What causes these so-called superbugs?" This question frames the students' learning experiences. Students use a graphic organizer to clarify important ideas from the video, including "species of interest," "MRSA," "antibiotic," and multiple-meaning words such as "resistance."

Over the next several days, students construct an initial explanatory model, which they test, revise, and refine, as they learn the influential factors of evolution through a series of activities such as Oh Deer!, a worm-eater simulation, and so on (see Passmore et al., 2013). They then use a graphic organizer to analyze

science classroom, they engage in science and engineering practices to figure out the phenomenon or design solutions to problems. As they experience science, they build an understanding of science to explain the phenomenon. Over the course of science instruction, students develop deeper and more sophisticated understanding of science.

Foundational to understanding science inquiry with ELs, the programmatic line of research by members of the Chèche Konnen team has involved the claims, evidence, and audience in three different texts with three different purposes, all related to MRSA, before finalizing their explanatory model about "how the species Staphylococcus aureus changed so that over 60 percent are methicillin resistant." In a final activity, students are given a new set of data about resistance to the antibiotic Vancomycin commonly used to treat MRSA and are asked to "apply your own understanding about adaptation and natural selection to explain with evidence how the percentage of bacteria resistant to Vancomycin changed from 1983 to 2001" (Lyon, 2016, p. 41). As an extension of this assignment, students are asked to communicate findings to a different audience, such as writing for a school paper or a local daycare center.

Throughout this series of activities, the teacher attends to students' simultaneous development of core ideas about natural selection and disciplinary practices, in this case, constructing evidence-based scientific explanations. ELs are supported through language scaffolds, such as cooperative learning structures, explicit vocabulary instruction as needed to support conceptual understanding and interpret and communicate findings, varied graphic organizers designed to home students in on key elements and key vocabulary related to a concept, and real-world contexts and students' own lived experiences as frames for learning. Students have "multiple modes of representation and thinking to use language and can practice interpreting and producing discipline-specific uses of language" (Lyon, 2016, p. 42). Walqui and Heritage (2012) described scaffolding for ELs in content area instruction as "the 'just right' kind of support required by students to engage in practice that helps them mature processes which are at the cusp of developing, while simultaneously engaging their agency" (p. 4). It is with this understanding of language development upon which the SSTELLA framework is founded. In the MRSA lesson, students are supported through appropriate scaffolds that progressively facilitate their construction of an explanatory model, while allowing students both "generativity and autonomy" within the academic tasks (Walqui and Heritage, 2012, p. 4).

---

[a]WIDA stands for the three states that were involved in the EAG grant that provided initial funding for the organization: Wisconsin (WI), Delaware (D), and Arkansas (A). Recently WIDA decided to stop using the acronym definition. See https://www.wida.us/aboutus/mission.aspx [August 2018].
SOURCE: Developed from commissioned paper *Secondary Science Education for English Learners* by Sara Tolbert (2018). Available: http://www.nas.edu/ELinSTEM [October 2018].

case studies of students from African American, Haitian, and Latino backgrounds in both bilingual and monolingual classrooms across elementary and secondary grades (Rosebery, Warren, and Conant, 1992; Warren et al., 2001). The Chèche Konnen research has used open-ended tasks to frame experimentation as an exploratory process of constructing meaning from emerging variables (Rosebery et al., 2010). By asking questions about what children do as they engage in experimental tasks, what resources they draw upon as they develop and evaluate ideas, and how children's scientific reasoning corresponds to the nature of experimentation practiced by scientists, these studies have provided evidence that ELs are capable of engaging in science inquiry.

ELs come into the science classroom with rich cultural and linguistic resources for scientific sense-making. Capitalizing on ELs' prior knowledge and interests is an important starting point for linking science and language (González, Moll, and Amanti, 2005; Tolbert and Knox, 2016). In the Chèche Konnen body of work, researchers explicitly consider the role of language in scientific sense-making by investigating how ELs' home languages and discourse styles can be used as resources to understand and gradually take ownership of the discourse patterns of scientific communities. For example, Hudicourt-Barnes (2003) demonstrated how argumentative discussion is a major feature of social interaction among Haitian adults and how this discourse pattern can then be leveraged as a resource for students as they practice argumentation in science class. More recent work by this group (Warren and Rosebery, 2011) has considered the value of viewing science learning as an intercultural process in which students and teachers negotiate the boundaries of race, culture, language, and subject matter in order to overcome the traditional inequalities that often persist in science classrooms with ELs.

Using large-scale and experimental or quasi-experimental designs, studies examined the impact of inquiry interventions on science and language development with ELs. Some interventions focused primarily on science learning while attending to language development (Llosa et al., 2016; Maerten-Rivera et al., 2016), others focused on both language development and science learning (August, Artzi, and Barr, 2016; August et al., 2009, 2014; Lara-Alecio et al., 2012), and still others focused primarily on ELs' language development in the context of science learning (Zwiep and Straits, 2013). To test the effectiveness of inquiry interventions with ELs, Estrella and colleagues (2018) conducted a meta-analysis of the effect of inquiry instruction on the science achievement of ELs in elementary school. An analysis of 26 articles confirmed that inquiry instruction produced significantly greater impacts on measures of science achievement for ELs compared to traditional science instruction. However, there was still a differential learning effect suggesting greater efficacy for non-ELs compared to ELs.

## Mathematical Practices

Research suggests that high-quality instruction for ELs that supports student achievement has two general characteristics (Gándara and Contreras, 2009): an emphasis on academic achievement (not only on learning English) and recognition of the meaning-making resources students bring to the classroom. Previous research shows that ELs, even as they are learning English, can participate in discussions where they grapple with important mathematical content (for examples of lessons, see Khisty, 1995, 2001; Khisty and Chval, 2002; Moschkovich, 1999, 2011; Pinnow and Chval, 2014). Moreover, research has described how teachers learn to recognize how ELs express their mathematical ideas as they are learning English and maintain a focus on mathematical reasoning as well as on language development (Khisty, 1995, 2001; Khisty and Chval, 2002; Moschkovich, 1999, 2011; Razfar, Khisty, and Chval, 2011).

Effective mathematics instruction for ELs includes and focuses on mathematical practices because these practices are central to developing full mathematical proficiency and expertise. For example, multiplication lessons are expected not to focus exclusively on the five strands of mathematical proficiency (see Chapter 3), but also to provide opportunities for students to participate in these mathematical practices—such as making sense of problems and looking for regularity—as well as mathematical discourse—reading word problems, explaining solutions orally and in writing, providing mathematical justification, and the like.

As described in Chapter 3, research describes high-quality mathematics instruction that is effective as having three central characteristics: teachers and students focus on mathematical concepts and connections among those concepts (Hiebert and Grouws, 2007), students wrestle with important mathematics (Hiebert and Grouws, 2007), and teachers use high cognitive demand mathematical tasks and maintain the rigor and cognitive demand of those tasks during lessons, for example, by encouraging students to explain their reasoning (American Educational Research Association, 2006; Stein, Grover, and Henningsen, 1996). The research suggests that mathematics lessons (1) include the full spectrum of mathematical proficiency (see Chapter 3), balance a focus on computational fluency with high-cognitive-demand tasks that require conceptual understanding and reasoning, and provide students opportunities to participate in mathematical practices (Moschkovich, 2013a, 2013b); (2) allow students to use multiple resources (such as modes of communication, symbol systems, registers, or languages) for mathematical reasoning (Moschkovich, 2013a, 2013b); and (3) support students in negotiating meanings for mathematical language grounded in student mathematical work.

In particular, for ELs, strong mathematics instruction focuses on uncovering, hearing, and supporting students' mathematical reasoning and supports their participation in these practices and is not focused on their accuracy in using language (Moschkovich, 2010, 2012). Effective instruction recognizes students' emerging mathematical reasoning and mathematical meanings learners construct, not on the mistakes they make or the obstacles they face. Instruction needs to first focus on assessing content knowledge as distinct from fluency of expression in English, so that teachers can then extend and refine students' mathematical reasoning (a central mathematical practice). If the focus is only on grammatical accuracy or vocabulary, mathematical reasoning may be missed. Mathematics instruction for ELs can be designed and implemented to provide ELs opportunities to actively engage in mathematical practices, such as making sense of problems, constructing arguments, and expressing structure and regularity.

In early mathematics classes, storytelling has been shown to be an effective teaching strategy that supports problem solving (Lo Cicero, Fuson, and Allexsaht-Snider, 1999; Lo Cicero, De La Cruz, and Fuson, 1999; Turner et al., 2009). Studying three primarily Latina/o kindergarten classrooms, one in which mathematics was taught in Spanish, one bilingual, and one in English as a second language, Turner and Celedón-Pattichis (2011) found that, although there was growth across all three classrooms in problem solving, students showed the most growth in solving word problems in the classroom where the teacher used storytelling twice as often; used the home language, Spanish, more often; and spent more time on a wide range of problem types. What is important to note is that all teachers drew from familiar ways of talking and negotiating meaning within students' cultural contexts (Delgado-Gaitan, 1987; Villenas and Moreno, 2001), telling and sharing authentic, storytelling conversations, and inviting young ELs to co-construct these stories when engaged in mathematical problem solving (Turner et al., 2009).

### Engage Students in Productive Discourse and Interactions with Others

For ELs, experiencing science and mathematics through engagement in the disciplinary practices is especially important, as the disciplinary practices are both cognitively demanding and language intensive. While engaging in the disciplinary practices, ELs comprehend (receptive language functions) and express (productive language functions) disciplinary ideas using their emerging English. For example, in science, the practice of developing and using models involves both science analytical tasks (e.g., make revisions to a model based on either suggestions from others or conflicts between a model and observation), receptive language functions (e.g., interpret the meaning of models presented in texts and diagrams), and productive language functions (e.g., describe a model using oral and/or written language as well as illustrations [Council of Chief State School Officers, 2012, pp. 27–28]). Swanson, Bianchini, and Lee (2014) found that a high school teacher who conceived of science as including both practices and discourse defined science discourse as generating and evaluating arguments from evidence, sharing ideas and understandings with others in public forums, and using precise language. In taking this approach, the teacher provided her EL students with multiple, scaffolded opportunities to articulate their ideas about natural phenomena; engage in the process of developing arguments from evidence; and read, interpret, and evaluate scientific information. Such instruction offers students repeated, extended access to participation in disciplinary practices such as conjecturing, explaining, and arguing with appropriate scaffolding.

## Scaffolding

Scaffolding for ELs is not simply one kind of support. Scaffolding can be provided at different levels (van Lier, 2004), in different settings (individual or collective), or for different pedagogical purposes (i.e., to support procedural fluency, conceptual understanding, or participation in classroom discussions, Moschkovich, 2015). It is not simply the ways in which tasks are structured to "help" the learner. Scaffolding is contingent upon the reaction of the learner to something new (Walqui, 2006). As such, scaffolding can occur as structure and as process (Walqui, 2006; Walqui and van Lier, 2010) and can be provided in multiple levels or time scales such as micro, meso, or macro (van Lier, 2004). Macro-level scaffolding involves the design of long-term sequences of work or projects, with recurring tasks-with-variations over a protracted time period. Meso-level scaffolding involves the design of individual tasks as consisting of a series of steps or activities that occur sequentially or in collaborative construction. Micro-level scaffolding involves contingent interactional processes of appropriation, stimulation, give-and-take in conversation, collaborative dialogue (Swain, 2000), and so on.

## Structuring Interaction

Gibbons (2004) pointed out that teachers plan activities, but rarely plan for how they will interact with students. In particular, interaction that involves shifting back and forth between registers can highlight the relationship between the specific task that students are engaged with and the general and more abstract disciplinary concepts that the students are learning. Haneda's (2000) case study of interaction between a teacher and two 3rd-grade ELs as they discussed an experiment on refraction describes how, with teacher support in interaction, one of the children was able to move beyond just recounting the procedures she had followed to also explain and reason about what she had done. The other student never reached this goal, suggesting that the move from recounting to explaining is quite challenging, as it calls for moving beyond concrete experiences and drawing on more abstract registers. McNeil (2012) found that after an instructional intervention, a 5th-grade teacher scaffolded her classroom talk in new ways, utilizing multiple new communicative moves that served to better engage her ELs in disciplinary discourse.

Research on interaction with ELs stresses the role of *contingent* responses in enabling learners to build their knowledge of language and subject matter. For example, Boyd and Rubin (2002) analyzed the kinds of interaction in the classroom that enable 4th- and 5th-grade ELs to produce what they call *student critical turns* (SCTs) in a literacy-rich science unit. They defined SCTs as coherent and topic-focused contributions of 10 seconds or more, and they studied the local discourse conditions that appear to foster production of SCTs. They found that contingent questioning by the teacher or other students at strategic junctures promoted extended contributions by ELs. The teacher initiated 58 percent of episodes that led to SCTs, and two-thirds of the time she had the turn of talk immediately prior to the SCT. Often the questions that preceded the SCTs were display questions that asked students to report on what they had learned. Although display questions are often considered less helpful to students than questions that authentically seek information, the researchers found that display questions could be contingently responsive teaching that pushes a student to elaborate on what has already been said. These questions pushed students to expand their thinking and talk. Authentic questions also worked this way, as did clarification requests.

Boyd and Rubin ask for reconsideration of the role of the often maligned Initiation-Response-Feedback (IRF[3]) participation structure, as these question-answer sequences can be used in different contexts to achieve different purposes. Gibbons (2004) noted that the Feedback move can increase the demands on a student and support language development by pushing the student to expand on what has been said. Cervetti, DiPardo, and Staley (2014) showed how a teacher used an IRF structure to adeptly nudge students to ask their own questions, make their own evaluations, and connect their contributions as they worked in an inquiry science context with 6th- and 7th-grade ELs. She used "shaping moves" that invited students into the discussion and encouraged collaborative listening, keeping the conversation going. The authors noted that IRF structures can be used strategically, striking "a balance...between more authoritative and more dialogic forms of discourse" (p. 560) as they engage students in participation that supports their conceptual understanding. (See Wells [1993] for further discussion of the potential of IRF participation structures to support language development.)

---

[3]Sometimes referred to as Initiation-Response-Feedback/Evaluation or IRE. Although these terms can be used interchangeably, the distinction is that the teacher provides an evaluation of the student's response in the third turn (Feedback) (Thoms, 2012).

## Disciplinary Talk and Talk Moves

Chapter 3 introduced the notion of linguistic *register* to highlight the ways students' language choice vary, depending on the activity, the interlocutors, and the modalities available for meaning-making. Herbel-Eisenmann, Steele, and Cirillo (2013) pointed out that not all talk is formal and whether students use more or less formal ways of talking depends on the context. They described how students may use more informal talk that involves pointing and reference to features of the situational context (e.g., "Why did you do *that*? When I did *this*, I got the wrong answer") when talking in a small group with writing or computations in front of them. That talk may become more formal when presenting a solution at the board (e.g., "When I multiplied by seven, I got the wrong answer"). And, finally, when presenting a final solution in writing, that talk would then become even more formal (e.g., "My calculation was initially wrong, but I changed the operation from multiplication to division and then the result made more sense").

Science talk formats and talk moves are one important way to support ELs to engage with locally relevant phenomena (Gallas, 1994; Herrenkohl and Guerra, 1998; Michaels and O'Connor, 2012). These moves make explicit the types of talk that are critical for making sense of phenomena collectively in the science classroom. Teachers can use a variety of formats (e.g., whole class, small group, pair work, and individual thinking time) and a set of moves to support particular kinds of reasoning. These moves include sharing; expanding or clarifying reasoning; listening to and understanding others' ideas; providing evidence and examples to support reasoning; or asking questions or making comments to agree with, add on to, or explain what someone else means. These strategies help students know how they can contribute productively to make sense of phenomena in the science classroom community. These strategies also address issues of equity, as they can help teachers monitor turn-taking to ensure that ELs have ample opportunities to participate in classroom discourse (Michaels and O'Connor, 2015).

Work on teacher talk moves in mathematics classrooms has documented how teachers support whole-class discussions (Chapin, O'Connor, and Anderson, 2003, 2009; Herbel-Eisenmann, Steele, and Cirillo, 2013; Michaels and O'Connor, 2015; Razfar and Leavitt, 2010, 2011). Chval (2012) reported on specific features of the discourse of one 5th-grade teacher who spoke and wrote sophisticated words. She used these words frequently and in the context of solving problems and supported students as they built understanding of the meanings of these words. These talk moves create opportunities for students to draw upon the linguistic resources they bring to class and move toward more formal registers. They also enable productive classroom discussions in mathematics (Anderson, Chapin, and

O'Connor, 2011). According to Anderson, Chapin, and O'Connor (2011), a productive classroom discussion supports students' mathematical understandings by proceeding through four steps:

- Step 1. Helping individual students clarify and share their own thoughts
- Step 2. Helping students orient to the thinking of other students
- Step 3. Helping students deepen their reasoning
- Step 4. Helping students to engage with the reasoning of others

Several "teacher moves" (Michaels and O'Connor, 2015) have been described that can support student participation in a discussion: revoicing, asking for clarification, accepting and building on what students say, probing what students mean, and using students' own ways of talking. Teachers can use multiple ways to scaffold and support more formal language, including revoicing student statements (Moschkovich, 2015).

Revoicing (O'Connor and Michaels, 1993) is a teacher move describing how an adult, typically a teacher, rephrases a student's contribution during a discussion, expanding or recasting the original utterance (Forman, McCormick, and Donato, 1997). Revoicing has been used to describe teacher talk moves in several studies (e.g., Herbel-Eisenmann, Drake, and Cirillo, 2009). A teacher's revoicing can support student participation in a discussion as well as introduce more formal language (see Box 4-4). First, it can facilitate student participation in general, by accepting a student's response, using it to make an inference, and allowing the student to evaluate the accuracy of the teacher's interpretation of the student contribution (O'Connor and Michaels, 1993). This teacher move allows for further student contributions in a way that the standard classroom Initiation-Response-Evaluation (IRE) pattern (Mehan, 1979; Sinclair and Coulthard, 1975) does not (although see above for studies that show such IRE/IRF interaction has a place in instruction for ELs).

The work cited above on talk moves can provide resources for teachers of STEM, with the important consideration that applying talk moves for instruction with ELs will require teachers to have experience, professional development, and resources that include ELs and consider issues particular to ELs, for example, the fact that the language ELs use may be different than that used by monolingual English speakers (Bunch, 2013; Moschkovich, 2007).

## Utilize Multiple Registers and Multiple Modalities

While communicating ideas with peers and the teacher, students use multiple modalities, including both linguistic and other semiotic modalities.

They draw on a variety of registers of talk and text, ranging from every-day to specialized. In addition, students participate in a range of different interactions. To communicate the growing sophistication of their ideas over the course of instruction, ELs use increasingly specialized registers adapting their language to meet the communicative demands of interactions in pair, small-group, and whole-class settings.

## Registers

To make sense of disciplinary concepts, students participate in partner (one-to-one), small-group (one-to-small group), and whole-class (one-to-many) settings. In doing so, they move fluidly across modalities (see below) and registers to meet the communicative demands of different interactions (Lee, Grapin, and Haas, 2018). Formal or school STEM disciplinary registers are one resource for students to express disciplinary reasoning, such as when making a presentation or developing a written account of a solution. However, informal registers are also important, especially when students are exploring a concept, learning a new concept, or discussing a problem in small groups. Informal language can be used by students (and teachers) during exploratory talk (Barnes, 1976/1992, 2008) or when working in a small group (Herbel-Eisenmann, Steele, and Cirillo, 2013). Such informal registers can reflect important student mathematical thinking (see Moschkovich, 1996, 1998, 2008, 2014). For example, in carrying out an investigation with a partner (one-to-one), ELs may use a more everyday register while pointing at a measurement instrument (e.g., "Put it on here"), as nonlinguistic modalities of gestures and objects serve as resources for meaning-making and communication (Grapin, 2018).

Specialized registers afford the *precision* necessary to communicate disciplinary meaning as students' disciplinary-specific ideas become more sophisticated. Precision privileges disciplinary meaning by focusing on how students use language to engage in the STEM practices. As Moschkovich (2012) described in the context of the mathematics classroom, precision goes beyond the use of specialized vocabulary of the content areas. In addition, precision does not imply linguistic accuracy, as "precise claims can be expressed in imperfect language" (Moschkovich, 2012, p. 22). Likewise, in the science classroom, precision goes beyond the use of specialized vocabulary to the communication of precise disciplinary meaning. For example, when engaging in argument from evidence, students communicate precise disciplinary meaning by supporting their claims with evidence and reasoning (Quinn, Lee, and Valdés, 2012). In the classroom, ELs can communicate precise disciplinary meaning using less-than-perfect English (Lee, Quinn, and Valdés, 2013).

In both mathematics and science classrooms, precision privileges disci-

## BOX 4-4
## Elementary Students Using Everyday Language
## as Resources and Teacher Revoicing

This example comes from a lesson in a 4th-grade bilingual classroom (33 students identified as Limited English Proficiency, urban school in California). In general, the teacher introduced topics first in Spanish and then later in English, using

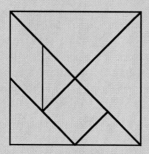

materials in both languages. Materials in both Spanish and English surrounded students and the desks were arranged in tables of four so that the students could work together.

Students had been working on a unit on two-dimensional geometric figures. For several weeks, instruction had included technical vocabulary, such as "radius," "diameter," "congruent," "hypotenuse," and the names of different quadrilaterals in both Spanish and English. Students had been talking about shapes and had been asked to point, touch, and identify different shapes. The teacher described this lesson as an ESL mathematics lesson, where students would be using English to discuss different shapes in the context of folding and cutting to make Tangram pieces as exhibited in the figure.

**Vignette**

1. Teacher:   Today we are going to have a very special lesson in which you really gonna have to listen. You're going to put on your best, best listening ears because I'm only going to speak in English. Nothing else. Only English. Let's see how much we remembered from Monday. Hold up your rectangles . . . high as you can. (Students hold up rectangles) Good, now. Who can describe a rectangle? Eric, can you describe it [a rectangle]? Can you tell me about it?

2. Eric:   A rectangle has . . . two . . . short sides, and two . . . long sides.

3. Teacher:   Two short sides and two long sides. Can somebody tell me something else about this rectangle, if somebody didn't know what it looked like, what, what . . . how would you say it.

4. Julian:   Paralela [holding up a rectangle, voice trails off].

5. Teacher:   It's parallel. Very interesting word. Parallel. Wow! Pretty interesting word, isn't it? Parallel. Can you describe what that is?

6. Julian:   Never get together. They never get together [runs his finger over the top side of the rectangle].

7. Teacher:   What never gets together?

8. Julian:   The parallela . . . they . . . when they go, they go higher [runs two fingers parallel to each other first along the top and base of the rectangle and then continues along those lines], they never get together.

9. Antonio:     Yeah!
10. Teacher:    Very interesting. The rectangle then has sides that will never meet. Those sides will be parallel. Good work. Excellent work.

The vignette shows that ELs can participate in discussions where they grapple with important mathematical content. Students were grappling not only with the definitions for quadrilaterals, but also with the concept of parallelism. They were engaged in mathematical practices because they were making claims, generalizing, imagining, hypothesizing, and predicting what will happen to two line segments if they are extended indefinitely. To communicate about these mathematical ideas, students used words, objects, gestures, and other students' utterances as resources.

This vignette illustrates several instructional strategies that can be useful in supporting student participation in mathematical discussions. Some of these strategies are (a) asking for clarification, (b) re-phrasing student statements, (c) accepting and building on what students say, and (d) probing what students mean. It is important to notice that this teacher did *not* focus directly on vocabulary development but instead on mathematical ideas and arguments as he interpreted, clarified, and rephrased what students were saying. This teacher provided opportunities for discussion by moving past student grammatical or vocabulary errors, listening to students, and trying to understand the mathematics in what students said. He kept the discussion mathematical by focusing on the mathematical content of what students said and did.

The excerpt illustrates a teacher revoicing student statements. In line 5, the teacher accepted Julian's response, revoicing it as "It's parallel," and probed what Julian meant by "parallela." In line 10, the teacher revoiced Julian's contribution in line 8: "the parallela, they" became "sides," and "they never get together" became "has sides that will never meet, those sides will be parallel."

Revoicing can support student participation in mathematical practices. A teacher can build on students' own use of mathematical practices or a student contribution can be revoiced to reflect new mathematical practices. Several mathematical practices are evident in Julian's original utterance in line 8. Julian was abstracting, describing an *abstract* property of parallel lines, and generalizing, making a *generalization* that parallel lines will *never* meet. In this case, the teacher's revoicing made Julian's claim more precise, introducing a new mathematical practice, attending to the precision of a claim. In line 10, the teacher's claim is more precise than Julian's claim because the second claim refers to the sides of a quadrilateral, rather than any two parallel lines.

Revoicing also provides opportunities for students to hear more formal mathematical language. The teacher revoiced Julian's everyday phrase "they never get together" as "has sides that will never meet" and "those sides will be parallel," both closer to academic language. This revoicing seemed to impact Julian who used the term "side(s)" twice when talking with another student in a later interaction, providing some evidence that revoicing supported this student's participation in both mathematical practices and more formal academic language.

SOURCE: Adapted from Moschkovich (1999, 2007, 2012, 2015).

plinary meaning regardless of the linguistic features used. Precision, then, is not an inherent quality of language itself, but rather, a function of what the language does or what effect it has in the context of engaging in disciplinary practices. In considering precision, it is crucial to clarify what is meant, and particularly what is considered precise language, since the word "language" can be used to mean different things. In the case of precision, the reference is not to the precision of individual words, but instead to longer constructions that enable claims to be more or less precise, even when the individual words in that claim may not be the single most perfect "mathy" or "sciency" word that an expert would use.

Moreover, the specialized register affords the *explicitness* necessary (e.g., fewer deictic words like "it" and "here") to communicate disciplinary meaning across physical and temporal contexts. Whereas one-to-one interactions allow students to check for comprehension in real time and clarify their meaning as needed, one-to-small group interactions and, to an even lesser extent, one-to-many interactions do not always offer such opportunities. For example, when presenting data to the class, ELs use a more specialized register as it affords the explicitness to ensure successful communication (e.g., "We recorded the weight of the substance."). Also, in one-to-many interactions, students can rely less on a shared frame of reference. Thus, whereas ELs may use a more everyday register in one-to-one interactions and one-to-small group interactions, they may need to move toward a more specialized register in one-to-many interactions.

## Multiple Modalities

As described in Chapter 3, *modalities* refer to the multiple channels through which communication occurs, including nonlinguistic modalities (e.g., gestures, pictures, symbols, graphs, tables, equations) as well as the linguistic modalities of talk (oral language) and text (written language). Multiple modalities are important in both the STEM disciplines and EL education. In the STEM disciplines, multiple modalities, especially visual representations (e.g., graphs, symbols, equations), are the essential semiotic resources used by scientists, mathematicians, and engineers to communicate their ideas (Lemke, 1998). They are not only important to support ELs but also are, in fact, central to participation in disciplinary practices.

In EL education, nonlinguistic modalities have traditionally been thought of as scaffolds for learning language, which has overshadowed their importance in content areas (Grapin, 2018). As STEM content areas expect all students to use multiple modalities strategically and in ways appropriate to each discipline, nonlinguistic modalities are not just compensatory for ELs. At the same time, multiple modalities serve to support ELs at the early stages of English language proficiency, as they engage in language-intensive practices, such as explaining causal mechanisms and arguing from evidence (Lee, Quinn, and Valdés, 2013). Thus, multiple modalities are essential to "doing" science and mathematics and are especially beneficial to ELs (Grapin, 2018). Recognizing the importance of multimodality in STEM content areas reorients the focus from what ELs lack in terms of language to the diverse meaning-making resources they bring to the classroom. Box 4-5 describes how ELs use different sets of linguistic resources to construct knowledge and express ideas in English and in their first language.

In the mathematics classroom, communication that moves beyond the written and oral world to incorporate diagrams, manipulatives, gestures, multiple representations, and technology can provide more avenues for ELs' participation (Dominguez, 2005; Fernandes, Kahn, and Civil, 2017; Sorto and Bower, 2017; Zahner and Gutiérrez, 2015; Zahner et al., 2012). Drawing on a situated multiliteracies approach, Takeuchi (2015) studied the participation of ELs in mathematics practices in an urban Canadian classroom, describing ELs' successful participation in classroom mathematics practices in relation to the context that supported their participation. Specifically, the teacher's use of multiple language and physical and symbolic tools supported her ELs, along with the teacher's affirmation of the students' identities as multimodal learners. Takeuchi calls for broadening the definition of language in mathematics classrooms as well as embracing students' identities that are shaped through classroom interactions with content and language.

In the science classroom, students use multiple modalities to engage in science and engineering practices (Grapin, 2018). For example, they use graphs and tables as they analyze and interpret data. Multiple modalities may be especially useful for supporting ELs to engage in language-intensive science and engineering practices, such as arguing from evidence and constructing explanations. ELs use drawings, symbols, and text to construct model-supported explanations of phenomena. As ELs build their understanding of science over the course of instruction, they make increasingly strategic use of multiple modalities. Specifically, they learn to consider how modalities help them communicate the increasing sophistication of their ideas. For example, students use arrows to represent relationships in a system, graphs and tables to represent patterns in data, or diagrammatic or computational models to explain causal mechanism.

## Leverage Multiple Meaning-Making Resources

By the time ELs come to school, they already possess a range of knowledge, values, and ways of looking at the world that have developed during their socialization into their families and communities that could be

**BOX 4-5**
**Problem Solving and Language Proficiency**

ELs use different sets of linguistic resources to construct knowledge and express ideas in English and in their first language. As the examples below show, the reasoning they use in solving science and mathematics problems and the sophistication of their discourse may vary depending on the language used. The examples are from a project that examined the responses of Grade 4 ELs to science and mathematics problems given in English and in their first language (Solano-Flores et al., 2001).

In the Erosion problem (National Assessment of Educational Progress, 1996b), Karina (a fictitious name) gives a correct answer in English and an incorrect answer in Haitian-Creole—her first language. The arguments supporting the response in each language are totally the opposite—in A, "mountains are not cacky;" in B, "the mountains do not look smooth (see Solano-Flores et al., 2001, p. 150).

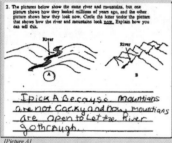

[Picture A].
*I pick A Because mountians are not cacky and now mountians are open to Let the River go through.*

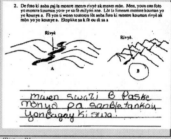

[Picture B].
*I choose B because the mountains do not look smooth.*

In the Gum Ball Machine Problem (National Assessment of Educational Progress, 1996a), Ming Ho (also a fictitious name) gives a correct answer in both English and in Chinese—his first language. However, important differences across language can be seen in different aspects of the responses. These aspects include the organization of ideas, the use of symbols (e.g., "percent" versus "%"), the precision with which the concepts are expressed (e.g., "the red were more" versus "50% in red"), and the accuracy with which relations are represented (e.g.,

leveraged to support science learning (Lee and Fradd, 1998) as well as mathematics learning. For example, Buxton and colleagues (2014) found that ELs had certain advantages in making use of the language of science, such as through the use of cognates, familiarity with multiple grammatical structures, and increased tenacity in trying to understand others' emergent science meaning-making.

"20/100, 30/100, 50/100" versus "1/5, 1/2, and 1/10"). The differences do not favor the student's response in one language or the other consistently across these aspects. The level of elaboration or sophistication is higher in English or in the first language for different aspects of the responses (Solano-Flores et al., 2001, p. 54). The skills needed for constructing arguments and representing information optimally are distributed across the two languages.

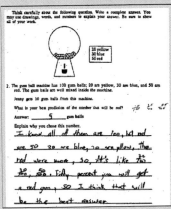

5 [gum balls].
I know all of them are 100, but red are 50 30 are blue, 20 are yellow, the red were more, so it's like 20/100, 30/100, 50/100. Fifty percent you will get a red gum, so I think that will be the best answer

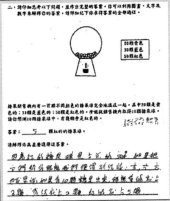

5 [gum balls].
Because there were 50% in red if we minimize the fractions, we would have the result 1/5, 1/2 and 1/10. That means if we picked 10, 3 would be yellow, 2 would be blue and 5 would be red.

This variation can be observed also across problems, when students are given multiple problems to solve. Not only do ELs have different sets of linguistic resources in each language, but also each science and each mathematics problem poses a unique set of content and linguistic demands in each language. Failure to take into account that the students' linguistic skills are distributed in their two languages may lead to underestimating ELs' progress, especially when they are schooled in English only—which is the case for the vast majority of ELs.

SOURCE: Based on Solano-Flores et al. (2001).

Research has documented a variety of language resources that ELs use to communicate mathematical ideas: their first language, everyday language, gestures, and objects. When communicating mathematically, students use multiple resources from experiences both in and out of school (Forman et al., 1998; Moschkovich, 2010; O'Connor, 1999). Everyday language, ways of talking, and experiences are resources students use as they participate in mathematical discussions (Moschkovich, 1996, 2010). For example, students have been documented using their first language to repeat an explanation or mixing Spanish and English ("translanguaging") to explain a mathematical idea (Moschkovich, 2002).

Several studies have described how students' use of home or everyday language is not a failure to be mathematically precise, but instead is a resource for communicating mathematical reasoning, making sense of mathematical meanings, and learning with understanding (Moschkovich, 2013a, 2013b). One promising instructional strategy is for teachers to hear how students use everyday language to communicate mathematical ideas and then build bridges from everyday language to more formal ways of talking (Pinnow and Chval, 2014). Teachers can build on the language students use by "revoicing" student contributions using more formal ways of talking (see Box 4-4), asking for clarification (Moschkovich, 1999), and probing for students' thinking (Herbel-Eisenmann, Steele, and Cirillo, 2013).

Civil and Hunter (2015) focused on relationships, use of home language, humor, and generalized cultural ways of being as resources to teach mathematics to ELs, claiming that "as we think of how to develop environments that support non-dominant students' participation in mathematical argumentation, we may want to learn from and build on students' cultural ways of being" (p. 308). Civil (2011, 2012) pointed to the richness of mathematical discussions when ELs are able to use their home languages but also the complexity when students are in situations where the language policy does not support the use of home languages. As Planas and Civil (2013) wrote, "students . . . have agency to use their home language as a resource in their learning of mathematics, while at the same time experiencing the political dimension of language when, for instance, they switch to English to report their mathematical thinking" (p. 370).

However, all too often, these intellectual and cultural resources are undervalued because teachers do not easily recognize them as being relevant or valuable (Moje et al., 2001). For example, in a paired study of 3rd-through 5th-grade ELs and their teachers, Buxton and colleagues (2013) found that ELs at all levels of English proficiency were able to provide a range of examples from home experiences that were directly connected to school science standards on topics ranging from measurement to energy transfer to the changing seasons. However, the majority of their science teachers, when viewing video recordings of the students discussing these science topics, were more likely to highlight linguistic or conceptual limitations than to focus on the relevant experiences that could be leveraged to support science learning. These studies concluded that recognition of ELs' academic strengths as well as limitations related to their prior knowledge is critical in enabling ELs to better gain the high status knowledge that is valued in school science.

Exploring ELs' science learning from another perspective, a body of literature highlights how the cultural beliefs and practices prevalent in some communities, including communities with sizable numbers of ELs, are sometimes discontinuous with Western scientific practices (Aikenhead, 2001; Bang, 2015; Riggs, 2005). This literature has shown that learning to recognize and value diverse views of the natural world can simultaneously promote academic achievement and strengthen ELs' cultural and linguistic identities in secondary schools.

## Provide Some Explicit Focus on How Language Functions in the Discipline

In addition to supporting concept learning over time and enabling learners to draw on multiple meaning-making resources in interaction in a variety of ways, good instruction for ELs also includes attention to language that goes beyond a focus on "words." Richardson Bruna, Vann, and Perales Escudero (2007) showed how a 9th-grade "EL Science" course teacher who sees her main goal as building vocabulary can constrain learning opportunities for ELs. Working with vocabulary alone meant that students were not engaged conceptually with the earth science knowledge at stake. The vocabulary-focused tasks tightly constrained classroom discourse, preventing ELs not only from talking like scientists, but also from thinking like scientists, and the teacher did not help students understand the relationships between the concepts being taught or provide students with new linguistic resources for conceptual understanding. The teacher's simplified understanding of her role as language instructor led to simplified science talk in the classroom, and simplified science learning by her EL students. The authors pointed out that integrating language and content instruction "means taking what is known about quality science education and infusing into those goals of cognitive development corollary goals of language development" (p. 52). That is, while studies have shown robust effects for the inclusion of vocabulary instruction in science learning, it is crucial that teachers provide opportunities for ELs to develop meaning by participating in disciplinary practices and by enabling students to learn not only individual words, but also their meaning, how to use them, and how to use them to construct claims and participate in further meaning-making and disciplinary practices.

A key tool for drawing attention to patterns of language is *metalanguage,* language about language. Metalanguage supports educational practice by offering a means of being explicit about how language presents the knowledge to be learned (Schleppegrell, 2013). Metalanguage can be both talk *about* language and technical terms for referring to language. Both forms of metalanguage can raise students' language awareness in relation to the purposes for which language is being used and the goals of the speakers/writers. Students can learn to recognize patterns in language and relate the patterns to the meanings they present, helping them recognize linguistic choices they can make in different contexts. Teachers can talk about language in relation to the demands of the curriculum; for example, by modeling how to write or speak in valued ways, or by deconstructing what is said or written to help learners recognize what it means (see Box 4-6). Meaningful metalanguage supports students to explore the ways speakers and writers use language, analyzing dense text to recognize how the wording means what it does. This kind of talk about text supports students in reading for comprehension as well as in engaging in critical ways with the texts they read and write (O'Hallaron, Palincsar, and Schleppegrell, 2015; Palincsar and Schleppegrell, 2014; Symons, 2017).

Paugh and Moran (2013) reported on how 3rd-grade students in an urban classroom, including ELs, used meaningful metalanguage in activities that involved speaking, reading, and writing as they engaged in a garden project in science. The teachers frequently asked students, "What do you notice about the language?" and made a focus on language an integral part of the activities. As the teachers looked closely at the seed packets they were asking students to read, they noticed that there were three different purposes represented: writing to describe and report about carrots; writing to persuade that carrots are good to eat; and writing to instruct how to plant the seeds. The children's attention was drawn to these different genre patterns as they identified the ways the authors used "*how to* verbs" (imperative mood) to tell them what to do as they read instructions for planting the garden, for example. Teachers also drew students' attention to language students could use when they wrote in their garden journals; for example, "sequence words" to recount the processes they had engaged in to prepare the garden. The class also focused on when they could best use "words about feelings" to report on their gardening experiences. The authors described the ways verb tense, pronouns, and time expressions can be in focus and be modeled for learners as they write a particular type of text. As this example shows, it is not necessary that linguistic meta-language be highly technical; the key criterion for use of language about language is that it is *meaningful* and enables learners to connect language and meaning to recognize how English works in presenting meanings of various kinds.

Symons (2017) showed how close attention to language features commonly found in informational science texts can support 4th-grade ELs in identifying and evaluating evidence. She illustrated how, using the metalanguage of *usuality* and *likelihood*, a teacher can facilitate discussions about the language choices that indicate the authors' level of certainty in the texts they read; this in turn supported students' evaluation of evidence. Symons also pointed to potential pitfalls of using metalanguage without clear understanding of the goals for science learning, as degrees of uncertainty expressed by an author do not make evidence inherently strong or weak, but relate to the claim being made. Symons noted that "[b]y explicitly highlighting features, forms, and patterns of language in texts as they are characterized and typified by genres, disciplines, and content, teachers encourage the linguistic consciousness-raising and attention needed to develop language (Ellis and Larsen-Freeman, 2006)." O'Hallaron, Palincsar, and Schleppegrell (2015) described new insights elementary grade teachers gained from thinking about how an author's perspective is infused into science texts, considering how an author can be cautious in making claims, and recognizing how an author positions the reader in particular ways through language choices. Teachers in that study reported that the insight that authors of informational texts present attitudes and judgments led to lively discussion in their classrooms with ELs.

As students engage with the new concepts they learn at school, attention to patterns in language can provide them with insights into the linguistic choices they can make to help them achieve the learning goals. This perspective also means that learners should not be restricted to simplified texts. Instead, teachers can help learners deconstruct challenging texts as they read and offer proactive support for making choices in writing. As an example, a teacher focused students on the way an author develops information in a science text in Gebhard, Chen, and Britton's (2014, p. 118) report on a 3rd-grade teacher helping the students analyze a model text about polar ice caps. The students' attention was drawn to the words *are melting* in the sentence *Polar ice caps are melting*. The next sentence used the notion of *melting* to introduce the effect of this process: ***This melting is causing the sea level to rise***. In continuing to analyze the language, students noted that the next sentence also drew on words from the previous sentence: *As a result of **this rising**, animals are losing their habitats*. The teacher drew students' attention to the ways this pattern of nominalization (*are melting -> This melting; to rise -> this rising*) enables the author to develop the topic over several sentences, helping students recognize how a sentence can take up information from a previous sentence and recast it in a way that helps the author develop a scientific explanation. This focus on language and use of metalanguage can be infused into instruction that engages students in activity, interaction, reading, and writing, providing support for ELs to learn how English works.

A key implication of this research is that although teachers of STEM content may not initially see language instruction as their purview, they can be motivated to learn to talk about discipline-specific language tied to achieving their broader instructional goals, and when they do so, they are

**BOX 4-6**
**Elementary Science**

In the following interaction, the teacher is holding a balance scale in her hand. Her 4th-grade student, Dai, is concerned that having a person hold the scale rather than placing it on a table could yield unreliable results. Dai is an EL in a classroom with some native speakers of English and some ELs. All students were intentionally given roles to help them learn to ask questions. However, they had difficulty forming and asking questions over the first several days of the study from which this example is taken (Herrenkohl and Mertl, 2010). In this case, Dai's role was to ask questions of other inquiry groups about the relationship between their predictions, theories, and results, a cornerstone of creating claims-evidence reasoning in science. He thinks that the results are not accurate in this case, which would impact the relationship between the predictions, theories, and results, but he cannot find a way to share his thinking in the form of a question.

| | | |
|---|---|---|
| 1. | Dai: | I can't make it a question. |
| 2. | Teacher: | It's hard, ok I'll tell you what, can you say the statement and then we'll all [the class] help you turn it into a question? Say what you wanna say and the rest of you guys, even though this isn't your role right now, listen to what he's gonna say and see if we can turn it into a question, go ahead. |
| 3. | Dai: | I only get, I can only say the answer. |
| 4. | Teacher: | Ok, then say the answer and let's see if we can turn the answer into a question, go ahead. |
| 5. | Dai: | I think because the scale is because when you put it down it's more comfortable, I guess. |
| 6. | Raul: | It's yeah it's flatter. |
| 7. | Dai: | Yeah. |
| 8. | Rich: | It's more comfortable? |
| 9. | Raul: | You mean. |
| 10. | Dai: | Flatter so it's more kinda. |
| 11. | Qing: | It's kinda balanced. |
| 12. | Raul: | Yeah it's almost balanced except that one's lower [on the balance scale]. |
| 13. | Dai: | Yeah. |
| 14. | Teacher: | But it's ok, so are you concerned that the way I had the scale. |
| 15. | Dai: | Yeah. |
| 16. | Teacher: | Wasn't giving accurate results? |
| 17. | Dai: | Yeah. |
| 18. | Teacher: | So do you see what I just did for you? You said what, you said it in a sentence form, ok, and I'm asking you a question, so I want, that's exactly what I want you guys to be doing (pause) so I asked him if he was concerned if it was the way I used the materials. |
| 19. | Dai: | Yeah. |
| 20. | Teacher: | Cuz that was givin' different results. |
| 21. | Dai: | Yeah it made it different. |

| 22. Teacher: | Good, good. |
|---|---|
| 23. Dai: | Because I guess it was [inaudible], like it goes in your hand like this and the scale just goes turning around. |
| 24. Teacher: | Ok you did it right, you did it absolutely right, the hardest thing to do is when you know something in your head but you're trying to get it outta somebody else's head, so you hafta take what you say and try to flip it into a question, Carson [another student]. I know you're looking at me like what is she talking about, but I want you guys to do what the teacher usually does, you know how the teacher usually asks the questions. |
| 25. Student: | Yeah. |
| 26. Teacher: | I don't want to be the one to ask the questions, I want you guys to ask the questions. |

This interaction involves important language and science learning. The teacher invites Dai to participate, even though he cannot do what she is asking him to do. In some classes, when a student says "I don't know" or "I can't do it," the teacher would move on to another student. For ELs to learn English, it is critical to gain access to the floor to have opportunities to use language to express ideas. Although Dai repeatedly says "yeah" throughout the exchange, he is showing evidence of receptive language as listening is also a form of participation. Students cannot learn English or use registers of English relevant to science without this type of opportunity. So the teacher starts by asking Dai to present what he considered "the answer" and says that the class will help him transform his answer into a question. In the process of sharing "the answer," Dai receives support from multiple students who indicate that they concur with his idea.

Dai is making a causal connection or claim when stating, "because when you put it down it's more comfortable." This leads to additional support from multipole studies. For example, when he uses the word "comfortable" to describe the balance scale, Raul offers the word "flatter" which Dai then uses to describe what he means when Rich seems confused by the use of "comfortable" in this context. The students are working together to come to understand Dai's scientific observation by settling on English terms to effectively communicate his idea. The teacher then introduces scientific terms like "accurate results" to build a bridge between the students' ideas and language and key scientific terminology. Throughout this interaction, the teacher positions students as resources for one another and encourages them to use their own ideas as starting points. She also uses metatalk (or talk about talk) to name her linguistic moves while highlighting the importance of students asking each other questions even though students often think of questioning as the teacher's job. This discussion expands opportunities for all students to share in creating and discussing important academic language in science. The teacher is setting the stage to transform students from question answerers to active listeners who ask important questions. These types of interactions are important for primary speakers of English learning scientific registers, and they are critical for ELs who are learning English while they learn these registers.

SOURCE: Based on Herrenkohl and Mertl (2010).

able to offer their ELs opportunities to learn language and content simultaneously. ELs learn the language of STEM subjects as they participate in STEM learning, especially when they are challenged and develop awareness about the ways language works to construct and present knowledge. Accomplishing this goal calls for the development of teachers' knowledge about language and STEM content in ways that rarely occur.

This is especially true of secondary school teachers of STEM subjects, as the culture of secondary school positions teachers as disciplinary experts, leading them in many cases to resist taking on instructional responsibility for issues such as language development that may seem to fall outside of their disciplinary mandate (for discussion, see Arkoudis, 2006). Secondary teachers are, understandably, highly focused on teaching their subject areas. At the same time, the language and concepts students are learning become increasingly complex and specialized, so teachers are best positioned to provide effective instruction in the uses of language specific to the disciplines. Lee and Buxton (2013) and Quinn, Lee, and Valdés (2012) pointed out that teachers can attend to both the disciplinary content and language demands inherent in the work students do and provide language support that helps learners respond to those demands. STEM content teachers and language teachers in K–12 classrooms can support the ongoing language development of ELs through a focus on patterns of language in their subject areas, offering their students opportunities to engage in noticing and attending to the ways the language works, comparing and contrasting language for different audiences and purposes, and broadening their linguistic repertoires for participation in learning.

## Word Problems: A Special Case for Mathematics

Mathematical word problems are a particular genre that deserves attention during instruction. Researchers in mathematics education have examined topics relevant to word problems, for example mathematical texts (O'Halloran, 2005), polysemy (Pimm, 1987), and differences between school mathematical discourse and mathematical discourse at home (Walkerdine, 1988). Especially relevant to word problems is the shift from seeing the mathematics register as merely technical mathematical language. The following word problem illustrates how challenges for learning do not just come from technical vocabulary:

> A boat in a river with a current of 3 mph can travel 16 miles downstream in the same amount of time it can go 10 miles upstream. Find the speed of the boat in still water.

The complexity involved in making sense of this word problem may not only be at the level of technical mathematical vocabulary but also may lie principally in the background knowledge (Martiniello and Wolf, 2012) for understanding and imagining the context or situation for the problem. In this case, the reader needs to imagine and understand that there is a boat traveling up and down a river, that the speed of the boat increases (by the speed of the current) when going downstream, decreases (by the speed of the current) when going upstream, and that the speed can be calculated as if it is being measured in still water (presumably a lake). The complexity lies not in understanding mathematical terms but in having the background knowledge to imagine the situation and knowing how to work with the information provided (Bunch, Walqui, and Pearson, 2014).

Although the vocabulary indexes background knowledge, that vocabulary is not specific to mathematics nor is it limited to what might be called mathematical terms. While words and phrases like *current, downstream, same amount, upstream*, and *still water* may be challenging for ELs (or for native speakers), these words would not typically be considered part of the specialized mathematics lexicon. The implications for mathematics instruction is that teachers cannot just teach what is perceived to be "mathematics" vocabulary and expect that to be sufficient for supporting ELs in learning how to solve word problems; they need to support students to make sense of problem situations. There is substantial research to support this recommendation and the importance of supporting students to make sense of problem situations albeit not specific to ELs (see, e.g., Jackson et al., 2013).

A glossary for non-mathematics words such as upstream, downstream, and the phrase "in still water" would certainly help. However, much of the linguistic complexity is not at the word level, but at the sentence level; in this example, in the use of multiple prepositional phrases (*in a river with a current of 3 mph*) and embedded constructions (*in the same amount of time [that] it can go 10 miles upstream*). Taking time to deconstruct a sentence like this to examine its meaningful segments can support learners in developing strategies for engaging with problems like this (Schleppegrell, 2007).

Martiniello (2008, 2010) found that understanding word problems that involve polysemous words (words with different meanings or connotations, deepening on the context provided by the text or discourse) can be challenging for ELs. Martiniello gave the following example: "Find the amount of money each fourth-grade class raised for an animal shelter using the table below." The word "raised" here refers to collecting funds. Other meanings are "raise your hands," "raise the volume," "raising the rent," or "receiving a raise." Martiniello found that "ELs tended to interpret the word raise as increase" and did not understand the connotation of raise in fund raising.

Martiniello and Shaftel both found that 4th-grade students struggled with specific categories of vocabulary. These included words with multiple meanings, slang or conversation words, and words learned in an English-speaking home (Martiniello, 2008; Shaftel et al., 2006). Martiniello (2008) concluded "it is important to distinguish between school and home related vocabulary as a potential source of differential difficulty for ELs." She suggested that since ELs learn English primarily at school, school-related words (i.e., students, notepad, pencil, ruler, school, day, colors) are likely to be more familiar than words related to the home (her examples are raking leaves, chore, wash dishes, vacuum, dust, rake, and weed). Martiniello's general recommendations for the assessment of word problems include avoiding unnecessary linguistic complexity not relevant to mathematics and addressing issues that are specific to ELs (e.g., home vocabulary, polysemy, familiarity). However, during initial instruction it may be important to carefully consider when and how to include different types of increasing linguistic complexity in more supportive settings in the classroom in order to provide ELs opportunities to learn to deal with particular aspects of linguistic complexity that is related to the mathematics content.

However, syntactic simplification of word problems is also problematic, as shortening sentences by eliminating words that establish connective relationships (e.g., because or therefore) can make text harder to read rather than easier (Davison and Kantor, 1982). In a study with Puerto Rican students learning English as a second language, researchers found that 8th-grade students' comprehension benefited from longer sentences that showed relationships rather than choppy sentences with simple syntax. Thus, sentences like, "If the manufacturer and the market are a long distance apart, then it can be a big expense for the manufacturer to get goods to market" were easier to understand than "Manufacturers must get goods to market. Suppose that the manufacturer and the market are a long distance apart. This can be a big expense" (Blau, 1982, p. 518).

### Engineering: A New Discipline Can Mean a Fresh Start

Though there is not yet research specific to ELs in K–12 engineering, research findings from other disciplines have the potential to inform engineering efforts. Educators can apply existing research about ELs in science and mathematics education (as well as other disciplines) to create engineering curricula, activities, and learning environments that embed effective classroom strategies from their inception. Design principles for inclusive curricula and lessons can be articulated to guide the development of engineering curricula and lessons that include and support ELs (Cunningham, 2018; Cunningham and Lachapelle, 2014). For example, ELs often benefit from a coherent narrative that ties activities together instead of participating in seemingly disjointed activities. Curricular units that provide a context and narrative thread can help ELs, and all students, navigate and connect the curricular activities to a relevant, larger purpose (Hammond, 2014). Similarly, designing curricula and activities to reduce up-front literacy demands can make engineering more accessible for children.

The three-dimensional learning described by the NGSS provides ample opportunities for language-rich classrooms in engineering and science. Using language in purposeful and meaningful ways, such as generating solutions to solve an engineering challenge, can help students develop facility with it. Engineering provides ways to accomplish three-dimensional learning by engaging students in authentic engineering (and science) practices, employing crosscutting concepts, and building understanding of disciplinary core ideas (Cunningham and Kelly, 2017). It can also be language intensive (Lee, Quinn, and Valdés, 2013)—well-designed engineering lessons will invite students to read, write, speak, and listen, as well as view and visually represent their ideas and designs. For example, as students design a water filter, they might research extant models and processes used around the world; share ideas for possible design features or solutions with their teammates verbally or through sketches; share ideas about which materials they would use, in what order, and why; come to consensus as a group and articulate a plan for their initial solution; draw and label a diagram they will use to construct the filter; interpret the data they collected and identify what worked well and what requires further development to achieve the desired goal; redesign and test their technology; and communicate with their classmates or a client about their recommended solution and the process they undertook to develop it.

## CURRICULUM

Curriculum materials play a critical role in education reform (Ball and Cohen, 1996), influencing both the content that is covered and the instructional approaches that are used in classrooms in intended and unintended ways. Research suggests that access to high-quality curricula, instruction, and teachers are effective in supporting the academic success of ELs learning English and content (American Educational Research Association, 2004; Gutiérrez, 2009, 2012). General characteristics of such environments are curricula that provide "abundant and diverse opportunities for speaking, listening, reading, and writing" and instruction that encourages "students to take risks, construct meaning, and seek reinterpretations of knowledge within compatible social contexts" (Garcia and Gonzalez, 1995, p. 424).

The design process for mathematics curriculum materials has not involved sufficient attention to language diversity and creating mathematical tasks and contexts that facilitate the participation of ELs (Chval, 2011).

Chval argued that the field needed to improve mathematics curriculum development and enhancement for ELs as "they [Latino students] also encounter barriers as they work with curriculum materials (Doerr and Chandler-Olcott, 2009)" (2011, p. 1).

Mathematics curriculum materials must include rich mathematical tasks and contexts that facilitate the participation of ELs and avoid reductionist approaches that do not sufficiently communicate mathematical complexity to ELs (Gutstein, 2003; Willey and Pitvorec, 2009). Yet, studies indicate that "curriculum materials incorporating these reforms may further disadvantage low-income, minority students, and Latinos specifically, and widen existing educational and social disparities between these students and middle-class White students (Lubienski, 2000, 2002; McCormick, 2005; Sconiers et al., 2003), especially if students are silent nonparticipants in the classroom" (Chval, 2011, p. 1).

Some researchers have investigated teachers' use of curriculum materials—the implemented curriculum—in classrooms with ELs (Chval, Pinnow, and Thomas, 2015; Riordan and Noyce, 2001; Webb, 2003). Chval, Pinnow, and Thomas (2015) conducted a professional development intervention with a 3rd-grade teacher that introduced approaches for enhancing mathematics curriculum for ELs. In this case, the teacher created new curriculum materials so that the ELs in her classroom could further their language development, extend the curriculum context, and encourage metacognitive thinking about mathematics. Rather than using a variety of contextual situations at the beginning of a mathematical unit, the teacher made a decision to focus on one context for a minimum of 2 weeks. As the year progressed, she began to create curriculum materials that involved more than one context so that the ELs would be comfortable and successful with standardized tests and curriculum materials in future grade levels that would reflect multiple contexts.

A few studies have examined curricular effectiveness determined by mathematics achievement for Latinos and ELs. The studies that have been conducted have examined different grade levels and curriculum materials using different methodologies and measures of student achievement. Different comparisons have been used, including Latinos versus other ethnic groups, ELs versus non-ELs using a specified set of curriculum materials, and ELs using Curriculum X versus ELs not using Curriculum X. These studies have various limitations such as not examining Latino ELs specifically, not including a sufficient sample of Latinos, not including a representative sample of Latinos, and not considering textbook integrity (Chval et al., 2009).

Science curriculum projects have played a large role in science education reforms since the Cold War and the launch of the Soviet Sputnik satellite (Rudolph, 2002). As researchers and curriculum developers have sought to better support teachers in using curriculum materials as intended, there has been a push toward the development of *educative curriculum materials* to help teachers more fully realize the intentions of the curriculum in promoting student understanding (Davis and Krajcik, 2005; Drake, Land, and Tyminski, 2014).

While high-quality science curriculum materials were difficult to find (Kesidou and Roseman, 2002), an added challenge involves how best to capitalize on the opportunities and meet the unique learning needs of ELs. For example, the National Science Foundation (1998) called for more "culturally and gender relevant curriculum materials" that recognize "diverse cultural perspectives and contributions so that through example and instruction, the contributions of all groups to science will be understood and valued" (p. 29). The fact that ELs are less likely to have access to such materials presents a barrier to equitable learning opportunities (Lee and Buxton, 2008).

Some studies focused on the development of curriculum materials with an explicit goal of better supporting science and language learning with ELs. August and colleagues (2009) designed and tested the Quality English and Science Teaching (QuEST) curriculum to simultaneously support the science knowledge and academic language development of middle-grade ELs. A controlled study of the QuEST intervention showed that use of the curriculum materials had a statistically significant positive effect on ELs' science knowledge and science vocabulary development. Bravo and Cervetti (2014) reported the impact of the Seeds of Science/Roots of Reading program on science and literacy with ELs. Fourth- and 5th-grade ELs in the treatment condition outperformed ELs in the comparison group in science understanding and science vocabulary, but not in science reading. Treatment teachers used more strategies to support ELs than did comparison teachers (Cervetti, Kulikowich, and Bravo, 2015). Lee and colleagues (2008, 2009) developed a curriculum for 3rd, 4th, and 5th grades, which reflected the evolution of the knowledge base of teaching science to ELs as well as the shifting policy contexts regarding ELs (e.g., English-only instructional policy) and science education (e.g., high-stakes testing and accountability policy). In later years of their research, effectiveness studies of the stand-alone, yearlong 5th-grade curriculum indicated positive effects on ELs' science achievement as measured by both the researcher-developed assessment and the state high-stakes science assessment and narrowing of science achievement gaps between ELs and non-ELs (Llosa et al., 2016; Maerten-Rivera et al., 2016).

While NGSS implementation requires high-quality instructional materials to meet the academic rigor for rapidly growing student diversity in the nation, developing such instructional materials presents challenges. The science education community is working to develop NGSS-aligned instructional materials. In addition to the evaluation guidelines that clarify key components and innovations for such materials (Achieve Inc., 2016, 2017; BSCS, 2017; Carnegie Corporation of New York, 2017), research-based NGSS-aligned instructional materials are being developed and shared.[4] Despite these recent efforts, research-based NGSS-aligned instructional materials are limited. Considering the language-intensive nature of science and engineering practices, the Framework (National Research Council, 2012) and the NGSS offer new opportunities to develop science curriculum that can promote both science learning and language development with ELs (e.g., Lee, Valdés, and Llosa, 2015–2019).

Additional curriculum design efforts (for both supplementary and mainstream curriculum) must be prioritized to provide opportunities for linguistically diverse students to successfully learn STEM in U.S. classrooms. Furthermore, little is known about the curriculum design process for existing science and mathematics materials that have considered ELs during the design and testing phases. The development of future STEM curriculum materials needs to involve research at every phase and the knowledge that is generated through this process needs to be disseminated to the field (Clements, 2007).

## SUMMARY

Teachers of STEM content to ELs are essential to ensuring that ELs learn STEM disciplinary concepts and practices, and, as such, they need to construct safe classroom communities that afford ELs with the opportunity to be successful in their STEM learning. To create these safe spaces, teachers need to be mindful of the beliefs that they may have with respect to ELs and STEM learning, as well as ensure that they positively position ELs in the classroom while drawing upon the rich experiences ELs bring to STEM. Moreover, as the newer content standards call for both sophistication in STEM learning as well as in English, the teacher needs to attend to both the content as well as the language. Collaboration with ESL teachers may play an important role in facilitating ELs progress as they engage in STEM subjects.

Given the committee's stance that language and content are inextricable, the instructional strategies proposed to foster ELs' learning of STEM disciplinary practices acknowledge this relationship. It is important to focus on engaging ELs in productive discourse as they are also engaging in the disciplinary practices. Teachers can focus on the language that is used in the disciplines to develop ELs' ability to utilize multiple registers and modalities

---

[4]For more information, see https://www.nextgenscience.org/resources/examples-quality-ngss-design [June 2018].

in the communication of their ideas. At the same time, this calls for leveraging the experiences that ELs bring to the classroom.

Overall, STEM subjects afford opportunities for ELs to simultaneously learn disciplinary content and develop language proficiency through engaging in the STEM disciplinary practices. By explicitly focusing on language in the teaching of STEM concepts and practices, teachers are able to encourage ELs to draw on their full range of linguistic and communicative competencies and use different modalities and representations to communicate their thinking, solutions, or arguments in STEM subjects.

## REFERENCES

Achieve, Inc. (2016). *Using Phenomena in NGSS-Designed Lessons and Units*. Washington, DC: Author.

Achieve, Inc. (2017). *Primary Evaluation of Essential Criteria (PEEC) for Next Generation Science Standards Instructional Materials Design*. Washington, DC: Author.

Aikenhead, G.S. (2001). Integrating western and aboriginal sciences: Cross-cultural science teaching. *Research in Science Education, 31*(3), 337–355.

American Educational Research Association. (2004). Closing the gap: High achievement for students of color. *Research Points, 2*(3). Available: http://www.aera.net/Portals/38/docs/Publications/Closing%20the%20Gap.pdf [June 2018].

American Educational Research Association. (2006). Do the math: Cognitive demand makes a difference. *Research Points, 4*(2).

Anderson, N., Chapin, S., and O'Connor, C. (2011). *Classroom Discussions in Math: A Facilitator's Guide to Support Professional Learning of Discourse and the Common Core, Grades K–6*. Sausalito, CA: Math Solutions.

Arkoudis, S. (2000). "I have linguistic aims and linguistic content": ESL and science teachers planning together. *Prospect, 15*(2), 61–71.

Arkoudis, S. (2003). Teaching English as a second language in science classes: Incommensurate epistemologies? *Language and Education, 17*(3), 161–173.

Arkoudis, S. (2006). Negotiating the rough ground between ESL and mainstream teachers. *International Journal of Bilingual Education and Bilingualism, 9*(4), 415–433.

August, D. Artzi, L., and Barr. C. (2016). Helping ELLs meet standards in English language arts and science: An intervention focused on academic vocabulary. *Reading and Writing Quarterly, 32*(4), 373–396.

August, D., Branum-Martin, L., Hagan, E., and Francis, D. (2009). The impact of an instructional intervention on the science and language learning of middle grade English language learners. *Journal of Research on Educational Effectiveness, 2*(4), 345–376.

August, D., Branum-Martin, L., Cárdenas-Hagan, E., Francis, D.J., Powell, J., Moore, S., and Haynes, E.F. (2014). Helping ELLs meet the common core state standards for literacy in science: The impact of an instructional intervention focused on academic language. *Journal of Research on Educational Effectiveness, 7*(1), 54–82.

Ball, D.L., and Cohen, D.K. (1996). Reform by the book: What is—or might be—the role of curriculum materials in teacher learning and instructional reform? *Educational Researcher, 24*(9), 6–8, 14.

Bang, M. (2015). Culture, learning, and development about the natural world: Advances facilitated by situative perspectives. *Educational Psychologist, 50*(3), 220–233.

Barnes, D. (1976/1992). *From Communication to Curriculum*. Portsmouth, NH: Boynton/Cook-Heinemann.

Barnes, D. (2008). Exploratory talk for learning. In N. Mercer and S. Hodgkinson (Eds.), *Exploring Talk in School: Inspired by the Work of Douglas Barnes* (pp. 1–16). Thousand Oaks, CA: Sage.

Becker, H. (2001). *Teaching ESL K–12: Views from the Classroom.* Boston: MA: Heinle & Heinle.

Bianchini, J. (2018). *Teachers' Knowledge and Beliefs about English Learners and Their Impact on STEM Learning.* Paper commissioned for the Committee on Supporting English Learners in STEM Subjects. Board on Science Education and Board on Children, Youth, and Families, Division of Behavioral and Social Sciences and Education. Available: http://www.nas.edu/ELinSTEM [October 2018].

Blau, E. (1982). The effect of syntax on readability for ESL students in Puerto Rico. *TESOL Quarterly, 16*(4), 517–528.

Boyd, M.P., and Rubin, D.L. (2002). Elaborated student talk in an elementary ESOL classroom. *Research in the Teaching of English, 36*(4), 495–530.

Bravo, M.A., and Cervetti, G.N. (2014). Attending to the language and literacy need of English learners in science. *Equity & Excellence in Education, 47*(2), 230–245.

BSCS. (2017). *Guidelines for the Evaluation of Instructional Materials in Science.* Colorado Springs, CO: Author.

Bunch, G.C. (2013). Pedagogical language knowledge: Preparing mainstream teachers for English learners in the new standards era. *Review of Research in Education, 37*(1), 298–341.

Bunch, G.C., Aguirre, J.M., and Téllez, K. (2009). Beyond the scores: Using candidate responses on high stakes performance assessment to inform teacher preparation for English learners. *Issues in Teacher Education, 18*(1), 103–128.

Bunch, G.C., Walqui, A., and Pearson, D.P. (2014). Complex text and new common standards in the United States: Pedagogical implications for English learners. *TESOL Quarterly, 48*(3), 533–559

Buxton, C., Allexsaht-Snider, M., Suriel, R., Kayumova, S., Choi, Y., Bouton, B., and Land, M. (2013). Using educative assessments to support science teaching for middle school English language learners. *Journal of Science Teacher Education, 24*(2), 347–366.

Buxton, C., Allexsaht-Snider, M., Aghasaleh, R., Kayumova, S., Kim, S., Choi, Y., and Cohen A. (2014). Potential benefits of bilingual constructed responses science assessments for understanding bilingual learners' emergent use of language of scientific investigation practices. *Double Helix, 2*(1), 1–21.

Callahan, R.M. (2005). Tracking and high school English learners: Limiting opportunity to learn. *American Educational Research Journal, 42*(2), 305–328.

Carlone, H.B., Haun-Frank, J., and Webb, A. (2011). Assessing equity beyond knowledge- and skills-based outcomes: A comparative ethnography of two fourth-grade reform-based science classrooms. *Journal of Research in Science Teaching, 48*(5), 459–485.

Carnegie Corporation of New York. (2017). *Instructional Materials and Implementation of NGSS: Demand, Supply, and Strategic Opportunities.* New York: ARLOSOUL: Visualize Innovation.

Celedón-Pattichis, S. (2018). *Mathematics Education and Young Dual Language Learners.* Paper commissioned for the Committee on Supporting English Learners in STEM Subjects. Board on Science Education and Board on Children, Youth, and Families, Division of Behavioral and Social Sciences and Education. Available: http://www.nas.edu/ELinSTEM [October 2018].

Cervetti, G.N., DiPardo, A., and Staley, S. (2014). Making room for exploratory talk: Science as a context for fostering academic discourse. *The Elementary School Journal, 114*, 547–572.

Cervetti, G.N., Kulikowich, J.M., and Bravo, M.A. (2015). The effects of educative curriculum materials on teachers' use of instructional strategies for English language learners in science and on student learning. *Contemporary Educational Psychology, 40,* 86–98.

Chapin, S.H., O'Connor, M.C., and Anderson, N.C. (2003). *Classroom Discussions: Using Math Talk to Help Students Learn* (1st ed.). Sausalito, CA: Math Solutions.

Chapin, S., O'Connor, C., and Anderson, N. (2009). *Classroom Discussions: Using Math Talk to Help Students Learn, Grades K–6* (2nd ed.). Sausalito, CA: Math Solutions.

Chval, K.B. (2011). Mathematics curriculum and Latino English language learners: Moving the field forward. In *Proceedings of the Practitioners and Researchers Learning Together: A National Conference on the Mathematics Teaching and Learning of Latinos/as* (pp. 100–116). Tucson, AZ: CEMELA-CPTM-TODOS.

Chval, K.B. (2012). Facilitating the participation of Latino English language learners: Learning from an effective teacher. In S. Celedón-Pattichis and N. G. Ramirez (Eds.), *Beyond Good Teaching: Advancing Mathematics Education for ELLs* (pp. 77–90). Reston, VA: National Council of Teachers of Mathematics.

Chval, K.B., and Chavez, O. (2011). Designing math lessons for English language learners. *Mathematics Teaching in the Middle School, 17*(5), 261–265.

Chval, K.B., and Pinnow, R.J. (2010). Pre-service teachers' assumptions about Latino/a English language learners in mathematics. *Teaching for Excellence and Equity in Mathematics, 2*(1), 6–13.

Chval, K.B., Pinnow, R.J., and Thomas, A. (2015). Learning how to focus on language while teaching mathematics to English language learners: A case study of Courtney. *Mathematics Education Research Journal, 27*(1), 103–127.

Chval, K.B, Chávez, Ó., Reys, B., and Tarr, J. (2009). Considerations and limitations related to conceptualizing and measuring textbook integrity. In J.T. Remillard, B.A. Herbel-Eisenmann, and G.M. Lloyd (Eds.), *Mathematics Teachers at Work: Connecting Curriculum Materials and Classroom Instruction* (pp. 70–84). London, UK: Routledge.

Chval, K.B., Pinnow, R.J., Smith, E., Rojas Perez, O. (2018). Promoting equity, access, and success through productive student partnerships. In. S. Crespo, S. Celedon-Pattichis, and M. Civil (Eds.), *Access and Equity: Promoting High Quality Mathematics in Grades 3–5.* Reston, VA: National Council of Teachers of Mathematics.

Civil, M. (2011). Mathematics education, language policy, and English language learners. In W.F. Tate, K.D. King, and C. Rousseau Anderson (Eds.), *Disrupting Tradition: Research and Practice Pathways in Mathematics Education* (pp. 77–91). Reston, VA: National Council for Teachers of Mathematics.

Civil, M. (2012). Mathematics teaching and learning of immigrant students. In O. Skovsmose and B. Greer (Eds.), *Opening the Cage* (pp. 127–142). Boston, MA: Sense Publishers.

Civil, M., and Hunter, R. (2015). Participation of non-dominant students in argumentation in the mathematics classroom. *Intercultural Education, 26*(4), 296–312.

Clements, D.H. (2007). Curriculum research: Toward a framework for "research-based curricula." *Journal for Research in Mathematics Education, 38*(1), 35–70.

Coady, M.R., Harper, C.A., and de Jong, E.J. (2016). Aiming for equity: Preparing mainstream teachers for inclusion or inclusive classrooms? *TESOL Quarterly, 50*(2), 340–368.

Cohen, E.G., and Lotan, R.A. (1995). Producing equal-status interaction in the heterogeneous classroom. *American Educational Research Journal, 32,* 99–120.

Cohen, E.G., and Lotan, R.A. (1997). *Working for equity in heterogeneous classrooms: Sociological theory in practice.* New York: Teachers College Press.

Cohen, E.G., and Lotan, R.A. (2014). Groupwork and language development *Designing groupwork: Strategies for heterogeneous classrooms* (3rd ed.). New York: Teachers College Press.

Council of the Chief State School Officers. (2012). *Framework for English Language Proficiency Development Standards Corresponding to the Common Core State Standards and the Next Generation Science Standards.* Washington, DC: Author.

Cunningham, C.M. (2018). *Engineering in Elementary STEM Education: Curriculum Design, Instruction, Learning, and Assessment.* New York: Teachers College Press.

Cunningham, C.M., and Kelly, G.K. (2017). Framing engineering practices in elementary school classrooms. *International Journal of Engineering Education, 33*(1B), 295–307.

Cunningham, C.M., and Lachapelle, C.P. (2014). Designing engineering experiences to engage all students. In S. Purzer, J. Strobel, and M. Cardella (Eds.), *Engineering in Pre-college Settings: Synthesizing Research, Policy, and Practices* (pp. 117–142). Lafayette, IN: Purdue University Press.

Davis, E., and Krajcik, J. (2005). Designing educative curriculum materials to promote teacher learning. *Educational Researcher, 34*(3), 3–14.

Davison, A., and Kantor, R.N. (1982). On the failure of readability formulas to define readable texts: A case study from adaptations. *Reading Research Quarterly, 17*(2), 187–209.

de Araujo, Z. (2017). Connections between secondary mathematics teachers' beliefs and their selection of tasks for English language learners. *Curriculum Inquiry, 47*(4), 363–389.

de Araujo, Z., Smith, E., and Sakow, M. (2016). Reflecting on the dialogue regarding the mathematics education of English learners. *Journal of Urban Mathematics Education, 9*(2), 33–48.

de Araujo, Z., Yeong I.J., Smith, E., and Sakow, M. (2015). Preservice teachers' strategies to support English learners. In T.G. Bartell, K.N. Bieda, R.T. Putnam, K. Bradfield, and H. Dominguez (Eds.), *Proceedings of the 37th Annual Meeting for the North American Chapter for the Psychology of Mathematics Education* (pp. 648–655). East Lansing: Michigan State University.

Deaton, C.C.M., Deaton, B., and Koballa, T. (2014). Teachers' awareness of their diverse classrooms: The nature of elementary teachers' reflections on their science teaching practice. *Action in Teacher Education, 36*(3), 211–233.

Delgado-Gaitan, M. (1987). Traditions and transitions in the learning process of Mexican children: An ethnographic view. In G. Spindler and L. Spindler (Eds.), *Interpretive Ethnography of Education: At Home and Abroad* (pp. 333–359). Hillsdale, NJ: Lawrence Erlbaum Associates.

Doerr, H.M., and Chandler-Olcott, K. (2009). Negotiating the literacy demands of standards-based curriculum materials: A site for teachers' learning. In J.T. Remillard, B.A. Herbel-Eisenmann, and G.M. Lloyd (Eds.), *Mathematics Teachers at Work: Connecting Curriculum Materials and Classroom Instruction* (pp. 283–301). New York: Routledge.

Dominguez, H. (2005). Articulation and gesticulation of mathematical knowledge during problem solving. *Bilingual Research Journal, 29*(2), 269–293.

Drake, C., Land, T.J., and Tyminski, A.M. (2014). Using educative curriculum materials to support the development of prospective teachers' knowledge. *Educational Researcher, 43*(3), 154–162.

Ellis, N.C., and Larsen-Freeman, D. (2006). Language emergence: Implications for applied linguistics. Introduction to the special issue. *Applied Linguistics, 27*(4), 558–589.

Empson, S.B. (2003). Low-performing students and teaching fractions for understanding: An interactional analysis. *Journal for Research in Mathematics Education, 34*(4), 305–343.

Estrella, G., Au, J., Jaeggi, S.M., and Collins, P. (2018). Is inquiry science instruction effective for English language learners? A meta-analytic review. *AERA Open, 4*(2), 1–23.

Faltis, C. (1993). Programmatic and curricular options for secondary schools serving limited English proficient students. *The High School Journal, 76*(2), 171–181.

Fernandes, A., Kahn, L.H., and Civil, M. (2017). A closer look at bilingual students' use of multimodality in the context of an area comparison problem from a large-scale assessment. *Educational Studies in Mathematics, 95*(3), 263–282.

Forman, E., McCormick, D., and Donato, D. (1997). Learning what counts as a mathematical explanation. *Linguistics and Education, 9*(4), 313–339.

Forman, E., Larreamendy-Joerns, J., Stein, M., and Brown, C. (1998). "You're going to want to find out which and prove it": Collective argumentation in a mathematics classroom. *Learning and Instruction, 8*(6), 527–548.

Gallas, K. (1994). *The Languages of Learning: How Children Talk, Write, Dance, Draw, and Sing Their Understanding of the World.* New York: Teachers College Press.

Gándara, P., and Contreras, F. (2009). *The Latino Education Crisis: The Consequences of Failed Social Policies.* Cambridge, MA: Harvard University Press.

Gándara, P., Maxwell-Jolly, J., Driscoll, A. (2005). *Listening to Teachers of English Language Learners: A Survey of California Teachers' Challenges, Experiences, and Professional Development Needs.* Berkeley, CA: Policy Analysis for California Education. Available: https://files.eric.ed.gov/fulltext/ED491701.pdf [June 2018].

Garcia, E., and Gonzalez, R. (1995). Issues in systemic reform for culturally and linguistically diverse students. *Teachers College Record, 96,* 418–431.

Gebhard, M., Chen, I., and Britton, B. (2014). "Miss, nominalization is a nomi-nalization": English language learners' use of SFL metalanguage and their literacy practices. *Linguistics and Education, 26*(3), 106–125.

Gibbons, P. (2004). Changing the rules, changing the game: A sociocultural perspective on second language learning in the classroom. In G. Williams and A. Lukin (Eds.), *The Development of Language* (pp. 196–216). London, UK: Continuum.

Gibbons, P. (2006). Steps for planning an integrated program for ESL learners in mainstream classes. In P. McKay (Ed.), *Planning and Teaching Creatively within a Required Curriculum for School-Age Learners* (pp. 215–233). Alexandria, VA: TESOL Press.

Gibbons, P. (2007). Mediating academic language learning through classroom discourse. In J. Cummins and C. Davison (Eds.), *International Handbook of English Language Teaching* (pp. 701–718). New York: Springer.

González, N., Moll, L., and Amanti, C. (2005). *Funds of Knowledge: Theorizing Practices in Households, Communities, and Classrooms.* New York: Routledge.

Grapin, S. E. (2018). Multimodality in the new content standards era: Implications for English learners. *TESOL Quarterly.* Available: https://onlinelibrary.wiley.com/doi/abs/10.1002/tesq.443?af=R [June 2018]. doi:10.1002/tesq.443.

Gutiérrez, R. (2009). Framing equity: Helping students "play the game" and "change the game." *Teaching for Excellence and Equity in Mathematics, 1*(1), 4–8.

Gutiérrez, R. (2012). Context matters: How should we conceptualize equity in mathematics education? In B. Herbel-Eisenmann, J. Choppin, D. Wagner, and D. Pimm (Eds.), *Equity in Discourse for Mathematics Education: Theories, Practices, and Policies* (pp. 17–34). New York: Springer.

Gutstein, E. (2003). Teaching and learning mathematics for social justice in an urban, Latino school. *Journal for Research in Mathematics Education, 34*(1), 37–73.

Hammond, Z. (2014). *Culturally Responsive Teaching and the Brain: Promoting Authentic Engagement and Rigor Among Culturally and Linguistically Diverse Students.* Thousand Oaks, CA: Corwin Press.

Haneda, M. (2000). Modes of student participation in an elementary school science classroom: From talking to writing. *Linguistics and Education, 10*(4), 1–27.

Hansen-Thomas, H. (2009). Reform-oriented mathematics in three 6th grade classes: How teachers draw in ELLs to academic discourse. *Journal of Language, Identity & Education, 8*(2–3), 88–106.

Harper, C.A., and de Jong, E.J. (2009). English language teacher expertise: The elephant in the room. *Language and Education, 23*(2), 137–151.

Harré, R., Moghaddam, F.M., Cairnie, T.P., Rothbart, D., and Sabat, S.R. (2009). Recent advances in positioning theory. *Theory & Psychology, 19*(1), 5–31.

Herbel-Eisenmann, B., Drake, C., and Cirillo, M. (2009). "Muddying the clear waters": Teachers' take-up of the linguistic idea of revoicing. *Teacher and Teacher Education, 25*(2), 268–277.

Herbel-Eisenmann, B., Steele, M., and Cirillo, M. (2013). (Developing) teacher discourse moves: A framework for professional development. *Mathematics Teacher Educator, 1*(2), 181–196.

Herrenkohl, L.R., and Guerra, M.R. (1998). Participant structures, scientific discourse, and student engagement in fourth grade. *Cognition and Instruction, 16*(4), 431–473.

Herrenkohl, L.R., and Mertl, V. (2010). *How Students Come to Be, Know, and Do: A Case for a Broad View of Learning.* New York: Cambridge University Press.

Hiebert, J., and Grouws, D.A. (2007). The effects of classroom mathematics teaching on students' learning. In F.K. Lester Jr. (Ed.), *Second Handbook of Research on Mathematics Teaching and Learning* (pp. 371–404). Charlotte, NC: Information Age.

Hudicourt-Barnes, J. (2003). The use of argumentation in Haitian Creole science classrooms. *Harvard Educational Review, 73*(1), 73–93.

Iddings, A.C.D. (2005). Linguistic access and participation: English language learners in an English-dominant community of practice. *Bilingual Research Journal, 29*(1), 165–183.

Jackson, K., Garrison, A., Wilson, J., Gibbons, L., and Shahan, E. (2013). Exploring relationships between setting up complex tasks and opportunities to learn in concluding whole-class discussions in middle-grades mathematics instruction *Journal for Research in Mathematics Education, 44*(4), 646–682.

Johnson, C.C., Bolshakova, V.L.J., and Waldron, T. (2016). When good intentions and reality meet: Large-scale reform of science teaching in urban schools with predominantly Latino ELL students. *Urban Education, 51*(5), 476–513.

Kesidou, S., and Roseman, J.E. (2002). How well do middle school science programs measure up? Findings from Project 2061's curriculum review. *Journal of Research in Science Teaching, 39*(6), 522–549.

Khisty, L. (1995). Making inequality: Issues of language and meaning in mathematics teaching with Hispanic students. In W. Secada, E. Fennema, and L. Adajain (Eds.), *New Directions for Equity in Mathematics Education* (pp. 279–297). New York: Cambridge University Press.

Khisty, L. (2001). Effective teachers of second language learners in mathematics. In M.H.-P. Den (Ed.), *Proceedings of the 25th Conference of the International Group for the Psychology of Mathematics Education* (Vol. 3) (pp. 225–232). Utrecht, The Netherlands: Freudenthal Institute.

Khisty, L., and Chval, K.B. (2002). Pedagogic discourse and equity in mathematics: When teachers' talk matters. *Mathematics Education Research Journal, 14*(3), 154–168.

Krajcik, J.S., and Czerniak, C. (2013). *Teaching Science in Elementary and Middle School Classrooms: A Project-based Approach* (4th ed.). London, UK: Routledge.

Krajcik, J.S., McNeill, K.L., and Reiser, B.J. (2008). Learning-goals-driven design model: Developing curriculum materials that align with national standards and incorporate project-based pedagogy. *Science Education, 92*(1), 1–32.

Lee, O., and Buxton, C. (2008). Science curriculum and student diversity: A framework for equitable learning opportunities. *The Elementary School Journal, 109*(2), 123–137.

Lee, O., and Buxton, C.A. (2013). Integrating science and English proficiency for English language learners. *Theory Into Practice, 52*(1), 36–42.

Lee, O., and Fradd, S.H. (1998). Science for all, including students from non-English-language backgrounds. *Educational Researcher, 27*(4), 12–21.

Lee, O., and Miller, E. (2016). Engaging in phenomena from project-based learning in a place-based context in science. In L.C. de Oliveira (Ed.), *The Common Core State Standards in Literacy in History/Social Studies, Science, and Technical Subjects for English Language Learners: Grades 6–12* (pp. 59–73). Alexandria: VA: TESOL International Association.

Lee, O., Lewis, S., Adamson, K., Maerten-Rivera, J., and Secada, W.G. (2008). Urban elementary school teachers' knowledge and practices in teaching science to English language learners. *Science Education, 92*(4), 733–758.

Lee, O., Maerten-Rivera, J., Buxton, C., Penfield, R., and Secada, W.G. (2009). Urban elementary teachers' perspectives on teaching science to English language learners. *Journal of Science Teacher Education, 20*(3), 263–286.

Lee, O., Quinn, H., and Valdés, G. (2013). Science and language for English language learners in relation to next generation science standards and with implications for common core state standards for English language arts and mathematics. *Educational Researcher, 42*(4), 223–233.

Lee, O., Valdés, G., and Llosa, L. (2015–2019). *Development of Language-Focused Three-Dimensional Science Instructional Materials to Support English Language Learners in Fifth Grade.* National Science Foundation, Discovery Research K-12.

Lee, O., Grapin, S., and Haas, A. (2018). How science instructional shifts and language instructional shifts support each other for English learners: Talk in the science classroom. In A. Bailey, C. Maher, and L. Wilkinson (Eds.), *Language, Literacy and Learning in the STEM Disciplines: How Language Counts for English Learners* (pp. 35–52). New York: Routledge.

Lee, O., Goggins, M., Haas, A., Januszyk, R., Llosa, L., and Grapin, S. (in press). Making everyday phenomena phenomenal: NGSS-aligned instructional materials using local phenomena with student diversity. In P. Spycher and E. Haynes (Eds.), *Culturally and Linguistically Diverse Learners and STEAM: Teachers and Researchers Working in Partnership to Build a Better Path Forward.* Charlotte, NC: Information Age.

Lemke, J.L. (1998). Multiplying meaning: Visual and verbal semiotics in scientific text. In J.R. Martin and R. Veel (Eds.), *Reading Science: Critical and Functional Perspectives on Discourses of Science* (pp. 87–113). New York: Routledge.

Lewis, J.L., Ream, R.K., Bocian, K.M., Cardullo, R.A., Hammond, K.A., and Fast, L.A. (2012). Con cariño: Teacher caring, math self-efficacy, and math achievement among Hispanic English learners. *Teachers College Record, 114*(7), 1–42.

Llosa, L., Lee, O., Jiang, F., Haas, A., O'Connor, C., Van Booven, C.D., and Kieffer, M.J. (2016). Impact of a large-scale science intervention focused on English language learners. *American Educational Research Journal, 53*(2), 395–424.

Lo Cicero, A.M., De La Cruz, Y., and Fuson, K. (1999). Teaching and learning creatively: Using children's narratives. *Teaching Children Mathematics, 5*(9), 544–547.

Lo Cicero, A.M., Fuson, K., and Allexsaht-Snider, M. (1999). Mathematizing children's stories, helping children solve word problems, and supporting parental involvement. In L. Ortiz-Franco, N. Gonzalez, and Y. De La Cruz (Eds.), *Changing the Faces of Mathematics: Perspectives on Latinos* (pp. 59–70). Reston, VA: National Council of Teachers of Mathematics.

Lubienski, S.T. (2000). Problem solving as a means toward mathematics for all: An exploratory look through a class lens. *Journal for Research in Mathematics Education, 31*(4), 454–482.

Lubienski, S.T. (2002). A closer look at black–white mathematics gaps: Intersections of race and SES in NAEP achievement and instructional practices data. *Journal of Negro Education, 71*(4), 269–287.

Lyon, E. (2016). The antibiotic resistance of MRSA: Teaching natural selection with literacy development for English learners. *Science Activities: Classroom Projects and Curriculum Ideas, 53*(1), 33–47.

Lyon, E., Tolbert, S., Solis, J., Stoddart, T., and Bunch, G. (2016). *Secondary Science Teaching for English Learners: Developing Supportive and Responsive Contexts for Sense-making and Language Development.* Lanham, MD: Rowman & Littlefield.

MacDonald, R., Miller, E., and Lord, S. (2017). Doing and talking science: Engaging ELs in the discourse of the science and engineering practices. In A.W. Oliveira and M.H. Weinburgh (Eds.), *Science Teacher Preparation in Content-Based Second Language Acquisition* (pp. 179–197). Cham, UK: Springer International.

Maerten-Rivera, J., Ahn, S., Lanier, K., Diaz, J., and Lee, O. (2016). Effect of a multiyear intervention on science achievement of all students including English language learners. *The Elementary School Journal, 116*(4), 600–623.

Martiniello, M. (2008). Language and the performance of English language learners in math word problems. *Harvard Educational Review, 78*(2), 333–368.

Martiniello, M. (2010). Linguistic complexity in mathematics assessments and the performance of English language learners. In *Research Monograph of TODOS: Mathematics for All. Assessing English-Language Learners in Mathematics* (Vol. 2, Monograph 2) (pp. 1–18). Washington, DC: National Education Association. Available: https://toma.memberclicks.net/assets/documents/Monographs/monographII_june19_2010.pdf [June 2018].

Martiniello, M., and Wolf, M.K. (2012). Exploring ELLs' understanding of word problems in mathematics assessments: The role of text complexity and student background knowledge. In S. Celedón-Pattichis and N. Ramirez (Eds.), *Beyond Good Teaching: Strategies That Are Imperative for English Language Learners in the Mathematics Classroom* (pp. 151–152). Reston, VA: National Council of Teachers of Mathematics.

McCormick, K. (2005). *Examining the Relationship between a Standards-based Elementary Mathematics Curriculum and Issues of Equity.* Unpublished doctoral dissertation, Indiana University.

McLeman, L., and Fernandes, A. (2012). Unpacking preservice teachers' beliefs: A look at language and culture in the context of the mathematics education of English learners. *Journal of Mathematics Education, 5*(1), 121–135.

McNeil, L. (2012). Using talk to scaffold referential questions for English language learners. *Teaching and Teacher Education, 28*(3), 396–404.

Mehan, H. (1979). *Learning Lessons: Social Organization in the Classroom.* Cambridge, MA: Harvard University Press.

Michaels, S., and O'Connor, C. (2012). *Talk Science Primer.* Cambridge, MA: TERC.

Michaels, S., and O'Connor, C. (2015). Conceptualizing talk moves as tools: Professional development approaches for academically productive discussions. In L.B. Resnick, C. Asterhan, and S. Clarke (Eds.), *Socializing Intelligence through Academic Talk and Dialogue.* Washington, DC: American Educational Research Association.

Moje, E.B., Collazo, T., Carrillo, R., and Marx, R.W. (2001). "Maestro, what is 'quality'?": Language, literacy, and discourse in project-based science. *Journal of Research in Science Teaching, 38*(4), 469–498.

Moll, L.C., Amanti, C., Neff, D., and Gonzalez, N. (1992). Funds of knowledge for teaching: Using a qualitative approach to connect homes and classrooms. *Theory into Practice, 31*(2),132–141.

Moschkovich, J.N. (1996). Moving up and getting steeper: Negotiating shared descriptions of linear graphs. *The Journal of the Learning Sciences, 5*(3), 239–277.

Moschkovich, J.N. (1998). Resources for refining conceptions: Case studies in the domain of linear functions. *The Journal of the Learning Sciences, 7*(2), 209–237.

Moschkovich, J.N. (1999). Supporting the participation of English language learners in mathematical discussions. *For the Learning of Mathematics, 19*(1), 11–19.

Moschkovich, J.N. (2002). A situated and sociocultural perspective on bilingual mathematics learners. *Mathematical Thinking and Learning, 4*(2–3), 289–212.

Moschkovich, J.N. (2007). Examining mathematical discourse practices. *For the Learning of Mathematics, 27*(1), 24–30.

Moschkovich, J.N. (2008). "I went by twos, he went by one:" Multiple interpretations of inscriptions as resources for mathematical discussions. *The Journal of the Learning Sciences, 17*(4), 551–587.

Moschkovich, J.N. (2010). *Language and Mathematics Education: Multiple Perspectives and Directions for Research.* Charlotte, NC: Information Age.

Moschkovich, J.N. (2011). Supporting mathematical reasoning and sense making for English learners. In M. Strutchens and J. Quander (Eds.), *Focus in High School Mathematics: Fostering Reasoning and Sense Making for All Students* (pp. 17–36). Reston, VA: National Council of Teachers of Mathematics.

Moschkovich, J.N. (2012). Mathematics, the common core, and language: Recommendations for mathematics instruction for English learners Aligned with the common core. Commissioned paper on Language and Literacy Issues in the Common Core State Standards and Next Generation Science Standards. In *Proceedings of "Understanding Language" Conference* (pp. 17–31). Palo Alto, CA: Stanford University.

Moschkovich, J.N. (2013a). Equitable practices in mathematics classrooms: Research based recommendations. *Teaching for Excellence and Equity in Mathematics, 5*, 26–34.

Moschkovich, J.N. (2013b). Principles and guidelines for equitable mathematics teaching practices and materials for English language learners. *Journal of Urban Mathematics Education, 6*(1), 45–57.

Moschkovich, J.N. (2014). Building on student language resources during classroom discussions. In M. Civil and E. Turner (Eds.), *The Common Core State Standards in Mathematics for English Language Learners: Grades K–8* (pp. 7–19). Alexandria, VA: TESOL Press.

Moschkovich, J.N. (2015). Scaffolding mathematical practices. *ZDM, The International Journal on Mathematics Education, 47*(7), 1067–1078.

National Academies of Sciences, Engineering, and Medicine. (2017). *Promoting the Educational Success of Children and Youth Learning English: Promising Futures.* Washington, DC: The National Academies Press.

National Assessment of Educational Progress (1996a). *The Nation's Report Card: 1996 Assessment Mathematics-Public Release, Grade 4.* Washington, DC: U.S. Department of Education.

National Assessment of Educational Progress (1996b). *The Nation's Report Card: 1996 Assessment Science-Public Release, Grade 4.* Washington, DC: U.S. Department of Education.

National Research Council. (1992). *Assessing Evaluation Studies: The Case of Bilingual Education Strategies.* Washington, DC: National Academy Press.

National Research Council. (2012). *A Framework for K–12 Science Education: Practices, Crosscutting Concepts, and Core Ideas.* Washington, DC: The National Academies Press.

National Science Foundation. (1998). *Infusing Equity in Systemic Reform: An Implementation Scheme.* Washington, DC: Author.

O'Connor, M.C. (1999). Language socialization in the mathematics classroom. Discourse practices and mathematical thinking. In M. Lampert and M. Blunk (Eds.), *Talking Mathematics* (pp. 17–55). New York: Cambridge University Press.

O'Connor, M.C., and Michaels, S. (1993). Aligning academic task and participation status through revoicing: Analysis of a classroom discourse strategy. *Anthropology and Education Quarterly, 24*(4), 318–335.

O'Halloran, K.L. (2005). *Mathematical Discourse: Language, Symbolism, and Visual Images.* London, UK: Continuum.

O'Hallaron, C.L., Palincsar, A.S., and Schleppegrell, M. (2015). Reading science: Using systematic functional linguistics to support critical language awareness. *Linguistics and Education, 32*(Pt. A), 55–67.

Palincsar, A., and Schleppegrell, M. (2014). Focusing on language and meaning while learning with text. *TESOL Quarterly, 48*(3), 616–623.

Pappamihiel, N.E. (2002). English as a second language students and English language anxiety: Issues in the mainstream classroom. *Research in the Teaching of English, 36*(3), 327–355.

Passmore, C., Coleman, E., Horton, J., and Parker, H. (2013). Making sense of natural selection. *The Science Teacher, 80*(6), 43–49.

Patchen, T., and Cox-Peterson, A. (2008). Constructing cultural relevance in science: A case study of two elementary teachers. *Science Education, 92*(6), 994–1014.

Paugh, P., and Moran, M. (2013). Growing language awareness in the classroom garden. *Language Arts, 90*(4), 253–267.

Pettit, S.K. (2013). Teachers' and students' beliefs about ELLs in mainstream mathematics classrooms. *Journal of Contemporary Research in Education, 1*(3), 130–143.

Pimm, D. (1987). *Speaking Mathematically: Communication in Mathematics Classrooms.* London, UK: Routledge.

Pinnow, R., and Chval, K. (2014). Positioning ELLs to develop academic, communicative, and social competencies in mathematics. In *The Common Core State Standards in Mathematics for English Language Learners, Grades K–8* (pp. 21–33). Alexandria, VA: TESOL Press.

Pinnow, R., and Chval, K. (2015). "How much you wanna bet?": Examining the role of positioning in the development of L2 learner interactional competencies in the content classroom. *Linguistics and Education, 30*, 1–11. doi:10.1016/j.linged.2015.03.004.

Planas, N., and Civil, M. (2013). Language-as-resource and language-as-political: Tensions in the bilingual mathematics classroom. *Mathematics Education Research Journal, 25*(3), 361–378.

Quinn, H., Lee, O., and Valdés, G. (2012). *Language Demands and Opportunities in Relation to Next Generation Science Standards for English Language Learners: What Teachers Need to Know.* Stanford, CA: Stanford University, Understanding Language. Available: http://ell.stanford.edu/sites/default/files/pdf/academic-papers/03-Quinn%20Lee%20Valdes%20Language%20and%20Opportunities%20in%20Science%20FINAL.pdf [June 2018].

Razfar, A., and Leavitt, D. (2010). *Building Mathematics Discussions in Elementary Classrooms with Latino/a English Learners.* Paper Presented at the Annual Meeting of the American Education Research Association, Denver, CO.

Razfar, A., and Leavitt, D. (2011). Developing metadiscourse: Building mathematical discussions in an urban elementary classroom. *The Canadian Journal of Science, Mathematics and Technology Education, 11*(2), 180–197.

Razfar, A., Khisty, L.L., and Chval, K.B. (2011). Re-mediating second language acquisition: A sociocultural perspective for language development. *Mind, Culture, and Activity, 18*(3), 195–215.

Richardson Bruna, K., Vann, R., and Perales Escudero, M. (2007). What's language got to do with it?: A case study of academic language instruction in a high school "English Learner Science" classroom. *Journal of English for Academic Purposes, 6*(1), 36–54.

Riggs, E.M. (2005). Field-based education and indigenous knowledge: Essential components of geoscience education for Native American communities. *Science Education, 89,* 296–313.

Riordan, J.E., and Noyce, P.E. (2001). The impact of two standards-based mathematics curricula on student achievement in Massachusetts. *Journal for Research in Mathematics Education, 32*(4), 368–398.

Roberts, S., Bianchini, J.A., Lee, J.S., Hough, S., and Carpenter, S. (2017). Developing an adaptive disposition for supporting English language learners in science: A capstone science methods course. In A.W. Oliveira and M.H. Weinburgh (Eds.), *Science Teacher Preparation in Content-based Second Language Acquisition* (pp. 79–96). Dordrecht, The Netherlands: Springer.

Rosebery, A.S., and Warren, B. (Eds.). (2008). *Teaching Science to English Language Learners: Building on Students' Strengths.* Arlington, VA: National Science Teachers Association Press.

Rosebery, A.S., Warren, B., and Conant, F.R. (1992). Appropriating scientific discourse: Findings from language minority classrooms. *Journal of Research in Science Teaching, 33,* 569–600.

Rosebery, A.S., Ogonowski, M., DiSchino, M., and Warren, B. (2010). "The coat traps all your body heat": Heterogeneity as fundamental to learning. *Journal of the Learning Sciences, 19*(3), 322–357.

Rudolph, J. (2002). *Scientists in the Classroom: The Cold War Reconstruction of American Science Education.* New York: Palgrave.

Schleppegrell, M.J. (2007). The linguistic challenges of mathematics teaching and learning: A research review. *Reading & Writing Quarterly, 23*(2), 139–159.

Schleppegrell, M.J. (2013). The role of metalanguage in supporting academic language development. *Language Learning, 63*(1), 153–170.

Sconiers, S., Isaacs, A., Higgins, T., McBride, J., and Kelso, C. (2003). *The ARC Center Tri-State Student Achievement Study.* Lexington, MA: Consortium for Mathematics and Its Applications.

Shaftel, J., Belton-Kocher, E., Glasnapp, D., and Poggio, G. (2006). The impact of language characteristics in mathematics test items on the performance of English language learners and students with disabilities. *Educational Assessment, 11*(2), 105–126.

Sinclair, J.M., and Coulthard, M. (1975). *Towards an Analysis of Discourse: The English Used by Teachers and Pupils.* London, UK: Oxford University Press.

Solano-Flores, G., Lara., J., Sexton, U., and Navarrete, C. (2001). *Testing English language Learners: A Sampler of Student Responses to Science and Mathematics Test Items.* Washington, DC: Council of Chief State School Officers.

Sorto, M.A., and Bower, R.S.G. (2017). Quality of instruction in linguistically diverse classrooms: It matters! In A. Fernandes, S. Crespo, and M. Civil (Eds.), *Access and Equity: Promoting High Quality Mathematics in Grades 6–8* (pp. 27–40). Reston, VA: National Council of Teachers of Mathematics.

Stein, M.K., Grover, B., and Henningsen, M. (1996). Building student capacity for mathematical thinking and reasoning: An analysis of mathematical tasks used in reform classrooms. *American Educational Research Journal, 33*(2), 455–488.

Swain, M. (2000). The Output Hypothesis and beyond: Mediating acquisition through collaborative dialogue. In J.P. Lantolf (Ed.), *Sociocultural Theory and Second Language Learning* (pp. 97–114). Oxford, UK: Oxford University Press.

Swanson, L.H., Bianchini, J.A., and Lee, J.S. (2014). Engaging in argument and communicating information: A case study of English language learners and their science teacher in an urban high school. *Journal of Research in Science Teaching, 51*(1), 31–64.

Symons, C. (2017). Supporting emergent bilinguals' argumentation: Evaluating evidence in informational science texts. *Linguistics and Education, 38,* 79–91.

Takeuchi, M. (2015). The situated multiliteracies approach to classroom participation: English language learners' participation in classroom mathematics practices. *Journal of Language, Identity and Education, 14*(3), 159–178.

Tan, M. (2011). Mathematics and science teachers' beliefs and practices regarding the teaching of language in content learning. *Language Teaching Research, 15*(3), 325–342.

Thoms, J.J. (2012). Classroom discourse in foreign language classrooms: A review of the literature. *Foreign Language Annals, 45*(s1), s8–s27.

Tolbert, S. (2016). Contextualizing science activity. In E. Lyon, S. Tolbert, J. Solís, S. Stoddart, and Bunch, G. (Eds.), *Secondary Science Teaching for English Learners: Developing Supportive and Responsive Learning Contexts for Sense-making and Language Development* (pp. 59–78). Lanham, MD: Rowman & Littlefield.

Tolbert, S. (2018). *Secondary Science Education for English Learners.* Paper commissioned for the Committee on Supporting English Learners in STEM Subjects. Board on Science Education and Board on Children, Youth, and Families, Division of Behavioral and Social Sciences and Education. Available: http://www.nas.edu/ELinSTEM [October 2018].

Tolbert, S., and Knox, C. (2016). "They might know a lot of things that I don't know": Investigating differences in preservice teachers' ideas about contextualizing science instruction in multilingual classrooms. *International Journal of Science Education, 38*(7), 1133–1149.

Turkan, S. (2018). *The Role of the ESL Teacher in Relation to Content Teachers.* Paper commissioned for the Committee on Supporting English Learners in STEM Subjects. Board on Science Education and Board on Children, Youth, and Families, Division of Behavioral and Social Sciences and Education. Available: http://www.nas.edu/ELinSTEM [October 2018].

Turner, E., and Celedón-Pattichis, S. (2011). Mathematical problem solving among Latina/o kindergartners: An analysis of opportunities to learn. *Journal of Latinos and Education, 10*(2), 146–169.

Turner, E., Celedón-Pattichis, S., Marshall, M., and Tennison, A. (2009). "Fíjense amorcitos, les voy a contar una historia": The power of story to support solving and discussing mathematical problems with Latino/a kindergarten students. In D.Y. White and J.S. Spitzer (Eds.), *Mathematics for Every Student: Responding to Diversity, Grades Pre-K–5* (pp. 23–41). Reston, VA: National Council of Teachers of Mathematics.

van Lier, L. (2004) *The Ecology and Semiotics of Language Learning.* Dordrecht, The Netherlands: Kluwer Academic.

Verplaetse, L.S. (2000). How content teachers allocate turns to limited English proficient students. *Journal of Education, 182*(3), 19–35.

Villenas, S., and Moreno, M. (2001). To valerse por si misma between race, capitalism and patriarchy: Latina mother–daughter pedagogies in North Carolina. *International Journal of Qualitative Studies in Education, 14*(5), 671–687.

Walkerdine, V. (1988). *The Mastery of Reason.* London, UK: Routledge.

Walqui, A. (2006). Scaffolding instruction for English language learners: A conceptual framework. *International Journal of Bilingual Education and Bilingualism, 9*(2), 159–180.

Walqui, A., and Heritage, M. (2012). *Instruction for Diverse Groups of English Language Learners.* Paper presented at the Understanding Language Conference, Stanford, CA. Available: http://ell.stanford.edu/publication/instruction-diverse-groups-ells [June 2018].

Walqui, A., and van Lier, L. (2010). *Scaffolding the Academic Success of Adolescent English Language Learners: A Pedagogy of Promise.* San Francisco, CA: WestEd.

Warren, B., and Rosebery, A.S. (2011). Navigating interculturality: African American male students and the science classroom. *Journal of African American Males in Education, 2*(1), 98–115.

Warren, B., Ballenger, C., Ogonowski, M., Rosebery, A., and Hudicourt-Barnes, J. (2001). Rethinking diversity in learning science: The logic of everyday sensemaking. *Journal of Research in Science Teaching, 38*(5), 529–552.

Webb, L. (2003). Ready to learn: teaching kindergarten students school success skills. *The Journal of Educational Research, 96*(5), 286–292.

Wells, G. (1993). Reevaluating the IRF sequence. *Linguistics and Education, 5*(1), 1–37.

Willey, C., and Pitvorec, K. (2009). *How Do You Know If What You're Doing Is Good for ELLs?* Presentation at the Chicago Mathematics Science Initiative Conference, May 2, Chicago, IL.

Yoon, B. (2008). Uninvited guests: The influence of teachers' roles and pedagogies on the positioning of English language learners in the regular classroom. *American Educational Research Journal, 45*(2), 495–522.

Zahner, W., and Gutiérrez, R.J. (2015). Using multiple representations of functions in mathematical discussions with English learners. In H. Hansen-Thomas, A. Bright, and L.C. de Oliveira (Eds.), *The Common Core State Standards in Mathematics for English Language Learners: High School* (pp. 107–122). Alexandria, VA: TESOL Press.

Zahner, W., Velazquez, G., Moschkovich, J.N., Vahey, P., and Lara-Meloy, T. (2012). Mathematics teaching practices with technology that support conceptual understanding for Latino/a students. *Journal of Mathematical Behavior, 31*(4), 431–446.

Zweip, S.G., and Straits, W.J. (2013). Inquiry science: The gateway to English language proficiency. *Journal of Science Teacher Education, 24*(8), 1315–1331.

# 5

# School-Family-Community: Contextual Influences on STEM Learning for English Learners

Decades of research and policy efforts have acknowledged that caregivers[1] may be key levers for improving children's educational success and that the involvement of caregivers has been associated with positive educational outcomes (Bryk et al., 2010; Epstein, 1995; Fan and Chen, 2001; Henderson and Mapp, 2002; Jeynes, 2015). Conventional roles for caregiver engagement have included checking homework, attending open houses, participating in parent-teacher conferences, and joining parent-teacher associations (Ishimaru et al., 2016), which can position caregivers as needing "remediation" in supporting their child's educational success (Baquendo-López, Alexander, and Hernandez, 2013; Barajas-López and Ishimaru, 2016). Ishimaru and colleagues (2016) acknowledged how studies of community-based reform have highlighted the powerful role that families and communities can play through "their culture and linguistic repertoires, lived experiences, social and economic 'funds of knowledge,' disciplinary understandings, social and cultural resources, community leadership, and ways of knowing" (p. 851; e.g., Bang et al., 2014; Gutiérrez and Rogoff, 2003; Heath, 1983; Ishimaru, Barajas-López, and Bang, 2015; Lareau, 2003; López, Scribner, and Mahitivanichcha, 2001; Moll et al., 1992; Valdés, 1996; Wang and Huguley, 2012; Warren et al., 2009). We draw from this broader discussion on underrepresented populations as few studies are specific to English learners (ELs).

---

[1]The term *caregiver* is used throughout this chapter instead of parents to acknowledge that not all children live with their biological parents and instead have other guardians in charge of their well-being.

In Chapter 4, we briefly introduced the notion that teachers' orientation(s) toward and preparation to work with ELs is associated with potential learning opportunities in science, technology, engineering, and mathematics (STEM) for these students. Here, we expand our discussion of this relationship, and highlight the important role of established connections between schools, families, and communities in supporting STEM learning for ELs.[2] We return to the notion of positioning of ELs in STEM and discuss how positioning that is based on views of the students' home culture can either be beneficial or detrimental to their learning. We then describe traditional models for family engagement that emerged from early reform efforts and the ways in which these models have positioned caregivers as having a passive role within the educational system. Because much of the literature is shaped on the perception of families and community, we discuss ways in which professional learning opportunities that afford teacher, family, and community interaction can positively impact the STEM learning environment for ELs. In the final section, we highlight the research on how building stronger connections between teachers and families and between schools and communities creates new contexts for mutual understanding, which, in turn, can enhance EL students' opportunities and motivation to engage in STEM learning.

## THE POSITIONING OF ENGLISH LEARNERS' CULTURES IN STEM

Carlone (2004) articulated how current classroom practices often perpetuate standards and methods that portray science and mathematics as "objective, privileged ways of knowing pursued by an intellectual elite" (p. 308), thus creating a disconnect with the ways of knowing that students from linguistically and culturally diverse backgrounds often bring to school. Olitsky (2006) illustrated the ways in which all students are routinely treated as homogenous when it comes to access, science and mathematics learning needs, and desired outcomes, regardless of the sociocultural, sociolinguistic, and sociopolitical factors that undergird current science and mathematics practices in U.S. public schools. Calabrese Barton (1998) called this a "one size fits all" educational mentality (p. 531) and critiqued the assumption that all students have equal access to science learning opportunities or that they have the same STEM learning goals.

Others have argued that for students to engage in academic discourse in the classroom, there is a requirement to embrace certain identity posi-

---

[2]This chapter includes content drawn from papers commissioned by the committee titled *Teachers' Knowledge and Beliefs about English Learners and Their Impact on STEM Learning* by Julie Bianchini (2018) and *Mathematics Education and Young Dual Language Learners* by Sylvia Celedón-Pattichis (2018).

tions, which many traditionally underrepresented students, including ELs, may feel ambivalent towards enacting (Brown, 2006; Paris, 2012a). In Lee's (2004) study of six 4th-grade teachers involved in a professional development project in a large urban district in the Southeast, teachers understood the community of scientists and of students to sometimes be in conflict. Such conflicts generally involved cultural values and practices related to the epistemology of science, and the teachers identified three areas of tension: (1) the *questioning and inquiry* central to science might not be encouraged in some cultures; (2) the *autonomy* needed to engage in inquiry might be in conflict with some cultures' respect for teachers' authority; and (3) the *movement between collaboration and independence* in science might conflict with some cultures' preference for group decision making (Cone et al., 2014; Lee, 2004). When ELs' home culture and the school culture are in disagreement, their abilities, aptitudes, and intents can easily be misjudged (Civil and Hunter, 2015; Oakes, 2005).

With the goal of unearthing underutilized academic resources that can empower students in STEM learning contexts, Tan and Calabrese Barton (2012) envisioned critical literacies that afford agency and opportunities to engage with science and mathematics in a variety of ways, while recognizing life experiences outside of school as valid sources of knowledge. These ideas rely on three principles of transformation: *transformation of discourses and practices, transformation of identities,* and *transformation of spaces for learning/doing science (and mathematics).* The transformation of discourses and practices entails de-privileging the authority of text and the teacher, shifting from representing science and mathematics content as final and complete, to "knowledge-in-the making," whereby students contribute to defining and situating the mathematical and scientific problems, methods, and limitations of evidence. In transforming identities, traditional narratives around who can do science and mathematics and the norms for participation are redefined. The identities of students that are established through their home language and culture are legitimized in the STEM classrooms as foundations for meaningful learning, and likewise, they are supported in developing a sense of their place and voice in tackling real-world issues. Lastly, the transformation in spaces for learning/doing science and mathematics affords opportunities to operate in identities and practices. Through STEM, students gain both the space and agency to alter the world to be more closely aligned to what they envision as more just (Tan and Calabrese Barton, 2012, p. 40).

There are powerful pedagogical models that enhance mainstream forms of STEM teaching and learning, in part by recognizing the experiences of those who are historically excluded by these mainstream models. One model proposes a less hierarchical dialogue between teachers and students, so that all students have a greater voice in the classroom (Moreno-

Lopez, 2005). In Cahnmann and Remillard's (2002) study of two 3rd-grade teachers involved in professional development opportunities, researchers found that both teachers were committed to making mathematics accessible and meaningful to their diverse students but had different approaches. Ms. Arieto worked to create a bridge between her students' home language and culture and the academic expectations of the school. She empathized with her students' life experiences and provided nurturing transitions from home to school, chose activities and tools that she believed would motivate students and connect to their culture and language, and used Spanish to introduce new mathematics concepts and reinforce learning in English. The second teacher, Ms. Kitcher, consistently engaged her students in reform-based mathematics, emphasizing mathematics concepts and explanations. She wanted her students to enjoy mathematics, see it as relevant, and see themselves as competent. However, she avoided making specific references to class and culture and assumed academic language was universal. In the end, the researchers concluded their study by recommending that teachers move to using both a mathematical and a cultural perspective in their teaching of diverse students, or what they called culturally contextualized instruction. Teachers of students who are typically underrepresented according to their social class and cultural and linguistic backgrounds need support to discover and take advantage of these potential instructional resources (Rosebery and Warren, 2008).

## CAREGIVER AND FAMILY INVOLVEMENT IN SCHOOLS

Early educational reforms used "parent involvement" as a way to remedy the underperformance of students, as the cause was deemed to lie outside of schools (Ishimaru et al., 2016). Activities of involvement were primarily in the form of a caregiver's participation in school open houses, parent-teacher conferences, and parent-teacher association meetings. These activities positioned parents as having a passive role (Baquedano-López, Alexander, and Hernandez, 2013) and led to caregivers and families from underrepresented communities feeling unwelcome, powerless, and marginalized in their children's schools (Delgado-Gauitan, 2004; Ishimaru et al., 2016; Lareau and Horvat, 1999; Lawrence-Lightfoot, 2003).

While the nature of home-school interactions understandably change as students progress through the grade levels, continued home-school connections are essential for positive student outcomes at all ages (Catsambis, 2001; Sanders, 2009). Caregivers often feel the greatest need to engage with their children's teachers in the elementary grades; however, the developmental challenges and the acceleration of academic demands in secondary schools means that ongoing home-school collaborations in support of adolescents remain critical (Patrikakou, 2004). Yet, when home-school collaboration does occur in support of secondary students, events for care-givers typically reach only a "narrow segment of the parent population and represent only select types of parental participation" (Gonzalez-DeHass and Willems, 2003, p. 89). Caregivers who are not members of this group are either explicitly or implicitly defined as "others," and this kind of "other-ing" can be viewed as institutional "cultural illiteracy" (Wainer, 2004) that often leads to institutional discriminatory practices toward ELs and their families. Deterministic and neglectful attitudes toward differences in school experiences can have a pathologizing effect on ELs, situating their academic struggles as a function of the challenges facing their immigrant families, without analyzing the roles that schools play as the bridge between com-munity inputs and student outcomes (Shields, 2004). Schools can thus find it easy to blame families for the academic struggles of ELs in the same way that policy makers find it easy to blame teachers for poor student perfor-mance (Garcia and Guerra, 2004).

## Traditional Views of Caregiver-School Relationships

Baquendano-López, Alexander, and Hernandez (2013) described sev-eral ways in which the relationship between caregivers and schools have been conceptualized by the following four programs: Caregivers as First Teachers: Early Learning Programs for Ages 0–5; Caregivers as Learners: Family Literacy Programs; Caregivers as Partners: Partnerships, Contracts, and Compacts; and Caregivers as Choosers and Consumers: School Choice.

In the early learning programs, building from the idea that ages 0 to 5 are critical to cognitive growth, the assumption was that for students to be successful in school, caregivers needed to prepare their children for educational success. This led to federally funded programs designed to assist caregivers in ensuring that they had the necessary preparation to be their child's first teacher. What is important to note is that early child-hood learning programs dictated the parental involvement practices and these program did not leverage the set of cultural practices from the child's families and/or communities. Family literacy programs became popular as a way to address home-school connections for districts and schools with culturally and linguistically diverse populations. Although family literacy programs encouraged families to read to their children and considered care-givers to be bearers of knowledge, the design of many programs was based on deficit assumptions about families and their cultural practices (Valdés, 1996; Whitehouse and Colvin, 2001). With Caregivers as Partners, schools and districts were required to share information with caregivers on school programs, academic standards, and assessments with the intent that care-givers would be more "knowledge partners" (Epstein and Hollifield, 1996). Moreover, it is known that caregivers make choices about their child's education: what schools to attend, the courses their child is placed in, special education services, language use, and testing. However, all of these choices are constrained by structural inequalities (Baquendano-López, Alexander, and Hernandez, 2013).

### Empowerment Approaches to Family and Community Involvement

Recently, there has been a recognition of the importance of moving beyond traditional caregiver involvement models toward a discourse of family engagement (Ishimaru et al., 2016; Warren et al., 2009). A range of powerful family engagement models have been proposed in the attempt to replace deficit orientations with asset-oriented views of typically under-represented youth, including ELs (Calabrese Barton et al., 2004; Civil and Andrade, 2003; Fournier, 2014; González, Moll, and Amanti, 2005). These models provide alternative roles that caregivers and teachers can adopt to support the academic and social development of these students (Carreón et al., 2005; Olivos, Jimenez-Castellanos, and Ochoa, 2011). For example, Fournier (2014) reframed "inclusion," placing significant value on the expertise and resources of students' caregivers, families, and communities to provide unique learning opportunities outside of the class-room, illustrating an authentic relationship between teachers and families. Additionally, the "ecologies of parent engagement" framework can be used to analyze the way caregivers make sense of their own engagement with schools (Calabrese Barton et al., 2004). This framework validates caregiv-ers' unique cultural capital to support academic learning, recognizing cul-tural and linguistic diversity as assets rather than as limitations on learning, and advocates for building reciprocal and authentic relationships between teachers and caregivers.

Ishimaru and colleagues (2016) suggested that "cultural brokers can play a critical role in bridging the racial, cultural, linguistic, and power divides between schools and nondominant [caregivers] and families" (p. 852). Cultural brokers can create spaces that help families to under-stand school culture, educate them on improving their child's achievement, connect them to institutional resources, and advocate for change (Ishimaru et al., 2016; Martinez-Cosio and Iannacone, 2007).

Building from the ideas presented in Chapter 4, the funds of knowledge paradigm is often used by educators as a transformative practice in con-necting homes and schools. In this theoretical framework, it was suggested that "only through the study of the sociopolitical, historical, and economic context of households could a static view of students' and families' culture be avoided, and as a consequence, the social and intellectual knowledge present in homes be recognized as viable resources to be leveraged in the classroom" (Baquendano-López, Alexander, and Hernandez, 2013, p. 37).

This particular view positions families to be stakeholders in their child's education and go beyond traditional roles of caregiver involvement. That is, educators can recognize that individuals participate in a range of communities in and out of school that can be leveraged for creating learning spaces that build on these skills and practices (Gutiérrez, 2008; Gutiérrez and Rogoff, 2003; Ishimaru, Barajas-López, and Bang, 2015; Lee, 2003).

Whereas most of the research on how to leverage community and family funds of knowledge to build instructional congruence and culturally sustaining pedagogies with ELs has focused predominantly on Hispanic communities, studies in other cultural, ethnic, and linguistic communities have provided additional insights (González, Moll, and Amanti, 2005; Ishimaru, Barajas-López, and Bang, 2015; Lee and Fradd, 1998; Paris, 2012b). For example, research involving Creole-speaking Haitian immigrant students and their families has pointed to cultural and linguistic assets, such as the use of argument patterns to be similar to scientific argumentation (Hudicourt-Barnes, 2003). Additionally, their affinity for multilingualism, multiculturalism, and communal responsibility may be related to the goal of civic engagement. The value they place on work ethic, academic success, and discipline also aligns with essential needs for STEM achievement (Buxton, Lee, and Mahotiere, 2009; Cone et al., 2014). Until more work is done to identify and acknowledge potential academic resources of these kinds, such cultural capital will continue to be underutilized in STEM classrooms (Ishimaru, Barajas-López, and Bang, 2015).

## SUPPORTING TEACHERS IN WORKING WITH FAMILIES AND COMMUNITIES

Teachers' attitudes about race, ethnicity, language, and socioeconomic status are critical factors that establish the parameters that influence the degree to which caregivers become involved in their children's schooling (Hoover-Dempsey and Sandler, 1997). To expect teachers to embrace linguistic and cultural differences as assets rather than as deficits requires teachers to engage in deep and self-critical analysis of how they perceive social and cultural differences in family-school interactions. Researchers who study inclusive science and mathematics education advocate for an alternative discourse around content area learning that values collaborative family-school interactions as a way to enhance all students' learning. Structuring opportunities for teachers to learn alongside their students and their students' caregivers is a promising approach toward this goal (Bernier, Allexsaht-Snider, and Civil, 2003; Buxton et al., 2016). In fact, interventions that engage teachers and caregivers with a science or mathematics focus have been shown to help teachers better understand their students' ways of thinking related to STEM concepts, have allowed teachers to recognize multiple ways of demonstrating content area learning, and have offered teachers new insights into how they can more efficiently work with traditionally underrepresented students and their families (see Bernier, Allexsaht-Snider, and Civil, 2003; Buxton, Allexsaht-Snider, and Rivera, 2012; Civil, 2012; Hammond, 2001; McCollough and Ramirez, 2012; Upadhyay, 2009).

## Teacher's Views of ELs' Home and Family Context

A small number of studies have looked at preservice teachers' beliefs about the mathematics education of ELs. However, extensive work by Fernandes on the development of MEELS (Mathematics Education of English Learners Scale) has addressed teachers' perceptions of parents and the home context (Fernandes and McLeman, 2012; Fernandes et al., 2017; McLeman, Fernandes, and McNulty, 2012). Findings from a survey report, administered to 215 preservice teachers, revealed the following:

1. 42 percent of preservice teachers agreed or strongly agreed that some ELs' home culture negatively impacts their mathematics learning.
2. 85 percent of preservice teachers agreed or strongly agreed that in general, parents from some cultures place a higher value on education than parents from other cultures.
3. About 33 percent of preservice teachers agreed or strongly agreed that ELs from some ethnicities are inherently better at mathematics than ELs from other ethnicities.

Thus, even orientations established prior to in-service tenure have major implications for whether ELs within instructional spaces led by these teachers will be positioned in ways that either benefit or impede their STEM learning.

Despite promising models to strengthen how ELs are positioned in STEM classrooms, there are persistent gaps in educators' understandings of how to partner effectively with diverse families and build on family and community-based aspects of science learning to support ELs' school-based STEM education. Traditionally, policy and standards documents have done little to provide guidance in this matter. For example, while organizations such as the National Science Teachers Association (2009) and UNESCO (Redding, 2000) do outline roles for families in supporting children's interests and aspirations related to STEM subjects, two important policy documents that are currently guiding the science education community in the United States, *A Framework for K–12 Science Education* (National Research Council, 2012) and the *Next Generation Science*

*Standards* (NGSS Lead States, 2013), have begun to acknowledge the role of families in influencing science education. Yet, families are critical in reaching global and national goals for expanding a STEM literate citizenry and a workforce that is equipped to solve challenging problems in arenas such as health, the environment, and social welfare, while also fostering economic development.

## Supporting Educators in Working with Families of ELs

Recent research involving teachers and culturally and linguistically diverse families demonstrates the potential for this work to enlighten STEM education, as well as the broader field of family-school-community engagement. Studies on equipping teachers to meet the needs of ELs revealed that improved skills in working with diverse families (e.g., Zeichner et al., 2016), increased ability to reflect on personal assumptions regarding diverse families (e.g., Smith, Smith-Bonahue, and Soutullo, 2014), and a broadened view of family diversity (e.g., Johnson, 2014) were competencies required to accomplish this goal. Common across these studies was the requirement for an increase in opportunities to reflect on personal assumptions about diversity and to have authentic interactions with families from backgrounds different from one's own. To this end, additional studies have emphasized that at least some teachers understand that their students come from diverse home cultures and recognize the need to not overgeneralize or stereotype (Lee, 2004). However, the majority of intervention-based research on family-school interactions that focused on teachers' experiences with families are free of academic content; studies with a particular focus on STEM content continue to be scarce.

Situating the teaching of science in informal settings with diverse children and families has been shown to be an effective tool in teacher education (Ciechanowski et al., 2015; Gaitan, 2006; Harlow, 2012; Sullivan and Hatton, 2011). Bottoms and colleagues (2017) showed how Family Math and Science Nights can be used to help elementary teacher candidates to understand and value their students' sociocultural and linguistic backgrounds. In this study, partnerships between universities and schools enabled preservice teachers to engage with families and experience first-hand bilingual communication and its power for families' and children's meaning-making. Through these interactions, preservice teachers shift their ideologies about the role of culture and language in schools.

Although teachers are expected to communicate effectively with families, teachers rarely have access to professional learning opportunities that support their efforts to work with families that are culturally and linguistically different from them (Upadhyay, 2009). Nieto's (2005) reconceptualization of the notion of highly qualified teachers is one of the few approaches focused on preparing teachers for working with the families of diverse students; it is redefined as five core features that are markedly different from the typical discourse around teacher qualifications whereby the focus is predominantly on content knowledge (e.g., Darling-Hammond, 2013). Instead, Nieto argues that highly qualified teachers are those who possess

1. *a sense of mission* to contribute to the common good,
2. *solidarity and empathy for students and their families* to affirm them in the classroom,
3. *the courage to question mainstream knowledge* to support critical thinking,
4. *improvisation* to negotiate teaching to meet their students' needs, and
5. *passion for social justice* to challenge the systemic inequalities that traditionally underrepresented students face in schools.

By problematizing the common definition of highly qualified teachers, when it comes to working with ELs, the most highly qualified teachers are those who focus on the formation of relationships as crucial for student learning (Nieto, 2003). Johnson and Bolshakova (2015) investigated five middle school science teachers as part of a 3-year professional development project on the role of culture in science pedagogy. Two teacher participants resisted the idea that culture was important to integrate into their science instruction; they held deep-seated views of what teaching should be, and thought their Latina/o students must conform to expectations in U.S. schools to be successful. The other three teacher participants came to see culture as a way to make students feel more welcomed and the science content more meaningful. They tried to transform their classrooms into safe and engaging places for learning, to build relationships with students, to make their content more culturally relevant, and to change their practice to be more inquiry-oriented and collaborative. These three teachers identified the following professional development experiences that enabled their shift in beliefs regarding culture: home visits, learning conversational Spanish, completing a course on culturally relevant pedagogy, and participating in professional development sessions monthly.

Buxton, Allexsaht-Snider, and Rivera (2012) showed how an instructional model that promoted both teacher and family agency supported and made visible new kinds of interactions among teachers, students, and families as they engaged in doing science together. Whereas many of the challenges that ELs and their families face are beyond teachers' control or influence, schools do have a responsibility to work to avoid reproducing the negative trends in who currently succeeds in science and mathematics and who does not (Gilbert and Yerrick, 2001; Oakes, Joseph, and Muir, 2003).

In the context of mathematics, Civil, Bratton, and Quintos (2005) examined immigrant caregivers' assumptions and experiences about their children's mathematics education as teachers and caregivers participated together in mathematics leadership development sessions to then implement workshops for the larger school district community. By shifting the hierarchical power dynamics common in teacher-caregiver relationships, the project helped teachers rethink mainstream views of caregiver involvement. The teachers found that when caregivers took on the role of facilitators of mathematics workshops for other families, they felt less inadequate.

At the heart of this work is the concept of caregivers as intellectual resources (Civil and Andrade, 2003). This view acknowledges caregivers' experiences with and knowledge about mathematics as resources that can support the students' school-based mathematics learning. However, Civil and Bernier (2006) discussed some of the tensions as well as opportunities that occur when caregivers act as co-facilitators of mathematics workshops and are supported in taking leadership roles. Caregivers became more familiar with the mathematics their children were learning and talked about advocating for the kinds of experiences that they thought were best for their children. They also shared their excitement to be able to talk to other caregivers about mathematics. In general, teachers were supportive of the idea of working alongside caregivers in facilitating workshops. But some teachers expressed reservations as they mentioned that they had received formal preparation as teachers while the caregivers had not. Additionally, work from Hammond (2001) examined both practicing and preservice elementary teachers engaged in a bilingual and cross-cultural professional development project at a school in California attended by students from Southeast Asian refugee families (Mien and Hmong) as well as from Central Asian, Mexican, and transient English-speaking families. Hammond found that teachers came to view caregivers as experts in traditional knowledge; however, some teachers assumed that caregivers wanted greater decision-making power at the school. On the contrary, caregivers simply wanted their traditional knowledge to be recorded and maintained.

## Supporting Educators in Working with ELs' Communities

Studies examining ELs' communities note that teachers primarily learn to recognize the importance of drawing on students' local communities and contexts as part of their teacher education or professional development experiences (Chval et al., 2015; Deaton et al., 2014; Lee, 2004). One study in particular examined teachers in relation to ELs' communities and identified both strengths and limitations in their knowledge, beliefs, and practices

(Bartell et al., 2010). In this study, 200 PreK–8 preservice mathematics teachers worked on a community mathematics exploration module as part of their mathematics methods course, which was intended to support teacher participants in designing and implementing effective instruction that builds on and integrates diverse students' mathematical knowledge bases. Researchers found that many preservice teachers entered the course with the belief that connecting to students' mathematics funds of knowledge was a valued teaching practice; however, they had little concrete understanding of how to do so. Additionally, some preservice teachers reported avoiding certain communities because of their negative reputations. By the end, all preservice teachers were able to develop mathematics problems that built on their students' multiple funds of knowledge, although some struggled with the mathematics involved or with knowing how to connect the community to instruction. Moreover, they came to feel more comfortable about engaging with all students' communities and identifying community contexts as resources.

The group of researchers in TEACH MATH has carried out a research program focused on the development of preservice teachers' ability to draw on community knowledge for mathematics instruction (Aguirre, Zavala, and Katanyoutanant, 2012; Turner et al., 2012). This multi-university project engages preservice elementary teachers in learning about the children's community funds of knowledge. The preservice teachers design mathematics lessons grounded in their community contexts while focusing on developing students' mathematical thinking. Turner and colleagues (2012) proposed a learning trajectory for preservice teachers that pays attention to how they make connections across different aspects of students' mathematical learning, and in particular to how they incorporate home and community funds of knowledge.

Building on the Funds of Knowledge for Teaching Project (González, Moll, and Amanti, 2005), Civil (2002, 2007) along with her colleagues (2001, 2002) applied the main ideas of that project to mathematics teaching and learning with a group of elementary and middle school teachers in schools with a majority of students of Mexican origin. The teachers conducted ethnographic visits with an eye on the mathematical potential for further development into classroom modules (Civil and Andrade, 2002). Examples of rich mathematical modules that are contextualized in the community funds of knowledge include a garden module (Civil, 2007; Kahn and Civil, 2001) and two construction modules (Ayers et al., 2001; Civil, 2002; Sandoval-Taylor, 2005). Through this work teachers developed relationships with some families and community members as they contributed their knowledge and expertise to an academic subject such as mathematics.

## BUILDING STRONGER CONNECTIONS
## FOR MUTUAL UNDERSTANDING

Research on Mexican American caregivers' perceptions about the teaching and learning of mathematics, with a particular focus on caregivers who went to school outside the United States and whose home language is Spanish, points to a need for schools and teachers in particular to develop an understanding of the different approaches to doing mathematics that caregivers may be sharing with their children (Acosta-Iriqui et al., 2011; Civil and Menéndez, 2011; Civil and Planas, 2010; Civil and Quintos, 2009).

### Immigrant Caregivers and U.S. Language Practices

The language of instruction can also present an obstacle for caregivers when attempting to help their children with homework and to support learning more broadly. Civil and Planas (2010) reported on caregivers' experiences when their children were in bilingual education settings, whereby the caregivers could be more engaged, could visit classrooms, and could help their children with homework. In contrast, as language policies in this context switched and limited access to bilingual education, caregivers felt an increased frustration, because they could no longer effectively help their children. Similarly, Acosta-Iriqui and colleagues (2011) reported on the impact of two different language policies (i.e., restricting bilingual education in Arizona versus promoting bilingual education in New Mexico) on caregivers' engagement in their children's mathematics education. In particular, caregivers in Arizona shared their frustration at how the language barrier limited how they could help their children, and also the emotional effect on their children as ELs when the instruction was restricted to English. Segregation from students who were not considered ELs was another result of the new language policy in Arizona. The impacted students as well as their caregivers expressed a desire to leave these environments as soon as possible; caregivers were particularly concerned that their children were not learning as much as they could, while the ELs were embarrassed to be in a segregated space (Civil and Menéndez, 2011). On the contrary, in New Mexico, bilingual education policies afford a continuous connection with culture and family; caregivers feel more encouraged when they understand what is being asked in the instructions for their children's homework, and this comfort is not because they do not want to learn English (Acosta-Iriqui et al., 2011). In fact, many Latino caregivers want to learn English, but find many obstacles along the way (e.g., responsibilities around the house, work schedules, current English learning structures for adults) (Acosta-Iriqui et al., 2011).

As part of a multifaceted professional learning framework for in-service middle and high school science and English as a second language teachers working with ELs, Buxton and colleagues (2015) and Allexsaht-Snider and colleagues (2017) developed a model of "steps to college through science bilingual family workshops" that brought teachers, students, and families together as co-learners with the motto that everyone has something to learn and everyone has something to teach. Immigrant caregivers gained increased confidence in their interactions with teachers, new ideas about advocating for their children, and built stronger relationships with other likeminded caregivers. Additionally, caregivers felt more comfortable going to school and meeting with teachers who they got to know in more meaningful ways due to their shared workshop participation. For their part, ELs gained new awareness of and appreciation for the commitment that their teachers and caregivers had to their academic success, as demonstrated by attending these Saturday workshops. Students benefited from the opportunity to share their school experiences and their academic and career aspirations with their teachers and caregivers in a welcoming space, while simultaneously learning about previously unknown academic and occupational pathways in science and engineering.

## The Dimensions of STEM Learning with Families

The range of ELs' experiences with STEM learning in family contexts that we have described thus far in this chapter illustrates the idea that learning can be viewed as a "life-long, life-wide, and life-deep" endeavor (Banks et al., 2007). This model of learning represents a promising practice and a framework for engaging families in STEM education in ways that foster curiosity, creativity, and problem-solving, while also promoting ownership of STEM practices and disciplinary discourse. Family-oriented STEM learning activities can occur in school settings as well as in out-of-school free learning spaces such as museums, parks, or the communities in which families live.

Research on informal or free-choice science learning contexts points to the importance of interactive and multifaceted caregiver engagement that acknowledges families' cultural practices. Ash (2004) has advocated for an alternative discourse around science learning within collaborative family interactions based on her investigations of dialogic inquiries among families, researchers, guides, and science exhibitions during museum and aquarium visits. Ash concluded that families engage with their children in dialogues through observing, questioning, and switching from everyday language to scientific language, practices that can also be followed in school science learning spaces. Rosebery and colleagues (2010) applied Bakhtin's notion of *heteroglossia* to propose the development of science learning settings that "conceptualize the heterogeneity of human cultural practices as fundamental to learning, not as a problem to be solved but as foundational in conceptualizing learning and in designing learning environments" (p. 2). As one concrete example, Tenenbaum and Callanan (2008) have conducted studies around science interactions in museums and in homes focusing on families of Mexican origin. Their findings indicate differences in style of interaction (e.g., explanatory talk) based on the caregivers' level of schooling. Overall, out-of-school programs can provide opportunities to engage with the content in the home language(s) (something that is sometimes limited or not allowed in school); they provide extended time for practice and exploration (ELs' instructional time in school can be limited if they are spending part of the school day learning English); and they can develop connections with family and community.

## SUMMARY

It is essential to acknowledge that all children, irrespective of their home culture and first language, arrive at school with rich knowledge and skills that have great potential as resources for STEM learning. Persistent family-school connections during K–12 schooling are essential for promoting students' educational attainment, and this is especially true for ELs and other traditionally underrepresented student populations. Despite widespread evidence of the necessity of caregiver engagement in schooling for the well-being of children, most school-supported teacher-caregiver interactions do little to facilitate meaningful teacher engagement with the families or communities of their ELs, especially in secondary schools. Cultural, linguistic, and social differences between teachers and immigrant caregivers are the most often-cited barriers to this collaboration, despite the desire on the part of all stakeholders for better communication and more productive engagement. Although teachers are expected to communicate effectively with families of all students, teachers rarely have access to professional learning opportunities that support their efforts to work with families that are culturally and linguistically different from themselves. While promising models for better family-school engagement that supports STEM learning for families of ELs now exist, both the research base and the infrastructure to build, sustain, and disseminate such models is largely lacking.

# REFERENCES

Acosta-Iriqui, J., Civil, M., Díez-Palomar, J., Marshall, M., and Quintos-Alonso, B. (2011). Conversations around mathematics education with Latino parents in two border-land communities: The influence of two contrasting language policies. In K. Téllez, J. Moschkovich, and M. Civil (Eds.), *Latinos/as and Mathematics Education: Research on Learning and Teaching in Classrooms and Communities* (pp. 125–148). Charlotte, NC: Information Age.

Aguirre, J.M., Zavala, M., and Katanyoutanant, T. (2012). Developing robust forms of pre-service teachers' pedagogical content knowledge through culturally responsive mathematics teaching analysis. *Mathematics Teacher Education and Development, 14*(2), 113–136.

Allexsaht-Snider, M., Vazquez Dominguez, M., Buxton, C., and Karsli, E. (2017). Figured worlds of immigrant fathers, sons, and daughters in steps to college through science bilingual family workshops. *Gender & Education, 28*, 1–17.

Ash, D. (2004). Reflective scientific sense-making dialogue in two languages: The science in the dialogue and the dialogue in the science. *Science Education 88*(6), 855–884.

Ayers, M., Fonseca, J.D., Andrade, R., and Civil, M. (2001). Creating learning communities: The "build your dream house" unit. In E. McIntyre, A. Rosebery, and N. Gonzalez (Eds.), *Classroom Diversity: Connecting Curriculum to Students' Lives* (pp. 92–99). Portsmouth, NH: Heinemann.

Bang, M., Curley, L., Kessel, A., Marin, A., Suzukovich, E. S., III, and Strack, G. (2014). Muskrat theories, tobacco in the streets, and living Chicago as Indigenous land. *Environmental Education Research, 20*(1), 37–55.

Banks, J.A., Au, K.H., Ball, A.F, Bell, P., Gordon, E.W, Gutiérrez, K.D., Heath, S.B., Lee, C.D., Lee, Y., Mahiri, J., Suad Nasir, N., Valdés, G., and Zhou, M. (2007). *Learning in and Out of School in Diverse Environments: Life-long, Life-wide, Life-deep.* Seattle: University of Washington, The Learning in Informal and Formal Environments Center. Available: http://life-slc.org/docs/Banks_etal-LIFE-Diversity-Report.pdf [June 2018].

Baquedano-López, P., Alexander, R., and Hernandez, S.J. (2013). Equity issues in parental and community involvement in schools: What teacher educators need to know. *Review of Research in Education, 37*, 149–182.

Barajas-López, F., and Ishimaru, A.M. (2016). "Darles el lugar": A place for nondominant family knowing in educational equity. *Urban Education*, 1–28.

Bartell, T.G., Foote, M.Q., Aguirre, J.M., Roth McDuffie, A., Drake, C., and Turner, E.E. (2010). Preparing preK-8 teachers to connect children's mathematical thinking and community based funds of knowledge. In P. Brosnan, D.B. Erchick, and L. Flevares (Eds.), *Proceedings of the 32nd Annual Meeting of the North American Chapter of the International Group for the Psychology of Mathematics Education* (pp. 1183–1191). Columbus: The Ohio State University.

Bernier, E., Allexsaht-Snider, M., and Civil, M. (2003). *Teachers, Parents, and Mathematics: Exploring Contexts for Collaboration and Partnership.* Paper presented at the Annual Meeting of the American Educational Research Association, Chicago, IL, April. Available: http://mathandparents.math.arizona.edu/papers/AERA_2003_Teachers.pdf [June 2018].

Bianchini, J. (2018). *Teachers' Knowledge and Beliefs about English Learners and Their Impact on STEM Learning.* Paper commissioned for the Committee on Supporting English Learners in STEM Subjects. Board on Science Education and Board on Children, Youth, and Families, Division of Behavioral and Social Sciences and Education. Available: http://www.nas.edu/ELinSTEM [October 2018].

Bottoms, S.I., Ciechanowski, K., Jones, K., de la Hoz, J., and Fonseca, A.L. (2017). Leveraging the community context of Family Math and Science Nights to develop culturally responsive teaching practices. *Teaching and Teacher Education, 61*, 1–15.

Brown, B.A. (2006). "It isn't no slang that can be said about this stuff": Language, identity, and appropriating science discourse. *Journal of Research in Science Teaching, 43*(1), 96–126.

Bryk, A.S., Sebring, P.B., Allensworth, E., Easton, J.Q., and Luppescu, S. (2010). *Organizing Schools for Improvement: Lessons from Chicago.* Chicago: University of Chicago Press.

Buxton, C.A., Allexsaht-Snider, M., and Rivera, C. (2012). Science, language, and families: Constructing a model of steps to college through language-rich science inquiry. In J. Bianchini, V. Akerson, A. Calabrese Barton, O. Lee, and A. Rodriguez (Eds.), *Moving the Equity Agenda Forward: Equity Research, Practice, and Policy in Science Education* (pp. 241–250). New York: Springer.

Buxton, C.A., Lee, O., and Mahotiere, M. (2009). The role of language in academic and social transition of Haitian children and their parents to urban U.S. schools. *Bilingual Research Journal, 31*(1–2), 47–74.

Buxton, C.A., Allexsaht-Snider, M., Kayumova, S., Aghasaleh, R., Choi, Y., and Cohen, A. (2015). Teacher agency and professional learning: Rethinking fidelity of implementation as multiplicities of enactment. *Journal of Research in Science Teaching, 52*(4), 489–502. doi:10.1002/tea.21223.

Buxton, C.A., Allexsaht-Snider, M., Hernandez, Y., Aghasaleh, R., Cardozo-Gaibisso, L., and Kirmaci, M. (2016). A design-based model of science teacher professional learning in the LISELL-B project. In A. Oliveira and M. Weinburgh (Eds.), *Science Teacher Preparation in Content-Based Second Language Acquisition* (pp. 179–196). New York: Springer.

Cahnmann, M.S., and Remillard, J.T. (2002). What counts and how: Mathematics teaching in culturally, linguistically, and socioeconomically diverse urban settings. *The Urban Review, 34*(5), 179–204.

Calabrese Barton, A. (1998). Reframing "science for all" through the politics of poverty. *Educational Policy, 12*(5), 525–541.

Calabrese Barton, A., Drake, C., Perez, J.G., St. Louis, K., and George, M. (2004). Ecologies of parental engagement in urban education. *Educational Researcher, 33*(4), 3–12.

Carlone, H.B. (2004). The cultural production of science in reform-based physics: Girls' access, participation, and resistance. *Journal of Research in Science Teaching, 41*(4), 392–414.

Carreón, G.P., Drake, C., and Barton, A.C. (2005). The importance of presence: Immigrant parents' school engagement experiences. *American Educational Research Journal, 42*(3), 465–498.

Catsambis, S. (2001). Expanding knowledge of parental involvement in children's secondary education: Connections with high school seniors' academic success. *Social Psychology of Education, 5*(2), 149–177.

Celedón-Pattichis, S. (2018). *Mathematics Education and Young Dual Language Learners.* Paper commissioned for the Committee on Supporting English Learners in STEM Subjects. Board on Science Education and Board on Children, Youth, and Families, Division of Behavioral and Social Sciences and Education. Available: http://www.nas.edu/ELinSTEM [October 2018].

Chval, K.B., Pinnow, R.J., and Thomas, A. (2015). Learning how to focus on language while teaching mathematics to English language learners: A case study of Courtney. *Mathematics Education Research Journal, 27*(1), 103–127.

Ciechanowski, K., Bottoms, S., Fonseca, A., St. Clair, T., and de la Hoz, J. (2015). Should Rey Mysterio drink Gatorade? Cultural competence in afterschool STEM programming. *Afterschool Matters Journal, 21*, 29e37.

Civil, M. (2002). Everyday mathematics, mathematician's mathematics, and school mathematics: Can we bring them together? *Journal for Research in Mathematics Education: Everyday and Academic Mathematics in the Classroom, 11*, 40–62.

Civil, M. (2007). Building on community knowledge: An avenue to equity in mathematics education. In N. Nasir and P. Cobb (Eds.), *Improving Access to Mathematics: Diversity and Equity in the Classroom* (pp. 105–117). New York: Teachers College Press.

Civil, M. (2012). Mathematics teaching and learning of immigrant students. In O. Skovsmose and B. Greer (Eds.), *Opening the Cage* (pp. 127–142). Boston, MA: Sense.

Civil, M., and Andrade, R. (2002). Transitions between home and school mathematics: Rays of hope amidst the passing clouds. In G. de Abreu, A.J. Bishop, and N.C. Presmeg (Eds.), *Transitions between Contexts of Mathematical Practices* (pp. 149–169). Boston, MA: Kluwer.

Civil, M., and Andrade, R. (2003). Collaborative practice with parents: The role of the researcher as mediator. In A. Peter-Koop, V. Santos-Wagner, C. Breen, and A. Begg (Eds.), *Collaboration in Teacher Education: Examples from the Context of Mathematics Education* (pp. 153–168). Boston, MA: Kluwer.

Civil, M., and Bernier, E. (2006). Exploring images of parental participation in mathematics education: Challenges and possibilities. *Mathematical Thinking and Learning, 8*(3), 309–330.

Civil, M., and Hunter, R. (2015). Participation of non-dominant students in argumentation in the mathematics classroom. *Intercultural Education, 26*(4), 296–312.

Civil, M., and Menéndez, J.M. (2011). Impressions of Mexican immigrant families on their early experiences with school mathematics in Arizona. In R. Kitchen and M. Civil (Eds.), *Transnational and Borderland Studies in Mathematics Education* (pp. 47–68). New York: Routledge.

Civil, M., and Planas, N. (2010). Latino/a immigrant parents voices in mathematics education. In E.L. Grigorenko and R. Takanishi (Eds.), *Immigration, Diversity, and Education*. New York: Routledge.

Civil, M., and Quintos, B. (2009). Latina mothers' perceptions about the teaching and learning of mathematics: Implications for parental participation. In B. Greer, S. Mukhopadhyay, S. Nelson-Barber, and A.B. Powell (Eds.), *Culturally Responsive Mathematics Education* (pp. 321–343). New York: Routledge.

Civil, M., Bratton, J., and Quintos, B. (2005). Parents and mathematics education in a Latino community: Redefining parental participation. *Multicultural Education, 13*(2), 60–64.

Cone, N., Buxton, C.A., Mahotiere, M., and Lee, O. (2014). Negotiating a sense of identity in a foreign land: Navigating public school structures and practices that often conflict with Haitian culture and values. *Urban Education, 49*(3), 263–296.

Darling-Hammond, L. (2013). Building a profession of teaching. In M.A. Flores, A.A. Carvalho, F. Ilídio Ferreira, and M.T. Vilaça (Eds.), *Back to the Future: Legacies, Continuities and Changes in Educational Policy, Practice and Research* (pp. 3–27). Boston, MA: Sense.

Deaton, C.C.M., Deaton, B., and Koballa, T. (2014). Teachers' awareness of their diverse classrooms: The nature of elementary teachers' reflections on their science teaching practice. *Action in Teacher Education, 36*(3), 211–233.

Delgado-Gaitan, C. (2004). *Involving Latino Families in Schools: Raising Student Achievement Through Home-School Partnerships*. Newbury Park, CA: Corwin Press.

Epstein, J.L. (1995). School/family/community partnerships: Caring for the children we share. *Phi Delta Kappan, 76*, 701–712.

Epstein, J.L., and Hollifield, J.H. (1996). Title I and school-family-community partnerships: Using research to realize the potential. *Journal of Education for Students Placed at Risk, 1*, 263–278.

Fan, X., and Chen, M. (2001). Parental involvement and students' academic achievement: A meta-analysis. *Educational Psychology Review, 13*(1), 1–22.

Fernandes, A., and McLeman, L. (2012). Interpreting and using gestures of English language learners in mathematics teaching. *Teaching for Excellence in Equity and Mathematics, 4*(1), 15–23.

Fernandes, A., Civil, M., Cravey, A., and DeGuzmán, M. (2017). Educating to empower Latina/os in mathematics in the New South. In S. Salas and P. Portes (Eds.), *U.S. Latinization: Education and the new Latino South* (pp. 67–88). New York: SUNY Press.

Fournier, G.M. (2014). The inclusion of parents and families in schooling: Challenging the beliefs and assumptions that lead to the exclusion of our students' first teachers. *Journal of Family Diversity in Education, 1*(2), 112–120.

Gaitan, C.D. (2006). *Building Culturally Responsive Classrooms: A Guide for K–6 Teachers.* Thousand Oaks, CA: Corwin.

Garcia, S.B., and Guerra, P.L. (2004). Deconstructing deficit thinking working with educators to create more equitable learning environments. *Education and Urban Society, 36*(2), 150–168.

Gilbert, A., and Yerrick, R. (2001). Same school, separate worlds: A sociocultural study of identity, resistance, and negotiation in a rural, lower track science classroom. *Journal of Research in Science Teaching, 38*(5), 574–598.

Gonzalez-DeHass, A.R., and Willems, P.P. (2003). Examining the underutilization of parent involvement in the schools. *School Community Journal, 13*(1), 85–99.

Gonzalez, N., Moll, L.C., and Amanti, C. (Eds.). (2005). *Funds of Knowledge: Theorizing Practices in Households, Communities, and Classrooms.* New York: Routledge.

Gutiérrez, K.D. (2008). Developing a sociocritical literacy in the third space. *Reading Research Quarterly, 43*(2), 148–164.

Gutiérrez, K.D., and Rogoff, B. (2003). Cultural ways of learning: individual traits or repertoires of practice. *Educational Researcher, 32*(5), 19–25.

Hammond, L. (2001). Notes from California: An anthropological approach to urban science education for language minority families. *Journal of Research in Science Teaching, 38,* 983–999.

Harlow, D. (2012). The excitement and wonder of teaching science: What preservice teachers learn from facilitating family science night centers. *Journal of Science Teacher Education, 23*(2), 199e220.

Heath, S.B. (1983). *Ways with Words: Language, Life and Work in Communities and Classrooms.* Cambridge, UK: Cambridge University Press.

Henderson, A.T., and Mapp, K.L. (2002). *A New Wave of Evidence: The Impact of School, Family, and Community Connections on Student Achievement.* National Center for Family & Community Connections with Schools, Southwest Educational Development Lab.

Hoover-Dempsey, K.V., and Sandler, H.M. (1997). Why do parents become involved in their children's education? *Review of Educational Research, 67*(1), 3–42.

Hudicourt-Barnes, J. (2003). The use of argumentation in Haitian Creole science classrooms. *Harvard Educational Review, 73*(1), 73–93.

Ishimaru, A.M., Barajas-López, F., and Bang, M. (2015). Centering family knowledge to develop children's empowered mathematics identities. *Journal of Family Diversity in Education, 1*(4), 1–21.

Ishimaru, A.M., Torres, K.E., Salvador, J.E., Lott, J., Williams, D.M.C., and Tran, C. (2016). Reinforcing deficit, journeying toward equity: Cultural brokering in family engagement initiatives. *American Educational Research Journal, 53*(4), 850–882.

Jeynes, W.H. (2015). A meta-analysis on the factors that best reduce the achievement gap. *Education and Urban Society, 47*(5), 523–554.

Johnson, L. (2014). Culturally responsive leadership for community empowerment. *Multicultural Education Review, 6*(2), 145–170.

Johnson, C.C., and Bolshakova, V.L.J. (2015). Moving beyond "those kids": Addressing teacher beliefs regarding the role of culture within effective science pedagogy for diverse learners. *School Science and Mathematics, 115*(4), 179–185.

Khan, L.H., and Civil, M. (2001). Unearthing the mathematics of a classroom garden. In E. McIntyre, A. Rosebery, and N. Gonzalez (Eds.), *Classroom Diversity: Connecting Curriculum to Students' Lives* (pp. 37–50). Portsmouth, NH: Heinemann.

Lareau, A. (2003). *Unequal Childhoods: Race, Class and Family Life.* Berkeley: University of California Press.

Lareau, A., and Horvat, E.M. (1999). Moments of social inclusion and exclusion race, class, and cultural capital in family-school relationships. *Sociology of Education, 72*(1), 37–53.

Lawrence-Lightfoot, S. (2003). *The Essential Conversation: What Parents and Teachers Can Learn from Each Other.* New York: Random House.

Lee, C.D. (2003). Editor's Introduction: Why we need to re-think race and ethnicity in educational research. *Educational Researcher, 32*(5), 3–5.

Lee, O. (2004). Teacher change in beliefs and practices in science and literacy instruction with English language learners. *Journal of Research in Science Teaching, 41*(1), 65–93.

Lee, O., and Fradd, S.H. (1998). Science for all, including students from non-English-language backgrounds. *Educational Researcher, 27*(4), 12–21.

López, G.R., Scribner, J., and Mahitivanichcha, K. (2001). Redefining parental involvement: Lessons from high-performing migrant-impacted schools. *American Education Research Journal, 38*, 253–288.

Martinez-Cosio, M., and Iannacone, R. (2007). The tenuous role of institutional agents. *Education and Urban Society, 39*(3), 349–369.

McCollough, C., and Ramirez, O. (2012). Cultivating culture: Preparing future teachers for diversity through family science learning events. *School Science and Mathematics, 112*(7), 443–451.

McLeman, L., Fernandes, A., and McNulty, M. (2012). Regarding the mathematics education of English learners: Clustering the conceptions of preservice teachers. *Journal of Urban Mathematics Education, 5*(2), 112–132.

Moll, L.C., Amanti, C., Neff, D., and Gonzalez, N. (1992). Funds of knowledge for teaching: Using a qualitative approach to connect homes and classrooms. *Theory into Practice, 31*(2), 132–141.

Moreno-Lopez, I. (2005). Sharing power with students: The critical language classroom. *Radical Pedagogy, 7*(2), 1–25.

National Research Council. (2012). *A Framework for K–12 Science Education: Practices, Crosscutting Concepts, and Core Ideas.* Washington, DC: The National Academies Press.

National Science Teachers Association. (2009). Position Statement: Parent Involvement in Science Learning. Available: http://www.nsta.org/about/positions/parents.aspx [September 2018].

NGSS Lead States. (2013). *Next Generation Science Standards: For States by States.* Washington, DC: The National Academies Press. doi:10.17226/18290.

Nieto, S. (2003). Challenging current notions of "highly qualified teachers" through work in a teachers' inquiry group. *Journal of Teacher Education, 54*(5), 386–398.

Nieto, S. (Ed.). (2005). *Why We Teach.* New York: Teachers College Press.

Oakes, J. (2005). *Keeping Track: How Schools Structure Inequality* (2nd ed.). New Haven, CT: Yale University Press.

Oakes, J., Joseph, R., and Muir, K. (2003). Access and achievement in mathematics and science. In J. Banks and C. Banks (Eds.), *Handbook of Research on Multicultural Education* (pp. 69–90). San Francisco, CA: Jossey-Bass.

Olitsky, S. (2006). Structure, agency, and the development of students' identities as learners. *Cultural Studies of Science Education, 1*(4), 745–766.

Olivos, E.M., Jimenez-Castellanos, O., and Ochoa, A.M. (2011). *Bicultural Parent Engagement: Advocacy and Empowerment.* New York: Teachers College Press.

Paris, D. (2012a). Become history: Learning from identity texts and youth activism in the wake of Arizona SB1070. *International Journal of Multicultural Education, 14*(2), 1–13. Available: http://ijme-journal.org/index.php/ijme/article/view/461/737 [June 2018].

Paris, D. (2012b). Culturally sustaining pedagogy: A needed change in stance, terminology, and practice. *Educational Researcher, 41*(3), 93–97.

Patrikakou, E. (2004). *Adolescence: Are Parents Relevant to Students' High School Achievement and Postsecondary Attainment.* Cambridge, MA: Harvard Family Research Project.

Redding, S. (2000). *Parents and Learning.* Geneva, Switzerland: UNESCO.

Rosebery, A.S., and Warren, B. (Eds.). (2008). *Teaching Science to English Language Learners: Building on Students' Strengths.* Arlington, VA: National Science Teachers Association.

Rosebery, A.S., Ogonowski, M., DiSchino, M., and Warren, B. (2010). "The coat traps all your body heat": Heterogeneity as fundamental to learning. *Journal of the Learning Sciences, 19*(3), 322–357.

Sanders, M. (2009). Collaborating for change: How an urban school district and a community-based organization support and sustain school, family, and community partnerships. *The Teachers College Record, 111*(7), 1693–1712.

Sandoval-Taylor, P. (2005). Home is where the heart is: A funds of knowledge-based curriculum module. In N. González, L. Moll, and C. Amanti (Eds.), *Funds of Knowledge: Theorizing Practice in Households, Communities, and Classrooms* (pp. 153–165). Mahwah, NJ: Lawrence Erlbaum Associates.

Shields, C.M. (2004). Dialogic leadership for social justice: Overcoming pathologies of silence. *Educational Administration Quarterly, 40*(1), 109–132.

Smith, S.C., Smith-Bonahue, T.M., and Soutullo, O.R. (2014). "My assumptions were wrong": Exploring teachers' constructions of self and biases towards diverse families. *Journal of Family Diversity in Education, 1*(2), 24–46.

Sullivan, J., and Hatton, M. (2011). Math and science night: A twist on the traditional event to engage families in exploring and learning through inquiry. *Science and Children, 48*(5), 58e63.

Tan, E., and Calabrese Barton, A. (2012). *Teaching Science & Mathematics for Empowerment in Urban Settings.* Chicago, IL: University of Chicago Press.

Tenenbaum, H.R., and Callanan, M.A. (2008). Parents' science talk to their children in Mexican-descent families residing in the USA. *International Journal of Behavioral Development, 32*(1), 1–12. doi:10.1177/0165025407084046.

Turner, E.E., Drake, C., Roth McDuffie, A., Aguirre, J.M., Bartell, T.G., and Foote, M.Q. (2012). Promoting equity in mathematics teacher preparation: A framework for advancing teacher learning of children's multiple mathematics knowledge bases. *Journal of Mathematics Teacher Education, 15*(1), 67–82.

Upadhyay, B. (2009). Teaching science for empowerment in an urban classroom: A case study of a Hmong teacher. *Equity & Excellence in Education, 42*(2), 217–232. doi:10.1080/10665680902779366.

Valdés, G. (1996). *Con respeto: Bridging the Distances Between Culturally Diverse Families and Schools.* New York: Teachers College Press.

Wainer, A. (2004). *The New Latino South and the Challenge to Public Education: Strategies for Educators and Policymakers in Emerging Immigrant Communities.* Los Angeles, CA: Tomas Rivera Policy Institute.

Wang, M.T., and Huguley, J.P. (2012). Parental racial socialization as a moderator of the effects of racial discrimination on educational success among African American adolescents. *Child Development, 83,* 1716–1731.

Warren, M., Hong, S., Rubin, C., and Uy, P. (2009). Beyond the bake sale: A community-based relational approach to parent engagement in schools. *The Teachers College Record, 111*(9), 2209–2254.

Whitehouse, M., and Colvin, C. (2001). "Reading" families: Deficit discourse and family literacy. *Theory into Practice, 40,* 212–219.

Zeichner, K., Bowman, M., Guillen, L., and Napolitan, K. (2016). Engaging and working in solidarity with local communities in preparing the teachers of their children. *Journal of Teacher Education,* 1–14.

# 6

# Preparing the Educator Workforce for English Learners in STEM

It is well documented that of the many factors that contribute to and hinder student learning, one of the most powerful is the role of teachers (e.g., Fullan and Miles, 1992; Spillane, 1999; see Chapters 2, 4, and 5). It has also long been known that large-scale changes in student learning goals, such as those changes brought about by the latest national standards, depend on teachers gaining new knowledge and skills that, in turn, require new visions of support and guidance for teachers across the span of their teaching careers (e.g., Ball and Cohen, 1999; Borko, 2004; Wilson, Floden, and Ferrini-Mundy, 2001). When it comes to the more specific context of preparing teachers of science, technology, engineering, and mathematics (STEM) to challenge English learners (ELs) as successful learners of STEM subjects, the knowledge base is newer and not as deep, but there is a solid and rapidly expanding body of research to draw on (e.g., Buxton and Lee, 2014; Civil, 2014; Turner and Drake, 2016).

How to effectively support teachers of STEM in successfully challenging their ELs is a multifaceted issue that must address a broad range of factors. These include differences across grade-level bands, STEM disciplines, program models, teacher experience, geographic region, and broad variations within EL student populations. Such variability requires a move beyond general frameworks and generic best practices for teacher learning toward models that center the unique assets and needs of ELs when learning STEM subjects. As noted throughout this report, emerging models highlight promising practices in need of further testing and refinement. Although the challenges for teachers of STEM working with ELs are substantial, and the unanswered questions are numerous, there is much to be optimistic about for those engaged in the work of teacher education in support of ELs in STEM. As described in Chapter 2, high-quality bilingual programs have been shown to yield positive student outcomes; however, in this chapter, we do not specifically attend to the preparation of bilingual teachers to teach STEM in these settings.

This chapter builds upon the ideas surrounding how to integrate content and language as articulated in Chapter 3 and the instructional strategies that can facilitate this as described in Chapter 4. Moreover, it builds upon interactions that teachers may have when leveraging ELs' assets by engaging with their students' families and communities, as presented in Chapter 5. We begin with describing specific issues associated with preservice teacher preparation followed by in-service preparation. We then describe themes that cut across the full spectrum of teacher learning opportunities and conclude the chapter with a discussion of specific needs for teacher educators.[1]

## PRESERVICE TEACHER PREPARATION

Many teacher education programs in the United States fail to adequately consider that in the 21st century, nearly all classrooms throughout the country include students whose first language is not English (Cochran-Smith et al., 2016). As described in more detail in Chapter 8, although there are a number of states that have policies that do require a minimum number of courses or specific certification to teach ELs, many teachers are unprepared to teach content to ELs (Ballantyne, Sanderman, and Levy, 2008; Darling-Hammond, 2006; Gándara, Maxwell-Jolly, and Driscoll, 2005; Villegas and Lucas, 2002). In science particularly, in a survey of elementary teachers, only 15 percent reported feeling adequately prepared to teach science to ELs (Banilower et al., 2013, Table 2.33). Secondary science teachers similarly do not feel prepared to teach science to ELs (Banilower et al., 2013, Table 2.33), and some have indicated that they would consult with English as a second language (ESL) teachers to meet the needs of these students (Cho and McDonnough, 2009; Chval and Pinnow, 2010).

Further, for teachers who work with immigrant and emergent bilingual students, the lack of a foundation for understanding the cultural, linguistic, and social class aspects of their pedagogical actions creates cultural distance between teachers and students who are different from themselves (Valencia, 2010). Educators' deficit views of immigrant and emergent bilingual stu-

---

[1]This chapter includes content drawn from papers commissioned by the committee titled *Teachers' Knowledge and Beliefs about English Learners and Their Impact on STEM Learning* by Julie Bianchini (2018), *Mathematics Education and Young Dual Language Learners* by Sylvia Celedón-Pattichis (2018), *Secondary Science Education for English Learners* by Sara Tolbert (2018), and *The Role of the ESL Teacher in Relation to Content Teachers* by Sultan Turkan (2018).

dents and their families are well documented (Adair, 2014; Eberly, Joshi, and Konzal, 2007), and such deficit thinking too often builds on preexisting public media and social representations of these students' limited possibilities rather than on meaningful firsthand experience.

Ball (1990, p. 12) wrote, "Prospective teachers, equipped with vivid images to guide their actions, are inclined to teach just as they were taught." In addition, teachers filter information about new ways of teaching, such as those acquired from methods courses and field experiences, through their prior knowledge and experience of being a student in K–12 classrooms as well as through their existing cultural expectations (Stein, Smith, and Silver, 1999). Moreover, preservice teachers enter their university coursework with strong beliefs about ELs and language as it relates to content instruction (Chval and Pinnow, 2010; Pinnow and Chval, 2015; Vomvoridi-Ivanovic and Chval, 2014). In this section, we describe research that is specific to supporting preservice teacher candidates in STEM to work with ELs.

### Self-Examination of Perceptions of Cultural and Linguistic Backgrounds

Teachers' own cultural, racial, ethnic, and social class backgrounds influence their instructional practices as well as other roles that teachers play for their students (e.g., mentor, role model, etc.). Thus, teacher education programs that explicitly focus on preservice teachers' backgrounds as related to their pedagogical practices, such as through community-based immersion programs for prospective teachers (see Box 6-1), can serve to bridge social and cultural gaps between teachers and their students (Ajayi, 2011). For example, Vomvoridi-Ivanovic's (2012) study of preservice teachers' use of cultural resources in an after-school bilingual mathematics club pointed to how the nature of the activity influenced the degree to which the preservice teachers attempted to make cultural connections. When the activities looked less like formal schoolwork, preservice teachers made more frequent cultural connections.

Cultural connections are also strengthened when preservice teachers have repeated opportunities to teach the same mathematics lesson repeatedly to small groups of students, to conduct task-based interviews with ELs, and to conduct the same interview with several children (Chval, 2004). Such approaches both enable preservice teachers to focus their attention on students' development of mathematical understanding and on how their actions impact that understanding. Preservice teachers reported that when given the chance to teach the same lesson to small groups of students multiple times, they were able to focus their attention on student thinking and communication rather than on classroom management. The preservice teachers had expected that every iteration of the same lesson would be the

---

**BOX 6-1**
**Learning through Immersion**

Many teachers are likely to have had limited experiences as learners of science, technology, engineering, and mathematics content in a language other than their home language. To develop an awareness of what this may be like, a strategy that teacher educators have used is to immerse teachers in a lesson taught in a language other than English. This approach can support teachers to be linguistically responsive (Lucas, Villegas, and Freedson-Gonzalez, 2008). Moreover, de Oliveira (2011) and Anhalt, Ondrus, and Horak (2007) presented similar experiences of engaging teachers in a mathematics lesson in a different language with the intent of eliciting participants' feelings about the experience and promoting discussion and reflection about implications for their own teaching of English learners (ELs). Another goal of these lessons in a different language was to provide the participants with a direct experience of strategies for how to teach mathematics to students whose home language is different from the language of instruction. Teachers were first presented content without much use of recommended strategies for ELs and then in the second part or lesson, they made use of many of those strategies. The goal was for the participants to notice the difference in supports between the two episodes to then promote a discussion on the different strategies. Both studies describe empathy and awareness among the teachers as a result of their participation in the lessons:

> Participants reported learning to develop "empathy for ELLs," to notice that "exposure to language ONLY doesn't work and repeating alone doesn't work," to realize that "it is not easy to stay interested when someone is trying to teach you something using another language" and "how easy it must be for our kids to feel overwhelmed." (de Oliveira, 2011, p. 61)

Moreover, "for these teachers, participating in these lessons seemed at some level to bridge the gap between the theoretical aspects of the reading assignments and everyday teaching" (Anhalt, Ondrus, and Horak, 2007, p. 21). Furthermore, these authors pointed to the potential of these experiences to help teachers question or revisit placement policies. In particular, one teacher questioned the placement of ELs in lower-level mathematics classes with the idea that would help them learn English since they already know the content. Through her experience in the lesson in Chinese, she had not paid any attention to the language because she already knew the content. As such, "this can result in placements in which students are repeating familiar mathematics content, leading to decreased engagement in classroom activities and discourse" (Anhalt, Ondrus, and Horak, 2007, p. 22).

SOURCE: Based on Anhalt, Ondrus, and Horak (2007) and de Oliveira (2011).

same and were surprised to find that every lesson was different because children's contributions and struggles took the lessons in different directions.

Siwatu (2007) found that preservice teachers felt more efficacious in their ability to help ELs feel like important members of their classroom community and in their ability to develop positive, personal relationships with their students than they did about their ability to communicate effectively about content learning with ELs. Chval and Pinnow (2010) found that preservice teachers, with limited knowledge about how to meet the needs of ELs, made assumptions that other educators with specialized knowledge and experience (i.e., translators, tutors, ESL specialists, parents, and peers) would be available to support ELs in their future classrooms. They also assumed that translating curriculum materials to the child's first language would be helpful, not realizing that some ELs may not be literate in the printed word in their native language, especially in the academic language of mathematics. Teacher preparation programs that include experiences specifically aimed at addressing the often implicit assumptions, beliefs, and expectations that teachers have in regard to working with ELs have the potential to address these and other misguided assumptions on the part of preservice teachers (Vomvoridi-Ivanovic and Chval, 2014).

Teacher education rarely includes an understanding of the role that ideology plays in teacher preparation in terms of cultural, linguistic, and social-class diversity (Bartolomé, 2004). There are political and ideological dimensions to education, particularly for vulnerable student populations, and these factors can have an adverse impact on teachers' work with these students (Bartolomé, 2010). For example, traditional views of mathematics hold it as a *universal language* that is transferable from one language to another (Remillard and Cahnmann, 2005). As a result, preservice teachers may assume that learning mathematics requires the ability to master a well-defined and *culture-free* body of knowledge (Boero, Douek, and Ferrari, 2008). This perspective limits the role of language in mathematics to mathematical vocabulary, notation, metaphors, and jargon. As Gutiérrez (2002) pointed out, an acceptance of the universality of mathematics has decreased the attention paid to students' cultural and linguistic backgrounds as they connect to mathematics, an area in critical need of further attention.

### Field Experiences and Community-Based Experiences

Equipping preservice teachers to teach STEM to ELs requires not only specific coursework on culturally responsive and equity-focused pedagogy, but also well-designed field experiences that align with and support the practices that preservice teachers learn in their coursework. Field experiences, although they may differ within and across institutions, are those designed with the intention to provide first-hand experience with what the job of teaching is like and to give practical reality to concepts encountered in university work (Wilson, Floder, and Ferrini-Mundy, 2001). For example, international or study-abroad field experiences have been associated with changes in preservice teachers' dispositions toward ELs (Li, 2007; Nero, 2009). In addition to the value of field experiences in school settings and abroad experiences, contact and collaboration with diverse ethnolinguistic communities in out-of-school settings can also support preservice teachers in considering how to teach STEM content to ELs (García et al., 2010; McDonald et al., 2011).

Gross and colleagues (2010) pointed to the importance of preservice teachers engaging in ongoing examination of their self-perceptions as teachers and their perceptions of ELs during field experiences. The researchers found that participants' teaching identities became more specific and elaborated over time during multiple field experiences in classrooms with large percentages of culturally and linguistically diverse students. Similarly, in a study of one elementary teacher preparation program that infused ESL preparation throughout the program, Harper and colleagues (2007) found that graduates reported high degrees of preparedness for and efficacy in working with ELs in classroom settings, and that their field experiences with ELs were cited as the most helpful component of the preservice preparation program in this regard.

Wilson, Floden, and Ferrini-Mundy (2001) reviewed the literature on field experiences and concluded that too often, field experiences are not well coordinated with the goals and content of the university-based course work that is meant to provide the foundation for success in the field experience. Moreover, when preservice teachers become overwhelmed with the challenges of learning to teach in field experience settings, they quickly revert to the norms and practices of the schools that they attended as students, even when those norms are quite different from those envisioned by university instructors in their teacher preparation program (Eisenhart, Behm, and Romagnano, 1991). Regardless of their subject matter preparation, preservice teachers who lack strong management and instruction are typically unable to focus on what students need to learn (Dutton Tillery et al., 2010).

Many of the promising possibilities for using field experiences to support preservice teachers learning to teach STEM subjects to ELs attempt to explicitly address the shortcomings of field experiences (Bollin, 2007). For example, Athanases and Martin (2006) described how they thoughtfully and intentionally integrated specific teacher education coursework on culturally responsive and equity-focused pedagogy with the corresponding field experiences that were meant to support preservice teachers in practicing those strategies. A key component of this approach was the role that field supervisors played as explicit equity mentors for the preservice teachers.

After-school programs provide another possible context for preservice teachers to gain new skills and experiences working with ELs, but such spaces have received little research attention. In one such example, Vomvoridi-Ivanovic (2012) described the benefits of bilingual preservice teachers using Spanish in a bilingual after-school mathematics club. However, she also pointed out the difficulties that these preservice teachers encountered in part due to their lack of experience using Spanish in mathematical contexts and in part due to the children's preference for English. Further study is needed about how field-based work can be used to specifically support preservice teachers of STEM to work with ELs; however, the limited work in this area shows promise.

### Integration of Learning How to Teach Disciplinary Content and Disciplinary Language

Preservice teachers often begin their preparation with limited views of what will be expected of them when it comes to teaching content to ELs. For example, Chval and Pinnow (2010) collected data from 51 preservice elementary mathematics teachers who were asked about teaching mathematics to ELs who moved to the United States from Central America and China. They describe three critical misconceptions held by the preservice teachers: (1) differential treatment of ELs based on their country of origin; (2) isolation of ELs rather than integration into a learning community; and (3) outsourcing to meet the needs of ELs rather than these needs being the responsibility of all teachers. The perceptions of these preservice teachers are in sharp contrast to research on best practices for teaching mathematics to ELs, which include (1) not reduce ELs to stereotypes about members of a cultural group, (2) promote active EL participation in mathematical discussions, and (3) recognize the resources that ELs use to express mathematical ideas in order to facilitate participation and learning of ELs (e.g., Khisty and Chval, 2002; Moschkovich, 2002). Nutta, Mokhtari, and Strebel (2012) described a model that was used to address these challenges to infusing EL instruction into existing general teacher education programs that currently lack support for preparing teachers to work with ELs. The key steps involved in this approach included winning faculty support, conducting an honest needs assessment, and developing capacity among teacher educators. One of the challenges described was how EL content could be incorporated into standard core courses in the teacher preparation program, such as human development, working with students with special needs, and social foundations courses, as well as across subject area courses.

The composition of the teacher education faculty also seems to influence the integration of language supports and supports for ELs more broadly in teacher preparation programs. For example, Lim and colleagues (2009) studied a range of teacher preparation programs and found that the presence of non-white full-time faculty in a teacher education program was positively correlated to more required coursework focused on engaging children and families from culturally and linguistically diverse backgrounds. Other contextual features of the teacher preparation program, such as its degree of urbanization, its governance structure, and whether or not the program had National Council for Accreditation of Teacher Education accreditation, were all associated with the amount of required coursework that was focused on working with bilingual children and ELs.

In the case of preparing preservice teachers to promote English language and literacy development for ELs in science, there is some evidence for the value of using inquiry-based pedagogies. For example, Shaw and colleagues (2014) described a modified elementary science methods course that also included professional development for cooperating teachers to improve teacher practice and student learning both for ELs and for non-ELs. The researchers concluded that the integration of science with language and literacy practices in an inquiry-driven process served to support preservice teachers in gaining skills to challenge ELs in their science classes while also improving the achievement of ELs in mastering science concepts and science writing. The study indicates that it is possible to begin to link the practices taught in preservice teacher preparation to novice teacher practice and to student learning outcomes.

A number of features associated with traditional STEM teacher education programs are detrimental to supporting ELs, including a failure to see the interconnectedness between first and second languages and cultures; fragmentation and isolation of language teaching and learning as separate for content teaching; a view of language learning that is over-reliant on vocabulary and grammar; and an implicit or explicit message that STEM subjects are culture free or based on a universal language. Moreover, little is known about the impact of the latest iterations of assessments of teacher candidates' readiness to teach and whether the assessment is a valid measure of new teachers' preparation to meet the needs of diverse learners (e.g., edTPA assessment adopted in many states; Baecher et al., 2017; Bunch, Aguirre, and Tellez, 2009, 2015; Ledwell and Oyler, 2016; Kleyn, López, and Makar, 2015). Gonzalez and Darling-Hammond (2000) pointed out that while programs that support ELs' access to challenging content can be enhanced through teaching strategies that provide multiple pathways to the understanding of language and content, most teacher preparation programs continue to be influenced by practices that are detrimental to ELs.

## IN-SERVICE TEACHER PROFESSIONAL DEVELOPMENT

When focused more specifically on preparing teachers to work effectively with ELs in the current context of standards-based disciplinary reforms, several models and frameworks have been proposed that highlight ways in which preparing to effectively teach ELs goes beyond general preparation for teaching well (e.g., Bunch, 2013; Lucas and Villegas, 2013; Turkan et al., 2014). Three of these frameworks were selected to highlight the need to prepare teachers to think in new ways about the integration of disciplinary language instruction with disciplinary content instruction.

One model, proposed by Bunch (2013), focuses on the purposeful integration of language and literacy into disciplinary STEM content instruction, as teachers and students engage in new ways of doing science and doing language together. These changing demands of STEM learning require teachers to develop enhanced *pedagogical language knowledge* (Galguera, 2011). Bunch argues that while there is broad agreement that teachers of ELs require new and deeper understandings about language, there is less agreement about what the exact nature of this enhanced linguistic understanding entails, as well as how it can best be developed. Bunch draws the distinction between pedagogical content knowledge about language, which represents the knowledge base possessed by effective teachers of a second language (i.e., ESL teachers), and pedagogical language knowledge, which highlights the knowledge base needed by content area teachers for integrating disciplinary language support with the other supports that facilitate learning of disciplinary content. While all content area teachers need to develop pedagogical language knowledge relevant to their discipline, such knowledge is critically important for teaching the disciplinary content areas to ELs.

In a similar effort to frame the preparation of content area teachers working with ELs, Lucas and Villegas (2013) proposed a model for the preparation of *linguistically responsive teachers*. Lucas and Villegas' model is composed of three orientations and four types of pedagogical knowledge and skills that the researchers found to be fundamental to the development of linguistically responsive teaching practices. The three orientations are (1) sociolinguistic consciousness, (2) valuing linguistic diversity, and (3) an inclination to advocate for ELs. The four types of pedagogical knowledge and skills to be developed by content area teachers in this model are (1) a broad repertoire of strategies for learning about the linguistic and academic backgrounds of ELs, (2) the ability to apply key principles of second language learning, (3) the ability to identify the language demands of classroom tasks, and (4) a broad repertoire of strategies for scaffolding instruction for ELs.

These orientations and skills are then mapped onto Feiman-Nemser's

(2001) central tasks, such as analyzing personal beliefs and preconceptions, developing an understanding of learners and learning, and developing the skills to study one's own teaching practice. Although this model shows alignment between the central task of developing subject matter knowledge for teaching and the skill of identifying classroom language demands of particular disciplines, it does not differentiate among those disciplinary demands. Thus, while highlighting more general linguistically responsive tasks for teachers, such as developing tools for analyzing academic language, it does not specifically aid teachers of STEM subjects in identifying STEM-specific language demands and supports. Still, Lucas and Villegas' model does important work to help move the field of content area teacher preparation toward a greater awareness of how to integrate teacher orientations and skills for supporting ELs from the outset of teacher preparation.

A third model, proposed by Turkan and colleagues (2014), develops an analytic framework for a teacher knowledge base that builds on current understandings of the role of language in teaching disciplinary content. This model of *disciplinary linguistic knowledge* (DLK) describes the knowledge base that is needed by teachers to facilitate ELs' understanding of the discourse within a given academic discipline. More specifically, this model of DLK includes two related components of teachers' knowledge as applied to disciplinary discourse: (1) teachers' ability to identify linguistic features of the disciplinary discourse, and (2) teachers' ability to model for ELs how to communicate disciplinary meaning through engaging students in using the language of the discipline, both orally and in writing. The first component is critical for making disciplinary content accessible for students to learn. The second component is critical for supporting students in expressing what they have learned. This distinction also helps point to the potential gap that may exist between a teacher's knowledge of disciplinary discourse and that teacher's ability to effectively challenge ELs in taking ownership of that discourse. Turkan et al. argue that the importance of understanding and applying the specialized knowledge base of DLK for teaching content to ELs is that it provides a framework to more clearly specify the role of teachers' knowledge about their students' language usage within the larger field of preparing teachers with the content knowledge needed for teaching effectively.

When taken together, these various models make the important point that when it comes to teaching ELs, context matters to such an extent that there may not be universal "best practices," while also validating the idea that the knowledge about disciplinary language that teachers need to support and challenge ELs is different from just good teaching. What is required is a combination of high-quality content area teaching plus preparation in integrating disciplinary language needed to support and challenge ELs (Ramirez and Celedón-Pattichis, 2012). Although not specifically STEM-focused, these models clearly frame the scope of work needed to effectively prepare teachers of STEM subjects to work with ELs who must learn enough English to engage with grade appropriate content while learning the various disciplinary discourses that are challenging to many native language speakers.

Although there is substantial overlap between the needs of those learning to teach and the needs of those currently teaching, when it comes to supporting ELs in STEM learning, the research highlights a few key themes that are especially relevant to the ongoing professional learning of teachers who already have STEM teaching experience and who may or may not be new to having ELs in their classes.

## Systemic Policy and Program Issues for Improving Professional Development

It has long been known that professional development can most effectively support practices when it is designed and presented in a systematic way. For example, the National Staff Development Council (NSDC; 2001) created a set of standards that support ongoing professional development with a commitment to rigorous learning that enhances "the knowledge, skills, attitudes, and beliefs necessary to create high levels of learning for all students" (National Staff Development Council, 2001, p. 2). The standards are organized into context standards (e.g., building learning communities involving leadership), process standards (e.g., research based; data driven), and content standards (e.g., aligned with content to be taught; integrates equity orientation).

In the specific case of improving professional development for teachers of STEM working with ELs, the National Clearinghouse for English Language Acquisition (NCELA) convened a Roundtable on Teacher Education and Professional Development of ELL Content Teachers in 2008, and subsequently, a report on what was known to be effective in this area of professional development (Ballantyne, Sanderman, and Levy, 2008). The report built on the NSDC standards mentioned above, highlighting the need for professional development that integrates relevant context, process, and content standards in a systemic way as central to improving professional development for teachers of STEM to ELs. More specifically, professional development on context standards highlight the need for integration of teacher learning communities focused on ELs' content area learning, administrator support based on increased knowledge of ELs, and a plan for acquiring additional resources based on the specific needs of local EL populations. Professional development on process standards highlight the need to follow research-based design and evaluation practices that are appropriate for ELs with attention to building lasting collaborations focused on ELs in which classroom teachers have an increased voice. Finally, when considering content standards, effective professional development for content area teachers working with ELs integrates a focus on equity, research-based teaching strategies, and strategies for enhancing family engagement (see Chapter 5).

A review, conducted by Khong and Saito (2014), highlighted the types of challenges that in-service teachers face when teaching ELs. The researchers concluded that social, institutional, and personal challenges, all of which extend beyond the classroom, are each relevant features that need to be addressed through systemic reform of which teacher professional development is one central component (see also Buxton, Kayumova, and Allexsaht-Snider, 2013; Newman, Samimy, and Romstedt, 2010). Ensuring adequate numbers of teachers who can be successful at meeting the STEM learning needs of ELs will necessitate effective professional development that takes intentional steps to retain teachers effective at working with underrepresented students. Many professional development programs for science and mathematics teachers fall short in this regard because they fail to consider teacher background, experience, knowledge, beliefs, and needs, instead treating teacher professional learning needs as homogenous (Loucks-Horsley et al., 2003). To build effective professional development systems requires adequate assessment of individual teachers' professional development needs, expectations, prior experiences, and constraints (Chval et al., 2008).

Rapid changes in policies and practices, both nationwide and at the state level, have led to ambiguity in language education policy, often resulting in instability and confusion for teachers (Walqui [2008] provided guidance on some priorities that could help teachers evaluate and improve the quality of instruction in their classroom). For example, Varghese and Stritikus (2005) studied bilingual teachers in two states, finding that many were looking for ways to become more involved in policy and decision making regarding the education of ELs. The researchers argued that gaining an understanding of language policy and decision-making processes is a greatly underdeveloped professional role for teachers who are experienced in supporting ELs in their classrooms. Despite this need, teacher professional learning that includes the dimension of policy advocacy is almost nonexistent and little is known about how to effectively build such a policy dimension into teacher professional learning.

### Build on Research-Based Practices to Improve Professional Development

One trend in professional development for in-service teachers that has been notable for some time is the tendency of school districts to contract with private individuals or companies to provide professional development for teachers (Ball, 2009). Often these are one-time workshops with limited or no follow-up that adhere to few if any of the characteristics of effective teacher learning models that have been discussed throughout this chapter. However, when teachers have adequate opportunities for professional development for teaching ELs and have more opportunities to teach ELs early in their teaching career, they are more effective as teachers of ELs (Boyd et al., 2009; Master et al., 2016).

Most teachers of STEM report that they are generally knowledgeable about the content in their curriculum at their grade level. For example, Lee and colleagues (2009) found that elementary teachers felt comfortable with their grade-level science content, with teaching that science to promote students' understanding and inquiry, and with talking about that content with their teaching peers. In contrast, the teachers reported rarely discussing student diversity, home culture, or home language in their own teaching or with other teachers at their schools. Moreover, Bowers and colleagues (2010) interviewed veteran teachers who mentioned that professional development programs would benefit from focusing on the use of metacognitive strategies and direct instruction regarding academic language.

Similarly, Molle (2013) studied the facilitation practices used in a professional development program for supporting ELs using three analytical lenses: participation context, ideological context, and content of the professional development work. As described in Box 6-2, Molle (2013) found that the value of using these different analytical lenses was that they provided rationales that supported the use of key research-based recommendations on effective professional development for educators of ELs. This model made it easier to make the case to district administrators for changes in the district approach to teacher professional development to support ELs.

The 5E instructional model in science education, which highlights strategies for students to Engage, Explore, Explain, Extend, and Evaluate their learning has been well documented as a successful framework for guiding teacher professional learning to support general reform-based practices (Bybee et al., 2006; Trowbridge and Bybee, 1996). Manzo and colleagues (2012) showed that the 5E model can also serve to frame professional development for secondary science teachers who are explicitly focused on increasing the participation and learning of ELs. The researchers found that after experienced science teachers practiced implementing the 5E model with their ELs, these students increased their engagement and use of explanation, and had increased opportunities to elaborate their understanding of science content.

Rather than arguing that experienced teachers need to implement reform-oriented practices with fidelity, Buxton and colleagues (2015) instead argued that professional learning for experienced teachers who are new to working with ELs needs to support those teachers in taking owner-

---

**BOX 6-2**
**Improve Professional Development for English Learner (EL)**
**Science, Technology, Engineering, and Mathematics**
**(STEM) Teachers: Build on Research-Based Practices**

Molle studied the work of one experienced facilitator, paying particular attention to a theme that is raised multiple times in this volume: that the education of ELs cannot be reduced to discussions of content learning and language learning without consideration of the sociocultural and sociopolitical aspects of how ELs and their needs are constructed by educators. That is, a key component of professional learning for teachers of STEM to ELs must include open and honest discussions of how societal discourse, including negative discourses about minoritized students, influence those students' educational opportunities, as well as how these discourses can be disrupted by educators.

During the 5-day meetings held over a 5-month period, the Content and Language Integration as a Means of Bridging Success (CLIMBS) program facilitator worked to: (1) facilitate the development of communities of practice among participants who work at the same school or district; and (2) use the WIDA English language proficiency standards to engage educators in thinking about the academic language and literacy needs of their ELs (WIDA Consortium, 2012). Molle considered these professional learning experiences through the lenses of participation, context, and content to highlight how the development of a professional development learning environment can serve to promote more equity-oriented teaching and learning.

**Context as participation:** One key aspect of the work of the facilitator for the CLIMBS project was to acknowledge and work with the tensions that always exist in professional communities if dissenting voices are not marginalized. The facilitator began by acknowledging that professional development opportunities for teachers of ELs typically bring together heterogeneous groups of stakeholders with differing areas of expertise, responsibilities, ideologies, and commitments related to ELs. This facilitator believed that the most impactful professional learning for teachers of ELs intentionally invokes ethical dilemmas and other tensions as a way to shift participants' perspectives about the abilities and experiences of ELs. The facilitator raised and addressed such tensions through a combination of the following strategies:

- Looking to build common ground from initially divergent opinions

---

ship and agency in terms of how they engage in professional learning and how they enact the recommended practices in their classrooms. Moreover, Chval and colleagues (2018) found that effective teachers of ELs learn to notice the types of interactions that support ELs in their content area learning and take these into account when observing students' partnership.

Despite the growing awareness that ELs bring many assets to the

- Challenging the basis on which an argument is founded rather than the argument itself
- Promoting the benefit of allowing divergent views to coexist rather than insisting on consensus

**Context as ideology:** The facilitator encouraged each participant in the training to develop their own ideological clarity about ELs as she systematically disrupted negative discourses about ELs, while also openly acknowledging that such discourses are prominent in the current U.S. sociocultural and sociopolitical context. She asked the educators to consider how these discourses were constraining their ability to fully perceive their EL students' academic knowledge and skills. The facilitator challenged participants whenever negative views of ELs were voiced in the workshops by using two main approaches:

1. Affirming both the resources and the potential that ELs bring to school
2. Emphasizing the responsibilities of all teachers, and of schools as social institutions, to support the language development of ELs as an integral part of their content learning

**Effects of policy:** The facilitator worked with participants on the distinction between the policies that influence EL student learning opportunities that were within the educators' direct control and those policies or factors that were outside the educators' sphere of influence. The facilitator argued that these discussions were an important feature of teacher professional learning to support ELs, as they were directly connected to:

- educators' sense of their capacity to effectively advocate for ELs; and
- educators' transformation of their professional relationships with peers and superiors (such as district staff) as they learned to become more effective advocates for ELs.

Molle concluded that the facilitation of professional development has the potential to transform the education of ELs, in part by shifting the relations between teachers and administrators by relying on research-based practices, such as affirming the importance of classroom teachers' judgment in creating the most successful learning environments possible for ELs.

SOURCE: Based on Molle (2013).

general education classroom, many teachers continue to hold deficit perspectives with regard to their ELs' learning potential in STEM subjects. Research on teachers' beliefs about and self-efficacy regarding teaching ELs in classrooms points to a clear need for continued professional development efforts to help all teachers learn to take an asset-oriented approach. Pettit (2011) identified factors, such as training in teaching ELs, years of teaching experience, and exposure to language diversity, that act as predictors of teachers' beliefs about ELs. Thus, not all experienced teachers hold views that are likely to help ELs to excel in their classes.

Building asset-oriented perspectives for teaching ELs often falls to school-based instructional coaches who routinely serve as facilitators of professional development for teachers working with ELs. While on-site coaches have the advantage of knowing the teachers and students at the school, Chien (2013) found that teachers who received professional development in this way reported limited usefulness due to a lack of follow up from the instructional coaches. Thus, limited access to high-quality and research-based professional development specifically targeted to meeting the needs and building on the strengths of ELs in STEM remains a substantial obstacle to ELs' success in STEM classrooms.

## CROSS-CUTTING THEMES FOR SUPPORTING TEACHERS OF STEM TO ELS

In this section, we describe research that addresses seven cross-cutting themes that are relevant to supporting all teachers of STEM subjects who work with ELs, regardless of the STEM discipline, grade-level band, English proficiency level of the students, or level of experience of the teacher. Although additional research is still needed to provide strong causal links between the strategies described and student outcomes, the review suggests that these strategies show promise. As such, the following themes for all teachers of STEM to consider include

- **Theme 1:** Explicit Integration of STEM Content and Disciplinary Language
- **Theme 2:** Use and Adaptation of Reform-Based Curriculum
- **Theme 3:** Shared Professional Learning Experiences for ESL and STEM Content Teachers
- **Theme 4:** Facilitation of Multilingual Instructional Approaches in STEM Classrooms
- **Theme 5:** Engagement with Families
- **Theme 6:** Use of Culturally Sustaining Pedagogies and Explicit Attention to Equity
- **Theme 7:** Targeted Teacher Learning around Common Societal Biases and Beliefs

### Explicit Integration of STEM Content and Disciplinary Language

Teachers of STEM require additional education around using and facilitating disciplinary discourse and how this can be integrated into their content area instruction, as it is now widely accepted that language development and content learning are interrelated (Snow and Brinton, 1997). Teachers can learn to orchestrate ways to move students from one language register to another. Because language is implicated in knowledge generation, this requires explicit knowledge about how the intentional use of language shapes students' meaning-making (see Chapters 3 and 4). The following studies present evidence for different models that support ways in which teachers can learn to explicitly integrate STEM content and disciplinary language.

A few large-scale studies of multiyear interventions point to positive outcomes of helping teachers more fully integrate language and content instruction. Lee and colleagues (2008) studied the development of elementary teachers' knowledge of science content, their teaching for understanding, their teaching of science inquiry, and their support for English language development (ELD). They found that after multiple years of professional development, the teachers' knowledge and practices were generally aligned with these four professional development goals of the intervention; however, the teachers' knowledge and practices fell short of the more ambitious instantiations of these goals.

Similarly, studies of the effects of teachers being trained to use the Sheltered Instruction Observation Protocol (SIOP) model have shown that these teachers' preparation improved the academic language performance of middle and high school ELs (e.g., Short, Fidelman, and Louguit, 2012). For example, Zwiep and colleagues (2011) studied a district's implementation of a blended science and ELD program, designed using many of the SIOP principles. The researchers found that this model prepared teachers to provide ELs with multiple opportunities to develop English language proficiency through participation in challenging inquiry-based science, and, in particular, they found that teachers' use of a combined science/ELD lesson plan format was a critical component to guide these teachers' efforts. However, the research base is not uniformly positive, with some studies showing no significant student outcomes (U.S. Department of Education, Institute of Education Sciences, and What Works Clearinghouse, 2013).

In another systemic, multiyear project, Stoddart and colleagues (2010) described a framework for preparing science teachers to work with ELs that is based on two bodies of sociocultural research: the CREDE Five Standards for Effective Pedagogy and the existing integrated science, language, and literacy instruction literature. The resulting ESTELL framework was used to prepare elementary teachers with five sets of socially, culturally, and linguistically responsive instructional practices: (1) practices for integrating science, language, and literacy development; (2) practices for engaging students in scientific discourse; (3) practices for developing scientific understanding; (4) practices for collaborative inquiry in science learning; and (5) practices for contextualizing science learning. The researchers found that teachers in the project learned to use these five sets of practices together to model linguistically responsive instruction that demonstrated the teachers' growth in awareness of students' specific linguistic demands while increasing teachers' ability to design and implement subject matter instruction integrated with language development activities.

Similar studies of mathematics teaching have pointed to the importance of teachers learning to engage ELs in discourse (e.g., eliciting vs. modeling) (Hansen-Thomas, 2009; Khisty and Chval, 2002). A 3-year professional development intervention by Chval, Pinnow, and Thomas (2015) provides evidence that suggests that content area teachers can improve their ability to engage and teach ELs effectively by developing as teachers of language as well as teachers of content. This intervention involved four components of the teachers' work: support for the development of mathematics, support for the development of language, enhanced tasks in curriculum materials, and facilitation of productive classroom interactions. Video data excerpts demonstrated the readiness with which both ELs and monolingual students engaged with talk about language, as teachers learned to create an environment where student ideas about both language and mathematics became important topics for clarification and discussion.

The use of genre-based pedagogies can prepare teachers to integrate explicit disciplinary language learning with content area learning. From a functional perspective on language, *genres* (see Chapter 3 for the earlier discussion on registers) are ways of getting things done or achieving a social purpose through language use. Thus, a genre-based pedagogy in a discipline like science or mathematics would highlight how language is used in that discipline to make grade-appropriate meaning at each level of schooling. Gebhard, Demers, and Castillo-Rosenthal (2008) used this approach in work with teachers to support the literacy practices of ELs (see Box 6-3). Educative assessment materials also have the potential to help teachers develop new strategies for integrating genre-based language and content teaching in STEM. For example, teachers learned to seek out and build upon how their students were using their emergent scientific language to make meaning, rather than focusing primarily on the gaps and limitations of their ELs' English language usage (Buxton et al., 2013).

Despite this emerging research, many teachers of STEM equate disciplinary language with disciplinary vocabulary. This limited view of language has been critiqued in instruction for ELs (e.g., Krashen, 2011). It has also been critiqued by researchers who study other aspects of vocabulary acquisition, such as proponents of a focus on general academic vocabulary (e.g., Snow, 2010). Yet, technical vocabulary is one key feature of disciplinary discourse in STEM subjects (Fang, 2005), and teachers can learn to support ELs' technical vocabulary development in ways that are contextualized to support meaning-making (Pollard-Durodola et al., 2012).

### Use and Adaptation of Reform-Based Curriculum

As students move through the grade levels, both the science concepts and the disciplinary language used to express and make meaning of those concepts become more abstract. This poses an increasing challenge for teachers of secondary school-aged ELs. Indeed, high school teachers of STEM subjects working with ELs claim that among their greatest needs are access to instructional materials that support ELs in learning grade-appropriate content plus the pedagogical training specifically designed to help them use these materials in effective ways (Cho and McDonnough, 2009).

Curriculum units designed to integrate instructional strategies that support language and content together can provide teachers with valuable tools to lead ELs to construct more sophisticated understanding of that content while also using more language to communicate their knowledge. For example, Weinburgh and colleagues (2014) showed how teacher educators engaged teachers in a summer school program to prepare them to adapt a set of inquiry-based instructional units to more effectively integrate language and science instruction in response to the goals of the Next Generation Science Standards (see Box 6-4; see also Brown and Ryoo, 2008; Brown, Ryoo, and Rodriguez, 2010). Similarly, Khisty (1993) argued that curriculum activities need to be "designed so that children . . . explore new experiences and acquire new information . . . and] are encouraged to employ their linguistic resources, thus mastering an expanding range of new register" (p. 197).

Lara-Alecio and colleagues (2012) designed and studied an intervention that combined ongoing professional development for middle school science teachers who worked with large numbers of ELs that was rooted in a series of integrated inquiry-based curriculum units. Teacher scaffolding embedded in the curriculum highlighted direct and explicit instruction in reading, writing, and vocabulary enrichment in English, take-home science activities for families, and review of lessons by university scientists to ensure rigorous, current, and accurate content. Research on the effectiveness of the intervention found that teachers who were trained in the use of these curricular materials were more successful as compared to teachers using the standard district curriculum.

In another longitudinal study that used curriculum units as a central component to integrate the teaching of science practices with the teaching of language of science practices, Buxton and colleagues (2015) found that when teachers were given agency to help create and adapt curriculum, as well as to make choices about the nature of the professional development

---

**BOX 6-3**
**Explicit Integration of Content and Disciplinary**
**Language in Elementary Contexts**

Gebhard, Demers, and Castillo-Rosenthal (2008) provided a clear example of how and why all teachers (and not just trained English as a second language [ESL] teachers) need to learn to analyze and build on the linguistic features of their students' emergent literacy practices. They argued that the current combination of demographic changes, accountability frameworks, and English-only mandates require all teachers to develop a greater awareness of the disciplinary genres that students are asked to produce in school and to develop a new set of pedagogical practices that are supportive of all students' academic literacy development. They made the case that knowledge of the role of genres (e.g., narratives, explanations, research reports, arguments) in building content knowledge is increasingly important for all teachers, and especially for teachers who themselves have limited experience learning, thinking, and making meaning in a second language.

Teachers in the program were taught to see the complexity in their elementary students' use of language practices by asking questions such as how students use talk, print, gestures, drawings, and other meaning-making tools in complementary and overlapping ways. Methodologically, the teachers were engaged in critical case study research in which they applied a conceptual framework based on the relationships between the texts that English learners (ELs) produce and the contexts (local, institutional, and historical) in which those texts are situated. The researchers found that teachers were able to use this "text-context analysis" to understand what their ELs were trying to communicate through their writing in ways that were not obvious to the teachers before analyzing the written texts in this way.

Specifically, teachers learned to make use of genre-based pedagogies through a process that included the following:

---

they engaged in, these teachers increased their implementation of reform-based practices to support ELs. Teachers showed increased willingness and ability to design and modify curriculum materials to meet the science learning needs of their ELs as a result of working collaboratively with researchers on strategies for adapting curriculum materials to challenge and support ELs (Cardozo Gaibisso, Allexsaht-Snider, and Buxton, 2017).

As Adamson, Santau, and Lee (2013) pointed out, teacher professional learning that is focused on supporting ELs often fails to attend to or to be explicitly aligned with reform-based curriculum. Further, when that teacher professional learning does align with reform-based curriculum, it may fail to extend beyond how to teach the disciplinary concepts and

- identifying an authentic audience with whom students could communicate about a specific topic to accomplish a purpose that the students found compelling;
- identifying an academic genre that was well suited to students achieving their purposes in writing about this topic for a specified audience;
- analyzing the salient linguistic features of this genre with attention to specialized vocabulary choices, grammatical structures, rhetorical conventions, and other genre norms;
- designing materials to support students in developing the ability to recognize and use genre-specific vocabulary, sentence structures, and rhetorical conventions (e.g., graphic organizers, guidelines for revision, assessment tools);
- providing students with multiple models and explicit instruction in analyzing the linguistic features of specified genres;
- providing opportunities for students to collaborate with each other and with teachers as they plan, draft, revise, and edit their texts;
- tracking changes in students' use of targeted, genre-specific practices as a way of reflecting on and modifying instruction and assessing student linguistic and academic development; and
- reflecting with students on the process of using academic language to attempt to enact social change (p. 288).

Although this example is not specific to STEM content, the broader issues apply. (For other examples specific to science and mathematics, see de Oliveira and Lan, 2014, and Fang, Lamme, and Pringle, 2010). Teachers who engaged in this work claimed that they felt more committed to engaging in advocacy not only for their bilingual students, but also for their ESL and bilingual teacher colleagues. They also gained greater awareness of how different genres can be made explicit for students who are being asked to use those linguistic features in new ways given the demands of new disciplinary standards, frameworks and assessments.

SOURCE: Based on Gebhard, Demers, and Castillo-Rosenthal (2008).

practices to also focus on students' language and culture. However, placing the expectation on teachers to adapt curriculum to better meet the needs of ELs requires significant professional learning and ongoing support that is currently quite rare in U.S. educational contexts.

### Shared Professional Learning Experiences for Teachers of STEM

The dual challenge that teachers face of learning to teach their disciplinary content in new reform-oriented ways while also learning to use language in new ways to meet the needs of all students including ELs is a daunting task for most teachers of STEM content (de Oliveira and Wilcox,

---

**BOX 6-4**
**Learn to Use and Adapt Reform-based Curriculum**

Weinburgh and colleagues (2014) described a study that tests the effectiveness of a model for integrating inquiry-based science and language, using a research-based instructional model applied to reform-based curriculum units for 5th-grade science. The study was developed in response to a tension that content area teachers who work with English learners (ELs) often feel when trained to use sheltered instruction approaches such as SIOP (Short, Vogt, and Echevarría, 2011). These models are meant to be used across all content areas but are misaligned in several ways with the current frameworks guiding STEM instruction. Particularly, elementary teachers working with ELs, who are taught methods in all subject areas, may get professional development with conflicting views about how best to support English language development and how to support STEM content area learning.

The 5R Instructional Model was developed to problematize several key practices common in sheltered instruction, such as the frontloading of vocabulary and the deliberate discussion of lesson objectives, recognizing that these practices are problematic in science instruction but are common in second language instruction. The components of the 5R model are *repeating, revealing, repositioning, replacing*, and *reloading* language. For example, in the 5R model, the alternative to frontloading vocabulary is to first let language emerge during the inquiry-based lesson and then to "reload" the essential language during a subsequent lesson.

Teachers in a 3-week summer school program for 5th-grade ELs learned to apply the 5R model as they adapted two curriculum units that were aligned with *A Framework for K–12 Science Education* (National Research Council, 2012) on the topics of erosion and wind energy/turbines. The researchers and teachers worked together to establish clear and explicit science, mathematics, and language objectives during the planning and adapting of the units, but these objectives were not made explicit to the students, as they would have been in typical sheltered

---

2017). Moreover, the role of ESL teachers has continued to evolve. One support structure that has proven to be effective in at least some contexts has been a closer integration of trained ESL teachers and paraprofessionals into STEM classrooms (Honigsfeld and Dove, 2010). For example, Harper and de Jong (2009) studied three different teacher education programs that claimed to integrate ESL teacher competencies throughout the general education curriculum (see Box 6-5).

Much of what the teacher education field already knows about preparing teachers from different disciplines to work together can be applied in the specific case of helping teachers of STEM content and ESL teachers work effectively together in supporting ELs' STEM learning. For example, Martin-Beltran and Peercy (2014) worked with pairs of elementary general-instruction. The research team conducted oral interviews with all students at the start and end of the summer program, with the key materials (stream table and wind turbine) present during the interview to act as stimuli for student responses. The analysis of the interviews clearly shows that after participating in the adapted curricular units, the students constructed more sophisticated understanding of the topics and used more disciplinary language to communicate their knowledge.

In addition to the *reloading* of language, the teachers learned, implemented, and came to see value in the other four Rs in the 5R model. Teachers *repeated* key words and phrases often as students engaged in the unit activities (rather that pre-teaching these). Teachers learned to *reposition* students' communication as students discussed what they were doing during and after investigations, with teachers guiding students to restate their initial ideas in ways that more clearly communicated their evolving thinking. Teachers learned to help students *replace* their initial use of colloquial language with grade-appropriate scientific language after (but not before) students had completed their investigations and had done what they could to describe what they had learned using their existing linguistic repertoires. Finally, teachers learned to *reveal* new vocabulary and phrases for concepts for which students had no existing language.

Weinburgh and colleagues (2014) concluded that the 5R Instructional Model can support teachers as they learn to enhance experiences for their ELs, in part by alleviating the confusion that teachers may feel about conflicting preparation for teaching inquiry-based science and sheltered instruction. The 5R model is not a rigid procedure, but rather a flexible way for teachers to adapt reform-based curricula so that ELs can engage meaningfully in conceptual as well as linguistic development. As the authors describe it, "the 5R model provides a 'space' in which science and language instruction can co-exist and complement one another" (p. 535).

SOURCE: Based on Weinburgh et al. (2014).

ists and ESL specialists to use collaboration strategies to make co-teaching processes more visible and explicit. Specifically, the teachers learned to: (1) communicate and build upon their own and their partner's teaching goals; (2) co-construct and adjust their knowledge base for teaching ELs; and (3) negotiate their ownership of space and voice during shared teaching activities. Thus, conceptualizing teacher collaboration as an opportunity for shared learning may allow co-teaching to become a more regular and integral part of teacher preparation for both ESL specialists and content-area teachers. However, it is important for ESL teachers collaborating with content teachers of STEM to have a shared vision for the integration of disciplinary content and language (Valdés, Kibler, and Walqui, 2014).

Pawan and Ortloff (2011) identified a set of factors that had the poten-

---

**BOX 6-5**
**Shared Professional Learning Experiences**

It is important that teacher preparation and ongoing professional development extend beyond strategies that are "just good teaching" for all students. Harper and de Jong (2009) made this point and highlighted the corresponding need for shared professional learning experiences for teachers of science, technology, engineering, and mathematics and for English as a second language (ESL) teachers.

Harper and de Jong studied cohorts of teachers who went through general preparation programs that included an ESL endorsement. They found that in these endorsement programs, the needed expertise was distilled down to basic concepts familiar to all teachers and applicable to all students, such as emphasizing the similarities between first and second language acquisition and the importance of valuing cultural diversity. This resulted in lists of good, general classroom teaching techniques, often referred to as "ESL strategies," such as using visuals to make concepts comprehensible and increasing wait time. They also found that unlike in the past, when ESL teachers and content teachers had clearly differentiated tasks, ESL and content teachers now share many of the same responsibilities, but that neither group of teachers is adequately prepared for this new reality. ESL teachers who work with ELs in content classrooms need new skills for assuming more collaborative and supporting roles, while teachers need new skills for integrating content and language instruction.

Harper and de Jong concluded that placement of ELs in classrooms has been based on the assumption that the needs of ELs are not significantly different from the needs of English-proficient students, and that this has resulted in the displacement of ESL specialist teachers and dependence on the instruction of minimally prepared content teachers who are prepared only with a generic toolkit of teaching strategies presumed to be effective for all students. As they describe it,

> ESL professional development for mainstream teachers must go beyond activities designed to increase comprehensible input and provide a welcoming environment. It must target more informed attitudes towards teaching linguistically and culturally diverse students, deeper understandings of second language and literacy development and of the language demands of content area texts and tasks, and more sophisticated approaches to integrating language and content instruction (p. 147).

As discussed elsewhere in this report, key components of this professional development should include high-quality field experiences that provide scaffolded practice identifying and building on English learners' (ELs') specific strengths and unique needs, as well as support for teachers at a more systemic level, such as through professional development for state, district, and school administrators to consider how policies and programs serve to include or exclude ELs. New teacher learning environments must be created that coordinate the knowledge and skills of both specialist ESL teachers and informed general educators.

SOURCE: Based on Harper and de Jong (2009).

tial to either sustain or hinder collaborations between ESL teachers and content teachers depending on how they were managed. Specific factors found to support collaborations included formally articulated procedures for collaboration, trust between teachers, and mutual respect for differentiated expertise. Specific barriers to collaboration included a lack of knowledge of the other partner's skills and abilities, a lack of coordination and communication structures in the school, and rigid, top-down decision making. Restructuring teacher education coursework to more specifically address collaboration between ESL and content teachers can lead to improvements in teachers' attitudes toward and practices for supporting ELs (DelliCarpini and Alonso, 2014; Dove and Honigsfeld, 2010).

However, as the number of ELs in STEM classrooms continues to increase, the number of trained ESL teachers becomes less and less sufficient to push in to all of the various STEM classes that would benefit from this support. Further, due to the selective pressures of accountability systems, most ESL teachers who work in content area classes tend to be assigned to language arts and mathematics classrooms, leaving science classrooms largely underserved. Although teacher educators are increasingly preparing general education teachers with some of the skills needed to work with ELs, this will not replace the need for more fully trained ESL teachers and the knowledge base that they possess (Liggett, 2010).

## Facilitation of Multilingual Instructional Approaches in STEM Classrooms

There is a need for teachers, most of whom are not bilingual, to learn how to make better use of their ELs' multilingual resources. While the historical focus of multilingualism in teacher education has been on compensating for the perceived deficits that students going to school in a second language face, Suárez-Orozco and Suárez-Orozco (2009) argued that this conversation can be reframed to highlight multilingual education as enrichment education for all. This framing positions ELs as having an asset of a broader range of linguistic resources that can be leveraged for making and communicating meaning when compared to monolingual students.

Translanguaging (the idea that multilingual individuals communicate and make meaning by drawing on their full repertoire of linguistic resources from all languages they speak) demonstrates that multiple languages and contexts cannot help but interact in complex ways; thus, learners benefit from encouragement to embrace the use of their full linguistic repertoires (see Chapters 3 and 4) in a free and dynamic way without restrictions (Otheguy, García, and Reid, 2015). This approach implies that teachers require training to work at the intersection of their students' diverse linguistic resources, necessitating a new focus in teacher education on supporting teachers in developing skills as language planners (Langman, 2014), and on ensuring that teachers do not limit opportunities in developing English and their home language.

In terms of teacher learning, there appears to be value in EL-specific university coursework that prepares teachers to support their students' usage of home language and other linguistic assets. For example, in a comparative study of strategies that general education teachers used to promote students' home language use, Karathanos (2010) found that teachers with at least three courses in EL-specific university preparation engaged in practices such as encouraging multilingual students to use all language resources with their classmates and seeking out multilingual materials for their students to a much greater extent than teachers without this preparation.

Although a growing body of research on instructional strategies and student learning highlights the value of translanguaging approaches to support and challenge ELs in their STEM learning, there has been little appetite in U.S. educational policy for embracing multilingual education or for prioritizing the recruitment and preparation of multilingual educators (Goldenberg and Wagner, 2015). Billings, Martin-Beltrán, and Hernández (2010) pointed out that teacher education programs have rarely stayed abreast of the newest ideas about how bilingualism and biliteracy develop or how teachers can be prepared to build upon the intellectual, linguistic, and cultural resources that bilingual learners possess. Similarly, Kibler and Roman (2013) found that while monolingual teachers did not typically hold negative views about their students' home languages, they also required substantial institutional support to move beyond simply accepting that students sometimes speak in their native languages in school to seeing student multilingualism as an academic asset. These teachers were not equipped to incorporate students' home language into their daily instruction. Emerging research in support of translanguaging approaches can lay the foundation for changes in how teachers of STEM come to think about the language resources that their ELs bring to the classroom.

## Engagement with Families

As described in Chapters 4 and 5, a persistent family-school connection is one of the strongest features to promote immigrant students' postsecondary education attendance and retention (Wimberly and Noeth, 2005). It has long been known that teachers play a central role in fostering a trusting collaboration with parents, and that teachers' attitudes, including those about race, ethnicity, language, and socioeconomic status, are critical factors (Hoover-Dempsey and Sandler, 1997). Research that focuses on teachers learning to work with diverse families continues to be rare (e.g., Symeou, Roussounidou, and Michaelides, 2012), and there are few programs designed to encourage preservice (e.g., McCollough and Ramirez, 2012) or in-service teachers (e.g., Bernier, Allexsaht-Snider, and Civil, 2003; Buxton, Allexsaht-Snider, and Rivera, 2012; Civil, 2016; Civil and Bernier, 2006; Civil, Bratton, and Quintos, 2005) to collaborate with the parents of immigrant students in their children's learning in STEM fields. Chapter 5 provides a deeper discussion of this critically important topic of how teachers and families can come together to support and challenge EL students.

## Use of Culturally Sustaining Pedagogies and Explicit Attention to Equity

Effective teachers of underrepresented students often share certain key characteristics, knowledge, and skills that allow them to be effective teachers for all children, regardless of their backgrounds (Grant and Gillette, 2006). One of these characteristics is the ability to use culturally sustaining pedagogies (Paris, 2012) to build on and recognize the value of the experiences and backgrounds that ELs and other underrepresented students bring to the classroom. For example, as described in the section on Facilitating Multilingual Instructional Approaches in STEM Classrooms, the use of translanguaging in the classroom enables students to draw on their full repertoire of linguistic resources. Teachers can be explicitly prepared to make use of such pedagogies.

Studies of "instructional congruence" by Lee and colleagues have long called for teachers of science to make meaningful connections to students' linguistic and cultural experiences and indicate that such congruence has a positive effect on student performance (e.g., Lee and Fradd, 1998; Lee et al., 2005). Similarly, in mathematics, Díez-Palomar, Simic, and Varley (2007) argued that "it is an important aspect of incorporating students' funds of knowledge into a culturally relevant mathematics curriculum for teachers to learn more about their students' lives and experiences" (pp. 28–29). Several projects supporting teachers in learning to build on ELs' funds of knowledge show that these approaches lead to engagement of children in problem-solving that is both meaningful and mathematically rigorous (Civil, 2007; Civil and Andrade, 2002; Turner and Bustillos, 2017).

Students' interests and passions, which can often be traced to cultural or community-based practices, can be leveraged to build student interest in STEM content while providing examples to teachers of what culturally sustaining pedagogies can look like. For example, Vazquez Dominguez, Allexsaht-Snider, and Buxton (2017) designed and taught a series of soccer and science investigations to promote interest and engagement in physical science learning for middle school ELs. They found that soccer, which was a passion for many of the middle school ELs they worked with, could be used to integrate ELs' cultural practices and passions with physical science content standards that students needed to learn in their science classroom, such as Newton's laws of motion and energy transformations. After being developed and tested with a middle school soccer team, these lessons were then integrated into teacher professional learning workshops as exemplars of culturally sustaining pedagogy (Buxton et al., 2016a,b).

As with curriculum, teachers can also learn to make their classroom assessments more culturally relevant in ways that can support ELs' academic success. For example, Siegel (2014) taught a group of preservice teachers to develop and test more equitable classroom assessments. Siegel found that this group of preservice teachers changed their understanding of equitable assessments from a simple view of equity as "fairness" to more sophisticated views of equity as actively providing the supports needed to motivate and challenge all students to share what they know, such as through the use of culturally relevant examples. These teachers' understanding of equitable assessments increased, but their actual assessment plans in their subsequent units often failed to demonstrate these new ideas about equity and cultural relevance. The work highlights the need to place more emphasis on developing critical understanding of equitable and culturally sustaining practices in teacher education to meet the needs of diverse learners.

As we have noted throughout this report, many teachers of STEM to ELs have only limited experiences of learning in a context where they are a linguistic or cultural minority. Without such experiences, it can be difficult to understand the importance of culturally sustaining pedagogies. Indeed, for teachers who have always been in the linguistic and cultural majority group, their own educational experiences have, in fact, been culturally and linguistically sustaining, but without ever making those practices explicit; rather, they just seem "normal." Thus, more research is needed on how teachers from culturally and linguistically dominant groups can learn to see how their own education was culturally and linguistically congruent.

### Targeted Teacher Learning around Common Societal Biases and Beliefs

As de Araujo, Smith, and Sakow (2016) made clear, the dominant narrative regarding ELs in STEM continues to be that ELs require support rather than challenge. Although seemingly a small difference, this taken-for-granted view has substantial consequences for the nature of the STEM learning experiences that ELs are likely to receive. For example, when teachers attempt to accommodate ELs, they may select tasks that are repetitive, procedurally focused, and devoid of context, based on their beliefs about the limitations of ELs' mathematical and linguistic abilities (de Araujo, 2017). These findings suggest a need to help teachers to critically examine the potential impact of their seemingly benign beliefs about ELs.

A small body of research examines practicing teachers' knowledge and beliefs about the need for professional development opportunities focused on working effectively with ELs in STEM (Cho and McDonnough, 2009; Gandára, Maxwell-Jolly, and Driscoll, 2005; Reeves, 2006). When taken together, these studies suggest that the majority of teachers of STEM believe that they would benefit from additional training on how to work more effectively with ELs in their classrooms. Gandára, Maxwell-Jolly, and Driscoll (2005), for example, surveyed 5,300 practicing K–12 teachers in California and found that professional development made a difference in how confident these teachers felt in their ability to meeting the challenges of teaching ELs. This was particularly true of teachers who received this in-service training through programs offered by a college or university, rather than by their school district. Elementary teachers identified ELD professional development as most useful, whereas secondary teachers identified professional development on cultural issues and strategies for teaching academic subjects as their greatest needs. Both groups thought that professional development on linguistics was too theoretical and the least useful, and they wanted more time to observe and collaborate with their colleagues as a central part of professional development. Many of the teachers surveyed claimed that over the past 5 years, they had participated in little or no professional EL training and that the quality of the training they had received was poor.

Few if any studies have explicitly examined the knowledge and beliefs of teachers of STEM subjects about their need to learn about ELs as part of their initial teacher education program. However, several studies about preservice and practicing teachers have compared teachers' knowledge and beliefs based on the type of bilingual or EL certification they are pursuing or have received as part of their teacher preparation (Gandára, Maxwell-Jolly, and Driscoll, 2005; Karathanos, 2010; Lee and Oxelson, 2006; Rios-Aguilar et al., 2012; Tolbert and Knox, 2016). These studies find that training in bilingual, ESL, or EL instruction has a positive impact on teachers' knowledge and beliefs about teaching ELs. Although it seems that teachers with any professional development focused on teaching ELs feel better able to teach ELs than teachers with no such training, more research is needed to understand the impact of these differences, particularly in the STEM disciplines.

## PREPARATION OF TEACHER EDUCATORS

In this section, we describe research that is specific to the work and preparation of the teacher educators who are preparing and supporting teachers who work with ELs. While research on teaching and teacher education are massive fields of inquiry, research on teacher educators, those who engage in the work of preparing teachers, is significantly less robust but growing (Levine, Howard, and Moss, 2014[2]). There are a number of important questions that are not fully answered about the work of teacher educators, such as: (1) how the skills of an effective teacher educator differ from the skills of an effective teacher; (2) where and how teacher educators develop those skills; and (3) whether today's teacher educators possess the skills and experiences needed to successfully prepare the next generation of teachers. This last question is particularly relevant to the topic of supporting ELs since many of today's teacher educators had their own K–12 classroom teaching experiences during a time when both the student demographics and the policy context of U.S. schools were quite different, and ELs were rarely present in mainstream STEM courses.

### Teacher Educators Need Their Own Professional Development

Teacher preparation programs that successfully prepare teachers who are effective with ELs and other minoritized students integrate issues of cultural and linguistic diversity throughout their courses and field experiences, rather than relegating these topics to a stand-alone course. Further, effective programs ensure that all methods faculty, field supervisors, and cooperating teachers are active participants in this integration process, rather than making issues of diversity and equity the responsibility of a few "equity oriented" faculty members (American Association for Colleges of Teacher Education, 2002). For a fully integrated approach to culturally and linguistically responsive teaching to function, all teacher educators need to regularly model best practices with respect to instructional strategies for working with diverse student populations, including ELs (see Chval, Pinnow, and Thomas, 2015; Estapa, Pinnow, and Chval, 2016). This, in turn, means that both newer and more experienced teacher educators need to engage in their own ongoing professional development and need continued access to appropriate resources and supports (O'Hara and Pritchard, 2008).

In the same way that general education teachers and ESL teachers benefit from coming together to plan for ways to meet the needs of EL students in their classes, teacher educators who teach general education and methods courses and those who teach TESOL courses can similarly benefit from coming together to co-plan and co-facilitate course work with teacher candidates (McCrary, Sennette, and Brown, 2011). Baecher and Jewkes (2014) found that bringing these two groups of teacher educators together resulted in increased understanding in both groups about how they could support each other's goals to enhance both general education

---

[2] The work by Levine and colleagues describes project PREPARE-ELLs (Preparing Responsive Educators Who Promote Access and Realize Excellence with English Language Learners).

and TESOL teacher candidates' beliefs and understandings of EL pedagogy during content area learning.

Some teacher education programs have developed faculty institutes to support teacher educators in better helping candidates prepare to work with ELs. Costa and colleagues (2005) described one such institute in which teacher education faculty, doctoral students, and teachers and paraprofessionals from local schools came together for a series of structured experiences and discussions. Costa found that this institute served as a catalyst for change, especially for the teacher educators, and led to greater efforts to infuse the general teacher education curriculum with explicit support for ELs (see also Nguyen et al., 2013). Similarly, Buxton and colleagues (2016b) examined the role of teacher educator participation in a teaching-focused research project that involved both veteran and novice teacher educators. They identified a set of principles for supporting teacher educators: (1) scaffolding co-design work involving teacher educators, teachers, and EL families in which the teacher educators make themselves vulnerable to the teachers' and families' expertise; and (2) giving novice teacher educators supported leadership opportunities to develop resources and models for working with and learning from teachers of ELs.

There are few studies of teacher preparation for "linguistic diversity" that systematically measure outcomes for teachers and fewer still that measure student outcomes. Most are descriptive in nature (Bunch, 2013; Lucas and Grinberg, 2008). This is a limitation for the preparation and professional learning of teacher educators, as not enough is known about program effectiveness in preparing teachers to support ELs in STEM learning to be useful in the professional learning of teacher educators.

## Teacher Educators Benefit from Collaboration

Teacher educators can gain new insights about effective ways to prepare teachers for working with ELs by more systematically observing and describing the professional development processes of the effective teachers with whom they work. Hutchinson and Hadjioannou (2011) described what they learned as teacher educators, as the teacher candidates they taught learned what they were and were not capable of doing in the classroom. Together the teachers and teacher educators learned that their peers struggled with similar issues and that they could use this camaraderie to construct a support network that they could continue to rely upon. The teachers and teacher educators all came to see more clearly how a multicultural and multilingual classroom environment could be an asset to supporting innovative teaching and learning.

Teacher educators' efforts to support preservice teachers learning to teach ELs can face multiple obstacles to success, with one of these being a lack of cohesion and collaboration within teacher preparation programs. Daniel and Peercy (2014) described an effort that met with only limited success. They found that while the teacher educators in the program they studied felt a responsibility to prepare their teacher candidates to effectively educate ELs, the teacher educators did not work collectively or cohesively toward this goal, in part due to a lack of leadership or a clearly articulated vision for their work together. Thus, a better understanding of how to build leadership and shared vision for supporting ELs within a teacher preparation program seems to be one necessary step for understanding how to support effective teacher educator professional learning.

## SUMMARY

The summary of research presented in this chapter highlights practices for preparing teachers to address the increased language and literacy demands embedded in the new generation of standards, curriculum, and assessments, while building on the assets and resources that ELs bring to STEM classrooms. Despite the persistence of deficit views of ELs in STEM subjects, a number of powerful professional learning models exist to debunk deficit perspectives and to prepare teachers at all levels to challenge and support students from linguistically and culturally diverse backgrounds to thrive in grade-appropriate STEM content classrooms. Many of these models have been described in this chapter, and many new models are currently being developed and studied. While the research base on the effectiveness of these models, especially regarding the relationships between teacher learning and student achievement, is still emergent, there are clearly a number of promising practices that have been summarized here. Many of these practices rely on a critical social justice orientation to teacher education that acknowledges the roles that power and privilege play when it comes to equitable STEM learning opportunities for ELs. Three decades ago, Giroux (1988) called for teacher education programs that were designed for both "empowering teachers and teaching for empowerment" (p. 158).

Although stronger and more targeted initial teacher education programs will be part of any solution to better meeting the needs of ELs in STEM, initial preparation will always be insufficient for teachers to overcome these challenges. Thus, there will continue to be great need for systemic efforts to work with practicing educators, local and central administrators, academics, lawmakers, local communities, families, and EL students themselves to create systems-level approaches to ensure that teachers have the training, support, and resources they need to help ELs succeed and thrive in STEM learning.

# REFERENCES

Adair, J.K. (2014). Examining whiteness as an obstacle to positively approaching immigrant families in U.S. early childhood educational settings. *Race Ethnicity and Education, 17*(5), 643–666. doi:10.1080/13613324.2012.759925.

Adamson, K., Santau, A., and Lee, O. (2013). The impact of professional development on elementary teachers' strategies for teaching science with diverse student groups in urban elementary schools. *Journal of Science Teacher Education, 24*(3), 553–571.

Ajayi, L. (2011). Exploring how ESL teachers relate their ethnic and social backgrounds to practice. *Race Ethnicity and Education, 14*(2), 253–275.

American Association for Colleges of Teacher Education. (2002). *Educators' Preparation for Cultural and Linguistic Diversity: A Call to Action.* Washington, DC: American Association for Colleges of Teacher Education Committee on Multicultural Education.

Anhalt, C.O., Ondrus, M., and Horak, V. (2007). Issues of language: Teacher insights from mathematics lessons in Chinese. *Mathematics Teaching in the Middle School, 13*(1), 18–23.

Athanases, S.Z., and Martin, K.L. (2006). Learning to advocate for educational equity in a teacher credential program. *Teaching and Teacher Education, 22*(6), 627–646.

Baecher, L., and Jewkes, A.M. (2014). TESOL and early childhood collaborative inquiry: Joining forces and crossing boundaries. *Journal of Early Childhood Teacher Education, 35*(1), 39–53.

Baecher, L., Artigliere, M., and Bruno, T. (2017). Leveraging the demands of edTPA to foster language instruction for English learners in content classrooms. *Journal of Educational Research and Practice, 7*(1), 111–124.

Ball, D.L. (1990). Breaking with experience in learning to teach mathematics: The role of a prospective methods course. *For the Learning of Mathematics, 10*(2), 10–16.

Ball, D.L., and Cohen, D.K. (1999). Developing practice, developing practitioners: Toward a practice-based theory of professional education. In G. Sykes and L. Darling-Hammond (Eds.), *Teaching as the Learning Profession: Handbook of Policy and Practice* (pp. 3–22). San Francisco, CA: Jossey Bass.

Ball, S.J. (2009). Privatising education, privatising education policy, privatising educational research: Network governance and the "competition state." *Journal of Education Policy, 24*(1), 83–99.

Ballantyne, K.G., Sanderman, A.R., and Levy, J. (2008). *Educating English Language Learners: Building Teacher Capacity. Roundtable Report.* Washington, DC: National Clearinghouse for English Language Acquisition. Available: https://files.eric.ed.gov/fulltext/ED521360.pdf [June 2018].

Banilower, E.R., Smith, P.S., Weiss, I.R., Malzahn, K.A., Campbell, K.M., and Weis, A.M. (2013). *Report of the 2012 National Survey of Science and Mathematics Education.* Available: http://www.horizon-research.com/2012nssme/wp-content/uploads/2013/02/2012-NSSME-Full-Report1.pdf [September 2018].

Bartolomé, L.I. (2004). Critical pedagogy and teacher education: Radicalizing prospective teachers. *Teacher Education Quarterly, 31*(1), 97–122.

Bartolomé, L.I. (2010). Preparing to teach newcomer students: The significance of critical pedagogy and the study of ideology in teacher education. *Yearbook of the National Society for the Study of Education, 109*(2), 505–526.

Bernier, E., Allexsaht-Snider, M., and Civil, M. (2003). *Teachers, Parents, and Mathematics: Exploring Contexts for Collaboration and Partnership.* Paper presented at Annual Meeting of American Educational Research Association, Chicago, IL. Available: http://mathandparents.math.arizona.edu/papers/AERA_2003_Teachers.pdf [June 2018].

Bianchini, J. (2018). *Teachers' Knowledge and Beliefs about English Learners and Their Impact on STEM Learning.* Paper commissioned for the Committee on Supporting English Learners in STEM Subjects. Board on Science Education and Board on Children, Youth, and Families, Division of Behavioral and Social Sciences and Education. Available: http://www.nas.edu/ELinSTEM [October 2018].

Billings, E.S., Martin-Beltrán, M., and Hernández, A. (2010). Beyond English development: Bilingual approaches to teaching immigrant students and English language learners. *Yearbook of the National Society for the Study of Education, 109*(2), 384–413.

Boero, P., Douek, N., and Ferrari, P.L. (2008). Developing mastery of natural language. *Handbook of International Research in Mathematics Education, 12,* 262–295. Available: http://citeseerx.ist.psu.edu/viewdoc/download?doi=10.1.1.457.4399&rep=rep1&type=pdf [June 2018].

Bollin, G.G. (2007). Preparing teachers for Hispanic immigrant children: A service learning approach. *Journal of Latinos and Education, 6*(2), 177–189.

Borko, H. (2004). Professional development and teacher learning: Mapping the terrain. *Educational Researcher, 33*(8), 3–15.

Bowers, E., Fitts, S., Quirk, M., and Jung, W. (2010). Effective strategies for developing academic English: Professional development and teacher practices. *Bilingual Research Journal, 33*(1), 95–110.

Boyd, D., Grossman, P., Lankford, H., Loeb, S., and Wyckoff, J. (2009). *Teacher Preparation and Student Achievement.* Available: https://files.eric.ed.gov/fulltext/ED509670.pdf [September 2018].

Brown, B.A., and Ryoo, K. (2008). Teaching science as a language: A "content-first" approach to science teaching. *Journal of Research in Science Teaching, 45*(5), 529–553.

Brown, B., Ryoo, K., and Rodriguez, J. (2010). Pathway towards fluency: Using "disaggregate instruction" to promote science literacy. *International Journal of Science Education, 32*(11), 1465–1493.

Bunch, G.C. (2013). Pedagogical language knowledge: Preparing mainstream teachers of English learners in the New Standards Era. *Review of Research in Education, 37*(1), 298–341. doi:10.3102/0091732X12461772.

Bunch, G.C., Aguirre, J.M., and Tellez, K. (2009). Beyond the scores: Using candidate responses on high stakes performance assessment to inform teacher preparation for English learners. *Issues in Teacher Education, 18*(1), 103–128.

Bunch, G.C., Aguirre, J.M., and Tellez, K. (2015). Integrating a focus on academic language, English learners, and mathematics: Teacher candidates' responses on the performance assessment for California teachers (PACT). *The New Educator, 11*(1), 79–103.

Buxton, C.A., and Lee, O. (2014). English language learners in science education. In N.G. Lederman and S.K. Abell (Eds.), *Handbook of Research in Science Education* (2nd ed.) (pp. 204–222). Mahwah, NJ: Lawrence Erlbaum Associates.

Buxton, C.A., Allexsaht-Snider, M., and Rivera, C. (2012). Science, language and families: Constructing a model of language-rich science inquiry. In J. Bianchini, V. Atkerson, A. Calebrese Barton, O. Lee, and A. Rodriguez (Eds.). *Moving the Equity Agenda Forward: Equity Research, Practice and Policy in Science Education* (pp. 241–259). New York: Springer.

Buxton, C.A., Kayumova, S., and Allexsaht-Snider, M. (2013). Teacher, researcher and accountability discourses shaping democratic practices for science teaching in middle schools. *Democracy & Education, 21*(2), article 2. Available: http://democracyeducationjournal.org/home/vol21/iss2/2 [June 2018].

Buxton, C.A., Allexsaht-Snider, M., Suriel, R., Kayumova, S., and Choi, Y. (2013). Using educative assessments to support science teaching for middle school English language learners. *Journal of Science Teacher Education, 24*(2), 347–366.

Buxton, C.A., Allexsaht-Snider, M., Kayumova, S., Aghasaleh, R., Choi, Y., and Cohen, A. (2015). Teacher agency and professional learning: Rethinking fidelity of implementation as multiplicities of enactment. *Journal of Research in Science Teaching, 52*(4), 489–502.

Buxton, C.A., Allexsaht-Snider, M., Hernandez, Y., Aghasaleh, R., Cardozo-Gaibisso, L., and Kirmaci, M. (2016a). A design-based model of science teacher professional learning in the LISELL-B project. In A. Oliveira and M. Weinburgh (Eds.), *Science Teacher Preparation in Content-Based Second Language Acquisition* (pp. 179–196). New York: Springer.

Buxton, C.A., Allexsaht-Snider, M., Suriel, R., Kayumova, S., Karsli, E., and Aghasaleh, R. (2016b). Reassembling science teacher educator professional learning in the LISELL-B project. In C.A. Buxton and M. Allexsaht-Snider (Eds.), *Supporting K–12 English Language Learners in Science: Putting Research into Teaching Practice* (pp. 69–92). New York: Routledge.

Bybee, R.W., Taylor, J.A., Gardner, A., Van Scotter, P., Powell, J.C., Westbrook, A., and Landes, N. (2006). *The BSCS 5E Instructional Model: Origins, Effectiveness, and Applications.* Colorado Springs: BSCS.

Cardozo-Gaibisso, L., Allexsaht-Snider M., and Buxton C.A. (2017). Curriculum in motion for English language learners in science: Teachers supporting newcomer unaccompanied youth. In L. de Oliveira and K. Campbell Wilcox (Eds.), *Teaching Science to English Language Learners: Preparing Pre-Service and In-Service Teachers* (pp. 7–29). London, UK: Palgrave Macmillan, Cham.

Celedón-Pattichis, S. (2018). *Mathematics Education and Young Dual Language Learners.* Paper commissioned for the Committee on Supporting English Learners in STEM Subjects. Board on Science Education and Board on Children, Youth, and Families, Division of Behavioral and Social Sciences and Education. Available: http://www.nas.edu/ELinSTEM [October 2018].

Chien, C.W. (2013). Analysis of an instructional coach's role as elementary school language teachers' professional developer. *Current Issues in Education, 16*(1), 1–12. Available: https://cie.asu.edu/ojs/index.php/cieatasu/article/download/1004/435 [June 2018].

Cho, S., and McDonnough, J. (2009). Meeting the needs of high school science teachers in English language learner instruction. *Journal of Science Teacher Education, 20*(4), 385–402.

Chval, K.B. (2004). Making the complexities of teaching visible for prospective teachers. *Teaching Children Mathematics, 11*(2), 91–96.

Chval, K.B., and Pinnow, R. (2010). Preservice teachers' assumptions about Latino/a English language learners. *Journal of Teaching for Excellence and Equity in Mathematics, 2*(1), 6–12.

Chval, K.B., Pinnow, R.J., and Thomas, A. (2015). Learning how to focus on language while teaching mathematics to English language learners: A case study of Courtney. *Mathematics Education Research Journal, 27*(1), 103–127. doi:10.1007/s13394-013-0101-8.

Chval, K., Abell, S., Pareja, E., Musikul, K., and Ritzka, G. (2008). Science and mathematics teachers' experiences, needs, and expectations regarding professional development. *Eurasia Journal of Mathematics, Science & Technology Education, 4*(1), 31–43.

Chval, K.B., Pinnow, R.J., Smith, E., and Rojas Perez, O. (2018). Promoting equity, access, and success through productive student partnerships. In S. Crespo, S. Celedon-Pattichis, and M. Civil (Eds.), *Access and Equity: Promoting High Quality Mathematics in Grades 3–5.* Reston, VA: National Council of Teachers of Mathematics.

Civil, M. (2007). Building on community knowledge: An avenue to equity in mathematics education. In N. Nasir and P. Cobb (Eds.), *Improving Access to Mathematics: Diversity and Equity in the Classroom* (pp. 105–117). New York: Teachers College Press.

Civil, M. (2014). Why should mathematics educators learn from and about Latina/o students' in-school and out-of-school experiences? *Journal of Urban Mathematics Education, 7*(2), 9–20. Available: http://citeseerx.ist.psu.edu/viewdoc/download?doi=10.1.1.869.9329& rep=rep1&type=pdf [June 2018].

Civil, M. (2016). STEM learning research through a funds of knowledge lens. *Cultural Studies of Science Education, 11*(1), 41–59. doi:10.1007/s11422-014-9648-2.

Civil, M., and Andrade, R. (2002). Transitions between home and school mathematics: Rays of hope amidst the passing clouds. In G. de Abreu, A.J. Bishop, and N.C. Presmeg (Eds.), *Transitions between Contexts of Mathematical Practices* (pp. 149–169). Boston, MA: Kluwer.

Civil, M., and Bernier, E. (2006). Exploring images of parental participation in mathematics education: Challenges and possibilities. *Mathematical Thinking and Learning, 8*(3), 309–330.

Civil, M., Bratton, J., and Quintos, B. (2005). Parents and mathematics education in a Latino community: Redefining parental participation. *Multicultural Education, 13*(2), 60–64.

Cochran-Smith, M., Ell, F., Grudnoff, L., Haigh, M., Hill, M., and Ludlow, L. (2016). Initial teacher education: What does it take to put equity at the center?. *Teaching and Teacher Education, 57*, 67–78. doi:10.1016/j.tate.2016.03.006.

Costa, J., McPhail, G., Smith, J., and Brisk, M.E. (2005). Faculty first: The challenge of infusing the teacher education curriculum with scholarship on English language learners. *Journal of Teacher Education, 56*(2), 104–118.

Daniel, S., and Peercy, M. (2014). Expanding roles: Teacher educators' perspectives on educating English learners. *Action in Teacher Education, 36*(2), 100–116.

Darling-Hammond, L. (2006). Constructing 21st-century teacher education. *Journal of Teacher Education, 57*(3), 300–314.

de Araujo, Z. (2017). Connections between secondary mathematics teachers' beliefs and their selection of tasks for English language learners. *Curriculum Inquiry, 47*(4), 363–389. doi:10.1080/03626784.2017.1368351.

de Araujo, Z., Smith, E., and Sakow, M. (2016). Reflecting on the dialogue regarding the mathematics education of English learners. *Journal of Urban Mathematics Education, 9*(2), 33–48.

de Oliveira, L.C. (2011). In their shoes: Teachers experience the needs of English language learners through a math simulation. *Multicultural Education, 19*(1), 59–62.

de Oliveira, L.C., and Lan, S-W (2014). Writing science in an upper elementary classroom: A genre-based approach to teaching English language learners. *Journal of Second Language Writing, 25*(1), 23–39.

de Oliveira, L.C., and Wilcox, K.C. (Eds.) (2017). *Teaching Science to English Language Learners: Preparing Pre-Service and In-Service Teachers.* London, UK: Palgrave Macmillan, Cham.

DelliCarpini, M.E., and Alonso, O.B. (2014). Teacher education that works: Preparing secondary-level math and science teachers for success with English language learners through content-based instruction. *Global Education Review, 1*(4), 155–178.

Díez-Palomar, J., Simic, K., and Varley, M. (2007). "Math is everywhere": Connecting mathematics to students' lives. *Journal of Mathematics and Culture, 1*(2), 20–36.

Dove, M., and Honigsfeld, A. (2010). ESL coteaching and collaboration: Opportunities to develop teacher leadership and enhance student learning. *TESOL Journal, 1*(1), 3–22.

Dutton Tillery, A., Varjas, K., Meyers, J., and Collins, A.S. (2010). General education teachers' perceptions of behavior management and intervention strategies. *Journal of Positive Behavior Interventions, 12*(2), 86–102.

Eberly, J.L., Joshi, A., and Konzal, J. (2007). Communicating with families across cultures: An investigation of teacher perceptions and practices. *School Community Journal, 17(2)*, 7–26.

Eisenhart, M., Behm, L., and Romagnano, L. (1991). Learning to teach: Developing expertise or rite of passage? *Journal of Education for Teaching, 17(1)*, 51–71.

Estapa, A., Pinnow, R.J., and Chval, K.B. (2016). Video as a professional development tool to support novice teachers as they learn to teach English language learners. *The New Educator, 12(1)*, 85–104.

Fang, Z. (2005). Scientific literacy: A systemic functional linguistics perspective. *Science Education, 89(2)*, 335–347.

Fang, Z., Lamme, L., and Pringle, R. (2010). *Language and Literacy in Inquiry-Based Science Classrooms, Grades 3-8*. Thousand Oaks, CA: Corwin Press and Arlington, VA: National Science Teachers Association.

Feiman-Nemser, S. (2001). From preparation to practice: Designing a continuum to strengthen and sustain teaching. *Teachers College Record, 103(6)*, 1013–1055.

Fullan, M.G., and Miles, M.B. (1992). Getting reform right: What works and what doesn't. *Phi Delta Kappan, 73(10)*, 745–752.

Galguera, T. (2011). Participant structures as professional learning tasks and the development of pedagogical language knowledge among preservice teachers. *Teacher Education Quarterly, 38*, 85–106.

Gándara, P., Maxwell-Jolly, J., and Driscoll, A. (2005). *Listening to Teachers of English Language Learners: A Survey of California Teachers' Challenges, Experiences, and Professional Development Needs*. Berkeley, CA: Policy Analysis for California Education.

García, E., Arias, M.B., Harris Murri, N.J., and Serna, C. (2010). Developing responsive teachers: A challenge for a demographic reality. *Journal of Teacher Education, 61(1-2)*, 132–142.

Gebhard, M., Demers, J., and Castillo-Rosenthal, Z. (2008). Teachers as critical text analysts: L2 literacies and teachers' work in the context of high-stakes school reform. *Journal of Second Language Writing, 17(4)*, 274–291.

Giroux, H. (1988) *Teachers as Intellectuals: Toward a Critical Pedagogy of Learning*. Granby, MA: Bergin & Garvey.

Goldenberg, C., and Wagner, K. (2015). Bilingual education: Reviving an American tradition. *American Educator, 39(3)*, 28–32.

Gonzalez, J.E., and Darling-Hammond, L. (2000). *Programs That Prepare Teachers to Work Effectively with Students Learning English* (ED447724). Washington, DC: ERIC Clearinghouse on Languages and Linguistics. Available: https://files.eric.ed.gov/fulltext/ED447724.pdf [June 2018].

Grant, C.A., and Gillette, M. (2006). A candid talk to teacher educators about effectively preparing teachers who can teach everyone's children. *Journal of Teacher Education, 57(3)*, 292–299.

Gross, L.A., Fitts, S., Goodson-Espy, T., and Clark, A.M. (2010). Self as teacher: Preliminary role identification of the potential teaching candidate. *Australian Journal of Teacher Education (Online), 35(2)*. doi:10.14221/ajte.2010v35n2.1.

Gutiérrez, R. (2002). Beyond essentialism: The complexity of language in teaching mathematics to Latina/o students. *American Educational Research Journal, 39(4)*, 1047–1088.

Hansen-Thomas, H. (2009). Reform-oriented mathematics in three 6th grade classes: How teachers draw in ELLs to academic discourse. *Journal of Language, Identity & Education, 8(2–3)*, 88–106. doi:10.1080/15348450902848411.

Harper, C.A., and de Jong, E. (2009). English language teacher expertise: The elephant in the room. *Language and Education, 23(2)*, 137–151.

Harper, C.A., Platt, E.J., Naranjo, C.J., and Boynton, S.S. (2007). Marching in unison: Florida ESL teachers and No Child Left Behind. *TESOL Quarterly, 41*(3), 642–651.

Honigsfeld, A., and Dove, M. (2010). *Collaboration and Co-teaching: Strategies for English Learners.* Thousand Oaks, CA: Corwin Press.

Hoover-Dempsey, K.V., and Sandler, H.M. (1997). Why do parents become involved in their children's education? *Review of Educational Research, 67*(1), 3–42.

Hutchinson, M., and Hadjioannou, X. (2011). Better serving the needs of limited English proficient (LEP) students in the mainstream classroom: Examining the impact of an inquiry-based hybrid professional development program. *Teachers and Teaching, 17*(1), 91–113.

Karathanos, K.A. (2010). Teaching English language learner students in U.S. mainstream schools: Intersections of language, pedagogy, and power. *International Journal of Inclusive Education, 14*(1), 49–65.

Khisty, L.L. (1993). A naturalistic look at language factors in mathematics teaching in bilingual classrooms. In *Proceedings of the Third National Symposium on Limited English Proficient Student Issues: Focus on Middle and High School Students.* Available: https://ncela.ed.gov/files/rcd/be019310/a_naturalistic_look.pdf [June 2018].

Khisty, L.L., and Chval, K.B. (2002). Pedagogic discourse and equity in mathematics: When teachers' talk matters. *Mathematics Education Research Journal, 14*(3), 154–168.

Khong, T.D.H., and Saito, E. (2014). Challenges confronting teachers of English language learners. *Educational Review, 66*(2), 210–225.

Kibler, A.K., and Roman, D. (2013). Insights into professional development for teachers of English language learners: A focus on using students' native languages in the classroom. *Bilingual Research Journal, 36*(2), 187–207.

Kleyn, T., López, D., and Makar, C. (2015). "What about bilingualism?" A critical reflection on the edTPA with teachers of emergent bilinguals. *Bilingual Research Journal, 38*(1), 88–106.

Krashen, S.D. (2011). *Free Voluntary Reading.* Santa Barbara, CA: ABC-CLIO. Available: https://www.slideshare.net/JerrySmith34/stephen-krashen-free-voluntary-reading-2011 [June 2018].

Langman, J. (2014). Translanguaging, identity, and learning: Science teachers as engaged language planners. *Language Policy, 13*(2), 183–200.

Lara-Alecio, R., Tong, F., Irby, B.J., Guerrero, C., Huerta, M., and Fan, Y. (2012). The effect of an instructional intervention on middle school English learners' science and English reading achievement. *Journal of Research in Science Teaching, 49*(8), 987–1011.

Ledwell, K., and Oyler, C. (2016). Unstandardized responses to a "standardized" test: The edTPA as gatekeeper and curriculum change agent. *Journal of Teacher Education, 67*(2), 120–134.

Lee, J.S., and Oxelson, E. (2006). "It's not my job": K–12 teacher attitudes toward students' heritage language maintenance. *Bilingual Research Journal, 30*(2), 453–477.

Lee, O., and Fradd, S.H. (1998). Science for all, including students from non-English-language backgrounds. *Educational Researcher, 27*(4), 12–21.

Lee, O., Deaktor, R.A., Hart, J.E., Cuevas, P., and Enders, C. (2005). An instructional intervention's impact on the science and literacy achievement of culturally and linguistically diverse elementary students. *Journal of Research in Science Teaching, 42*(8), 857–887.

Lee, O., Lewis, S., Adamson, K., Maerten-Rivera, J., and Secada, W.G. (2008). Urban elementary school teachers' knowledge and practices in teaching science to English language learners. *Science Education, 92*(4), 733–758.

Lee, O., Maerten-Rivera, J., Buxton, C., Penfield, R., and Secada, W.G. (2009). Urban elementary teachers' perspectives on teaching science to English language learners. *Journal of Science Teacher Education, 20*(3), 263–286.

Levine, T., Howard, E., Moss, D. (Eds.) (2014). *Preparing Classroom Teachers to Succeed with Second Language Learners: Lessons from a Faculty Learning Community.* New York: Routledge.

Li, L.F. (2007). Teacher dispositions: Finding a way to identify with struggling language learners. *Journal for the Liberal Arts and Sciences, 11*(3), 39–41. Available: https://eric.ed.gov/?id=ED507908 [June 2018].

Liggett, T. (2010). "A little bit marginalized": The structural marginalization of English language teachers in urban and rural public schools. *Teaching Education, 21*(3), 217–232.

Lim, C.I., Maxwell, K.L., Able-Boone, H., and Zimmer, C.R. (2009). Cultural and linguistic diversity in early childhood teacher preparation: The impact of contextual characteristics on coursework and practica. *Early Childhood Research Quarterly, 24*(1), 64–76.

Loucks-Horsley, S., Love, N., Stiles, K., Mundry, S., and Hewson, P. (2003). *Designing Professional Development for Teachers of Science and Mathematics.* Thousand Oaks, CA: Corwin Press.

Lucas, T., and Grinberg, J. (2008). Responding to the linguistic reality of mainstream classrooms. In S. Feiman-Nemser, M. Cochran-Smith, D.J. McIntyre, and K.E. Demers, (Eds.), *Handbook of Research on Teacher Education: Enduring Questions in Changing Contexts* (3rd ed.) (pp. 606–636). New York: Routledge.

Lucas, T., and Villegas, A.M. (2013). Preparing linguistically responsive teachers: Laying the foundation in preservice teacher education. *Theory Into Practice, 52*(2), 98–109.

Lucas, T., Villegas, A.M., and Freedson-Gonzalez, M. (2008). Linguistically responsive teacher education: Preparing classroom teachers to teach English language learners. *Journal of Teacher Education, 59*(4), 363–373.

Manzo, R.D., Cruz, L., Faltis, C., and de la Torre, A. (2012). Professional development of secondary science teachers of English learners in immigrant communities. *Association of Mexican American Educators Journal, 5*(1), 41–48.

Martin-Beltran, M., and Peercy, M. (2014). Collaboration to teach English language learners: Opportunities for shared teacher learning. *Teachers and Teaching, 20*(6), 721–737.

Master, B., Loeb, S., Whitney, C., and Wyckoff, J. (2016). Different skills? Identifying differentially effective teachers of English language learners. *The Elementary School Journal, 117*(2), 261–284.

McCollough, C., and Ramirez, O. (2012). Cultivating culture: Preparing future teachers for diversity through family science learning events. *School Science and Mathematics, 112*(7), 443–451. doi:10.1111/j.1949-8594.2012.00158.x.

McCrary, D.E., Sennette, J., and Brown, D.L. (2011). Preparing early childhood teachers for English language learners. *Journal of Early Childhood Teacher Education, 32*(2), 107–117.

McDonald, M., Tyson, K., Brayko, K., Bowman, M., Delport, J., and Shimomura, F. (2011). Innovation and impact in teacher education: Community-based organizations as field placements for preservice teachers. *Teachers College Record, 113*(8), 1668–1700.

Molle, D. (2013). Facilitating professional development for teachers of English language learners. *Teaching and Teacher Education, 29*(1), 197–207.

Moschkovich, J.N. (2002). A situated and sociocultural perspective on bilingual mathematics learners. *Mathematical Thinking and Learning, 4*(2–3), 189–212.

National Research Council. (2012). *A Framework for K–12 Science Education: Practices, Crosscutting Concepts, and Core Ideas.* Washington, DC: The National Academies Press.

National Staff Development Council. (2001). *NSDC's Standards for Staff Development.* Oxford, OH: Author.

Nero, S. (2009). Inhabiting the other's world: Language and cultural immersion for U.S.-based teachers in the Dominican Republic. *Language, Culture and Curriculum, 22*(3), 175–194.

Newman, K.L., Samimy, K., and Romstedt, K. (2010). Developing a training program for secondary teachers of English language learners in Ohio. *Theory Into Practice, 49*(2), 152–161.

Nguyen, H.T., Benken, B.M., Hakim-Butt, K., and Zwiep, S.G. (2013). Teaching and learning in higher education: Enhancing faculty's preparation of prospective secondary teacher candidates for instructing English language learners. *International Journal of Teaching and Learning in Higher Education, 25*(3), 305–315.

Nutta, J.W., Mokhtari, K., and Strebel, C. (2012). *Preparing Every Teacher to Reach English Learners: A Practical Guide for Teacher Educators.* Cambridge, MA: Harvard Education Press.

O'Hara, S., and Pritchard, R.H. (2008). Meeting the challenge of diversity: Professional development for teacher educators. *Teacher Education Quarterly, 35*(1), 43–61.

Otheguy, R., García, O., and Reid, W. (2015). Clarifying translanguaging and deconstructing named languages: A perspective from linguistics. *Applied Linguistics Review, 6*(3), 281–307.

Paris, D. (2012). Culturally sustaining pedagogy: A needed change in stance, terminology, and practice. *Educational Researcher, 41*(3), 93–97.

Pawan, F., and Ortloff, J.H. (2011). Sustaining collaboration: English-as-a-second-language, and content-area teachers. *Teaching and Teacher Education, 27*(2), 463–471.

Pettit, S.K. (2011). Teachers' beliefs about English language learners in the mainstream classroom: A review of the literature. *International Multilingual Research Journal, 5*(2), 123–147.

Pinnow, R., and Chval, K. (2015). "How much you wanna bet?": Examining the role of positioning in the development of L2 learner interactional competencies in the content classroom. *Linguistics and Education, 30*, 1–11. doi:10.1016/j.linged.2015.03.004.

Pollard-Durodola, S.D., González, J.E., Simmons, D.C., Taylor, A.B., Davis, M.J., Simmons, L., and Nava-Walichowski, M. (2012). An examination of preschool teachers' shared book reading practices in Spanish: Before and after instructional guidance. *Bilingual Research Journal, 35*(1), 5–31.

Ramirez, N., and Celedón-Pattichis, S. (2012). Understanding second language development and implications for the mathematics classroom. In S. Celedón-Pattichis and N. Ramirez (Eds.), *Beyond Good Teaching: Advancing Mathematics Education for ELLs* (pp. 19–37). Reston, VA: National Council of Teachers of Mathematics.

Reeves, J.R. (2006). Secondary teacher attitudes toward including English-language learners in mainstream classrooms. *The Journal of Educational Research, 99*(3), 131–143.

Remillard, J.T., and Cahnmann, M. (2005). Researching mathematics teaching in bilingual bicultural classrooms. In T. McCarty (Ed.), *Language, Literacy, and Power in Schooling* (pp. 169–187). Hillsdale, NJ: Lawrence Erlbaum Associates.

Rios-Aguilar, C., Gonzalez Canche, M.S., and Moll, L.C. (2012). A study of Arizona's teachers of English language learners. *Teachers College Record, 114*(9), 1–33.

Shaw, J.M., Lyon, E.G., Stoddart, T., Mosqueda, E., and Menon, P. (2014). Improving science and literacy learning for English language learners: Evidence from a pre-service teacher preparation intervention. *Journal of Science Teacher Education, 25*(5), 621–643.

Short, D.J., Fidelman, C.G., and Louguit, M. (2012). Developing academic language in English language learners through sheltered instruction. *TESOL Quarterly, 46*(2), 334–361.

Short, D.J., Vogt, M., and Echevarría, J. (2011). *The SIOP Model for Teaching Science to English Learners.* Boston, MA: Pearson.

Siegel, M.A. (2014). Developing preservice teachers' expertise in equitable assessment for English learners. *Journal of Science Teacher Education, 25*(3), 289–308.

Siwatu, K.O. (2007). Preservice teachers' culturally responsive teaching self-efficacy and outcome expectancy beliefs. *Teaching and Teacher Education, 23*(7), 1086–1101.

Snow, C.E. (2010). Academic language and the challenge of reading for learning about science. *Science, 328*(5977), 450–452.

Snow, M.A., and Brinton, D.M. (Eds.). (1997). *The Content-Based Classroom: Perspectives on Integrating Language and Content.* White Plains, NY: Longman.

Spillane, J.P. (1999). External reform initiatives and teachers' efforts to reconstruct their practice: The mediating role of teachers' zones of enactment. *Journal of Curriculum Studies, 31*(2), 143–175.

Stein, M.K., Smith, M.S., and Silver, E.A. (1999). The development of professional developers: Learning to assist teachers in new settings in new ways. *Harvard Educational Review, 69*(3), 237–269.

Stoddart, T., Solis, J., Tolbert, S., and Bravo, M. (2010). A framework for the effective science teaching of English language learners in elementary schools. In D.W. Sunal, C.S. Sunal, and E.L. Wright (Eds.), *Teaching Science with Hispanic ELLs in K–16 Classrooms* (pp. 151–181). Charlotte, NC: Information Age.

Suárez-Orozco, C., and Suárez-Orozco, M. (2009). Educating Latino immigrant students in the twenty-first century: Principles for the Obama administration. *Harvard Educational Review, 79*(2), 327–340.

Symeou, L., Roussounidou, E., and Michaelides, M. (2012). "I feel much more confident now to talk with parents": An evaluation of in-service training on teacher–parent communication. *School Community Journal, 22*(1), 65–88. Available: https://pdfs.semanticscholar.org/c4d0/47157b1a7ca7e5c049dac89edf8b146a0a78.pdf [June 2018].

Tolbert, S. (2018). *Secondary Science Education for English Learners.* Paper commissioned for the Committee on Supporting English Learners in STEM Subjects. Board on Science Education and Board on Children, Youth, and Families, Division of Behavioral and Social Sciences and Education. Available: http://www.nas.edu/ELinSTEM [October 2018].

Tolbert, S., and Knox, C. (2016). "They might know a lot of things that I don't know": Investigating differences in preservice teachers' ideas about contextualizing science instruction in multilingual classrooms. *International Journal of Science Education, 38*(7), 1133–1149. doi:10.1080/09500693.2016.1183266

Trowbridge, L.W., and Bybee, R.W. (1996). *Teaching Secondary School Science: Strategies for Developing Scientific Literacy.* Englewood Cliffs, NJ: Merrill, an Imprint of Prentice Hall.

Turkan, S. (2018). *The Role of the ESL Teacher in Relation to Content Teachers.* Paper commissioned for the Committee on Supporting English Learners in STEM Subjects. Board on Science Education and Board on Children, Youth, and Families, Division of Behavioral and Social Sciences and Education. Available: http://www.nas.edu/ELinSTEM [October 2018].

Turkan, S., De Oliveira, L.C., Lee, O., and Phelps, G. (2014). Proposing a knowledge base for teaching academic content to English language learners: Disciplinary linguistic knowledge. *Teachers College Record, 116*(3).

Turner, E.E., and Bustillos, L.M. (2017). Qué observamos aquí? Qué preguntas tienen?: Problem solving in Ms. Bustillos's second-grade bilingual classroom. In *Access and Equity: Promoting High Quality Mathematics in PK–2* (pp. 45–63). Reston, VA: National Council of Teachers of Mathematics.

Turner, E.E., and Drake, C. (2016). A review of research on prospective teachers' learning about children's mathematical thinking and cultural funds of knowledge. *Journal of Teacher Education, 67*(1), 32–46.

U.S. Department of Education, Institute of Education Sciences, and What Works Clearinghouse. (2013). *English Language Learners Intervention Report: Sheltered Instruction Observation Protocol® (SIOP®).* Available: http://whatworks.ed.gov [August 2018].

Valdés, G., Kibler, A.K., and Walqui, A. (2014). *Changes in the Expertise of ESL professionals: Knowledge and Action in an Era of New Standards.* Alexandria, VA: TESOL International Association.

Valencia, R. (2010). *Dismantling Contemporary Deficit Thinking: Educational Thought and Practice.* New York: Taylor & Francis.

Varghese, M.M., and Stritikus, T. (2005). "Nadie me dijo Nobody told me": Language policy negotiation and implications for teacher education. *Journal of Teacher Education, 56*(1), 73–87.

Vazquez Dominguez, M., Allexsaht-Snider, M., and Buxton, C. (2017). Connecting soccer to middle school science: Latino students' passion in learning. *Journal of Latinos and Education, 17*(3), 225–237.

Villegas, A.M., and Lucas, T. (2002). *Educating Culturally Responsive Teachers.* Albany: State University of New York Press.

Vomvoridi-Ivanovic, E. (2012). "Estoy acostumbrada hablar ingles": Latin@ preservice teachers' struggles to use Spanish in a bilingual afterschool mathematics program. *Journal of Urban Mathematics Education, 5*(2), 87–111.

Vomvoridi-Ivanovic, E., and Chval, K.B. (2014). Challenging beliefs and developing knowledge in relation to teaching English language learners: Examples from mathematics teacher education. In B. Cruz, C. Ellerbrock, A. Vasquez, and E. Howes (Eds.), *Talking Diversity with Teachers and Teacher Educators: Exercises and Critical Conversations Across the Curriculum* (pp. 115–130). New York: Teachers College Press.

Walqui, A. (2008). The development of teacher expertise to work with adolescent English language learners: A model and a few priorities. In L.S. Verplaetse and N. Migliacci (Eds.), *Inclusive Pedagogy for English Language Learners.* New York: Lawrence Erlbaum Associates.

Weinburgh, M., Silva, C., Smith, K.H., Groulx, J., and Nettles, J. (2014). The intersection of inquiry-based science and language: Preparing teachers for ELL classrooms. *Journal of Science Teacher Education, 25*(5), 519–541.

WIDA Consortium. (2012). *Amplification of the English Language Development Standards.* Madison, WI: Board of Regents of the University of Wisconsin System. Available: http://www.wida.us/standards/eld.aspx [June 2018].

Wilson, S.M., Floden, R.E., and Ferrini-Mundy, J. (2001). *Teacher Preparation Research: Current Knowledge, Gaps, and Recommendations.* Seattle, WA: Center for the Study of Teaching and Policy.

Wimberly, G.L., and Noeth, R.J. (2005). *College Readiness Begins in Middle School.* ACT Policy Report. Iowa City, IA: ACT, Inc. Available: http://citeseerx.ist.psu.edu/viewdoc/download?doi=10.1.1.508.5566&rep=rep1&type=pdf [June 2018].

Zwiep, S.G., Straits, W.J., Stone, K.R., Beltran, D.D., and Furtado, L. (2011). The integration of English language development and science instruction in elementary classrooms. *Journal of Science Teacher Education, 22*(8), 769–785.

# 7

# Assessing STEM Learning
# among English Learners

This chapter discusses the role that assessment plays or potentially can play in ensuring English learners' (ELs') successful access to science, technology, engineering, and mathematics (STEM). Assessment of STEM subjects, as with other academic areas, can be separated into two broad assessment approaches. Measurement-driven (i.e., macro-level) assessment is used summatively for large-scale accountability of student performances and for evaluating learning across broad intervals (e.g., annual progress). Performance data-driven (i.e., micro-level) assessment can be used for summative purposes at the classroom level, or can provide formative feedback to inform teaching and learning as it happens (Black, Wilson, and Yao, 2011; see Figure 7-1).

Within these broad assessment approaches, the discussion addresses several challenges in EL testing practice and policy. The first challenge concerns large-scale assessment and has to do with the fact that language is the means through which tests are administered. Professional organizations consistently have recognized that scores on tests confound, at least to some extent, proficiency in the content being assessed and proficiency in the language in which that content is assessed (American Educational Research Association, American Psychological Association, and National Council on Measurement in Education, 2014). This limitation, which is always a concern in the testing of any student population, is especially serious for ELs. While there is a wealth of information on the academic achievement of ELs in tests from large-scale assessment programs, the majority of current testing practices with ELs are ineffective in eliminating language proficiency in the language of testing as a factor that negatively affects the performance

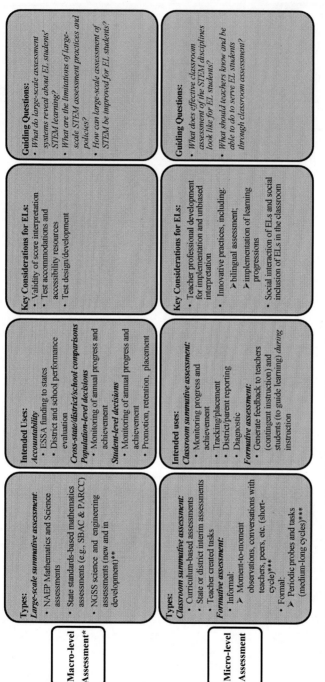

**Macro-level Assessment***

**Types:**
*Large-scale summative assessment:*
- NAEP Mathematics and Science assessments
- State standards-based mathematics assessments (e.g., SBAC & PARCC)
- NGSS science and engineering assessments (new and in development)**

**Intended Uses:**
*Accountability*
- ESSA funding to states
- District and school performance evaluation

*Cross-state/district/school comparisons*
*Population-level decisions*
- Monitoring of annual progress and achievement

*Student-level decisions*
- Monitoring of annual progress and achievement
- Promotion, retention, placement

**Key Considerations for ELs:**
- Validity of score interpretation
- Test accommodations and accessibility resources
- Test design/development

**Guiding Questions:**
- *What do large-scale assessment systems reveal about EL students' STEM learning?*
- *What are the limitations of large-scale STEM assessment practices and policies?*
- *How can large-scale assessment of STEM be improved for EL students?*

**Micro-level Assessment**

**Types:**
*Classroom summative assessment:*
- Curriculum-based assessments
- State or district interim assessments
- Teacher created tasks

*Formative assessment:*
- Informal:
  ➤ Moment-to-moment observations, conversations with teachers, peers, etc. (short-cycle)***
- Formal:
  ➤ Periodic probes and tasks (medium-long cycles)***

**Intended uses:**
*Classroom summative assessment:*
- Monitoring progress and achievement
- Tracking/placement
- District/parent reporting
- Diagnostic

*Formative assessment:*
- Generate feedback to teachers (contingent instruction) and students (to guide learning) *during* instruction

**Key Considerations for ELs:**
- Teacher professional development for implementation and unbiased interpretation
- Innovative practices, including:
  ➤ bilingual assessment;
  ➤ implementation of learning progressions
- Social interaction of ELs and social inclusion of ELs in the classroom

**Guiding Questions:**
- *What does effective classroom assessment of the STEM disciplines look like for EL students?*
- *What should teachers know and be able to do to serve EL students through classroom assessment?*

**FIGURE 7-1** STEM assessment and English learners in U.S. schools.

* Black, P., Wilson, M., and Yao, S. Y. (2011). Road maps for learning: A guide to the navigation of learning progressions. *Measurement: Interdisciplinary Research & Perspective, 9*(2-3), 71-123.

** For example, Washington Comprehensive Assessment of Science (operational 2017-18), California Science Test (operational Spring 2019), Massachusetts Comprehensive Assessment System. See also, National Research Council (2014). *Developing Assessments for the Next Generation Science Standards.* Washington, DC: The National Academies Press.

*** Wiliam, D. (2006). Formative assessment: Getting the focus right. *Educational Assessment, 11*(3-4), 283-289.

of these students on tests. This in turn poses a limit to the extent to which appropriate generalizations can be made about ELs' academic achievement based on test scores.

The second challenge concerns classroom summative assessment and formative assessment—assessment *for* learning. The past decade has witnessed a tremendous increase in the number of investigations and publications that examine how teachers can obtain information about their students' progress and, based on that information, adjust their teaching to ensure that learning goals are met. Classroom summative assessment includes more frequent monitoring of student progress on standardized measures such as state or district interim assessments, implementation of commercial curriculum-based assessments, or teacher-made end-of-unit tests. Formative assessment entails generating feedback on student learning using formal activities (such as giving quizzes or assignments that involve the entire class and that are carried out in a purposeful and planned manner) and/or informal activities (such as requesting participation in classroom discussions, or observing student-to-student discussions and asking questions to probe student understanding of the topic).

Much of the research on classroom summative and formative assessment has been conducted without considering linguistic diversity in the classroom. With a few exceptions, research is mostly silent about the linguistic factors that may shape effectiveness in formative assessment, or it appears to implicitly assume equal proficiency in the language of instruction among all students in class. As a consequence, the extent to which current knowledge on formative assessment is applicable to linguistically diverse classrooms still needs more research.

The chapter has two main sections. The first examines what is known about ELs on STEM large-scale assessments, the limitations of available information on EL achievement, and the factors that contribute to these limitations. The second section examines what is known about ELs and classroom assessment practices for the STEM disciplines, including teacher preparation and credentialing.

## ENGLISH LEARNERS IN LARGE-SCALE
## STEM ASSESSMENT PROGRAMS

Legal mandates to include ELs in large-scale assessment programs are intended to ensure that states produce indicators of academic achievement for ELs. The quality of such indicators depends, to a large extent, on the ability of assessment systems to support these students to gain access to the content of items in spite of the fact that they are in the process of developing proficiency in the language in which they are tested. It also depends on the ability of assessment systems to consider this developing proficiency as critical to making valid interpretations of test scores for these students.

Test scores from assessment programs consistently show that ELs lag behind their non-EL counterparts in science and mathematics achievement (see Chapter 2). Multiple factors may contribute to this achievement gap; among them is the exclusion of proficient ELs from the EL subgroup and, more importantly, the limited opportunities these students have to benefit from STEM instruction delivered in a language that they are still developing. This section focuses on the limited effectiveness of assessment systems to properly address the complexity of EL student populations in a consistent and cohesive manner (see for review, Bailey and Carroll, 2015).

### Participation of ELs in National and State Assessment

The inclusion of ELs in large-scale assessment programs has been shaped by changes in legislation and different ways of interpreting and implementing that legislation. The No Child Left Behind Act (NCLB)[1]—another reauthorization of the Elementary and Secondary Education Act (ESEA)[2]—contained requirements for schools to meet growth requirements and report status regarding progress toward learning English according to English-proficiency standards aligned to academic standards. The goal of this effort was to align language proficiency standards under Title III to the language needed to learn academic content under Title I. A potentially unfortunate consequence of these requirements is that they may have unintentionally promoted practices that do not distinguish between the characteristics of developing English as a second language and learning the formal and academic aspects of English language encountered in content areas.

States were required to adopt standards that targeted knowledge and skills in mathematics and English language arts deemed necessary to access and succeed in college (e.g., Common Core State Standards [National Governors Association Center for Best Practices and Council of Chief State School Officers, 2010]). As part of the American Recovery and Reinvestment Act,[3] Race to the Top—a federal grant intended to promote innovation in education at the state and local levels (U.S. Department of Education, 2017)—funded two state assessment consortia, the Partnership for Assessment of Readiness for College and Careers (PARCC) and the Smarter Balanced Assessment Consortium (Smarter Balanced). These two assessment consortia are required to administer and provide reports on assessments tied to state standards in mathematics and English/language arts once a year in Grades 3–8 and once in high school.

---

[1]No Child Left Behind Act of 2001. Public Law 107-110.

[2]Elementary and Secondary Education Act of 1965. Public Law 89-10.

[3]American Recovery and Reinvestment Act of 2009. Public Law 111-5.

Along with the assessment consortia and their focus on mathematics, four major recent developments have contributed to define the current assessment scene for ELs as it concerns STEM broadly. First is the Every Student Succeeds Act[4]—the latest reauthorization of ESEA, which includes both an indicator of progress in English language proficiency and indicators of academic content achievement within the same accountability system. It also requires states to report on the languages most used by their ELs and to make efforts to assess students in those languages (see Solano-Flores and Hakuta, 2017).

The second development is the creation of new English language development or proficiency (ELD/P) standards by states and consortia that attempt to align with the uses of language in the most recent academic content standards, and newer ELD/P assessments to match these standards (e.g., WIDA Consortium World-Class Instructional Design Assessment, 2007). These assessment efforts have opened the possibility for states to make sound decisions concerning the identification of ELs and supporting them based on aspects of language that are relevant to learning content (Council of Chief State School Officers, 2012). They may also contribute to helping educators to meet the academic language demands inherent to college and career readiness (see Frantz et al., 2014; Valdés, Menken, and Castro, 2015).

The third recent development in STEM education is the Next Generation Science Standards (NGSS), which set expectations for knowledge and skills for students in grades K–12. The NGSS provide a conceptual organization for large-scale assessment frameworks (NGSS Lead States, 2013). Sufficient consideration of ELs' needs in the development of NGSS-based assessments will depend on the extent to which the intersection of content and the linguistic demands of science content are addressed (see Lee, Quinn, and Valdés, 2013).

Finally, a fourth important recent development relevant to ELs has to do with the requirement for states to formalize college- and career-readiness expectations for their students. ESSA allows more flexibility in state accountability systems, which allows more states to refine their accountability systems to include college readiness (see Council of Chief State School Officers, 2012). An important outcome of this development is the link between Common Core standards and the criteria used by colleges to make placement decisions for developmental courses. For example, about 200 colleges are using Smarter Balanced high school test scores assessing the Common Core (including mathematics) as part of their measure to inform decisions on whether students are ready for credit-bearing courses or need to take developmental courses (Smarter Balanced Assessment Consortium, 2017a).

---

[4]Every Student Succeeds Act of 2015. Public Law 114-95 § 114 Stat. 1177 (2015–2016).

## Limitations of Current Large-Scale Testing Policies and Practices

Low performance of ELs on large-scale tests can be regarded as reflecting the challenges inherent to learning in a second language, living in poverty, receiving inadequate support to learn both English and academic content, and having limited opportunities to learn. Performance differences between ELs and non-ELs are further complicated by the routine practice of excluding former ELs who have gained proficiency in English from the EL reporting subgroup. This creaming from the top within the EL subgroup diminishes the performance of the EL subgroup and exacerbates differences between ELs and non-ELs (Saunders and Marcelletti, 2013). At the same time, including former ELs in the EL subgroup masks the performance of those ELs who have not yet gained proficiency in English. Both comparisons are important and useful but address different questions of importance to educators and policy makers, as well as to parents and students.

In addition to those sources of low performance in large-scale assessment tests, a discussion of STEM assessment for ELs needs to take into consideration multiple limitations in current testing policies and practices: (1) EL identification and classification practices; (2) the validity of generalizations of test scores for ELs; (3) the process of test development, review, and adaptation; (4) the use of testing accommodations; and (5) the reporting and documentation of ELs' performance and test scores.

### Identifying and Classifying ELs

Decisions relevant to STEM assessment for ELs are affected by the process of identifying students and deciding on their level of proficiency in English. Results from this process determine who is tested and how (e.g., the kinds of testing accommodations ELs receive when they are given tests in large-scale content assessment programs). Legal definitions of English language learners (e.g., as students who speak a language other than English at home and who may not benefit fully from instruction due to limited proficiency in the language of instruction, as contained in NCLB) help states and school districts to make classification decisions needed to comply with legal mandates concerning ELs. Yet these definitions are not technical and may render erroneous classifications—some students may be wrongly classified as ELs, while certain ELs may wrongly not be identified as ELs (Solano-Flores, 2009; see also National Academies of Sciences, Engineering, and Medicine, 2017). Because states have different criteria to implement legislation regarding the definition of ELs, whether a student is regarded or not as being an EL depends, at least to some extent, on the state in which a given student lives. Remarkable collaborative efforts involving states and other stakeholders have recently been undertaken to support states in developing a statewide, standardized definition of ELs (Linquanti et al., 2016). Given the new requirements in Every Student Succeeds Act for states to adopt standardized, statewide EL entrance and exit procedures and criteria, more states are moving to adopt entrance and exit criteria focused squarely on the English language proficiency construct that can be applied consistently by schools and districts across the state.

To complicate matters, testing practices and practices concerning reporting and using information on English proficiency are not sensitive to the tremendous heterogeneity of EL populations. Of course, an important source of this heterogeneity stems from the wide diversity of ELs' first languages (while Spanish is the first language of the vast majority of ELs in the United States, there are hundreds of other languages used by ELs). However, the kind of linguistic heterogeneity that is perhaps most important in the assessment of ELs is the heterogeneity that exists across students in oral language, reading, and writing skills. This diversity is present in both English and in students' first language and is evidenced even among speakers of the same language. Failure to properly address this diversity has a great negative impact on the effectiveness of any action intended to support ELs.

These differences are not captured by overall categories of English proficiency, whose use fails to recognize the strengths a given EL student may have in English. While assessment systems may report English proficiency for different language modes (i.e., listening, speaking, reading, writing), this information is not necessarily available to educators or the professionals in charge of making placement or testing accommodation decisions for use during STEM assessment or is not given in ways easy for teachers to interpret and use during STEM instruction (see Zwick, Senturk, and Wang, 2001).

## Validity Concerns

Another limitation in current STEM testing practices for ELs concerns validity. For the purposes of this report, *validity* can be defined as the extent to which reasonable generalizations can be made about students' knowledge or skills based on the scores produced by a test (see Kane, 2006). The fact that limited proficiency in the language of testing constitutes a threat to the validity of test score interpretations has been widely recognized for a long time.

A large body of research has identified language as a source of construct irrelevant variance—variation in test scores due to factors that do not have to do with the knowledge or skill being assessed (e.g., Abedi, 2004; Avenia-Tapper and Llosa, 2015; Solano-Flores and Li, 2013). Many of these factors have to do with linguistic complexity; for example, complexity due to the use of unfamiliar and morphologically complex words, words with multiple meanings, idiomatic usages, and long or syntactically complex sentences in texts and accompanying test items and directions (Bailey et al., 2007; Noble et al., 2014; Shaftel et al., 2006; Silliman, Wilkinson, and Brea-Spahn, 2018). However, underrepresentation of the content construct is a concern, as well, if all linguistic complexity is unreflexively removed from assessments (Avenia-Tapper and Llosa, 2015). If communication of STEM is part of the target construct of the assessment, then some degree of linguistic complexity representing the texts, tests, and discourse of STEM classrooms could be desirable on content assessments (e.g., Bailey and Carroll, 2015; Llosa, 2016). Indeed it may not be possible to present higher-level STEM content in language that is not complex.

An important source of construct irrelevant variance has to do with dialect and culture. Tests are administered in so-called Standard English, which is a variety of English commonly used in formal and school texts and carries high social prestige. There is evidence that indicates that the lack of correspondence between the Standard English used in tests and the variety of English used by ELs produces a large amount of measurement error (Solano-Flores and Li, 2009). Due to limited experience in life, younger students may be more sensitive to these dialect differences.

An additional set of validity threats concerns culture and the contextual information (e.g., fictitious characters, stories, situations) used in science and mathematics items with the intent to make them more relatable and thus more meaningful to students. A study found that at least 70 percent of released National Assessment of Educational Progress science items for Grades 4 and 8 provided contextual information, both in the form of text and illustrations. Correlation data suggest that some of those contextual characteristics influence student performance (Ruiz-Primo and Li, 2015; see also Martiniello, 2009). Evidence from research conducted with small samples of science and mathematics items suggests that the contextual information of items reflects mainstream, white, middle-class culture (Solano-Flores, 2011). Certainly, not sharing the communication styles, values, resources, ways of living, objects, or situations of another cultural group does not necessarily mean that an individual is incapable of understanding contextual information. Yet it is not clear to what extent responding to test items that picture situations that are not part of one's everyday life makes students feel alienated and to what extent that feeling may impact performance. After all, how meaningful something is to a person is not only a matter of familiarity, but also a matter of the person's identification with a community and their level of social participation in that community (Rogoff, 1995).

## Test Development, Review, and Adaptation

Key to properly addressing the linguistic and cultural challenges relevant to validly testing ELs appears to be the process of test development. Ideally, when tests are developed properly, draft versions of items are tried out with samples of pilot students drawn from the target population of examinees. This process involves examination of student responses and even interviews and talk-aloud protocols that provide evidence on the ways in which students interpret items and the reasoning and knowledge they use to respond to them. Based on this information, the content, context, and text of items are refined through an iterative process of review and revision (Trumbull and Solano-Flores, 2011). Even when the target population of students does not include ELs, many of the refinements concern linguistic features (e.g., colloquial words that are not used by students in the ways in which test developers assumed).

Unfortunately, there is no certainty that this process of development takes place for a substantial proportion of items used in large-scale assessment. Of course, many items may undergo a process of formal scrutiny in which committees of reviewers examine them and systematically identify sources of potential bias (Hambleton and Rodgers, 1995; Zieky, 2006). Yet experts' reviews are only partially sensitive to the features of items that may pose an unnecessary challenge to students due to linguistic and cultural issues (Solano-Flores, 2012).

To complicate matters, even when items are pilot tested with samples of students, ELs are rarely included in those student samples. Underlying this exclusion is the assumption that little information on the reasoning ELs use when they respond to items can be obtained from them due to their limited English proficiency. Yet there is evidence that most ELs can participate in cognitive interviews and communicate with test developers (Kachchaf, 2011). Non-ELs and ELs may differ on the sets of linguistic features that may hamper their understanding of items. This simple notion is extremely important, as there is evidence that even changing one word or slightly rephrasing an expression in science items may make a difference on whether an item is or is not biased against linguistic minority students (Ercikan, 2002).

Regarding test review, an important aspect of EL assessment is the analysis of item bias. Using item response theory (a psychometric theory of scaling), potential bias in an item can be examined by comparing the level of difficulty of the item for ELs and for non-ELs after controlling for group performance differences on the overall test score. If the item is more difficult for the sample of ELs than for the sample of non-ELs in spite of the fact that their overall test scores are similar, that case is considered as evidence that the item functions differentially for the two populations—it is biased against ELs (Bailey, 2000/2005; Camilli, 2013; Martiniello, 2009). While this procedure has been available for several decades, the extent to which it is used routinely in large-scale assessment programs and with respect to the heterogeneity of the samples of students compared is unclear. One reason that explains why it may not be used with substantial numbers of items is that item response theory-based item bias analysis is costly and time consuming (Allalouf, 2003). To complicate matters, the effectiveness of this procedure may be limited by the characteristics of the student populations. There is evidence that the rate of detection of biased items declines as the samples of ELs' heterogeneity increases (Ercikan et al., 2014; Oliveri, Ercikan, and Zumbo, 2014).

## Testing Accommodations

Legislation contains provisions on accommodations in tests for ELs and special education students. These accommodations are modifications made on the format of tests or the ways in which they are administered. These modifications are intended to minimize factors related to the condition of being an EL that could adversely affect the student's test performance, but which are not relevant to the constructs being measured. Thus, valid accommodations remove the impact of construct irrelevant variance on test performance without giving the students who receive them an unfair advantage over non-ELs who are not provided with those accommodations (see Abedi, Hofstetter, and Lord, 2004). Examples of testing accommodations used by states include: allowing students extra time to complete the test, assigning students preferential seating, simplifying the text of items, providing students with printed dictionaries and glossaries, and providing them with translations of the test. An investigation on the use of accommodations (Rivera et al., 2006) counted a total of more than 40 testing accommodations used by states with ELs, many of which were shown by the authors to be inappropriate and likely to fail to address the linguistic needs of ELs. The study also found that accommodations for ELs and accommodations for students with disabilities are often confused. For example, schools may be given lists of authorized accommodations without distinguishing which ones are for each of these two groups of students (Rivera et al., 2006). As a result, ELs may receive accommodations such as providing enhanced lighting conditions or large font size, which are intended for visually impaired students.

In spite of the good intentions that drive their use, there are many technical and practical issues that need to be resolved before testing accommodations can reasonably be expected to serve the function for which they have been created. An important issue is the defensibility of the implied assumptions about the students' skills and needs. Because EL populations are very heterogeneous, some accommodations may be effective only for some students. For example, allowing extra time to complete the test will help only students who truly take longer reading and comprehending the text of test items than typical test-takers. If ELs are not literate in their first language or have not had schooling in their first language, they may be equally slow, or even slower in completing a test given in their first language (see Chia and Kachchaf, 2018). Also, dictionaries or glossaries might benefit only those students who have the skills needed to efficiently locate words alphabetically ordered, and translation will benefit only those students who have received formal instruction in their first language and know how to read in it.

Several reviews and meta-analyses have been conducted with the intent to shed light on the effectiveness of different types of accommodations for ELs (Abedi, Hofsteteter, and Lord, 2004; Kieffer et al., 2009; Pennock-Roman and Rivera, 2011; Sireci, Li, and Scarpati, 2003; Wolf et al., 2008, 2012). The results indicate that very few accommodations are effective and those that are effective are only moderately effective insofar as they reduce only a small portion of the achievement gap between ELs and non-ELs. Also, there is evidence that, in the absence of accurate and detailed information about students' skills and needs, assigning accommodations to what educators or school administrators believe is the best accommodation for their students, or randomly assigning them to any accommodation render similar results (Kopriva et al., 2007). Thus, limited proficiency in English should not be assumed to be entirely removed as a source of measurement error in large-scale assessment programs simply because testing accommodations are used with ELs.

An important aspect often neglected in examining testing accommodation effectiveness is implementation (see Ruiz-Primo, DiBello, and Solano-Flores, 2014). Assessment programs' specifications concerning the accommodations that states or schools are authorized to provide are not specific on the ways in which those accommodations have to be created or provided (Solano-Flores et al., 2014). Test translation is a case in point. Research shows that translations can alter the constructs (skills, knowledge) being measured by tests (Hambleton, 2005). Research also shows that translating tests is a very delicate endeavor that, in addition to qualified translators, needs to involve content specialists and teachers who teach the content assessed, and who must engage in a careful process of review and revision (Solano-Flores, 2012; Solano-Flores, Backhoff, and Contreras-Niño, 2009). Thus, it is possible that many accommodations are not properly created or provided to students, and it is possible that schools and states vary considerably in their approaches to matching students to accommodations, as well as in the fidelity with which accommodations are implemented.

As large-scale assessment programs transition from paper-and-pencil to computer-based formats, a wide range of devices emerge that, if developed carefully, have the potential to effectively reduce limited proficiency in English as a source of measurement error in testing (Abedi, 2014). The term *accessibility resource* is becoming increasingly frequent in the literature on EL assessment. An accessibility resource can be defined as a device available for students to use when they need it, and which reacts to each individual student's request, for example, by displaying an alternative representation of the text of the item or part of this text (see Chia et al., 2013).

During the past few years, Smarter Balanced[5] has been developing accessibility resources for ELs in mathematics assessment (Chia et al., 2013; Chia and Kachchaf, 2018; Solano-Flores, Shade, and Chrzanowski, 2014). Pop-up text glossaries are an example of these accessibility resources. The text of the item highlights select words or strings of words that are available for translation. When the student clicks on one of those words or strings of words, its translation in the student's first language pops up next to it. Unlike a conventional glossary printed on paper, a pop-up text glossary is sensitive to each individual student's need in that it is activated only when the student needs it.

This capability to react to the student is critical to designing accessibility resources that are sensitive to individual needs. Other accessibility resources, such as pictorial and audio representations of selected words, are being designed using this capability (see Smarter Balanced Assessment Consortium, 2017b). These accessibility resources hold promise as an alternative to testing accommodations intended to support ELs in gaining access to the content of items. The methods for their sound design and use are currently being investigated.

### Reporting and Documentation

Reporting the results of tests poses intricate challenges to supporting ELs to have access to STEM. For decades, test score reporting has been identified as critical to ensuring that assessment programs effectively inform policy and practice (Klein and Hamilton, 1998; Ryan, 2006). Loopholes in legislation or inappropriate interpretation or implementation of legislation concerning the use of measures of academic achievement can lead to unfair practice. For example, NCLB legislation mandated that states measured adequate yearly progress in reading, science, and mathematics, and report

---

[5]The Smarter Balanced Assessment Consortium distinguishes between universal tools, designated supports, and accommodations. Under Smarter Balanced's framework, most EL-related accessibility resources are considered designated supports. See Stone and Cook (2018) for a detailed discussion.

this progress in a disaggregated manner for different groups, one of which was students classified as limited English proficient (LEP). Due to their limited proficiency in English, these students start school with lower scores than their native English-using peers. According to these requirements, many LEP students with substantial yearly progress in the mentioned content areas would also likely have increased their English proficiency and placed out of the LEP category, becoming reclassified as fluent English proficient. As mentioned, as a consequence, school reports for LEP students could never reflect the actual progress of students in this group because they would no longer belong to that reporting category (Abedi, 2004; Saunders and Marcelletti, 2013).

Of special importance is the kind of information about ELs that is included in technical reports and scientific papers. As discussed before, EL populations are linguistically heterogeneous, even within the same linguistic group of students who are users of the same given language. Along with English proficiency in the different language modalities (i.e., listening, speaking, reading, and writing), first language, literacy in a first language, schooling history, ethnicity, age, socioeconomic status, and geographical region are variables that contribute to this heterogeneity. Unfortunately, information on the samples of students according to those variables and the sizes of those samples often goes unreported. Contributing to this limitation is the fact that no EL population sampling frameworks are available that support institutions and researchers in specifying and drawing representative samples of ELs based on critical sociodemographic variables.

Perhaps the most important aspect yet to be properly addressed in reporting and documentation is heterogeneity in English language proficiency and how content area achievement performance covaries with English proficiency. Aggregating achievement results across language proficiency categories complicates inferences about EL achievement because of the positive covariation between English proficiency and content area achievement measured in English (see Hopkins et al., 2013). In such contexts, the aggregate performance is a function of both the performance of students in each proficiency category and the percentage of ELs in different categories, which complicates the interpretation of comparisons across schools and districts in the same state, and comparisons over time in the same school or district.

It is easy to construct examples where the performance in each proficiency category is better in School A than in School B, and yet school B has better overall performance because School B has a larger percentage of its ELs in higher levels of English proficiency. This problem, known as the Simpson's paradox (Blyth, 1972; Wagner, 1982), can occur in the EL context because the percentage of students at different levels of proficiency varies from school to school and over time for reasons outside of the control of the schools. Aggregation of achievement results across language proficiency categories and the lack of information on other sources of heterogeneity within the EL populations make it impossible to determine how reasonable are the generalizations that can be made about ELs' STEM performances on large-scale assessment of STEM or to properly inform practice and policy for these students.

## CLASSROOM SUMMATIVE AND FORMATIVE STEM ASSESSMENT WITH ENGLISH LEARNERS

In this section, we focus on the micro-level assessment that occurs during instruction in STEM classrooms (see Figure 7-1), specifically on what is known about effective classroom assessment of the STEM disciplines for ELs. We discuss what teachers would benefit from knowing and being able to do to serve ELs through formative assessment. Classroom assessment is important for teacher use in instructional planning and student-level decision making (e.g., Noyce and Hickey, 2011). In addition to the problematic implementation of large-scale assessment of STEM subjects with ELs (outlined in the previous section), large-scale assessment, with its design for signaling strengths and weaknesses in student learning, is not focused on suggesting what kinds of assistance students will need from their teachers to further that learning. This is the role that classroom assessment is designed to play.

There is renewed interest in classroom assessment of the academic content areas as part of a balanced assessment system under ESSA (2015). Such a balance is inclusive of both classroom and large-scale assessment approaches; information on student learning produced by classroom assessment ideally complements that produced by large-scale assessment and together they can form an academic achievement assessment system that fulfils the *comprehensive, coherent,* and *continuous* recommended assessment framing of *Knowing What Students Know* (National Research Council, 2001; see also Black, Wilson, and Yao, 2011; Songer and Ruiz-Primo, 2012). At the same time, there has been an increased interest and visibility around how classroom assessment can be brought into the discussion of educational measurement considerations more broadly, especially in the areas of assessment validity, reliability, and feasibility, which have traditionally been under the purview of large-scale assessment approaches (see Bennett, 2010; Mislevy and Durán, 2014; Wilson, 2016).

In the area of EL student assessment research specifically, classroom assessment is argued to better suit the learning needs of ELs for whom large-scale assessments have limitations on validity (e.g., Cheuk, Daro, and Daro, 2018). In some instances, there is a suggestion that ELs are failing to answer correctly despite their abilities to otherwise show their content knowledge and skills, for example, in the area of science multiple-choice tests (Noble et al., 2014). The promise of classroom summative and formative assessment for ELs is that students can demonstrate their content knowledge and language, and language practices are used in authentic contexts encountered during content learning (e.g., Mislevy and Durán, 2014). One of the goals of classroom assessment can be teasing apart STEM knowledge from language used in the display of that knowledge.

Furthermore, large-scale assessments of STEM may inadequately provide tractable information that teachers can use for their instruction of ELs (e.g., Abedi, 2010). Durán (2008) has argued that there are "inherent limits of large-scale assessments as accountability tools for ELs as a means for directly informing a deep understanding of students' learning capabilities and performance that can be related to instructions and other kinds of intervention strategies supporting ELL schooling outcomes" (p. 294). A pertinent illustration of these limitations can be found in the recent research of Rodriguez-Mojica (2018) working in the area of English language arts. She has shown the range of appropriate academic speech acts (i.e., the communicative intents performed by a speaker) naturally occurring in the "real-time talk" between emerging bilingual students. Many of the students who were successfully engaged in interactive classroom activities in English were otherwise deemed to be struggling with English language proficiency and reading on state-wide standardized assessments.

Rodriguez-Mojica's findings from the discourse analysis of student-to-teacher and peer interactions lend credence to Durán's suggestion that "assessments can be designed to work better for these students, if we take care to have assessments do a better job of pinpointing skill needs of students developmentally across time, better connect assessments to learning activities across time and instructional units, and better represent the social and cultural dimensions of classrooms that are related to opportunities to learn for ELL students" (Durán, 2008, p. 294; see also Mislevy and Durán, 2014; Wilson and Toyama, 2018). Indeed, there is a small body of research that suggests that classroom-level approaches to assessing STEM disciplines constitute alternative designs that may "work better" for ELs (e.g., Siegel, 2007). However, there are very few studies focusing expressly on ELs and the classroom assessment of their knowledge of the STEM disciplines, particularly of mathematics, engineering, and technology. Where necessary, we have included relevant findings from general education studies of this topic, considering likely implications for ELs and encouraging the urgently needed studies of STEM classroom assessment to fill this lacuna in the EL research base.

## Types of Classroom Assessment

Black and Wiliam (2004) cautioned that "[t]he terms classroom assessment and formative assessment are often used synonymously, but . . . the fact that an assessment happens in the classroom, as opposed to elsewhere, says very little about either the nature of the assessment or the functions that it can serve" (p. 183). On this point, Black, Wilson, and Yao (2011) further delineated the different characteristics that classroom assessment can take on. Classroom assessment can have an evaluative function when it adds to the summative information of large-scale academic achievement assessments with interim assessment and teacher-created assessments that may be given at shorter intervals than the annual large-scale assessments (e.g., Abedi, 2010). These classroom summative assessments give teachers and districts information on how well students have acquired certain topics sooner than year-end testing so that modifications to instruction, curricula, or planning of future lessons can be made in a more timely fashion. These purposes of classroom assessment contrast with formative assessment that instead may comprise both formal and informal observations of student work and student discussions, student self- and peer assessment, and teacher analysis of student responses to in-the-moment questions or preplanned probes, among other activities (e.g., Ruiz-Primo, 2011, 2017). These are all examples of an assessment approach designed with feedback to individual student learning as a primary target so that instructional responses can be personalized to the immediate needs of learners (e.g., Erikson, 2007; Heritage, 2010; Ruiz-Primo and Brookhart, 2018).

Our discussion of these two forms of assessment takes into account the nature of empirical evidence that is valued in research on classroom assessment. Whereas research on large-scale assessment tends to use quantitative research methods and research on classroom assessment tends to utilize modest to small-scale quantitative, qualitative, or mixed-methods approaches to research, there are no set of methods specific to large-scale or classroom-based assessment (see Ruiz-Primo et al., 2010; Shavelson et al., 2008). Yet, it is safe to say that, while randomized controlled trials are highly valued in research on large-scale assessment, they are not common in research on classroom assessment due, to a large extent, to the need to be sensitive to classroom context. As a result of this sensitivity to context, studies of classroom assessment may involve different treatments across classrooms—an approach intended to ensure ecological validity, for example through capturing in detail the characteristics of a classroom teachers' authentic assessment routines and practices with ELs.

## Classroom Summative Assessment of STEM with English Learners

There are a number of important initiatives for the summative assessment of STEM subjects at the classroom level. For example, Smarter Balanced has developed interim assessments of mathematics aligned with both the Common Core and the annual summative assessment, to be administered and scored locally by classroom teachers. In another initiative, the Gates Foundation-supported Mathematics Assessment Project successfully supported classroom summative assessment task adoption and design by secondary teachers.[6] However, there is scant literature on the effectiveness of classroom summative assessment practices in STEM specifically designed with ELs in mind. Some studies have reported on classroom assessment strategies, although few reported findings address the question of effectiveness. A larger body of literature reports on the creation of classroom assessments by researchers as a means of assessing the effectiveness of new STEM intervention or curricula for ELs (e.g., Llosa, et al., 2016; see also Wilson and Toyama, 2018). However, because evaluation of the technical quality of the assessments for use with ELs is not a predominant target of the research, we have not included these studies here.

As far back as the early 1990s, Short called on integrated assessment to match integrated language and content instruction (Short, 1993). She illustrated this approach with different examples of alternative assessment tasks from a number of content areas, including several integrated language and mathematics tasks. Rather than relying on one type of classroom assessment, Short advocated using several types that span summative and formative purposes (i.e., the teacher's anecdotal notes of how students draw diagrams to solve word problems and students' own self-assessments used to generate formative feedback). The summative purposes include classroom assessments that *evaluate* the students' performance on a task such as a written essay in which students are asked to explain how other students solved an algebraic word problem. Adding to this repertoire of alternative mathematics assessment with young ELs, Lee, Silverman, and Montoya (2002) found that students' drawings could reveal students' comprehension of mathematics word problems helping to separate out the linguistic challenges of mathematics word problems from student comprehension of the mathematical concepts in the word problems.

In a rare large-scale study focused on mathematics assessment and including measures of effectiveness, Shepard, Taylor, and Betebenner (1998) examined the outcomes on the Rhode Island Mathematics Performance Assessment with 464 4th-grade ELs among other student groups. Items on the assessment included matching stories with data in graphic form,

---

[6]See http://www.map.mathshell.org [October 2018].

representing numbers with base 10 stickers, and representing tangrams with numbers. Students were also required to explain their answers, and a rubric was created for scoring the tasks. Results of the study showed that the assessment was highly correlated with the concurrently administered Metropolitan Achievement Test, a standardized assessment of mathematics knowledge. Promisingly, ELs were found to be less far behind non-ELs on the performance assessment than on the Metropolitan Achievement Test, and very little differential item functioning between the student groups on the performance assessment tasks was observed. However, the authors raised the issue of the adequacy of the scoring rubric and the impact of students' abilities to explain on their mathematics scores. Elsewhere, Pappamihiel and Mihai (2006) also raised the issue of rubrics used in classroom assessments with ELs and recommended to teachers that the language of rubrics be culturally sensitive and the feedback useful and in language understandable by ELs.

Addressing EL classroom assessment in both mathematics and science, the ONPAR project[7] has demonstrated several techniques effective for measuring the mathematics and science knowledge and abilities of ELs. ONPAR tasks engage students in conveying their mathematical and scientific understanding through a variety of representational formats beyond traditional text-based demonstrations, including technology-enhanced assessments that do not place high language demands on ELs (e.g., Kopriva, 2014). ONPAR uses multisemiotic approaches to task creation, including inquiry-based performances, dynamic visuals, auditory supports, and interaction with stimuli to support ELs' situational meaning. For example, in a series of experimental studies and cognitive labs with 156 elementary through high school-aged ELs and non-ELs, Kopriva and colleagues (2013) found evidence that ELs were able to demonstrate their science knowledge more effectively. Consistent with findings reported by Shepard, Taylor, and Betebenner (1998), the ELs in the ONPAR studies scored higher on ONPAR tasks than they did on a traditional assessment of the same content knowledge. Important for science construct validity, there were no differences in performance on the ONPAR tasks and the traditional assessment for non-ELs and ELs with high levels of English language proficiency.

A different science assessment initiative by Turkan and Liu (2012) presents a mixed set of findings for EL classroom assessment. The authors studied the inquiry science performances of 313 7th- and 8th-grade ELs and more than 1,000 of their non-EL peers. Using differential item functioning analysis to test for the effects of EL status on the performance assessment, the authors found that non-ELs significantly outperformed the ELs overall. Turkan and Liu warned that "in addition to the produc-

---

[7]See http://www.onpar.us [September 2018].

tion demands placed on ELLs by inquiry science assessments, the wording of prompts in these assessments may also prove challenging for ELLs, which might influence student performance" (p. 2347). However, the study also captured complexities that speak to the necessity for cultural sensitivity and an awareness of student backgrounds during assessment development that might optimize their performances. For example, the differential item functioning analyses revealed an item that favored ELs. This item provided a graphic representation of a science concept within a familiar context. Furthermore, while a constructed response task may seemingly add language challenges for a student acquiring English, Turkan and Liu reported evidence that this task type provided an opportunity for ELs to convey their scientific reasoning in their own words. Collectively, the findings of this study provide direction for assessment developers and teachers who, the authors cautioned, need to be aware of the likelihood of complex "interactions between linguistic challenges and science content when designing assessment for and providing instruction to ELLs" (p. 2343).

The remaining studies of classroom summative assessment with ELs reviewed here were also conducted in the science field. Work by Siegel (2007), who studied the assessment of life sciences in middle school classrooms, suggests ways in which classroom assessments might be best designed to optimize student performance. She modified existing writing tasks by adding visual supports and dividing prompts into smaller units. Using a pre-post test design, Siegel was able to document that ELs with high levels of English language proficiency, along with their non-EL peers, scored higher on the modified classroom assessments. Similarly, Lyon, Bunch, and Shaw (2012) found the students were able to navigate the demanding communicative situation of the performance assessments. The assessments required students to modify their language use to fit a range of participation configurations (e.g., whole group, small group, one-to-one) in order to interpret and present their science knowledge as well as use language to engage interpersonally with other students. However, echoing the findings of Siegel (2007), Lyon, Bunch, and Shaw (2012) wondered how well students with lower English language proficiency than their case study students would be able to participate in such assessments. The question is not trivial, as there is evidence that, along with language, epistemology (ways of knowing) and culturally determined practices influence students' interpretations of science and mathematics test items (Basterra, Trumbull, and Solano-Flores, 2011; Turkan and Lopez, 2017).

This evidence speaks to the need for careful interpretations of students' performance on assessment activities, if those activities are to accurately provide information about student progress toward learning goals (Solano-Flores and Nelson-Barber, 2001). Teachers evaluating their ELs may not have sufficient cultural awareness or familiarity with students' epistemologies and practices. Also, they may be biased against the culturally bounded responses their ELs offer to specific tasks and regard them as incorrect (Shaw, 1997). Consistently, there is evidence that, in evaluating students' responses to mathematics tasks, teachers tend to fail to give proper consideration to the cultural background of their ELs (Nguyen-Le, 2010). Moreover, there is evidence that teachers who have the same ethnic and cultural backgrounds as their ELs tend to articulate a more complex and sophisticated reasoning about the ways in which culture and language influence students' interpretations of items and their responses to those items. However, both these teachers and their teacher counterparts who do not share the ELs' ethnic and cultural backgrounds are equally limited in their ability to address culture in their interpretations of specific scenarios (Nguyen-Le, 2010). These findings indicate that, while necessary, the participation of educators who share ethnic or cultural background with their students in assessment endeavors is not sufficient to properly address the complex and subtle cultural influences that shape student performance in classroom STEM assessment.

### Classroom Formative Assessment of STEM with English Learners

Formative assessment involves gathering data or evidence of student learning *as* learning occurs so that teachers and students can benefit from the information generated during real-time instruction (i.e., short cycle formative assessment) or after reflection for modifying later lessons or future curricula choices (i.e., medium or long cycles) (e.g., Black and Wiliam, 1998, 2009; Heritage, 2010; Swaffield, 2011).

Formative assessment can occur in a variety of ways (Ayala et al., 2008; Ruiz-Primo and Furtak, 2007). As Heritage and Chang (2012) pointed out, "These include informal methods during the process of teaching and learning that are mostly planned ahead of instruction but can occur spontaneously (e.g., observations of student behavior, written work, representations, teacher student interactions and interactions among students) as well as more formal methods (e.g., through administering assessments that are specifically designed for formative purposes for ELL students)" (p. 2). Formal methods of formative assessment may involve giving students commercially available or teacher-created assessments such as quizzes and checklists (Shavelson, 2006). As long as the information they generate is used to inform instruction, rather than to summarize students' performances with a score or grade, these formal assessments also meet the definition of formative assessment recently revised by the Formative Assessment for Teachers and Students State Collaborative on Assessment and Student Standards (2017) of the Council of Chief State School Officers:

> Formative assessment is a planned, ongoing process used by all students and teachers during learning and teaching to elicit and use evidence of student learning to improve student understanding of intended disciplinary learning outcomes and support students to become self-directed learners.

Those who view formative assessment as an approach, rather than as formal tests or tasks administered to students, treat it as a process for generating information about where student learning currently is and where it needs to go next to meet a learning goal (e.g., Hattie and Timperley, 2007; Ruiz-Primo and Furtak, 2007). For example, through episodes of close questioning of ELs' thinking and planning around their persuasive writing, teachers are able to grasp in what ways they can scaffold learning to take the students to the next level of understanding (Furtak and Ruiz-Primo, 2008; Heritage and Heritage, 2013; Ruiz-Primo and Furtak, 2006). The line between instruction and assessment here is blurred: Where instruction stops and assessment starts during such interactions is not clear and may not be relevant. By being in such sustained conversations with a student, formative assessment is especially suited to assessing ELs' content thinking and learning (Alvarez et al., 2014; Bailey, 2017; Bailey and Heritage, 2014; Solano-Flores, 2016). Only when they are interacting with students in real time are teachers in a position to modify their own language as well as scaffold their students' language comprehension and production needs if and when those needs occur. In combination, these linguistic adjustments can seamlessly assist in the display of a student's content knowledge and abilities (Bailey, 2017).

Formative assessment also suits the assessment of STEM with ELs in several additional ways. For example, teachers may ask their students to express their ideas with drawings and to explain those ideas in their own words. Potentially, this approach not only allows students to demonstrate learning in multiple ways, but also allows informal triangulation of data (Alvarez et al., 2014; Ruiz-Primo, Solano-Flores, and Li, 2014). However, research is needed that allows proper identification of the ways in which these resources can be used effectively with ELs. Unfortunately, research and practice involving the use of visual (non-textual) resources in assessment wrongly assumes that visual information is understood in the same ways by all individuals and is not sensitive to the multiple variations of visual representations (see Wang, 2012) or the abstractness of many concepts.

Mixed-methods research conducted with science teachers of secondary-level general education students has found that written scaffolding (e.g., "focusing" sentence frames such as "What I saw was_____" and "Inside [the balloon] the particles were_____," and "connecting" sentence frames such as "Evidence for _____comes from the [activity or reading] because_____." p. 686) embedded in the formative assessment of written science explanations successfully increased the explicitness of the explanations from students at all levels of science achievement (Kang, Thompson, and Windschitl, 2014). Quantitative analyses revealed that contextualizing the focal science phenomena in the writing tasks was the most effective scaffold alone, even when used in combination with other proven scaffolding types such as providing rubrics, answer checklists, and sentence frames, and allowing students to diagram their explanatory models, as well as explain in writing. Qualitative analysis of the students' writing illustrated how contextualization (e.g., students selecting a geographic location of their own choosing to explain seasonal changes) along with combinations of the other scaffolds in this assessment meant that the "students were invited to engage in a high level of intellectual work" (Kang et al., 2014, p. 696).

This work can be informative for designing effective formative assessment opportunities with ELs. First, by knowing at what level of comprehension a student is making meaning of STEM content through the student's oral articulation of that content, a teacher can then devise a contingent pedagogical response: that is, the teacher can tailor the next steps of instruction to match the content and language needs of the student (Bailey, 2017). This approach is consistent with findings that using both written and oral prompts in teaching contributes to understanding where students are in their learning (Furtak and Ruiz-Primo, 2008). This may take the form of translating key STEM concepts into a student's first language, allowing students to make connections to their own cultural contexts, and supporting STEM instruction with images, graphics, manipulatives, and other relevant objects and material from everyday life.

Second, to be inclusive of ELs, formative assessment can be viewed as a form of social interaction through language (Ruiz-Primo, Solano-Flores, and Li, 2014). Formative assessment practices can lead to establishing "a talking classroom" (Sfard, 2015), and thus such practices can also provide a rich(er) language environment for ELs to participate (Ruiz-Primo, Solano-Flores, and Li, 2014; Solano-Flores, 2016) as they learn the STEM disciplines.

Third, formative assessment can foster students' agency in their STEM content learning, through a key focus on self-assessment and peer assessment made by formative assessment approaches (Heritage, 2013a). Research with the K–12 general population has documented the efficacy of self-assessment in particular on student learning outcomes (e.g., Andrade and Valtcheva, 2009; McMillan and Hearn, 2008). There is also some evidence of positive outcomes of formative assessment approaches that include student self- and peer assessment for EL learning in disciplines that are not STEM related (e.g., Lenski et al. [2006] in the area of literacy).

Self-directed learners are able to monitor and plan for their own learning through the feedback they generate for themselves with self-assessment. Related to the second point above, ELs who are also self-directed learners may be in a position to create their own English language-learning opportunities by not waiting for language learning chances to come to them. Rather, they can deliberately seek out additional language exposure throughout the school day, including during their STEM classes (Bailey and Heritage, 2018).

There has been a small number of studies on the effectiveness of formative approaches to assessment of mathematics and science with ELs specifically. The TODOS: Mathematics for ALL initiative conducted a series of research studies on the effectiveness of the interactive interview as a means of uncovering students' mathematical understanding. In one study, four 6th-grade Spanish-English bilingual students (their English language proficiency status was not reported) took part in multistage interactive interviews. Following an oral think-aloud to approximate a problem solution, students initially independently wrote draft responses to tasks focused on fractions, mixed numbers, percentages, and proportional reasoning. The interviews encouraged students to consider different problem solutions, test and revise their hypotheses, and use all their linguistic resources (e.g., both Spanish and English) for solving the tasks. Analyses of these interviews showed that this formative assessment approach "provided the means to develop student agency through problem solving, support and encourage mathematical innovation, and cultivate a shared sense of purpose in mathematics" (Kitchen, Burr, and Castellón, 2010, p. 68). While this assessment format yielded promising results with students who were Spanish-English bilinguals, the authors cautioned that the interview format is lengthy and requires a substantial time investment on the part of teachers (Castellón, Burr, and Kitchen, 2011).

In the area of science assessment, one recent mixed-methods study implemented "educative assessments" that were writing rich assessments for Grades 4 through 8. Educative assessments are designed to support teachers' instructional decision making, particularly in this instance with ELs in the areas of inquiry practices, academic language, and science content, which fits formative assessment as defined here (Buxton et al., 2013). These assessments were implemented as one component of the Language-Rich Science Inquiry for English-language Learners (LISELL) project. The assessments were found to support "teachers in diagnosing their students' emergent understandings. . . . And interpretation of assessment results led to changes in teachers' instructional decision making to better support students in expressing their scientific understandings" (Buxton et al., 2013, p. 347). Specifically, the teachers were able to support their students in building connections from everyday language (both English and Spanish) to disciplinary discourse during their science learning. However, Buxton and colleagues noted the necessary time required and the scaffolding that the teachers needed from the project during focus group sessions to draw conclusions about their students' learning.

In a study of two 9th-grade science classrooms in Canada, Slater and Mohan (2010a) reported how an ESL teacher and a science teacher collaborated to formatively assess their ELs to help improve their "use of English *in* and *for* science" (p. 93). The science teacher had a mix of English-only and more proficient ELs, whereas the ESL teacher had a class of relatively newcomer students who were beginning to acquire English. The newcomer ELs were predominantly users of Chinese as a first language. Both adopted a register approach to unpacking the language of science so that students could use all of their available linguistic resources to demonstrate their content knowledge. The science teacher focused on formatively assessing students' acquisition of the science register in his class through problem-solving, whereas the ESL teacher focused on explicit teaching and assessing of the knowledge structures of the register, namely the language underlying cause-effect reasoning, and problem-solving/decision-making in science to prepare her students for transfer to the science teacher's classroom. Slater and Mohan explained that "[w]hen teachers assess learners' knowledge of science, in [Systemic Functional Grammar] terms they are assessing whether the learners have built up the meaning potential of the science register and can apply it to relevant situations and texts" (p. 92).

Slater and Mohan (2010b) argued that oral explanations provide teachers with the requisite information they need to scaffold student learning. Moreover, these authors provided a clear example of formative assessment being ideally suited to EL pedagogy that integrates language and content learning; only by being engaged in an approach to formative assessment that requires oral discourse to generate evidence of science learning are teachers also able to build on what their students say contingently. This not only helps develop students' English language proficiency, but also works to further their explanations of "their understanding of cause and effect in order to further their content knowledge" (Slater and Mohan, 2010b, p. 267).

Also using students' explanations as the basis of generating evidence of learning, a study of kindergarten teachers illustrated how through intervention, they increased their implementation of simultaneous formative assessment of ELs' science and language knowledge (Bailey, Huang, and Escobar, 2011). This 3-year research-practice partnership assisted teachers in intentionally planning for and then putting into practice formative assessment with Spanish-dominant ELs by implementing three components of a formative assessment approach: (1) setting learning goals for science and language based on state science and ELD standards during lesson planning and using self-reflection guides; (2) making success criteria explicit to students during lessons so that they were aware of the desired goals; and (3) evoking evidence of student learning in both science and language learning using diverse ways, including through closely observing students engaged in different tasks and activities, questioning student comprehension and understanding, and inferring student understanding through the questions students asked them and other students. This small-scale qualitative study can only be suggestive of the impacts of formative assessment implementation on science and language learning, but it revealed that, over time, formative assessment was more frequently adopted and enabled teachers to identify gaps between current levels of student science and language understanding and the desired learning goals, as well as documented increased student engagement and talk during science lessons over the same time period.

In a recent review of formative assessment practices in science instruction, Gotwals and Ezzo (2018) also reported that teachers' use of scientific phenomena (e.g., observable events that allow students to develop predictions and explanations) to anchor their instruction provides opportunities for rich language use and engagement in science classrooms. These discussions in turn provide opportunities for formative assessment of student scientific understanding. This review also highlights the close connections between science instruction and assessment when a formative approach is adopted.

Bailey and Heritage (2018) provided several clinical examples of formatively assessing ELs in both mathematics and science among other content areas, also primarily with an emphasis on explanation as a cross-curriculum language practice. These examples provide elaborated descriptions of how teachers who have experience with implementing a formative approach to assessment pay close attention to both the current status of students' content learning and the kinds of language students use to exhibit their understanding (both orally and in written tasks). Only with this simultaneous focus, the authors argued, can teachers effectively develop contingent teaching that takes account of the integration of content and language: that is, make in-the-moment decisions to either make modifications to any content misconceptions or language ambiguities to complete the formative feedback loop, or to move on to presenting students with a suitably calibrated subsequent challenge. The centrality of this feedback loop in formative assessment is discussed in the next section.

## The Central Role of Feedback in Formative Assessment

Generating feedback so that teachers know what to teach next or which pedagogical moves to choose and provide feedback to students about how their learning is progressing is central to formative approaches to assessment (Ruiz-Primo, 2017). In a review of effectiveness, Hattie and Timperley (2007) defined the purpose of effective feedback as reducing the gap between a student's current understanding and a desired learning goal. Effective feedback provides answers to three main questions for the student (and the teacher): "Where am I going?" "How am I going?" and "Where to next?" (p. 86). Feedback that was effective was coupled with instruction-enhanced learning, whereas feedback that involved praise only was not effective for learning.

Effective feedback makes partners out of the student and the teacher, giving each a role in response to the same assessment information (e.g., Heritage, 2010; Kitchen, Burr, and Castellón, 2010; Li et al., 2010; Ruiz-Primo and Li, 2012, 2013). While most studies of the positive effects of feedback on the accuracy of students' own assessment of their performance have been conducted with adult and adolescent learners, van Loon and Roebers (2017) reported encouraging findings with German-speaking 4th- and 6th-grade students in Switzerland. Students studied concepts and their definitions, and they were then tested on their knowledge and asked to self-assess their performances. Feedback was effective in improving the accuracy of their self-assessments. The authors even reported that initial age differences in selecting what aspects of their work needed restudying went away after students received feedback on how to improve their definitions. These findings indicate that students used information from feedback to make themselves not only better self-evaluators but also better regulators of their own learning.

### Use of Learning Progressions with Formative Assessment

For over a decade, there has been much interest within the assessment field in the development of learning progressions, also known as trajectories of learning in some STEM disciplines (Shavelson, 2009; Wilson, 2009). Progressions have been used to guide classroom assessment, particularly formative approaches to assessment. Learning progressions are useful to formative approaches to assessment because they can provide the necessary details of how student thinking about a domain develops over time with instruction and experience with tasks and thus guide teachers in their choice of what next to teach and in their feedback to students on what next to learn.

There is variation in the design of learning progressions; some are hypothesized incremental developments in a domain often based on syntheses of research on children's conceptual knowledge, whereas others are empirically derived from authentic student performances (see Briggs et al., 2006). Some are designed to reference the academic content standards, others are based on "big ideas" or concepts within a domain of learning, and yet others are based on the analysis of the curriculum to be taught. If they are empirically based, learning progressions are designed to trace pathways of learning for a particular domain that students have demonstrated on tasks devised for that purpose that may also have been informed by the research on children's conceptual knowledge of a domain (Confrey and Maloney, 2010). When they are not empirically based, these ideas are based on logical analyses (Ayala et al., 2008; Ruiz-Primo, 2016; Ruiz-Primo and Li, 2012).

If they are well devised and implemented, learning progressions can be a framework to integrate assessment (both summative and formative) with instruction and can take account of developmental theories of learning (see National Research Council, 2005; Wilson and Toyama, 2018). However, the course of a progression is not developmentally inevitable for every student. Instead, a learning progression offers a sequence of "expected tendencies" along a continuum of increasing expertise (Confrey and Maloney, 2010). While most students will follow the different phases of the progression if it is well researched and designed, proponents of learning progressions point out that due to individual variation in student development and instructional experience, it is not expected that all students exhibit every growth point along the route to greater expertise (e.g., Heritage, 2008). Indeed, learning progressions are descriptions of typical development of a domain and are not intended for students and teachers to follow lockstep through each phase if students have already progressed to more sophisticated levels of understanding and skill.

Moreover, in contrast with state and professional organizations' standards for mathematics and science, many learning progressions or trajectories are not tied to specific grades or to a particular scope and sequence for learning, which is an important consideration for implementation with ELs who may have different pathways to arrive at successful STEM content learning. The learning of ELs with strong literacy skills but still emerging oral English skills, the learning of newcomers with extensive schooling experiences in their first language, or the learning of ELs with interrupted schooling may all be better understood with a learning progression of a specific domain (e.g., proportional reasoning, force and motion) rather than with summative or formative assessments of STEM content tied to a curriculum that is aligned to specific grade-level academic standards that may be out of synchrony with an EL's school experience.

Unfortunately, much of the work on progressions to date has focused on science and mathematics learning in general education contexts rather than with ELs specifically and has been articulated as a "promising approach" to evidence-based educational reform (see Corcoran, Mosher, and Rogat [2009] for discussion of science learning progressions and Daro, Mosher, and Corcoran [2011] for discussion of mathematics learning progressions).

Working in the area of mathematics, for example, Confrey (2012) and her colleagues have elaborated a learning trajectory for equipartitioning to capture the initial informal thinking of students about fairly sharing objects and single wholes as it evolves into the more complex understanding of sharing multiple wholes and "the equivalence of the operation $a \div b$, the quantity $a/b$, and the ratio $a/b$:1" (Wilson et al., 2014, p. 151). Subsequent professional learning with the equipartitioning trajectory enabled teachers to become aware of their students' mathematical thinking and where it fits on the trajectory. Becoming familiar with the trajectory also allowed teachers to increase their own knowledge of mathematics, although this was mediated by the teachers' prior mathematical knowledge for teaching (Wilson et al., 2014).

In a review of learning progressions in science learning (including example progressions for buoyancy, atomic molecular theory, and tracing carbon in ecosystems), Corcoran, Mosher, and Rogat (2009) explained that ideally learning progressions "are based on research about how students' learning actually progresses—as opposed to selecting sequences of topics and learning experiences based only on logical analysis of current disciplinary knowledge and on personal experiences in teaching. These hypotheses are then tested empirically to assess how valid they are (Does the hypothesized sequence describe a path most students actually experience given appropriate instruction?)" (p. 8).

With notable exceptions in a recent volume on STEM and ELs (Bailey, Maher, and Wilkinson, 2018), few studies have expressly included ELs in their descriptions of learning progression development and implementation. In that volume, Covitt and Anderson (2018) described a program of research in the science field that uses clinical interviews and written assignments with K–12 and university students in order to develop a comprehensive learning progression framework. Student oral and written performances in the genres of scientific discussion, namely explanation, argument, and prediction, show trajectories from less sophisticated informal discourse in these genres to more sophisticated scientific discourse. The authors pointed out how ELs are faced with the challenge of acquiring not only a new language for day-to-day purposes, but also the characteristics of these different scientific genres. Also adopting a learning progression approach to describe alignment among science and literacy curriculum, instruction, and summative and formative assessment in the same volume, Wilson and Toyama (2018) articulated how the implementation of learning progressions with ELs may possibly differ from that of non-ELs. First, ELs may follow the same learning progression as non-ELs but are systematically at lower anchoring points as measured by assessment items of tasks. Second, ELs may follow the same learning progression but assessment items behave differently for ELs (i.e., as revealed by differential item functioning

## BOX 7-1
### Example of Formative Assessment during a Mathematics Lesson in a Dual-Language Classroom

Ms. Garcia regularly uses one-on-one conferences with her 1st- and 2nd-grade students to obtain actionable information about their language use during her teaching of mathematics. The image below shows the template she uses to make notes about sentence structures in the context of mathematics problem solving during the conferences. The notes are organized under the headings of language feature, evaluating sentence structure, sentence structure modeled, and student response after modeling. There is also a space for her to write the next steps she wants the student to take. Once she has made notes, she uses the Dynamic Language Learning Progression to determine the "best fit" so she can decide on next steps. For this particular student, we see on her template in the figure below that one of her next steps was to "provide more opportunities for the use of complex sentences Model for support (Partner with Sean. Work on paraphrasing with prompts)."

SOURCE: Adapted from Bailey, Heritage, and Cardenas (forthcoming).

[DIF] analysis of summative assessments). Third, ELs may follow a different progression from non-ELs. These hypotheses can guide future research on the creation and validation of learning progressions in STEM with ELs.

Finally, Wylie and colleagues (2018) examined proportional reasoning in mathematics and language progressions in tandem. The language progressions for word-, sentence-, and discourse-level features had previously been empirically derived from both ELs' and non-ELs' oral and written performances on explanations tasks for the Dynamic Language Learning Progressions (DLLP) project (Bailey, 2017; Bailey and Heritage, 2014, forthcoming) and had been used by teachers as an interpretive framework for their formative assessment of language in the content areas (Bailey and Heritage, 2017). (See Box 7-1 for an example of how an elementary teacher of a dual-language classroom had created her own tool to guide her next-steps pedagogical moves as a result of using the sentence structure progression.) Wylie and colleagues (2018) placed written explanations of the mathematical reasoning of 6th- and 7th-grade students on both the proportional reasoning and language progressions to produce four interpretative quadrants of intersectional performance. They noted that few non-EL students could convey high levels of mathematical understanding without corresponding high levels of written explanation abilities, which has implications for ELs as well. The simultaneous use of STEM and language progressions appeared to be absent in the literature for either ELs or non-ELs prior to this initial effort. Although dual progressions for multiplication and language were also applied to the writing of a 6th-grade EL student as a proof of concept, the current state of research in this area is too much in its infancy to know how useful this technique will be for generating feedback to ELs and teachers on progress in the STEM disciplines and their related language learning.

### Limitations of Classroom Summative and Formative Assessment with ELs

In the field of early childhood education, the Migration Policy Institute recently concluded, "Together, the lack of longitudinal research and dearth of multilingual assessments complicate efforts to ensure that [. . .] programs are adequately preparing students..." (McNamara, 2016). A similar conclusion can be drawn from the review of available research on classroom assessments and assessment practices for evaluating the STEM preparation of K–12 ELs. With few exceptions (e.g., Wilson and Toyama, 2018), there has been little attempt at building a systemic congruence between large-scale and classroom assessment. The ideal of a *comprehensive, coherent,* and *continuous* assessment system (National Research Council, 2001) has yet to be realized. Both summative and formative assessments could yield richer information when mutual links among ELD standards, math or science standards, and classroom STEM-related instructional tasks are considered together.

Moreover, effective classroom summative and formative assessment will require robust teacher professional development for effective implementation (Lyon, 2013). Several studies point to what this might take in terms of teacher preparation and continued professional supports. This support may come in the form of professional learning communities or communities of learning to create sustainable venues for teachers to discuss interpretations of assessment information, acquire knowledge of learning progression tied to formative assessment, and enhance strategies for addressing EL learning in terms of both their language and STEM content knowledge and skills (e.g., Bailey and Heritage, forthcoming; Buxton et al., 2013). These studies also found that classroom assessment involves an investment in time. This is not simply time for teachers to build their familiarity with assessment techniques, but also sustained amounts of time to carry out assessment often with individual students.

There are important criticisms of learning progressions and the role they can play in both effective instruction and formative assessment. These criticisms stem in part from concerns that learning progressions may be erroneously implemented as prescriptive sequences of acquisition rather than as descriptive guides to the general course of development of a domain (e.g., Goldenberg, 2015). Learning may occur gradually, but it may not be a linear process. This may be especially true of language learning that occurs in the real-world context of the classroom rather than neatly falling along a simple-to-more complex continuum (Velasco, 2015). Until more research is conducted on the validity of learning progressions in effective instruction and formative assessment approaches with ELs, the implementation of STEM and language learning progressions remain a promising practice with ELs.

Teacher bias in assessment of students may also be of particular concern with classroom assessment of student learning. Teachers need to build familiarity with the cultural backgrounds of their students so that they do not come to erroneous conclusions about their students' STEM understanding. Teachers also need to build expertise with data use as a result of generating the amounts of information yielded by classroom summative and formative assessment. Addressing teacher bias will be just one aspect of the validity of classroom assessments that needs to be established. Application of NGSS and the college- and career-ready standards for mathematics initiatives to ELs' STEM classroom summative assessment also waits validation. Establishing the validity of formative assessment approaches will be particularly challenging given their more qualitative and informal nature. However, Heritage (2013b) has suggested how formative assessment validity can be considered differently from traditional notions of validity, reliability, and feasibility.

## Teacher Preparation and Certification Examinations

To be successfully implemented, any improvement in assessment practices for ELs needs to be supported by proper training for decision makers, school administrators, and educators. This training needs to address the heterogeneity of EL populations and the limitations of testing accommodations and accessibility resources as forms of support for ELs. The preparation of teachers and the examinations required of those seeking credentials and certification need to be designed to support and evaluate teachers as they become critical assessment users, task designers, and interpreters of student performances. Teachers also need greater familiarity with data use and support in becoming critical assessment users (e.g., questioning the validity of assessments not developed or normed with students who might not share the backgrounds and educational opportunities of their students). Teachers need to critically interpret and integrate information from assessment with other sources of information (e.g., linguistic knowledge, experience, practices) on their ELs' STEM learning (Chrzanowski, 2015; Lyon, 2013). Moreover, STEM-specific teaching examinations can be designed to assess teacher STEM knowledge, their pedagogy of STEM, and teacher pedagogy of STEM specifically for ELs. This would be tantamount to promoting enhanced teacher skills for the benefit of ELs through teacher certification examinations. Existing limitations of teacher examinations and certification processes may stem from the fact that teachers of English as a foreign language and bilingual teachers are viewed as equivalent in their roles and responsibilities, and the requisite knowledge, skills, and abilities for effectively fulfilling these roles are considered equivalent. Certification exams also undervalue the importance of teachers' sensitivity to the social and cultural aspects of being an EL along with language considerations that contribute to teachers' effectiveness with ELs. Incorporating the knowledge, skills, and abilities that enable teachers to provide socially and culturally responsive instruction to ELs would improve the examination and certification process for both kinds of teacher.

Teacher certification examinations of STEM have improved in their degree of coverage of important constructs, as well as in their integration of academic language and inclusion of EL instructional strategies. One such examination is the edTPA, which is a widely available teacher candidate assessment now used in most states (American Association of Councils for Teacher Education, 2018). This examination is based on the former Performance Assessment for California Teachers (PACT) that has integrated a focus on mathematics, academic language, and EL students for all teacher candidates (Bunch, Aguirre, and Téllez, 2015). As Castellano and colleagues (2016) pointed out, "The Performance Assessment for California Teachers (PACT) is the first assessment of teaching to include mastery of AL [academic language] knowledge by teachers not specializing in teaching ELLs. The decision to include AL teaching proficiency on the PACT followed from a combination of important considerations, including the need to provide a rich education to the diverse California student population" (p. 5).

Teacher certification examinations for STEM teaching could be reviewed to determine whether the examination content is up to date on EL assessment issues and knowledge, and whether they effectively capture the assessment literacy teachers will need, both in terms of interpreting the results of state-wide, large-scale STEM assessments, and at the local level in which they are implementing classroom summative and formative assessment approaches (Bailey, Maher and Wilkinson, 2018).

## SUMMARY

Important improvements are needed if large-scale assessment programs and classroom assessment practices are to produce accurate indicators of ELs' STEM achievement and if these indicators are to effectively inform policy and practice. If STEM assessment is to serve ELs, the following are important considerations: "inappropriate definitions of (EL) populations and English proficiency; failure to include these students in the entire process of assessment development; limited participation of language specialists in the process of item writing; and the use in large-scale assessment programs of testing accommodations that are linguistically ineffective" (Songer and Ruiz-Primo, 2012, p. 688). In order for these transformations to take place, revising existing practices is crucial. Needed changes concern the methods used to address the characteristics of ELs, to develop STEM assessment instruments, to analyze and interpret information produced by tests, and to prepare teachers to effectively design and interpret STEM assessments in their classrooms. Although the move away from accommodations in favor of accessibility resources is viewed positively, the implementation of accommodations must also improve in those situations where accommodations are provided.

While there is evidence that formative assessment approaches, particularly those that encourage student self- and peer assessment, have positive outcomes for learning, this evidence comes from the area of literacy, not STEM, and has not systematically included EL students. The studies of STEM and formative assessment of EL students, while limited, suggest that the nature of formative assessment lends itself to creating a "talking classroom" that is both supportive of greater language exposure for students and a desired condition of formative assessment so that teachers can observe student interactions and engagement to make judgements about student understanding and progress.

Two key aspects of formative assessment emerge from the literature: the role of feedback for teachers and students and the use of learning progressions as an interpretive framework for student performance on tasks. Much of this work is conducted with non-EL students, and the few studies that do include EL students tend to be small scale or report clinical applications of formative assessment. Nevertheless, formative assessment stands to become *transformative* assessment for EL students and their teachers that could lead to a greater degree of self-regulated learning for students who are engaged in self-assessment as a component of formative assessment. For teachers, learning progressions used as an interpretive framework for formative assessment have highlighted the need for greater STEM knowledge on the part of teachers to be able to work well with learning progressions used in formative assessment. Lastly, although teacher certification exams have improved in recent years in their coverage of important constructs and the integration of academic language, their coverage of the knowledge, skills, and abilities to provide socially and culturally responsive instruction to ELs and of current EL classroom assessment is unclear.

## REFERENCES

Abedi, J. (2004). The *No Child Left Behind Act* and English language learners: Assessment and accountability issues. *Educational Researcher, 33*(1), 4–14.

Abedi, J. (2010). Research and recommendations for formative assessment with English language learners. In H.L. Andrade and G.J. Cizek (Eds.), *Handbook of Formative Assessment* (pp. 181–197). New York: Routledge.

Abedi, J. (2014). The use of computer technology in designing appropriate test accommodations for English language learners. *Applied Measurement in Education, 27*(4), 261–272.

Abedi, J., Hofstetter, C., and Lord, C. (2004). Assessment accommodations for English language learners: Implications for policy-based empirical research. *Review of Educational Research, 74*(1), 1–28.

Allalouf, A. (2003). Revising translated differential functioning items as a tool for improving cross-lingual assessment. *Applied Measurement in Education, 16*(1), 55–73.

Alvarez, L., Ananda, S., Walqui, A., Sato, E., and Rabinowitz, S. (2014). *Focusing Formative Assessment on the Needs of English Language Learners.* San Francisco, CA: WestEd.

American Association of Councils for Teacher Education. (2018). *edTPA FAQ.* Available: http://edTPA.aacte.org [August 2018].

American Educational Research Association, American Psychological Association, and National Council on Measurement in Education. (2014). *Standards for Educational and Psychological Testing.* Washington, DC: Joint Committee on Standards for Educational and Psychological Testing.

Andrade, H., and Valtcheva, A. (2009). Promoting learning and achievement through self-assessment. *Theory Into Practice, 48*(1), 12–19.

Avenia-Tapper, B., and Llosa, L. (2015). Construct relevant or irrelevant? The role of linguistic complexity in the assessment of English learner's science knowledge. *Educational Assessment, 20*(2), 95–111.

Ayala, C., Shavelson, R.J., Ruiz-Primo, M.A., Brandon, P.R., Yin, Y., Furtak, E.M., Young, D.B., and Tomita, M. (2008). From formal embedded assessments to reflective lessons: The development of formative assessment studies. *Applied Measurement in Education, 21*(4), 315–334.

Bailey, A.L. (2000/2005). Language analysis of standardized achievement tests: Considerations in the assessment of English language learners. In J. Abedi, A.L. Bailey, and F.A. Butler (Eds.), *Assessing English Language Learners: Considerations from Three Perspectives* (CSE Technical Report 663). Los Angeles: University of California, National Center for Research on Evaluation, Standards, and Student Testing.

Bailey, A.L. (2017). Progressions of a new language: Characterizing explanation development for assessment with young language learners. *Annual Review of Applied Linguistics, 37,* 241–263. doi:10.1017/S0267190517000113.

Bailey, A.L., and Carroll, P.E. (2015). Assessment of English language learners in the era of new academic content standards. *Review of Research in Education, 39*(1), 253–294.

Bailey, A.L., and Heritage, M. (2014). The role of language learning progressions in improved instruction and assessment of English language learners. *TESOL Quarterly, 48*(3), 480–506.

Bailey, A.L., and Heritage, M. (2017). Imperatives for teacher education: Findings from studies of effective teaching for English language learners. In M. Peters, B. Cowie, and I. Menter (Eds.), *A Companion to Research in Teacher Education* (pp. 697–712). Berlin, Germany: Springer.

Bailey, A.L., and Heritage, M. (2018). *Self-Regulation in Learning: The Role of Language and Formative Assessment.* Cambridge, MA: Harvard Education Press.

Bailey, A.L., and Heritage, M. (forthcoming). *Progressing Students' Language Day-by-Day.* Thousand Oaks, CA: Corwin Press.

Bailey, A.L., Heritage, M., and Cardenas, G. (2018). Discourse features of the DLLP. In A.L. Bailey and M. Heritage (Eds.), *Developing Students' Language Day-by-Day* (Chapter 6). Thousand Oaks, CA: Corwin Press.

Bailey, A.L., Huang, Y.D., and Escobar, M. (2011). I can explain: Academic language for science among young English language learners. In P.E. Noyce and D.T. Hickey (Eds.), *New Frontiers in Formative Assessment* (pp. 143–158). Cambridge, MA: Harvard Education Press.

Bailey, A.L., Maher, C., and Wilkinson, L. (Eds.) (2018). *Language, Literacy and Learning in the STEM Disciplines: How Language Counts for English Learners.* New York: Routledge Publishers.

Bailey, A.L., Butler, F.A., Stevens, R., and Lord, C. (2007). Further specifying the language demands of school. In A.L. Bailey (Ed.), *The Language Demands of School: Putting Academic English to the Test* (pp. 103–156). New Haven, CT: Yale University Press.

Basterra, M., Trumbull, E., and Solano-Flores, G. (Eds.). (2011). *Cultural Validity in Assessment: Addressing Linguistic and Cultural Diversity.* New York: Routledge.

Bennett, R.E. (2010). Cognitively Based Assessment of, for, and as Learning (CBAL): A preliminary theory of action for summative and formative assessment. *Measurement, 8*(2–3), 70–91.

Black, P., and Wiliam, D. (1998). Assessment and classroom learning. *Assessment in Education: Principles, Policy and Practice, 5*(1), 7–73.

Black, P., and Wiliam, D. (2004). Classroom assessment is not (necessarily) formative assessment (and vice-versa). *Teachers College Record, 106*(14), 183–188.

Black, P., and Wiliam, D. (2009). Developing the theory of formative assessment. *Educational Assessment, Evaluation, and Accountability, 21*(1), 5–31.

Black, P., Wilson, M., and Yao, S.Y. (2011). Road maps for learning: A guide to the navigation of learning progressions. *Measurement: Interdisciplinary Research & Perspective, 9*(2–3), 71–123.

Blyth, C.R. (1972). On Simpson's paradox and the sure-thing principle. *Journal of the American Statistical Association, 67*(338), 364–366.

Briggs, D., Alonzo, A., Schwab, C., and Wilson, M. (2006). Diagnostic assessment with ordered multiple choice items. *Educational Assessment, 11*(1), 33–63.

Bunch, G., Aguirre, J.M., and Téllez, K. (2015). Integrating a focus on academic language, English learners, and mathematics teacher candidates' responses on the performance assessment for California teachers (PACT). *The New Educator, 11*(1), 79–103.

Buxton, C.A., Allexsaht-Snider, M., Suriel, R., Kayumova, S., Choi, Y.J., Bouton, B., and Baker, M. (2013). Using educative assessments to support science teaching for middle school English-language learners. *Journal of Science Teacher Education, 24*(2), 347–366.

Camilli, G. (2013). Ongoing issues in test fairness. *Educational Research and Evaluation: An International Journal on Theory and Practice, 19*(2–3), 104–120.

Castellano, K.E., Duckor, B., Wihardini, D., Telléz, K., and Wilson, M. (2016). Assessing academic language in an elementary mathematics teacher licensure exam. *Teacher Education Quarterly, 43*(1), 3–17.

Castellón, L.B., Burr, L., and Kitchen, R.S. (2011). English language learners' conceptual understanding of fractions: An interactive interview approach as a means to learn with understanding. In K. Téllez, J.N. Moschkovich, and M. Civil (Eds.), *Latinos and Mathematics Education: Research on Learning and Teaching in Classrooms and Communities* (pp. 259–282). Charlotte, NC: Information Age Publishing.

Cheuk, T., Daro, P., and Daro, V. (2018). The language of mathematics and summative assessment: Interactions that matter for English learners. In A.L. Bailey, C.A. Maher, and L.C. Wilkinson (Eds.), *Language, Literacy and Learning in the STEM Disciplines: How Language Counts for English Learners* (pp. 187–205). New York: Routledge.

Chia, M., and Kachchaf, R. (2018). Designing, developing, and implementing an accessible computer-based national assessment system. In S. Elliott, R.J. Kettler, P. Beddow, and A. Kurtz (Eds.), *Handbook of Accessible Instruction and Testing Practices: Issues, Innovations, and Applications* (pp. 75–91). New York: Springer.

Chia, M., Hock, M., Vallenzuela, S., and Paul, J. (2013). *Providing Accessible Assessments in Next Generation Assessments.* Presented at Symposium at the Annual Conference of the National Conference on Student Assessment, Washington, DC.

Chrzanowski, A.M. (2015). Teachers as critical users of assessment for emergent bilingual students. Doctoral dissertation. School of Education, University of Colorado Boulder. https://scholar.colorado.edu/cgi/viewcontent.cgi?article=1073&context=educ_gradetds [August 2018].

Confrey, J. (2012). Better measurement of higher-cognitive processes through learning trajectories and diagnostic assessments in mathematics: The challenge in adolescence. In V. Reyna, M. Dougherty, S.B. Chapman, and J. Confrey (Eds.), *The Adolescent Brain: Learning Reasoning, and Decision Making* (pp. 155–182). Washington, DC: American Psychology Association.

Confrey, J., and Maloney, A. (2010, June). The construction, refinement, and early validation of the equipartitioning learning trajectory. In *Proceedings of the 9th International Conference of the Learning Sciences* (vol. 1, pp. 968–975). Chicago, IL: International Society of the Learning Sciences.

Corcoran, T.B., Mosher, F.A., and Rogat, A. (2009). *Learning Progressions in Science: An Evidence-based Approach to Reform.* London, UK: Consortium for Policy Research in Education.

Council of Chief State School Officers. (2012). *Framework for English Language Proficiency Development Standards Corresponding to the Common Core State Standards and the Next Generation Science Standards.* Washington, DC: Author.

Covitt, B., and Anderson, C.W. (2018). Assessing scientific genres of explanation, argument, and prediction. In A.L. Bailey, C.A. Maher, and L.C. Wilkinson (Eds.), *Language, Literacy and Learning in the STEM Disciplines: How Language Counts for English Learners* (pp. 206–230). New York: Routledge.

Daro, P., Mosher, F., and Corcoran, T. (2011). *Learning Trajectories in Mathematics: A Foundation for Standards, Curriculum, Assessment, and Instruction.* Available: http://www.cpre.org/images/stories/cpre_pdfs/learning%20trajectories%20in%20math_ccii%20report.pdf [June 2018].

Durán, R.P. (2008). Assessing English-language learners' achievement. *Review of Research in Education, 32*(1), 292–327.

Ercikan, K. (2002). Disentangling sources of differential item functioning in multi-language assessments. *International Journal of Testing, 2*(3-4), 199–215.

Ercikan, K., Roth, W.-M., Simon, M., Sandilands, D., and Lyons-Thomas, J. (2014). Inconsistencies in DIF detection for sub-groups in heterogeneous language groups. *Applied Measurement in Education, 27*(4), 275–285.

Erikson, F. (2007). Some thoughts on "proximal" formative assessment of student learning. *Yearbook of the National Society for the Study of Education, 106*(1), 186–216. doi:10.1111/j.1744-7984.2007.00102.x.

Formative Assessment for Students and Teachers State Collaborative on Assessment and Student Standards. (2017). *Revising the Definition of Formative Assessment.* Available: https://www.michigan.gov/documents/mde/New_FAST_SCASS_definition_paper_June_27_2017_601106_7.pdf [June 2018].

Frantz, R.S., Bailey, A.L., Starr, L., and Perea, L.M. (2014). Measuring academic language proficiency in school-age language proficiency assessments under new college and career readiness standards in the United States. *Language Assessment Quarterly, 11*(4), 432–457.

Furtak, E., and Ruiz-Primo, M.A. (2008). Making students' thinking explicit in writing and discussion: An analysis of formative assessment prompts. *Science Education, 92*(5), 799–824.

Goldenberg, C. (2015). How might existing learning progressions help or hinder English language learners/emergent bilinguals in meeting the demands of the Common Core State Standards? In G. Valdés, K. Menken, and M. Castro (Eds.), *Common Core and ELLs/Emergent Bilinguals: A Guide for All Educators* (pp. 72–76). Philadelphia, PA: Caslon.

Gotwals, A.W., and Ezzo, D. (2018). Formative assessment: Science and language with English language learners. In A.L. Bailey, C.A. Maher, and L.C. Wilkinson (Eds.), *Language, Literacy and Learning in the STEM Disciplines: How Language Counts for English Learners.* New York: Routledge.

Hambleton, R.K. (2005). Issues, designs, and technical guidelines for adapting tests into multiple languages and cultures. In R.K. Hambleton, P.F. Merenda, and C.D. Spielberger (Eds.), *Adapting Educational and Psychological Tests for Cross-Cultural Assessment* (pp. 3–38). Mahwah, NJ: Lawrence Erlbaum Associates.

Hambleton, R., and Rodgers, J. (1995). Item bias review. *Practical Assessment, Research & Evaluation, 4*(6), 1–3. Available: http://PAREonline.net/getvn.asp?v=4&n=6 [September 2018].

Hattie, J., and Timperley, H. (2007). The power of feedback. *Review of Educational Research, 77*(1), 81–112.

Heritage, M. (2008). *Learning Progressions: Supporting Instruction and Formative Assessment.* Washington, DC: Council of Chief State School Officers.

Heritage, M. (2010). *Formative Assessment and Next-Generation Assessment Systems: Are We Losing an Opportunity?* Washington, DC: Council of Chief State School Officers.

Heritage, M. (2013a). *Formative Assessment: A Process of Inquiry and Action.* Cambridge, MA: Harvard Education Press.

Heritage, M. (2013b). Gathering evidence of student understanding. In J.H. McMillan (Ed.), *SAGE Handbook of Research on Classroom Assessment* (pp. 179–196). Thousand Oaks, CA: SAGE.

Heritage, M., and Chang, S. (2012). *Teacher Use of Formative Assessment Data for English Language Learners.* Los Angeles: University of California, National Center for Research on Evaluation, Standards, and Student Testing.

Heritage, M., and Heritage, J. (2013). Teacher questioning: The epicenter of instruction and assessment. *Applied Measurement in Education, 26*(3), 176–190.

Hopkins, M., Thompson, K.D., Linquanti, R., Hakuta, K., and August, D. (2013). Fully accounting for English learner performance: A key issue in ESEA reauthorization. *Educational Researcher, 42*(2), 101-108.

Kachchaf, R.R. (2011). *Exploring Problem-Solving Strategies on Multiple-Choice Science Items: Comparing Native Spanish-Speaking English Language Learners and Mainstream Monolinguals.* Unpublished doctoral dissertation. University of Colorado Boulder. Available: https://core.ac.uk/download/pdf/54848999.pdf [September 2018].

Kane, M.T. (2006). Validation. In R.L. Brennan (Ed.), *Educational Measurement* (4th ed., pp. 17–64). Westport, CT: American Council on Education and Praeger.

Kang, H., Thompson, J., and Windschitl, M. (2014). Creating opportunities for students to show what they know: The role of scaffolding in assessment tasks. *Science Education, 98*(4), 674–704.

Kieffer, M.J., Lesaux, N.K., Rivera, M., and Francis, D.J. (2009). Accommodations for English language learners taking large-scale assessments: A meta-analysis on effectiveness and validity. *Review of Educational Research, 79*(3), 1168–1201.

Kitchen, R.S., Burr, L., and Castellón, L.B. (2010). Cultivating a culturally affirming and empowering learning environment for Latino/a youth through formative assessment. In R.S. Kitchen, and E. Silver (Eds.), *Assessing English Language Learners in Mathematics* (A Research Monograph of TODOS: Mathematics for All) (pp. 59–82). Washington, DC: National Education Association.

Klein, S.P., and Hamilton, L. (1998). *Large Scale Testing Current Practice and New Directions.* Santa Monica, CA: The RAND Corporation.

Kopriva, R.J. (2014). Second-generation challenges for making content assessments accessible for ELLs. *Applied Measurement in Education, 27*(4), 301–306.

Kopriva, R.J., Emick, J.E., Hipolito-Delgado, C.P., and Cameron, C.A. (2007). Do proper accommodation assignments make a difference? Examining the impact of improved decision making on scores for English language learners. *Educational Measurement: Issues and Practice, 26*(3), 11–20.

Kopriva, R., Winter, P., Triscari, R., Carr, T.G., Cameron, C., and Gabel, D. (2013). *Assessing the Knowledge, Skills, and Abilities of ELs, Selected SWDs, and Controls on Challenging High School Science Content: Results from Randomized Trials of ONPAR and Technology-Enhanced Traditional End-of-Course Biology and Chemistry Tests.* Available: http://iiassessment.wceruw.org/research/researchPapers/Assesing%20KSAs%20ONPAR%20HS%20Exper%20Study%20Results%203%205%2013.pdf [June 2018].

Lee, O., Quinn, H., and Valdés, G. (2013). Science and language for English language learners in relation to Next Generation Science Standards and with implications for Common Core State Standards for English language arts and mathematics. *Educational Researcher, 42*(4), 223–233.

Lee, F. Y., Silverman, F. L., and Montoya, P. (2002). Assessing the math performance of young ESL students. *Principal, 81*(3), 29–31.

Lenski, S.D., Ehlers-Zavala, F., Daniel, M.C., and Sun-Irminger, X. (2006). Assessing English-language learners in mainstream classrooms. *The Reading Teacher, 60*(1), 24–34.

Li, M., Quynn, J.A., Ruiz-Primo, M.A., Tasker, T., Minstrell, J., Anderson, R.A. (2010, April). *Secondary Science Teachers Written Feedback Practices in Students Notebooks.* Paper presented at the Annual Meeting of the American Educational Research Association, Denver, CO. Available: http://www.aera.net/Publications/Online-Paper-Repository/AERA-Online-Paper-Repository/Owner/143621 [September 2018].

Linquanti, R., Cook, H.G., Bailey, A.L., and MacDonald, R. (2016). *Moving Toward a More Common Definition of English Learner: Collected Guidance for States and Multi-state Assessment Consortia.* Washington DC: Council of Chief State School Officers.

Llosa, L. (2016). Assessing students' content knowledge and language proficiency. In E. Shohamy and I. Or (Eds.), *Encyclopedia of Language and Education* (vol. 7, pp. 1–12). New York: Springer International.

Llosa, L., Lee, O., Jiang, F., Haas, A., O'Connor, C., Van Booven, C.D., and Kieffer, M.J. (2016). Impact of a large-scale science intervention focused on English language learners. *American Educational Research Journal, 53*(2), 395–424.

Lyon, E.G. (2013). What about language while equitably assessing science? Case studies of preservice teachers' evolving expertise. *Teaching and Teacher Education, 32*, 1–11. doi:10.1016/j.tate.2012.12.006.

Lyon, E.G., Bunch, G.C., and Shaw, J.M. (2012). Language demands of an inquiry based science performance assessment: Classroom challenges and opportunities for English learners. *Science Education, 96*(4), 631–651.

Martiniello, M. (2009). Linguistic complexity, schematic representations, and differential item functioning for English language learners in math tests. *Educational Assessment, 14*(3), 160–179.

McMillan, J.H., and Hearn, J. (2008). Student self-assessment: The key to stronger student motivation and higher achievement. *Educational Horizons, 87*(1), 40–49.

McNamara, K. (2016). *Dual Language Learners in Head Start: The Promises and Pitfalls of New Reforms.* Washington, DC: Migration Policy Institute. Available: http://www.migrationpolicy.org/article/dual-language-learners-head-start-promises-and-pitfalls-new-reforms [June 2018].

Mislevy, R.J., and Durán, R.P. (2014). A sociocognitive perspective on assessing EL students in the age of Common Core and Next Generation Science Standards. *TESOL Quarterly, 48*(3), 560–585.

National Academies of Sciences, Engineering, and Medicine. (2017). *Promoting the Educational Success of Children and Youth Learning English: Promising Futures.* Washington, DC: The National Academies Press.

National Governors Association Center for Best Practices, and Council of Chief State School Officers. (2010). *Common Core State Standards.* Washington, DC: Author.

National Research Council. (2001). *Knowing What Students Know: The Science and Design of Educational Assessment.* Washington DC: National Academy Press.

National Research Council. (2005). *How Students Learn: History, Mathematics, and Science in the Classroom.* Washington, DC: The National Academies Press.

NGSS Lead States (2013). *Next Generation Science Standards: For States, by States.* Washington, DC: The National Academies Press.

Nguyen-Le, K. (2010). *Personal and Formal Backgrounds as Factors Which Influence Linguistic and Cultural Competency in the Teaching of Mathematics.* Doctoral dissertation. School of Education, University of Colorado Boulder.

Noble, T., Rosebery, A., Suarez, C., and Warren, B. (2014). Science assessments and English language learners: Validity evidence based on response processes. *Applied Measurement in Education, 27*(4), 248–260.

Noyce, P.E., and Hickey, D.T. (Eds.). (2011). *New Frontiers in Formative Assessment*. Cambridge, MA: Harvard Education Press.

Oliveri, M.E., Ercikan, K., and Zumbo, B.D. (2014). Simulating the effect of linguistic heterogeneity on the accuracy of detection of differentially functioning items between linguistic groups. *Applied Measurement in Education, 27*(4), 286–300.

Pappamihiel, N.E., and Mihai, F. (2006). Assessing English language learners' content knowledge in middle school classrooms. *Middle School Journal, 38*(1), 34–43.

Penock-Roman, M., and Rivera, C. (2011). Mean effects of test accommodations for ELLs and non-ELLs: A meta-analysis of experimental studies. *Educational Measurement: Issues and Practice, 30*(3), 10–28.

Rivera, C., Collum, E., Willner, L.N., and Sia, Jr. J.K. (2006). Study 1: An analysis of state assessment policies regarding the accommodation of English language learners. In C. Rivera and E. Collum (Eds.), *State Assessment Policy and Practice for English Language Learners: A National Perspective* (pp. 1–136). Mahwah, NJ: Lawrence Erlbaum Associates.

Rodriguez-Mojica, C. (2018). From test scores to language use: Emergent bilinguals using English to accomplish academic tasks. *International Multilingual Research Journal, 12*(1), 31–61.

Rogoff, B. (1995). Observing sociocultural activity on three planes: Participatory appropriation, guided participation, and apprenticeship. In J.V. Wertsch, P. del Río, and A. Alvarez (Eds.), *Sociocultural Studies of Mind*. New York: Cambridge University Press.

Ruiz-Primo, M.A. (2011). Informal formative assessment: The role of instructional dialogues in assessing students' learning. *Special Issue in Assessment for Learning Studies of Educational Evaluation, 37*(1), 15–24.

Ruiz-Primo, M.A. (2016). Implementing high quality assessment for learning: Mapping as a professional development tool for understanding the *What to learn, Why to learn it*, and *How to learn it*. In D. Laveault and L. Allal (Eds.), *Assessment for Learning—Meeting the Challenge of Implementation* (pp. 219–236). New York: Springer International.

Ruiz-Primo, M.A. (2017). Informal assessment. In M. Peters (Ed.), *Encyclopedia of Educational Philosophy and Theory* (vol. 2, pp. 1142–1147). Singapore: Springer.

Ruiz-Primo, M.A., and Brookhart, S. (2018). *Using Feedback to Improve Learning*. New York: Routledge.

Ruiz-Primo, M.A., and Furtak, E.M. (2006). Informal formative assessment and scientific inquiry: Exploring teachers' practices and student learning. *Educational Assessment, 11*(3–4), 205–263.

Ruiz-Primo, M.A., and Furtak, E.M. (2007). Exploring teachers' informal formative assessment practices and students' understanding in the context of scientific inquiry. *Journal of Educational Research in Scientific Teaching, 44*(1), 57–84.

Ruiz-Primo, M.A., and Li, M. (2012). Examining formative feedback in the classroom context: New research perspectives. In J.H. McMillan (Ed.), *Handbook on Research on Classroom Assessment* (pp. 215–232). Los Angeles, CA: SAGE Publications.

Ruiz-Primo, M.A., and Li, M. (2013). Analyzing teachers' feedback practices in response to students' work in science classrooms. Special Issue on Using Evidence to Take Action: Strategies Teachers Use to Deconstruct Student Work. *Applied Measurement in Education, 26*(3), 163–175.

Ruiz-Primo, M.A., and Li, M. (2015). The relationship between item context characteristics and student performance: The case of the 2006 and 2009 PISA science items. *Teachers College Record, 117*(1), 010306.

Ruiz-Primo, M.A., DiBello, L., and Solano-Flores, G. (2014). *Supporting the Implementation of the Next Generation Science Standards (NGSS) through Research: Assessment.* Available: https://narst.org/ngsspapers/assessment.cfm [June 2018].

Ruiz-Primo, M.A., Solano-Flores, G., and Li, M. (2014). Formative assessment as a process of interaction through language: A framework for the inclusion of English Language Learners. In P. Colbert, C. Wyatt-Smith, and V. Klenowski (Eds.), *The Enabling Power of Assessment* (pp. 265–282). Heidelberg, Germany: Springer-Verlag.

Ruiz-Primo, M.A. Furtak, E., Ayala, C., Yin, Y., and Shavelson. R.J. (2010). Formative assessment, motivation, and science learning. In G.J. Cizek, and H. Andrade (Eds.), *Handbook of Formative Assessment* (pp. 139–158). New York: Routledge, Taylor & Francis Group.

Ryan, J. (2006). Practices, uses, and trends in student test score reporting. In S.M. Downing and T.M. Haladyna (Eds.), *Handbook of Test Development* (pp. 677–710). Mahwah, NJ: Lawrence Erlbaum Associates.

Saunders, W.M., and Marcelletti, D.J. (2013). The gap that can't go away: The catch-22 of reclassification in monitoring the progress of English learners. *Educational Evaluation and Policy Analysis, 35*(2), 139–156.

Sfard, A. (2015). Why all this talk about talking classrooms? Theorizing the relation between talking and learning. In L.B. Resnick, C.S.C. Asterhan, and S.N. Clarke (Eds.), *Socializing Intelligence through Academic Talk and Dialogue* (pp. 245–254). Washington, DC: American Educational Research Association.

Shaftel, J., Belton-Kocher, E., Glasnapp, D., and Poggio, G. (2006). The impact of language characteristics in mathematics test items on the performance of English language learners and students with disabilities. *Educational Assessment, 11*(2), 105–126.

Shavelson, R.J. (2006). On the integration of formative assessment in teaching and learning: Implications for new pathways in teacher education. In F. Oser, F. Achtenhagen, and U. Renold (Eds.), *Competence-Oriented Teacher Training: Old Research Demands and New Pathways* (pp. 63–78). Utrecht, The Netherlands: Sense.

Shavelson, R.J. (2009). Reflections on learning progressions. *Learning Progressions in Science*, 13–26. Available: https://link.springer.com/chapter/10.1007/978-94-6091-824-7_2 [June 2018].

Shavelson, R.J., Young, D., Ayala, C., Brandon, P., Furtak, E., Ruiz-Primo, M.A., Tomita, M., and Yin, Y. (2008). On the impact of curriculum-embedded formative assessment on learning: A collaboration between curriculum and assessment developers. *Applied Measurement in Education, 21*(4), 295–314.

Shaw, J.M. (1997). Threats to the validity of science performances assessments for English language learners. *Journal or Research in Science Teaching, 34*(7), 721–743.

Shepard, L., Taylor, G., and Betebenner, D. (1998). *Inclusion of Limited-English-Proficient Students in Rhode Island's Grade 4 Mathematics Performance Assessment* (Center for the Study of Evaluation Technical Report 486). Los Angeles: University of California.

Short, D. (1993). Assessing integrated language and content instruction. *TESOL Quarterly, 27*(4), 627–656.

Siegel, M.A. (2007). Striving for equitable classroom assessments for linguistic minorities: Strategies for and effects of revising life science items. *Journal of Research in Science Teaching, 44*(6), 864–881.

Silliman, E.R., Wilkinson, L. C., and Brea-Spahn, M. (2018). Writing the science register and multiple levels of language implications of English learners. In A.L. Bailey, C.A. Maher, and L.C. Wilkinson (Eds.), *Language, Literacy and Learning in the STEM Disciplines: How Language Counts for English Learners* (pp. 115–140). New York: Routledge.

Sireci, S.G., Li, S., and Scarpati, S. (2003). *The Effects of Test Accommodation on Test Performance: A Review of the Literature* (Research Report 485). Amherst, MA: Center for Educational Assessment.

Slater, T., and Mohan, B. (2010a). Cooperation between science teachers and ESL teachers: A register perspective. *Theory Into Practice, 49*(2), 91–98.

Slater, T., and Mohan, B. (2010b). Towards systematic and sustained formative assessment of causal explanations in oral interactions. In A. Paran and L. Sercu (Eds.), *Testing the Untestable in Language Education* (vol. 17, pp. 256–269). Bristol, UK: Multilingual Matters.

Smarter Balanced Assessment Consortium. (2017a). *Higher Education Approved.* Available: http://www.smarterbalanced.org/about/higher-education [November 2017].

Smarter Balanced Assessment Consortium. (2017b). *Illustration Glossary Implementation Readiness.* Available: http://www.smarterapp.org/irp/IRP-Illustration-Glossary-TestPackage.html [May 2018].

Solano-Flores, G. (2009). The testing of English language learners as a stochastic process: Population misspecification, measurement error, and overgeneralization. In K. Ercikan and W.M. Roth (Eds.), *Generalizing from Educational Research* (pp. 33–48). New York: Routledge.

Solano-Flores, G. (2011). Assessing the cultural validity of assessment practices: An introduction. In M.R. Basterra, E. Trumbull, and G. Solano Flores (Eds.). *Cultural Validity in Assessment: Addressing Linguistic and Cultural Diversity* (pp. 3–21). New York: Routledge.

Solano-Flores, G. (2012). *Translation Accommodations Framework for Testing English Language Learners in Mathematics.* Available: https://portal.smarterbalanced.org/library/en/translation-accommodations-framework-for-testing-english-language-learners-in-mathematics.pdf [June 2018].

Solano-Flores, G. (2016). *Assessing English Language Learners: Theory and Practice.* New York: Routledge.

Solano-Flores, G., and Hakuta, K. (2017). *Assessing Students in Their Home Language.* Available: https://stanford.app.box.com/s/uvwlgjbmeeuokts6c2wnibucms4up9c2 [June 2018].

Solano-Flores, G., and Li, M. (2009). Language variation and score variation in the testing of English language learners, native Spanish speakers. *Educational Assessment, 14*(3-4), 1–15.

Solano-Flores, G., and Li, M. (2013). Generalizability theory and the fair and valid assessment of linguistic minorities. *Educational Research and Evaluation, 19*(2–3), 245–263.

Solano-Flores, G., and Nelson-Barber, S. (2001). On the cultural validity of science assessments. *Journal of Research in Science Teaching, 38*(5), 553–573.

Solano-Flores, G., Backhoff, E., and Contreras-Niño, L.A. (2009). Theory of test translation error. *International Journal of Testing, 9*(2), 78–91.

Solano-Flores, G., Shade, C., and Chrzanowski, A. (2014). *Item Accessibility and Language Variation Conceptual Framework.* Available: https://portal.smarterbalanced.org/library/en/item-accessibility-and-language-variation-conceptual-framework.pdf [June 2018].

Solano-Flores, G., Wang, C., Kachchaf, R., Soltero-Gonzalez, L., and Nguyen-Le, K. (2014). Developing testing accommodations for English language learners: Illustrations as visual supports for item accessibility. *Educational Assessment 19*(4), 267–283.

Songer, N.B., and Ruiz-Primo, M.A. (2012). Assessment and science education: Our essential new priority? *Journal of Research in Science Teaching, 49*(6), 683–690.

Stone, E.A., and Cook, L.L. (2018). Fair testing and the role of accessibility. In S. Elliott, R.J. Kettler, P. Beddow, and A. Kurtz (Eds.), *Handbook of Accessible Instruction and Testing Practices: Issues, Innovations, and Applications* (pp. 59–74). New York: Springer.

Swaffield, S. (2011). Getting to the heart of authentic assessment for learning. *Assessment in Education: Principles, Policy and Practice, 18*(4), 433–449.

Trumbull, E., and Solano-Flores, G. (2011). Addressing the language demands of mathematics assessments: Using a language framework and field-based research findings. In M.R. Basterra, E. Trumbull, and G. Solano-Flores (Eds.), *Cultural Validity in Assessment: Addressing Linguistic and Cultural Diversity* (pp. 218–253). New York: Routledge.

Turkan, S., and Lopez, A., (2017). Helping English language learners access the language and content of science through the integration of culturally and linguistically valid assessment practices. In L.C. de Oliveira and K.C. Wilcox (Eds.), *Teaching Science to English Language Learners* (pp. 163–190). Basingstoke, UK: Palgrave Macmillan.

Turkan, S., and Liu, O.L. (2012). Differential performance by English language learners on an inquiry-based science assessment. *International Journal of Science Education, 34*(15), 2343–2369.

U.S. Department of Education. (2017). *Race to the Top Assessment Program.* Available: http://www2.ed.gov/programs/racetothetop-assessment/awards.html [June 2018].

Valdés, G., Menken, K., and Castro, M. (2015). *Common Core, Bilingual and English Learners: A Resource for Educators.* Philadelphia, PA: Caslon.

van Loon, M.H., and Roebers, C.M. (2017). Effects of feedback on self-evaluations and self-regulation in elementary school. *Applied Cognitive Psychology, 31*(5), 508–519.

Velasco, P. (2015). What are language learning progressions and why are they important to educators. In G. Valdés, K. Menken, and M. Castro (Eds.), *Common Core and ELLs/Emergent Bilinguals: A Guide for All Educators.* Philadelphia, PA: Caslon.

Wagner, C.H. (1982). Simpson's paradox in real life. *The American Statistician, 36*(1), 46–48.

Wang, C. (2012). *The Use of Illustrations in Large-Scale Science Assessment: A Comparative Study.* Doctoral dissertation. University of Colorado Boulder. Available: https://core.ac.uk/download/pdf/54849364.pdf [August 2018].

WIDA Consortium World-Class Instructional Design Assessment (2007). *English Language Proficiency Standards and Resource Guide: Prekindergarten through Grade 12.* Madison: Wisconsin Center for Education Research and the Board of Regents of the University of Wisconsin System.

Wiliam, D. (2006). Formative assessment: Getting the right focus. *Educational Assessment, 11*(3–4), 283–289.

Wilson, M. (2009). Measuring progressions: Assessment structures underlying a learning progression. *Journal of Research in Science Teaching, 46*(6), 716–730.

Wilson, M. (2016). The importance of classroom assessment. *National Council on Measurement in Education Newsletter, 24*(2), 2–3.

Wilson., M., and Toyama, Y. (2018). Formative and summative assessments in science and literacy integrated curricula: A suggested alternative approach. In A.L. Bailey, C.A. Maher, and L.C. Wilkinson (Eds.), *Language, Literacy and Learning in the STEM Disciplines: How Language Counts for English Learners* (pp. 231–260). New York: Routledge.

Wilson, P.H., Sztajn, P., Edgington, C., and Confrey, J. (2014). Teachers' use of their mathematical knowledge for teaching in learning a mathematics learning trajectory. *Journal of Mathematics Teacher Education, 17*(2), 149–175.

Wolf, M.K., Kao, J.C., Herman, J., Bachman, L.F., Bailey, A.L., Bachman, P.L., Farnsworth, T., and Chang, S.M. (2008). *Issues in Assessing English Language Learners: English Language Proficiency Measures and Accommodation Uses: Literature Review (Part 1 of 3)* (Report 731). Los Angeles, CA: University of California, National Center for Research on Evaluation, Standards, and Student Testing, Graduate School of Education and Information.

Wolf, M.K., Kao, J.C., Rivera, N.M., and Chang, S.M. (2012). Accommodation practices for English language learners in states' mathematics assessments. *Teachers College Record, 114*(3), 1–26.

Wylie, C., Bauer, M, Bailey, A.L., and Heritage, M. (2018). Formative assessment of mathematics and language: Applying companion learning progressions to reveal greater insights to teachers. In A.L. Bailey, C.A. Maher, and L.C. Wilkinson (Eds.), *Language, Literacy and Learning in the STEM Disciplines: How Language Counts for English Learners* (pp. 143–168). New York: Routledge.

Zieky, M. (2006). Fairness reviews in assessment. In S.M. Downing and T.M. Haladyna (Eds.), *Handbook of Test Development* (pp. 359–376). Mahwah, NJ: Lawrence Erlbaum Associates.

Zwick, R., Senturk, D., and Wang, J. (2001). An investigation of alternative methods for item mapping in the National Assessment of Educational Progress. *Educational Measurement: Issues & Practice, 20*(2), 15–25.

# 8

# Building Capacity to Transform Science, Technology, Engineering, and Mathematics (STEM) Learning for English Learners

This chapter outlines practical implications for district and school leaders as they work to implement the new directions for STEM learning for English learners (ELs) presented in previous chapters. As Penuel and colleagues (2011) noted, an important strategy for promoting such implementation efforts, and for ensuring their sustainability, is to build capacity through intentional efforts to develop policies, processes, and practices that help an innovation travel through a system. As described in Chapter 2, the United Nations Development Programme (2009) defines capacity-building as: "the process through which individuals, organizations and societies obtain, strengthen and maintain the capabilities to set and achieve their own development objectives over time" (p. 5). Central to such capacity building is transformation, or the changing of mindsets and attitudes, that is generated and sustained over time (United Nations Development Programme, 2009). Following this definition, we view capacity building as more than the allocation of resources and engagement in implementation efforts; it also requires the questioning of broader policies and practices and concerted efforts to shift them.

Given that implementation researchers have long found that capacity can serve as both a resource and a constraint for change (e.g., Darling-Hammond, 1993; Penuel et al., 2011), the first half of this chapter outlines aspects of federal and state policy and practice that enable or constrain district and school capacity-building efforts focused on transforming STEM learning opportunities for ELs. These features of the broader educational landscape are important considerations in district and school capacity building, as they may present levers for change or warrant critique and revisions. The second half of the chapter describes how some districts and schools in the United States have worked to build capacity related to EL and STEM education within the current policy landscape.

It is important to note that existing research does not offer sufficient causal evidence related to the effectiveness of different approaches for improving EL outcomes across districts and schools. As such, the committee reviewed research on instructional reform more broadly, as well as the available descriptive evidence related to policies and practices for ELs. Further, we relied on presentations made during committee meetings and the expertise of committee members, especially those who have worked with districts and schools to develop their EL and STEM-related capacity. Therefore, the findings presented in this chapter should be read as suggestive of what matters in EL STEM capacity building rather than a firm set of guidelines.

## FEDERAL AND STATE POLICY CONSIDERATIONS

In addition to offering a vision for STEM education that considers the role that language plays in the learning of content, previous chapters in this report described the complexities inherent in integrating content and language in the classroom. The challenges educators face in facilitating such integration are in many ways related to the larger U.S. policy context that has historically treated language learning as separate from the learning of content. These aspects of federal and state policy are described below, in addition to relevant shifts in policy that have opened up opportunities for considering language and content integration in STEM subjects.

### Federal Accountability and Assessment Requirements

Accountability policy under the federal No Child Left Behind Act (NCLB) of 2002 shined a light on the education of ELs, defining ELs as a subgroup in Title I accountability and requiring EL inclusion in statewide achievement testing and data reporting. This policy was meant to ensure that districts and schools monitored and attended to student achievement in reading/language arts and mathematics, as well as high school graduation rates. For all students, however, this high-stakes accountability policy led to an emphasis on reading and mathematics instruction to the exclusion of other content areas, like science (Dee and Jacob, 2010). For ELs, given that English language proficiency fundamentally influences performance on assessments administered in English, students at beginning levels of English proficiency often cannot demonstrate their knowledge of content on standardized tests (Abedi and Gándara, 2006; Martiniello, 2008), notwithstanding concerns with the reliability and validity of such assessments for ELs outlined in Chapter 7. Furthermore, the way in which the EL subgroup is defined in federal policy results in a constantly fluctuating subgroup as ELs continuously enter and exit through identification and reclassification processes. This fluctuation places unfair expectations on educators to demonstrate improved academic performance on an index that is unstable because it is based on a constantly shifting population (Hopkins et al., 2013).

Under NCLB, districts and schools receiving Title III funding were also required to monitor and report ELs' annual progress in learning English and attainment of English language proficiency. Title III accountability provisions, combined with Title I high-stakes accountability emphasizing testing in English, thus afforded no incentives for districts or schools to use primary language instruction or assessments, and instead emphasized rapid English acquisition (Gándara and Baca, 2008; Menken and Solorza, 2014). In many ways, these policies reified long-standing assumptions in the field that ELs need to acquire English before learning academic content (Canagarajah, 2015). Furthermore, the separation of accountability for ELs' academic progress and language proficiency between Title I and Title III ignored the connection between language and academic development (Working Group on ELL Policy, 2015).

The lack of attention to language and content integration in NCLB was addressed, at least to some extent, in the more recent Every Student Succeeds Act (ESSA) signed into law in late 2015. Rather than splitting accountability for ELs' academic progress and language proficiency development between Title I and Title III, ESSA moved Title III accountability for English language progress and proficiency fully into Title I. Title I provisions now require states to administer and report school performance on annual assessments of core content as well as English language proficiency, and to determine long-term goals for progress in both areas. In terms of core content, ESSA maintains the requirement that students participate in statewide achievement testing in reading/language arts and mathematics in Grades 3–8 and once in high school, with some exceptions allowed for recently arrived ELs. ESSA also continued the requirement put forward in NCLB that states assess science at least once in each of Grades 3–5, 6–9, and 10–12 (Penfield and Lee, 2010), and added reporting requirements for science assessment results. With respect to English language proficiency, ESSA allows states to consider ELs' time in U.S. schools and initial proficiency when setting expected timeframes for language development. Overall, these changes attend to EL inclusion in mathematics and science testing and reporting and offer more realistic expectations for English language proficiency development. Nevertheless, researchers argue that more accurate expectations for ELs' academic progress would also account for correlations between ELs' level of English language proficiency and their scores on content-based achievement tests (Hopkins et al., 2013). They assert that accountability systems that do not consider the relationship between language development and academic achievement will thus continue to overestimate achievement gaps and may negatively impact district and school ratings (Robinson-Cimpian, Thompson, and Umansky, 2016).

At the state level, ESSA requires the development of statewide accountability plans that include multiple measures of student performance and opportunity to learn (see Section 1111(c)(4)(B) of the act). In addition to the achievement and English language proficiency requirements mentioned above, states are required to include the following in their accountability plans:

1. another "valid and reliable statewide academic indicator" for elementary and middle schools, which can be a measure of student growth;
2. the 4-year adjusted cohort graduation rate for high schools (states may add an extended adjusted cohort graduation rate if they choose); and
3. at least one other measure of school quality or student success that is valid, reliable, and comparable across the state, such as student engagement, educator engagement, student access to advanced coursework, postsecondary readiness, school climate and safety, or other measures.

These additional indicators and measures have the potential to bring important information to bear on whether or not ELs have equitable access to STEM courses, as well as their opportunities to learn in STEM subjects. For example, the inclusion of course access and completion as a statewide measure of school quality or student success (#3 above) could reveal the extent to which ELs at the secondary level have equitable access to core content and college preparatory coursework, including STEM-related subjects (Callahan and Hopkins, 2018; Robinson-Cimpian, Thompson, and Umansky, 2016). At the elementary level, including a measure of instructional time provided in core content areas (i.e., reading/language arts, mathematics, science) would provide similar information and indicate the extent to which ELs are exposed to STEM content in the primary grades.

### English Language Proficiency and Content Standards

Beyond accountability and assessment requirements, Title I provisions require that states adopt rigorous college- and career-ready standards in reading/language arts, mathematics, and science, as well as corresponding English language proficiency standards that reflect the skills and practices

ELs need to engage with academic standards. As the Council of Chief State School Officers (CCSSO, 2012) pointed out, many states are in the process of developing or adopting English language proficiency standards that align with content standards such as the Common Core State Standards and Next Generation Science Standards (NGSS). As noted in Chapter 2 of this report, these shifts represent a step forward in terms of compelling policy makers and practitioners to attend simultaneously to content and language, and thus for transforming teaching and learning environments for ELs in STEM subjects.

These policy changes require effective implementation to facilitate positive change in ELs' trajectories. Further, as Bunch, Kibler, and Pimental (2012) pointed out, "Any discussion about potential affordances [of standards implementation] for ELs must consider variation among ELs, including age, grade level, native languages, language proficiency levels, literacy background both in English and other languages, and quality of previous schooling" (p. 2). Research is needed that examines how districts and schools implement integrated language and content standards, and whether and how such integration facilitates improvement in outcomes for diverse groups of ELs. Moreover, as many scholars have pointed out, these shifts necessitate that all PreK–12 educators engage in rigorous standards-aligned content and language instruction (Santos, Darling-Hammond, and Cheuk, 2012); thus, the development of capacity to serve ELs in STEM subjects is a critical issue for English as a second language, bilingual, and content area teachers (Valdés, Kibler, and Walqui, 2014).

### English Learner Reclassification

ESSA provisions under Title III also require that states adopt standardized entry and exit procedures for identifying and reclassifying English learners. In states (e.g., California, Florida, Oregon, Texas) that have allowed school districts to define their own exit criteria, a reclassified EL in one district may still be considered a current EL in a neighboring district (Linquanti, 2001; Parrish et al., 2006; Tanenbaum et al., 2012). These variations can be problematic in terms of access to services (Goldenberg and Rutherford-Quach, 2010) as well as students' long-term outcomes (Hill, Weston, and Hayes, 2014). Whereas some states (e.g., New York, Washington) have long relied solely on ELs' performance on a standardized English language proficiency assessment and require that ELs score above an established cut-point to be considered for reclassification, others (e.g., California) also required a passing score on content-based assessments (e.g., a standardized English language arts test).

As noted in Chapter 2, although removing content-based criteria for adjusting reclassification cut-points may increase reclassification rates and afford ELs increased access to STEM coursework; the success of ELs in those courses will depend on district and school capacity to address ELs' linguistic and academic needs in those courses, which is presently uneven (Cimpian, Thompson, and Makowski, 2017). In light of these complexities, some states are exploring innovative approaches to EL reclassification. For example, California is considering using the state English language proficiency test, as is required under ESSA, in addition to employing methods that provide impact data on the relationship of English language proficiency test scores to English language arts and mathematics test scores to inform the setting of cut-points (Cook et al., 2012). Further, they are collaborating with EL researchers to develop a teacher-administered language use observation protocol (Molle et al., 2016) that would inform teachers' recommendations.

While states consider their reclassification guidelines, it will be important to attend to their effects on currently and formerly designated ELs' access to and outcomes in STEM at the district and school level. Findings from a series of regression discontinuity studies point out that, depending on the services available in districts and schools, a misplaced reclassification threshold can lead to substantial negative effects on EL achievement, course-taking, and graduation, for either students who remain ELs or those who are reclassified (Carlson and Knowles, 2016; Cimpian, Thompson, and Makowski, 2017; Robinson, 2011; Robinson-Cimpian and Thompson, 2016; Umansky, 2016). Moreover, mere placement in coursework is not enough to facilitate EL access to STEM content and providing instruction that ensures ELs' successful completion of STEM courses requires local capacity development (Kanno and Kangas, 2014; Thompson, 2017).

## Funding

Funding choices at state and local levels affect the degree to which ELs have equitable access to STEM courses and rigorous language and content instruction. Overall, the cost of educating ELs varies between districts and schools depending on the characteristics of the EL population, the programs and services provided, and personnel costs (Sugarman, 2016). Federal funding for ELs under Title III of ESSA is distributed to states based on their overall share of ELs, as determined by state English language proficiency assessments, and on the number of immigrant students served, as indicated by the American Community Survey. Many states also provide supplementary funding to school districts using a weighted formula based on the size of their EL populations. Some states base the amount of funding that districts receive on ELs' grade level and/or language proficiency level, or the types of services provided. Each of these funding mechanisms is based on the number of currently classified ELs, and thus depends on state identification and reclassification criteria. As Wixom (2015) pointed out, "State funding systems have the potential to incentivize districts to shuffle ELs around different programs depending on funding availability, exit ELs from language programs too quickly or let students remain in EL programs longer than they should" (p. 4). Each of these practices has potentially negative effects on ELs access to STEM courses and content.

At the local level, districts distribute state funding for ELs in a variety of ways. Some districts allocate funds to schools on a per-pupil basis, while others allocate staff positions to schools based on enrollment, with ELs receiving greater funding based on need. Moreover, whereas some districts maintain authority over school funding and staffing, others allow school leaders to make these decisions.

### Instructional Policies and Programs

Although state policies related to ELs typically focus on finance, identification, reclassification, performance monitoring, standards, and educator quality (Wixom, 2015), some states also set policy related to the use of home languages for instructional purposes (National Academies of Sciences, Engineering, and Medicine, 2017). Differences in state policy in this area have implications for the kinds of programs available to ELs and their subsequent outcomes. As described in Chapter 2, ELs who are enrolled in bilingual programs and who attend school in states with bilingual policies tend to perform better in mathematics and science as measured by standardized achievement tests (López et al., 2014; McEneaney, López, and Nieswandt, 2014; Steele et al., 2017; Valentino and Reardon, 2015). Although some states (e.g., Connecticut, Illinois, New Jersey, New York, and Texas) mandate that districts with more than 20 ELs at the same grade level from the same language background provide bilingual programming, other states (e.g., California, Arizona, Massachusetts) passed English-only policies that decreased bilingual programs statewide. California and Massachusetts amended these mandates in 2017, with California also implementing an EL Road Map that outlines a comprehensive approach to EL education and affirms ELs' multilingual abilities (California Department of Education, 2018). Nonetheless, Arizona maintains its English-only policy and further requires that ELs participate in 4 hours of daily English Language Development instruction, often to the exclusion of meaningful content instruction (Gándara and Hopkins, 2010).

State policy related to EL instruction shapes policy and practice at the local level. Given that school districts play key roles in setting and implementing instructional policy in the United States (Honig, 2006; Spillane, 1996), the programs designed and implemented by district leaders often serve as local language policies that guide the provision of services for ELs

(Hopkins, 2016). In designing programs that attend to ELs' language and content needs, district leaders wrestle with what some have described as conflicting principles set forth by two relevant Supreme Court cases: *Brown* and *Lau*.[1] While *Brown* declared that the provision of separate educational settings was not equal, *Lau* argued that differential treatment was necessary when failure to do so would deny students—specifically ELs—access to an equitable education (Thompson, 2013). To address the requirements of both *Brown* and *Lau*, some states mandate that districts provide both designated and integrated ELD instruction, with the former addressing ELs' language development for a specific time period, often in a separate classroom, and the latter including ELs in content (e.g., STEM) courses with integrated language instruction.

Aligned with these policies, a majority of districts and schools, especially in states that do not require or offer support for bilingual programming, implement pull-out ESL programs at the elementary level or ELD course tracks at the secondary level. These programs focus on developing ELs' English language proficiency in separated environments. Content instruction is then provided to ELs in integrated classrooms either when they are deemed proficient enough in English to be successful, or when a teacher can provide sufficient attention to language development. Educators rely on these approaches, which tend to separate language and content and exclude ELs from content area instruction for a variety of reasons, including: (1) they assume that ELs need to attain a certain level of proficiency in English before engaging in content area coursework (Met, 1994; Minicucci and Olsen, 1992); (2) the constraints of scheduling mean that ELs in ESL or ELD courses do not have sufficient time during the school day for content courses, especially at the secondary level (Callahan, Wilkonson, and Muller, 2010); and (3) most content teachers are not prepared to work with ELs (Ballantyne et al., 2008; Gándara et al., 2005).

At the elementary level, this siloed approach emerges in how ESL services are conceptualized, as they tend to supplant, or at best supplement, language arts instruction; thus, attention to language development in content areas like mathematics and science can be limited. Implications of these separated structures are that: (1) ESL teachers assume primary responsibility for EL learning, (2) content teachers lack sufficient preparation to provide properly challenging instruction and experiences to ELs, and (3) there is little coordination or collaboration between teachers (Hopkins, Lowenhaupt, and Sweet, 2015). Nonetheless, there is a growing prevalence of co-teaching approaches in U.S. elementary schools, where ESL specialists and general education teachers collaborate to deliver linguistically respon-

---

[1]Brown v. Board of Education of Topeka, 347 U.S. 483 (1954) and Lau v. Nichols, 414 U.S. 563 (1974).

sive content instruction (Bell and Baecher, 2012; Dove and Honinsfeld, 2012; Valdés, Kibler, and Walqui, 2014). At the secondary level, ELs are often less likely to take STEM courses (Callahan, Wilkson, and Muller, 2010) or are enrolled in less rigorous content classes with underprepared teachers (Dabach, 2015). As argued in prior chapters, these practices can foreclose opportunities for developing the language of the STEM subject areas, and they can have serious implications for graduation and college entry if ELs are not able to access the courses they need to graduate high school in a timely manner.

### Graduation Requirements

States are also responsible for outlining high school graduation requirements. While these requirements vary in their rigor and content coverage, they generally mandate completion of a certain number of units in English, math, science, social studies, physical education, art, and foreign language. Many ELs at the secondary level have difficulty fulfilling these requirements because they are required to demonstrate sufficient proficiency in English or complete English language development prerequisites. This is especially true for newcomers at the high school level, who are often placed in non-credit-bearing courses as they learn English (Callahan, 2005). This practice makes it challenging for high school newcomers to complete high school, especially when state policies preclude ELs from continuing in their studies past a certain age (e.g., 18 or 21), or require that students attend alternative or vocational schools after aging out. As a recent CCSSO report points out (Umansky et al., 2018), educators have found that meeting high school graduation requirements before aging out is particularly challenging for newcomers who arrive with limited or interrupted formal education, including refugees.

Notwithstanding these challenges, a potential opportunity related to high school graduation for ELs is the implementation of the Seal of Biliteracy in many states. The Seal of Biliteracy is "an award made by a state department of education or local district to recognize a student who has attained proficiency in English and one or more other world languages by high school graduation" (American Council on the Teaching of Foreign Languages, 2015, p. 2). Some states, such as Oregon, provide opportunities for ELs to receive world language credit to acknowledge their native language skills, which affords ELs more access to STEM classes and improves their chances of graduating on time (Greenberg Motamedi and Jaffery, 2014).

## Teacher Preparation

As has been stated previously in this report, another key issue in transforming STEM learning for ELs is the capacity of the workforce to teach language and content in integrated settings. Given that most content teachers have received little preparation to work with ELs (Ballantyne et al., 2008; Gándara et al., 2005), some states have initiated course requirements and teacher certification policies focused on EL instruction. Although all states offer ESL certificates, only 21 states require specialized certification to teach ELs, and 7 states have no such requirements (López, Scanlan, and Gundrum, 2013). Other states fall somewhere in between; for example, Missouri and Pennsylvania require that all preservice teachers complete a 3-hour course related to teaching ELs, yet this requirement does not apply to practicing teachers. Overall, these policy differences mean that some states have fewer teachers who have the skills necessary to design rigorous instruction for ELs in STEM subjects. In some locales, the lack of content teachers qualified to work with ELs can be more pronounced at the secondary level; in one Connecticut district, for example, ELs in Grades K–1 were much more likely to be taught by EL-certified teachers than ELs in Grades 9–12 (79% compared to 31% [Parker, O'Dwyer, and Irwin, 2014]).

There is also insufficient infrastructure for equipping STEM teachers to work with ELs, and professional development related to teaching ELs in the content areas is not required for STEM teachers who serve ELs. It should be noted that while institutions of higher education, Regional Educational Labs, and county offices of education attempt to fill these gaps in STEM for ELs through state- or federally funded programs (e.g., the National Professional Development program funded by the Office for English Language Acquisition), these efforts are by no means equally distributed across or within states.

## CAPACITY BUILDING AT THE DISTRICT AND SCHOOL LEVEL

The first section of this chapter outlined how federal and state policy approaches both enable and constrain the integration of language and STEM content. District and school leaders wrestle with these challenges and opportunities as they work to design and implement equitable instructional and assessment practices for ELs in grades PreK–12, the ideals of which have been outlined in previous chapters. Research on instructional reform more broadly may be helpful in these efforts. This research consistently shows that top-down reform models are neither transformative nor sustainable, and that both organizational and individual capacity development are needed to facilitate large-scale instructional change (e.g., Hargreaves and

Fullan, 2012; Spillane, Hopkins, and Sweet, 2017; Spillane and Thompson, 1997).

In this section, we present a framework for district and school capacity building for transforming EL learning in STEM that is based around continuous instructional improvement cycles. We then describe how some districts and schools have (and have not) intentionally and strategically designed and developed systemic change across aspects of this framework. To do so, we draw on the available research literature, as well as committee members' experiences working in and with districts and schools undertaking efforts to improve ELs' access to and experiences in STEM. Although we describe each component of the framework separately, these components are best considered holistically in order to facilitate systemic transformation.

## A Framework for Continuous Instructional Improvement for ELs in STEM

In a study of six U.S. school districts demonstrating different levels of progress with ELs, the Council of Great City Schools characterized EL improvement efforts as complex, in that they require explicit and continuous attention to interactions between and among a range of organizational and instructional policies and practices (Horwitz et al., 2009). Although focused on improvements in language arts and reading instruction, the districts they studied that made significant strides with respect to addressing instructional equity and quality for ELs attended to these policies and practices with focused, coherent, strategic, and sustained continuous improvement efforts. The lessons from such efforts have important implications for teaching ELs in STEM subjects.

Scholars studying systemic science education reform in U.S. school districts describe three interrelated areas around which such continuous improvement efforts align: organizational culture, educators' capability, and policy and management (Blumenfeld et al., 2000). Organizational culture encompasses local norms, routines, and practices that shape district and school culture as well as expectations for educator professionalism, collaboration, and reflection. Educators' capability considers educators' beliefs and expertise that influence their ability to implement curriculum, strategies, and other practices. Finally, continuous improvement efforts are supported by appropriate policies and management, which may include funding, resources, scheduling, staffing, and allocation of responsibility.

Indeed, a recent study examining large-scale reform efforts to transform science teacher quality for Latino ELs in Grades 4–8 showed that when these three areas are achieved and aligned, significant growth in teacher quality and science achievement is possible (Johnson, Bolshakova, and Waldron, 2016). Based on this scholarship, as well as committee exper-

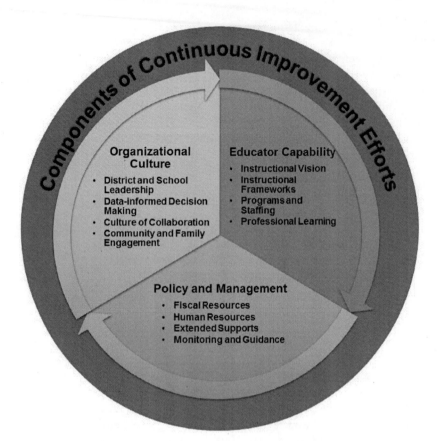

**FIGURE 8-1** Components of continuous improvement efforts.

tise, we developed a framework outlining the components of continuous improvement efforts for local systems leaders to consider as they work to facilitate instructional equity and quality for ELs in STEM education (see Figure 8-1). In the sections that follow, we describe each component in more detail, and provide examples from school districts across the United States undertaking such efforts.

## Organizational Culture

Improving student learning in deep and sustained ways requires "reciprocal accountability" (Elmore, 2004), where all community stakeholders (e.g., district and school leaders, teachers, families, students) take individual and joint responsibility for owning and executing an instructional improvement plan. Too often, accountability is operationalized punitively from the top down (Ladd, 2017). When accountability is reciprocal, however, all stakeholders are responsible to each other for achieving common goals. Committee members who have worked in school districts engaged in continuous improvement efforts, have observed that resources are in place to facilitate capacity-building, processes are transparent and inclusive, and roles and expectations are clearly defined. Moreover, everyone's work is evaluated so that appropriate action can be taken to improve performance when capacity or will is lacking (Bryk et al., 2010; Futernick, 2010). Overall, the extant literature suggests that establishing an organizational culture based on reciprocal accountability for ELs in STEM requires attention to district and school leadership, data-informed decision making, norms of interaction, and community and family engagement, as detailed below.

## District and School Leadership

Elfers and Stritikus (2014) noted that when research on educational leadership includes ELs (e.g., Frattura and Capper, 2007; Skrla et al., 2004), it tends to focus on "broader questions of equity and social justice for diverse students" (p. 307). Although these questions are undoubtedly important, these studies less frequently document the specific approaches taken by district and school leaders as they redesign their organizations with ELs' linguistic and cultural assets in mind. As such, our focus in this section is on practical strategies district and school leaders can use to transform ELs' STEM learning, which have diversity, equity, and inclusion at their core.

*Central office leadership.* Continuous improvement efforts focused on implementing instructional policies and practices call on central office leaders to build districtwide capacity for change (Cuban and Usdan, 2003; Honig, 2006). In terms of EL education, Elfers and colleagues (2013) conducted a qualitative case study in four districts engaging in deliberate improvement efforts focused on EL instruction and noted that central office leaders made explicit efforts to resolve the fragmentation that typically exists between central office departments. The study committee members have observed that these efforts often entail elevating EL-focused central office leaders to executive director or assistant superintendent positions, so that they can participate in cabinet decisions related to instructional priorities, accountability measures and performance targets, fiscal allocations, and human resources development and deployment.

Moreover, in districts where committee members have collaborated, the role of the EL Department often shifts from compliance and monitoring to developing policy and providing instructional guidance. To facilitate this change, some districts establish their EL Department comparable in status to their Curriculum and Instruction Department, whereas other districts integrate the EL Department into Curriculum and Instruction. In either case, no longer is the EL Department "under the umbrella of 'special programs'" (Elfers et al., 2013, p. 168). Instead, as has been observed by committee members, EL departments in these districts are supervised by a chief academic officer who facilitates EL and STEM integration by setting time-bound goals for co-constructed products (e.g., curriculum, instructional strategies, professional learning sessions) and allocating time and resources for cross-departmental communication. These processes ensure that EL-related issues are represented in STEM-focused instructional planning meetings, and that all staff share responsibility for EL success. For example, leaders with EL expertise work alongside STEM content experts to develop instructional frameworks, plan and deliver professional development, and communicate with school leaders.

One study of school districts demonstrating success with ELs noted that these collaborative organizational structures allowed for the distribution of EL-related expertise across content experts (Horwitz et al., 2009). Though focused on English language arts, these findings suggest that attention to district-level routines may be important for ensuring that STEM experts have opportunities to develop EL-related expertise, and vice versa. In fact, in some districts where committee members have observed success with EL populations, the creation of integrated structures and responsibility sharing resulted in policy change related to time allocations for science instruction and protected time for mathematics instruction in elementary schools. This integrated approach contrasts with the approach observed in one descriptive study, where district work routines prohibited the EL department and EL specialists from participating in STEM-related curriculum discussions and limited opportunities for teachers to learn how to transform learning for ELs in mathematics (Hopkins et al., 2015; see Box 8-1).

*School leadership.* In addition to bringing ELs into the center of work at the district central office, open and consistent communication between district and school leadership is an important condition for capacity building. Such communication can help engage leaders "in a mutual and reinforcing blend of efforts that set direction and mobilize resources" (Elfers et al., 2013, p. 169). Just as district leaders redesign structures for language and content integration, school leaders engaged in capacity building look to move or reassign staff, invest in the capabilities of existing staff, and foster a culture of collaboration.

Studies examining components of inclusive school environments for ELs have shown that, rather than viewing the ESL teacher and program as primarily responsible for EL learning, school leaders create structures that emphasize a school culture of shared responsibility for EL instruction (Brooks, Adams, and Morita-Mullaney, 2010; Theoharis and O'Toole, 2011). Whereas some leaders opt to shift from pull-out ESL instruction models to integrated co-teaching models with language and content teachers (see Chapters 4 and 6), others reallocate resources to ensure that all general education staff are dually certified in ESL and content instruction (Theoharis and O'Toole, 2011). In both models, ELs are equitably distributed across classrooms, rather than clustered by language or proficiency level, and bilingual paraprofessionals are assigned to general education rather than ESL classrooms (Elfers and Stritikus, 2014). Both approaches require the design of structures and routines that afford teachers opportunities to collaborate and learn from one another about language and content instruction (Education Trust-West, 2018; Hopkins, Lowenhaupt, and Sweet, 2015). Overall, these shifts are taken up while communicating a compelling rationale for moving beyond a fragmented approach and articulating the ways in which EL education is central to district and school reform efforts (Elfers and Stritikus, 2014).

Importantly, research suggests that elementary and secondary leaders face different challenges as they organize to transform STEM learning for ELs. Given that elementary schools tend to emphasize language arts and mathematics instruction, school leaders at that level wrestle with how to amplify science as a core instructional area (Alarcón, 2012). At the secondary level, on the other hand, instructional alignment and integration tends to be a challenge given that larger numbers of teachers are often involved in serving ELs (Elfers and Stritikus, 2014). Nonetheless, when school leaders are committed to changing practice and invest in the professional development of all teachers, school capacity to teach ELs in STEM subjects can be developed (Elfers and Stritikus, 2014).

### Data-Informed Decision Making

District and school leadership teams spearheading efforts to improve STEM instruction for ELs engage in data-informed and inquiry-driven decision-making processes. Equity audits, a civil rights concept applied to education by Skrla and colleagues (2004), are a promising tool for assisting leaders in engaging in "systemic equity," in which they operate to ensure that all students have equitable learning opportunities (Scott, 2001, p. 6). Scholars recommend that leaders collect and analyze a range of data related to achievement equity, programmatic equity, and teacher quality equity to identify where inequities may be present in the system, understand their root causes, and inform improvement efforts. District and school leaders work together to gather and analyze demographic and performance

---

**BOX 8-1**
**The Role of District Leadership in the**
**Integration of Language and Content**

Hopkins, Lowenhaupt, and Sweet (2015) illustrated the important role that district and school leaders play in designing organizational structures that facilitate the integration of language and content within schools. The study took place in Twin Rivers, a mid-size rural school district in a new immigrant destination in the Midwest where English learners (ELs) represented 21 percent of the elementary school (Grades K–6) population. In Twin Rivers, district leaders outlined a "continuum of English learner support" that mandated the provision of a specific number of minutes of pull-out English as a second language (ESL) instruction depending on students' language proficiency level. During this pull-out period, ESL teachers typically focused on supplementing language arts instruction, and ESL curriculum materials were purchased from the same publisher as the district-adopted language arts curriculum. On the other hand, district leaders mandated that ELs at all proficiency levels take part in mathematics instruction in the general education classroom, though they provided few professional learning opportunities for teachers to develop capacity to teach ELs in math.

In the context of these district mandates, schools implemented routines that positioned ESL teachers as language arts instructors, and they were often left out of grade-level meetings focused on mathematics. These leadership decisions limited opportunities for ESL and general education teachers to interact, learn from one another, and collaborate around the integration of language and mathematics content. The patterns of teachers' interaction across the content areas are shown in the figure below for one Twin Rivers elementary school (Pine Elementary School) where ELs represented 38 percent of the student body (ESL teachers are circled nodes). Whereas ESL teachers at this school were well-integrated into their school's language arts instructional network, and in fact served as brokers of language arts–related information between teachers, they were completely iso-

---

data, observe in classrooms, shadow principals and conduct school walk-throughs, and survey teachers, parents, and students.

Data points relevant to informing EL and STEM improvement efforts include student academic performance and grades, English language proficiency growth, reclassification rates, attendance rates, graduation rates, program enrollment, course-taking and completion patterns, and teacher qualifications and years of experience. Initial data analyses can inform such questions as:

- Do ELs have equitable access to STEM content and coursework?
- How well are ELs at different levels of language proficiency faring in STEM subjects?

lated in the mathematics network, resulting in greater fragmentation of the network overall. This isolation meant that general education teachers had no opportunities to learn from ESL teachers about mathematics instruction, and vice versa. Thus, district and school leaders' policy decisions can either facilitate or hinder teacher collaboration, with implications for the integration of language and content instruction in content areas like mathematics.

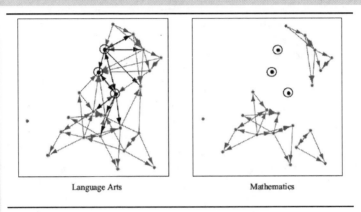

Language Arts    Mathematics

*Figure 1.* **Pine Elementary advice and information networks.**
*Note.* English as a Second Language teachers are circled.

SOURCE: Adapted from Hopkins, Lowenhaupt, and Sweet (2015). Reprinted by permission of SAGE.

- Do ELs have access to highly qualified and experienced STEM teachers? How does access to STEM content vary by ELs' language background, or by their prior level of schooling?
- How are ELs enrolled in bilingual programs or courses performing in STEM subjects compared to ELs enrolled in English-only programs or courses?
- How well are reclassified ELs doing in STEM subjects?
- How is EL access to and performance in STEM subjects related to attendance and/or high school graduation rates?

In conducting such analyses, it is important to look at results holistically, as Robinson-Cimpian, Thompson, and Umansky (2016) pointed out in their analysis of EL-related policies and practices. For example, schools with higher reclassification rates may not necessarily serve ELs better, as they may be removing services too soon, resulting in lower performance for reclassified ELs in STEM courses. Further, as outlined in Chapters 2 and 7, appropriate assessments are typically not available and/or used for ELs; thus, data related to EL performance may not represent all that students are capable of and may require EL expertise to be interpreted.

In engaging in data analysis efforts that attend to ELs' inclusion in STEM opportunities, district leaders can move their focus on ELs from policy compliance to educational equity and quality. The information gathered via an equity audit helps district and school leaders identify policies and practices that are stalling or generating success for ELs and make decisions about where to intervene in the system (e.g., district or school level, elementary or secondary), and for whom (e.g., recently arrived ELs, long-term ELs, reclassified ELs, ELs with interrupted formal education, ELs from particular language backgrounds, dual identified ELs). Based on scholarship on educational leadership (e.g., Mintrop, 2016), systems interventions can draw on design-based inquiry approaches, where changes are designed and implemented, then adapted as necessary around iterative data collection and analysis cycles.

In districts showing success with their ELs, instructional leadership teams at the district and school level gather and analyze data at least three times each year. At the secondary level, district and school leaders regularly examine EL reclassification rates, course-taking trends, and success rates. They study the extent to which ELs are included in college preparatory and Advanced Placement mathematics and science courses and their rate of success, failure, or drop-out. They look at students currently classified as ELs and those who have been reclassified to ensure all current and former ELs have equitable access to STEM coursework and are on track to graduate. They then study course enrollment and instructional practices, the core curriculum and its enactment in the classroom, instructional resources (in English and other languages), and assessments. In addition, district and school staff can shadow ELs to understand their experiences in STEM, and observe how teachers engage ELs in STEM discourse in the classroom (Education Trust-West, 2018). These ongoing data collection and analysis efforts help districts identify problematic course placement and sequencing for ELs, thus informing decisions to transform classrooms for ELs in STEM that minimize their isolation and ensure both equitable course access and high-quality learning opportunities.

Emerging scholarship on research-practice partnerships (RPPs) in education suggests that collaborations with researchers may be especially helpful in district and school continuous improvement processes. In collaboration with researchers, district and school leaders can ensure data quality, receive support for data collection and analysis, engage in program evaluation, and connect to the broader evidence base to inform ongoing improvement efforts (Coburn and Penuel, 2016; Thompson et al., 2017). For example, based on their collaborative data analysis, researchers working with leaders from the Oregon Department of Education found that ELs with disabilities were much less likely to be reclassified than other ELs (Thompson et al., 2017), which is informing a design-based project to understand how districts address this issue, to develop tools and processes for reclassifying ELs with disabilities, and to engage in cycles of inquiry to refine these tools and processes.

## Culture of Collaboration

Practicing reciprocal accountability and data-driven decision making requires an organizational culture that values and facilitates collaboration among all stakeholders. Districts engaged in systemic transformation for ELs invite representatives from many stakeholder groups to engage in the planning, implementation, and oversight of improvement efforts. They establish a culture of collaborative problem solving, experimentation, and learning through formal organizational structures and professional networks. With respect to networks, districts engaged in continuous improvement focused on EL education facilitate peer networks in which leaders uncover, analyze, and respond effectively to problems of policy and practice. Such networks can facilitate information exchange and access to research and can promote leaders' professional learning and development (Umekubo, Chrispeels, and Daly, 2015). On the other hand, sparse leadership networks can constrain the exchange of information and inhibit district change efforts (Finnigan, Daly, and Che, 2013). Developing peer networks across school systems can help to facilitate a culture of collaboration in which leaders plan and implement changes that strengthen system-wide policies, programs, and practices that transform STEM learning for ELs.

Moreover, the integration of language and content across local systems often requires the development of new policies and practices related to curriculum development, materials selection, assessment, instruction, and professional development. Facilitating these changes requires collaboration between STEM leaders and leaders in literacy and English language development to revise, adapt, or create new practices and tools that support schools in teaching ELs in STEM. These leadership teams might include central office mathematics, science, technology, literacy, and language specialists, as well as instructional coaches or other teacher leaders, or even university partners. These diverse teams meet regularly to develop integrated instructional frameworks (more on this below), design curricula and associated assessments, and plan professional development. These processes help to ensure coordination across the system, while also allowing for site-based needs to be considered. In Oakland Unified School District, for example, the Oakland Language Immersion Advancement in Science (OLAS) partnership brings together instructional teams from five dual-language elementary schools, the district's science and EL departments, and external partners (e.g., the Bay Area Writing Project), who work together to integrate science and language instruction and design integrated lesson plans that attend to both science and ELD standards (Feldman and Malagon, 2017).

Within schools, designing for the kind of high-quality teaching and learning described in previous chapters also requires collaboration among content and language teachers (Alarcón, 2012; Valdés, Kibler, and Walqui, 2014). As an example, Ciechanowksi (2014) described how a team including a language specialist and classroom teacher, with assistance from a researcher, designed interconnected science and language instruction for a 3rd-grade dual language class. In after-school planning meetings, the team analyzed its ELD and science curricula and developed a series of lessons that "promote[d] classroom conversation to leverage a variety of language types in extended discourse around [science] topics" (p. 239). Through its collaborative analysis, the team identified ways to scaffold various linguistic functions (e.g., explaining) to facilitate ELs' participation in science investigations, an approach that highlights the importance of language in meaning-making (see Chapter 3). The team's diverse expertise in linguistics, science, instructional strategies, and disciplinary discourses enabled it to integrate the two curricula, and ELs demonstrated significant gains in both language and content as a result of its integrated unit planning and co-teaching approach.

On the other hand, several studies have shown how ELD teachers tend to be marginalized in their schools when a culture of collaboration is not fostered in districts and schools, and when language and content teachers do not have opportunities to work together to examine curricula and jointly plan instruction and assessment (Arkoudis, 2006; Davison, 2006; McClure and Cahnmann-Taylor, 2010). Such marginalization often results in ELD teacher isolation, which can be especially problematic when content area teachers have not been equipped to serve ELs and could benefit from opportunities to collaborate with language specialists (Hopkins, Lowenhaupt, and Sweet, 2015).

## Community and Family Engagement

Beyond developing a culture of collaboration between district and school staff focused on teaching ELs in STEM, organizational cultures in districts showing success with ELs (as observed by committee members) foster community and family engagement. They develop an ecosystem for EL STEM education that leverages assets in the community and in students' homes. In terms of community, district and school partnerships with intermediary organizations can facilitate learning opportunities for leaders, teachers, and students (see Box 8-2). Such partnerships can strengthen the quality and amount of science instruction provided to ELs. For example, several San Francisco Bay Area school districts partner with the BaySci network, the Lawrence Hall of Science, the Exploratorium, and Inverness Research to offer leadership seminars, a teacher leadership academy, and group planning meetings (Feldman and Malagon, 2017). An evaluation of this partnership revealed increases in the quality and quantity of science instruction and in student engagement in the majority of participating districts (Remold et al., 2014).

Community partnerships can also afford ELs with access to resources, as well as mentoring opportunities and internships that expose them to workplace experiences and enhance STEM learning and language use. For example, Calipatria Unified School District in California, which is geographically distant from science institutions, partners with the Research and Education Cooperative Occultation Network to provide ELs at the high school level with access to an astronomer's telescope with which they can make planetary observations and conduct astronomy research (Feldman and Malagon, 2017). Students then videotape observations from the telescope and send their results to university partners in St. Louis and Arizona.

These kinds of partnerships also provide ELs and their families with opportunities to learn about current and evolving career opportunities and expose ELs and their parents to the skills and practices needed to be successful in postsecondary STEM education. Committee experience suggests that external partnerships focused on STEM learning for ELs usually have a district-based coordinator who establishes relationships with museums, businesses, industry, professional organizations, and universities and works with them to develop activities that introduce and deepen students' and families' understandings of STEM. Activities might include speaker series, field trips, mentorships, internships, and conferences for teachers, students, and families. For example, in Oakland Unified School District, student groups, including ELs from each school, attend a yearly "Dinner with a Scientist" event.

In districts and schools where committee members have worked, the people engaged in continuous improvement focused on transforming learning for ELs in STEM tend to view family engagement from a collaborative perspective. They go beyond traditional engagement strategies such as hosting parent-teacher conferences and parent education or volunteer activities (Carreón, Drake, and Barton, 2005; Lowenhaupt, 2014) and recognize the importance of building families' understanding of STEM education and what is needed for their children to actively participate in STEM courses and activities. By taking a relational approach (Warren et al., 2009), they

---

**BOX 8-2**
**Science, Technology, Engineering, and Mathematics**
**(STEM) Partnerships in Support of High School**
**English Learners (ELs)—New York Example**

High schools that have significant success graduating college- and career-ready EL students create trajectories of opportunities that these students follow toward successful academic and life outcomes. These schools offer their students a rigorous college preparatory program with relevant STEM partnerships that enrich students' motivation, interests, and learning in their postsecondary lives. The staffs of these schools believe that with adequate support, all students will master college preparatory coursework and have the tools to succeed in their postsecondary lives. These schools build cohesive team members who share and understand the school's mission in supporting students' academic and social-emotional development and design learning opportunities so that students maximize their language and disciplinary knowledge development in and out of the school day. In addition, resources, structures, supports, and partnerships are developed in alignment to their visions of high expectations for ELs.

These schools forge lasting partnerships with external organizations that are purposefully and carefully selected and designed to augment and improve the existing practices at the school. The schools work strategically with organizations to expand opportunities for students to:

- Bolster the academic and extracurricular opportunities they offer to students
- Offer college-level courses, so that students often graduate with college credits
- Provide mentoring or internship opportunities
- Provide intensive college counseling and guidance including college visits, application support, and mentorships

Each high school's vision drives the type of partnerships secured. Common features of the external partnerships include

- alignment to vision and mission of the school;
- relevance to students' needs, interests and aspirations;

---

work with families so that the families can serve as advocates for their children to be included in college preparatory STEM courses and in STEM-related experiences. Building on the aforementioned external partnerships, committee members have observed that these districts offer families experiences such as parent ambassadorships, visits to STEM institutions, multicultural programming, college and career planning, and financial aid courses. Some of these efforts began as innovations supported by philanthropic

- capacity to enrich and augment learning, guidance, and exposure to college and career pathways; and
- open communication, collaborative construction, and continuous refinement of the partnership and the opportunities afforded to students and families.

Manhattan Bridges High School in New York City offers students the opportunity to take experiential STEM coursework that prepares them for postsecondary success. Students can choose between two STEM academies—engineering or information technology (IT). The school has partnerships with the National Academy Foundation to offer these two career and technical education (CTE) academies for students. Students who successfully complete the IT program can receive industry certifications (e.g., in A+ and IC3) by the time they graduate, and students in the engineering academy have access to industry internships and credit-bearing college courses. The power of these CTE academies is that they help students to see the immediate purpose of what they are learning in school for their future career aspirations.

In their pre-engineering or IT classes, students complete hands-on projects such as breaking down a computer or formatting a hard drive from scratch. Everything they learn in the classroom has a direct connection to a real-world career application. Even if they decide not to pursue careers in engineering or IT, they have built a repertoire of knowledge and skills—tools and resources to rely on in the future. Most important, these experiences help students to understand why they are in school and how their hard work is helping them to prepare for college or career.

Families and caregivers also see the value of the career academies for motivating their students. One parent of a 10th-grade student explained that he chose the school for his son because of its focus on mathematics and engineering. These experiences have motivated and prepared his son toward a career path of becoming a car designer. The parent credited the engineering academy's courses with helping his son to develop a vision for his future and to stay motivated to achieve his career goals (Santos et al., 2018).

SOURCE: Based on Santos et al. (2018).

foundations, but are sustained by the district and partnering organizations after a period of implementation and demonstrated success. Overall, these partnerships can help to create a rich ecosystem of STEM learning for educators, students, and families that may not otherwise be possible given policy and funding constraints outlined in the first part of this chapter.

## Educator Capability

As noted in previous chapters, efforts to improve STEM education for ELs, and all students, require deepening educators' understandings of content and language instruction and attending to their beliefs about the nature of EL and STEM education. Improvement efforts that overlook these aspects of educator capability are less likely to be taken up in a widespread manner than those that attend explicitly to them (Lee and Luykx, 2005). Committee members' experiences in school districts suggest that attending to the development of educators' knowledge and beliefs requires a coherent instructional vision and articulated framework that guides districtwide improvement efforts, including program implementation and staffing decisions, as well as opportunities for professional learning.

### Instructional Vision

An instructional vision can be defined as "beliefs about the education of children and the expressed . . . goals . . . for the school district to accomplish these beliefs" (Petersen, 1999, p. 6). In school districts where committee members have observed progress on state assessments and graduation rates for ELs, continuous improvement efforts are guided by a clear vision for EL instruction that is grounded in principles of diversity, equity, and inclusion and articulates goals for language and content integration that are aligned to rigorous language and content standards. Committee experience suggests that this instructional vision is most often developed by an EL-focused leadership team that includes representatives from all instructional departments (e.g., curriculum and instruction, special education, community and family engagement, and school support services) and operational departments (e.g., human resources, budget office) in the central office, as well as school leaders and teachers, union representatives, members of institutions of higher education, and relevant community partners. Some district leaders also include students and families on the vision development team to ensure their voices, hopes, and aspirations are included.

Leveraging results from equity audits and other data collection and analyses (see Data-Informed Decision Making above), the vision development process engages team members in a variety of learning experiences that strengthen their understandings of ELs, their experiences in schools, and their success in STEM subjects. To engage in vision development, leadership teams are often provided the time and space to engage in capacity development and planning by top district leaders (e.g., superintendents, chief academic officers, board members). The vision they develop focuses district priorities and guides strategic improvement efforts for ELs in STEM. For example, committee members have observed that some districts demonstrating gains for ELs in STEM have equity-oriented visions for ELs that are evidence- and research-based and move away from deficit-oriented models that require ELs to demonstrate proficiency in English before engaging in STEM content. Some of these districts shifted from intervention-based practices toward high expectations and instructional rigor so that ELs are college- and career-ready upon high school graduation. Some districts also include biliteracy as a goal, especially in states offering the Seal of Biliteracy to high school students.

This visioning process is critical for developing an instructional framework focused on transforming STEM learning for ELs across the PreK–12 pipeline. As has been illustrated in districts undergoing mathematics instructional reform, an instructional framework serves as a guide for implementation of a district's instructional vision, and articulates alignment among standards, curriculum, and assessments (Hopkins and Spillane, 2015).

## Instructional Frameworks

Instructional frameworks in districts where committee members have observed success with ELs in STEM tend to focus on three principles: opportunity to learn, asset orientation, and student autonomy. First, instructional frameworks inform the development of demanding core academic curriculum that is aligned to both college- and career-readiness standards and English language proficiency standards and ensures equitable practices to assess ELs' content learning and language development. Second, they acknowledge that ELs' backgrounds, cultures, and home languages are assets for learning. Third, instructional frameworks are designed to build ELs' autonomy within and between grade levels and guide the development of challenging learning experiences that provide opportunities for regular feedback. This three-pronged approach can help move districts away from implementing models based on a minimum number of required minutes of ELD instruction geared to meet compliance requirements, toward offering quality instruction for ELs that is aligned to research-informed principles.

Embedded across all areas of a district's instructional framework is a clear and coherent language development approach designed to provide ELs with challenging, personalized, high-quality, rigorous, grade-level standards-based instruction. Such instruction is aligned to PreK–12, anchored in the district's vision for ELs, and reflects the teaching and learning expectations in both content and language standards. A robust language development approach calls for ELs, and all students, to have ample opportunities to simultaneously develop content area knowledge, analytical practices, and discipline-specific academic language (Heritage, Walqui, and Linquanti, 2015). Grade-level expectations are maintained for ELs in STEM classrooms using research-informed strategies, such as deliberate and appropriate scaffolds that build on students' cultural and linguistic assets and connects their prior knowledge to new learning, purposeful and embedded language instruction, and formative assessment. Such approaches strive to develop student autonomy by affording ELs multiple and varied opportunities to engage in disciplinary discourse and comprehend and use language for a variety of purposes. Importantly, this approach to language development in STEM subjects is communicated across the system to all stakeholders, including leaders, teachers, family members, and students.

Districts with a clear language development approach require all educators to be responsible for the design and implementation of high-quality EL STEM instruction. Central office leaders understand that language and content learning cannot be separated, and they work together to develop curriculum, resources, and professional development to build educators' capacities to integrate language and content. As has been described in previous chapters, each content area or discipline has specific ways of using language to reason or develop arguments, to explain ideas and cite evidence, to comprehend and produce texts that communicate conceptual understanding, and to engage in analytic practices. ELs need to be apprenticed into these practices through active engagement in authentic STEM learning opportunities. Districts that have been successful in implementing these practices articulate coherent visions and frameworks, then prioritize building the understanding and capacity of all educators to deliver on the approach.

Research on elementary mathematics reform describes how curriculum development teams, including central office leaders and teachers from across the district, engage with state standards to articulate a reform-oriented framework that guides the selection of instructional materials as well as the development of instructional units and associated assessments (Hopkins and Spillane, 2015). Instructional coaches and teacher leaders engaged in framework development help to lead implementation efforts, which are supported by teacher professional development activities. Districts working to develop instructional frameworks specifically for ELs in STEM might find California's integrated English language arts and English language development framework helpful as starting points (California Department of Education, 2015), as well as associated resources for integrating the ELD standards into math and science teaching and learning (Lagunoff et al., 2015). District leaders can support their staff in adopting or developing high-quality curriculum materials that integrate ELD and STEM rather than serve as add-on interventions. Attention to the adoption of instructional materials is critical, as these materials are highly influential on student learning yet their selection is often under the purview of district and school leaders (Koedel and Polikoff, 2017).

## Programs and Staffing

In addition to articulating a vision that informs the development of an instructional framework to align standards, curriculum, assessment, and professional development, school districts engage in efforts to implement this framework via programs and staffing. Although research points to the benefit of bilingual programs for improving ELs' achievement in math and science (López, McEneaney, and Nieswandt, 2015; McEneaney, López, and Nieswandt, 2014; Steele et al., 2017; Valentino and Reardon, 2015), the reality is that the programs that districts implement vary by EL population size and diversity, and by the extent to which resources are present to facilitate EL inclusion. For example, districts serving small and relatively new EL populations that speak many languages may spend resources on ESL pull-out or push-in models to attend to ELs' needs in STEM classrooms. On the other hand, school districts with large and long-standing EL populations that tend to speak one or two languages may have bilingual pathways in place for students across PreK–12 that attend to language and content for ELs and other students.

Given these variations in EL instructional models, the ways in which language and content are integrated to transform STEM learning opportunities for ELs will necessarily require different allocations of instructional time, resources, and staffing. A few districts demonstrating gains for ELs on standardized science assessments in California have created integrated ELD and science instructional blocks at the elementary level to leverage connections between science and language, and to ensure there is dedicated instructional time for science (Feldman and Malagon, 2017). To support these efforts, teachers receive significant professional development related to the integration of science, literacy, and ELD in classrooms where English is the language of instruction. Feldman and Malagon (2017) noted that this integrated approach to teaching science and ELD has been adopted in districts that are organized around both English-dominant and bilingual instructional models at the elementary level.

Similarly, at the secondary level, districts demonstrating gains for ELs schedule dedicated and uninterrupted time for integrated ELD and STEM instruction (Feldman and Malagon, 2017). These arrangements allow for either an ELD teacher to co-teach with a STEM teacher in an extended class period, or for the teachers to co-teach a regular period, and then the ELD teacher has additional time for integrated language and science or math learning. These models require that ELD and STEM teachers have time and resources dedicated to co-planning, and to developing a shared understanding of language and STEM instruction that align with the pedagogical approaches described in earlier chapters (see also Valdés, Kibler, and Walqui [2014] for a discussion of the role of the ESL professional in standards-based reform). On the other hand, coherent, sound bilingual instructional models with qualified teachers with advanced bilingual capabilities may be particularly beneficial at the secondary level for recently arrived ELs. A demonstration project in southern California, for example, used a binational curriculum to offer college preparatory STEM courses to recently arrived ELs in Spanish, which provided students access to STEM classes and allowed them to stay on track to graduate while they learned English (Hopkins et al., 2013; see Box 8-3). Bilingual STEM teachers offered these courses and received professional development related to the integration

---

**BOX 8-3**
**Example of Transformative Science, Technology, Engineering, and Mathematics (STEM) Learning for Recently Arrived English Learners (ELs) in High School**

Transforming STEM learning for recently arrived ELs (i.e., newcomers) at the secondary level is challenging, as many districts and schools are not equipped to facilitate access to rigorous content instruction for students who are in the process of learning English. A demonstration project led by Dr. Patricia Gándara of the UCLA Civil Rights Project/Proyecto Derechos Civiles took up this challenge in four high schools in Southern California serving large numbers of Spanish-speaking newcomers, the vast majority of whom were from Mexico. Project Secondary On-line Learning (SOL) recruited bilingual math and science teachers in each school and provided professional development and on-the-job coaching to facilitate their implementation of an online Mexican curriculum provided in collaboration with the Colegio de Bachilleres. Given that the curriculum was aligned to state graduation requirements, its implementation facilitated students' access to rigorous content via a structure and language with which they were familiar and allowed them to complete college preparatory coursework while they learned English. Project SOL researchers also collaborated with the WRITE Institute to support teachers' integration of language and content instruction, and to foster the development of teachers' academic literacy in Spanish. Beyond classroom-based supports, Project SOL staff worked with teachers to develop a Newcomer Club at each school, where students had access to peer tutoring and college-related information. Additionally, the project engaged parents and families via Parents for Quality Education (PIQE), which provided workshops related to navigating the U.S. education system and understanding requirements for high school graduation and college admittance. This multipronged approach not only leveraged newcomers' linguistic assets in the classroom, but also provided them with access to school-based personnel and other resources and information that ensured their success in STEM.

SOURCE: Based on committee experience and Hopkins et al. (2013).

of language and content, as well as opportunities to develop the language skills necessary to offer rigorous STEM instruction in Spanish.

Regardless of instructional program, ensuring proper placement of ELs into STEM classes is important. In districts where committee members have observed attention to course placement at the elementary level, district and school leaders create structures so that designated or pull-out ELD does not take away from content instruction, and push-in ELD are allocated across all content areas, including STEM. At the secondary level, ELs are placed into STEM classes with both equity and access in mind to ensure placement into appropriate coursework as well as the provision of resources to facilitate their success, such as highly qualified teachers. In Washington state, school districts offer world language credits to ELs for demonstrating proficiency in their first language, which opens up space in their schedules to take advanced-level classes, and to retake them as necessary (Greenberg Motamedi and Jaffery, 2014).

Across all program types, districts in which committee members have observed success with ELs in STEM pay particular attention to the recruitment and retention of instructional staff with STEM expertise. District and school leaders build staff capacity to teach STEM and to integrate ELD and content instruction, and they ensure that ELs are placed into the classrooms of these educators. Instructional staff include teachers with STEM expertise, many of whom are also bilingual, as well as paraprofessionals who have expertise in STEM and/or are bilingual (Erbstein, 2016). District and school leaders are careful to ensure that teachers with content certification are working with those with language expertise to co-construct and/or co-teach lessons that include appropriate scaffolds for ELs and are collaborating with paraprofessionals to ensure instructional alignment. School counselors are also critical staff members in these districts, as they can ensure proper placement of ELs in STEM courses and in classrooms with teachers or teams of teachers who are well-equipped to meet EL needs (see National Academies of Sciences, Engineering, and Medicine [2017] for the preparation of counselors and principals).

## Professional Learning

As noted in Chapter 6, the majority of ELs are placed in classrooms with teachers who have limited preparation related to how to deliver integrated language and content instruction aligned to college- and career-ready standards. To address this challenge, some districts build certification processes internally or partner with universities to increase educator capabilities. For example, after struggling to fill teacher vacancies in their dual language programs, Portland Public Schools partners with Portland State University to offer staff members the opportunity to earn a master's degree in elementary education with a bilingual/English to Speakers of Other Languages (ESOL) endorsement or in secondary education with a world language endorsement (e.g., Spanish) while they simultaneously work as classroom teachers, full-time substitutes, or paraprofessionals (Garcia, 2017). As another example, a decades-long school-university partnership in Chula Vista, California, is structured such that university faculty offer professional development to teachers in the school related to implementing standards-based content instruction with ELs, and the school places preservice teacher candidates from the university in their classrooms to generate a pipeline of well-qualified teachers who are prepared to employ the kinds of linguistically responsive and culturally sustaining approaches described in Chapter 6 (Alfaro et al., 2014; Garcia, 2017).

In other districts where committee members have worked, mathematics and science leaders in the central office work with EL specialists to develop job-embedded teacher professional development that seeks to augment the quality and quantity of extended academic conversations in classrooms. Professional development activities focus on developing teachers' knowledge and skills related to facilitating academic discussions in each content area, and teachers learn how to implement a classroom culture with disciplinary discussion norms, routines, strategies, and peer feedback in consultation with coaches or other instructional leaders. In other cases, committee members have observed teachers learning STEM content during professional development sessions, as well as how to facilitate STEM inquiry using disciplinary discussion and how to use tools such as science notebooks to promote writing. To monitor teachers' implementation of these approaches, some of these districts have used a protocol similar to instructional rounds that brings teams of teachers and principals into classrooms to examine practices, identify trends, and target and plan for improvements in practice. Finally, some districts have joined community-wide initiatives to pool resources as they engage in these efforts; several districts in San José, California, for example, joined a collaborative with the Santa Clara County Office of Education, where teachers participate in symposia on standards-based math instruction and form teams that analyze student work, examine data, and reflect on issues of equity and access for ELs with a math coordinator and instructional coaches (Education Trust-West, 2018; see Box 8-4).

Although all teachers would benefit from professional development opportunities that attend to explicit integration of STEM content and disciplinary language, the professional learning needs of elementary and secondary teachers may differ somewhat. Whereas elementary teachers may need more support for learning STEM content than secondary teachers of STEM, secondary STEM teachers may require more exposure to ELD instructional strategies and resources than elementary teachers. Related to

## BOX 8-4
## Designing Teacher Professional Learning in Support of Integrated Science and English Language Development

Several districts in California have increased the percentage of ELs meeting elementary science standards. To improve the quantity and quality of science instruction for ELs in elementary classrooms, these districts engage teachers in sustained professional learning initiatives to build their capacity to integrate science and English language development (ELD). For example, in Calipatria Unified School District (USD), all teachers have been prepared to integrate content concepts and practices with ELD in all subjects, including science. In addition, they expect students to take 2 to 3 years of science in high school. In Oakland USD, science specialists together with ELD specialists partner with multiple science institutions to integrate science learning with language instruction and strengthen the capacity of educators to facilitate language and science learning in their schools. Oak Grove School District partners with the Sobrato Early Academic Language program to increase the quantity and quality of science through thematic science and social studies units that infuse best practices for EL learning including bilingual language development. These districts have used dedicated ELD time to increase science learning for ELs by engaging students in high-quality science instruction that integrated science and language development.

Strategies employed by districts to increase the quality and quantity of integrated science and ELD include increased science instructional time for ELs by integrating science and ELD; providing high-quality, job-embedded professional learning for teachers and administrators to build science content knowledge and capacity to integrate research evidence–based ELD strategies; partnering with science institutions to support teacher professional learning; and aligning fiscal resources to better support the efforts (see National Academies of Sciences, Engineering, and Medicine [2017] for additional information of professional development for administrators).

In these districts, teachers have integrated science and ELD goals for students and have formulated approaches for reaching them whether instruction is in English or in bilingual settings. Language development approaches are designed to build students' capacities to engage in rich science discussions and to produce multimodal texts to meet disciplinary purposes (e.g., explain phenomena, model a process, or substantiate a claim).

Strong and sustained professional learning structures for teachers and leaders include summer institutes and on-site coaching. The summer institute professional learning sessions delve into scientific investigations, concepts and practices, science vocabulary instruction, language functions within the disciplinary discourse practices, and science talk norms. On-site coaching supports application of new learnings, lesson planning, and shifts in classroom practices.

SOURCE: Based on Feldman and Malagon (2017).

the latter, a study described how rural math and science teachers who took part in an ELD-focused professional development and acquired their ESL certificates served as peer mentors for their content specialist colleagues (Hansen-Thomas and Richins, 2015). Through targeted collaboration efforts, teachers served as mentors for their colleagues in the integration of STEM and ELD instruction at their schools. This example illustrates how teachers benefit from both formal and informal opportunities to develop their expertise to serve ELs in STEM, through professional development activities and coursework as well as through on-the-job collaboration with colleagues.

## Policy and Management

As Blumenfeld and colleagues (2000) suggested, the foundations of any efforts to foster organizational cultures and develop educator capabilities to teach ELs in STEM are policies and management structures that allocate funding and other resources to support them. In districts where committee members have observed success with ELs in STEM, district and school leaders create policies that are aligned to the instructional vision and allocate fiscal and human resources and extended supports to ensure realization of those policies. Moreover, efforts to monitor progress and offer guidance are employed to allow for continuous improvement.

### Fiscal Resources

Generally, recent analyses suggest that the explicit integration of language and content instruction via co-teaching or bilingual models may be more cost-effective than fragmented ESL pull-out approaches (Sugarman, 2016). At the secondary level in particular, Sugarman (2016) noted that standalone ESL courses incur costs but do not confer graduation credits to students, in comparison to the integrated co-teaching of ELD and STEM or the provision of bilingual content courses. As described above, school districts receive a combination of federal, state, and local funding for EL education, and district and school leaders are tasked with deciding how to allocate funding across schools. Although the allocation of fiscal resources for EL STEM education varies within and between school districts depending on the extent to which resource distribution is centralized (Sugarman, 2016), research points to the value of blending district and school involvement in resource allocation and decision making. In a district with a high degree of centralized decision making, for example, resources were equitably distributed to schools based on need, yet school leaders could appeal to district leaders for more resources (e.g., funding to hire an EL instructional coach) if they provided evidence of need (Elfers and Stritikus, 2014). Moreover, decisions to replace ineffective programs with different programs, or to reallocate program funds to staffing or professional development, were made collectively by district and school leaders. On the other hand, in school districts where resources were more decentralized, there was less consistency in the allocation of fiscal resources for ELs, and resource allocation was most connected to the district's vision for EL instruction in schools with leaders knowledgeable about effective EL instruction (Elfers and Stritikus, 2014).

## Human Resources

In districts where committee members have observed positive gains for ELs in STEM, leaders prioritize the alignment of fiscal and human resources. Human resources staff review for appropriate credentials in STEM content and ELD or ESL, and they seek educators with bilingual skills by recruiting inside and outside the country. Some districts in Elfers and Stritikus' (2014) study went beyond state credentialing requirements and developed their own systems for screening personnel to assess their bilingual abilities and to determine whether newly hired teachers and paraeducators could meet the demands of their programs. Other districts in this study focused on augmenting the skills of their existing staff and negotiated with state agencies for funding assistance to be able to offer ESL certificate courses to teachers. These teachers were then prepared to deliver EL-focused professional development to others in the district, including paraprofessionals. Paraprofessionals received extensive onboarding and follow-up training so they were prepared to work with ELs in content classrooms.

Beyond instructional staff, some school districts use extra funding to hire community or parent liaisons whose work focuses on newcomer integration, translation services, and other mechanisms that foster home-school connections (Garcia and Carnock, 2016). Other districts ensure that each school has a bilingual secretary to welcome parents and students (Elfers and Stritkus, 2014). Finally, bilingual school counselors are present in some districts and schools to ensure ELs have access to program and course information and are appropriately placed in schools and classrooms such that they have access to rigorous STEM coursework while they are learning English.

## Extended Supports

Given the challenges many districts and schools face in meeting ELs' diverse needs within the constraints of the regular school day, some have opted to allocate funding and resources to provide ELs with extended supports that afford them additional opportunities to engage with STEM content. As described above, some of these opportunities are facilitated by community partners and include afterschool or summer programs (Feldman and Malagon, 2017). Others are facilitated by teachers, such as efforts among elementary science teachers in Arizona to develop afterschool clubs and summer camps focused on STEM content for ELs in Grades K–5 (Kelly, 2016). At the secondary level, the Boston International High School headmaster acquired additional funding to allow teachers to work extended hours on select days of the week to tutor ELs one-on-one or in small groups (Castellón et al., 2015). These afterschool interventions were developed and assessed during collaborative teacher meetings on early release days each week to ensure students received targeted and timely content instruction. A national survey of programs and services for high school ELs showed that, in addition to afterschool programs, high schools offer summer school, remediation classes, and credit recovery (Lewis and Gray, 2016). These extended supports are often necessary to facilitate ELs' access to STEM content and coursework, and they are most successful when supported by fiscal and human resources and aligned to the district's instructional vision.

Beyond extended instructional time, many districts serving large populations of recently arrived ELs allocate additional resources to acquire background information that facilitates proper course placement (Umansky et al., 2018). In addition to initial English language proficiency assessments, some districts use native language and mathematics assessments, coupled with transcript evaluations when possible, so that newcomers can be placed in STEM classes appropriate to their language abilities and prior schooling experiences. These types of intake processes are often facilitated by bilingual liaisons and counselors, which again requires the alignment of fiscal and human resources to ensure these staff members are supported and prepared for this work.

## Monitoring and Guidance

Continuous improvement efforts focused on teaching ELs in STEM are often guided by actionable improvement and monitoring plans that allow stakeholders to monitor progress and communicate the impact of new policies and practices. This work can be facilitated by an oversight committee that includes district leadership responsible and accountable for results in addition to critical community leaders. Members represent a range of programs and groups, including secondary and elementary supervisors, human resources, parent engagement, instructional technology, student support services, curriculum, instruction, assessment, financial services, communications, local universities, and teachers' unions. This group of stakeholders might engage in data collection and analysis to monitor district and school progress in facilitating ELs' access to and progress in STEM (see "Data-driven Decision Making" above) and offer guidance with respect to program design and redesign, staffing, professional development, and resource allocation. They may also gather information pertaining to legal requirements for serving ELs and ensure that the district and schools are meeting these obligations.

In general, although an oversight committee oversees implementation, provides guidance, and makes recommendations for resource allocation, schools have some latitude in how they use their human and fiscal resources to transform instruction for ELs in STEM subjects. In school districts that are successful in serving ELs, central office leadership holds tight to its instructional vision, defines core and supplemental instructional programs, and outlines competencies required of educators. District leaders build tools and professional learning opportunities for teachers, principals, and central office staff to support and deepen implementation of new instructional policies and practices. Still, schools have flexibility in how they implement the pedagogical shifts required in each classroom, and district leaders monitor progress by establishing implementation and student outcome targets and uses data and continuous improvement cycles to study results and progress.

## SUMMARY

Systemic reform is needed to ensure that ELs receive equitable opportunities to engage in STEM subjects. Policies at all levels—federal, state, and local—can impact these opportunities by either facilitating access or serving as a barrier. For example, as described in this chapter as well as Chapter 2, the ways in which ELs are identified and reclassified can potentially skew the interpretation of STEM academic achievement for ELs. Moreover, policies at the local level can influence the distribution of funding as well as the preparation and placement of STEM teachers in schools and districts. Throughout this chapter, a framework for continuous instructional improvement for ELs in STEM has been outlined that attends to three core aspects of organizational culture, educator capability, and policy and management. Although three areas are described as inclusive of distinct components, these components are interrelated and represent an interconnected web that has the potential to shape the development of equitable STEM learning opportunities for ELs within and across districts and schools. The development of such systems is necessary to leverage the opportunities, and to address the challenges, presented by federal and state educational policies.

# REFERENCES

Abedi, J., and Gándara, P. (2006). Performance of English language learners as a subgroup in large-scale assessment: Interaction of research and policy. *Educational Measurement: Issues and Practice, 25*(4), 36–46.

Alarcón, M.H. (2012). *Urban School Leadership for Elementary Science Education: Meeting the Needs of English Language Learners.* Ph.D. dissertation. University of Texas at San Antonio.

Alfaro, C., Durán, R., Hunt, A., and Aragón, M.J. (2014). Steps toward unifying dual language programs, common core state standards, and critical pedagogy: Oportunidades, estrategias y retos. *Association of Mexican American Educators Journal, 8*(2), 17–30.

American Council on the Teaching of Foreign Languages. (2015). *Guidelines for Implementing the Seal of Biliteracy.* Available: https://www.actfl.org/sites/default.files/pdfs [August 2018].

Arkoudis, S. (2006). Negotiating the rough ground between ESL and mainstream teachers. *International Journal of Bilingual Education and Bilingualism, 9*(4), 415–433.

Ballantyne, K.G., Sanderman, A.R., and Levy, J. (2008). *Educating English Language Learners: Building Teacher Capacity.* Washington, DC: National Clearinghouse for English Language Acquisition.

Bell, A.B., and Baecher, L. (2012). Points on a continuum: ESL teachers reporting on collaboration. *TESOL Journal, 3*(3), 488–515.

Blumenfeld, P., Fishman, B.J., Krajcik, J., Marx, R.W., and Soloway, E. (2000). Creating usable innovations in systemic reform: Scaling up technology-embedded project-based science in urban schools. *Educational Psychologist, 35*(3), 149–164.

Brooks, K., Adams, S.R., and Morita-Mullaney, T. (2010). Creating inclusive learning communities for ELL students: Transforming school principals' perspectives. *Theory into Practice, 49*(2), 145–151.

Bryk, A.S., Sebring, P.B., Allensworth, E., Luppesco, S., and Easton, J.Q. (2010). *Organizing Schools for Improvement: Lessons from Chicago.* Chicago, IL: University of Chicago Press.

Bunch, G., Kibler, A., and Pimental, S. (2012). *Realizing Opportunities for English Learners in the Common Core English Language Arts and Disciplinary Literacy Standards.* Available: http://ell.stanford.edu/sites/default/files/pdf/academic-papers/01_Bunch_Kibler_Pimentel_RealizingOpp%20in%20ELA_FINAL_0.pdf [June 2018].

California Department of Education. (2015). *English Language Arts/English Language Development Framework for California Public Schools.* Sacramento: Author.

California Department of Education. (2018). *English Learner Roadmap.* Available: https://www.cde.ca.gov/sp/el/rm/ [August 2018].

Callahan, R.M. (2005). Tracking and high school English learners: Limiting opportunity to learn. *American Educational Research Journal, 42*(2), 305–328.

Callahan, R.M., and Hopkins, M. (2018). Using ESSA to improve secondary English learners' opportunities to learn through course taking. *Journal of School Leadership, 27*(5), 755–766.

Callahan, R.M., Wilkinson, L., and Muller, C. (2010). Academic achievement and course taking among language minority youth in U.S. schools: Effects of ESL placement. *Educational Evaluation and Policy Analysis, 32*(1), 84–117.

Canagarajah, S. (2015). TESOL as a professional community: A half-century of pedagogy, research, and theory. *TESOL Quarterly, 50*(1), 7–41.

Carlson, D., and Knowles, J.E. (2016). The effect of English language learner reclassification on student ACT scores, high school graduation, and postsecondary enrollment: Regression discontinuity evidence from Wisconsin. *Journal of Policy Analysis and Management, 35*(3), 559-586.

Carreón, G.P., Drake, C., and Calabrese Barton, A. (2005). The importance of presence: Immigrant parents' school engagement experiences. *American Educational Research Journal, 42*(3), 465–498.

Castellón, M., Cheuk, T., Greene, R., Mercado-Garcia, D., Santos, M., Skarin, R., and Zerkel, L. (2015). *Schools to Learn From: How Six High Schools Graduate English Language Learners College and Career Ready.* Stanford, CA: Stanford Graduate School of Education.

Ciechanowksi, K.M. (2014). Weaving together science and English: An interconnected model of language development for emergent bilinguals. *Bilingual Research Journal, 37*(3), 237–262.

Cimpian, J.R., Thompson, K.D., and Makowski, M. (2017). Evaluating English learner reclassification policy effects across districts. *American Educational Research Journal, 54*(S1), 255S–278S.

Coburn, C.E., and Penuel, W.R. (2016). Research-practice partnerships in education: Outcomes, dynamics, and open questions. *Educational Researcher, 45*(1), 48–54.

Cook, G., Linquanti, R., Chinen, M., and Jung, H. (2012). *National Evaluation of Title III Implementation Supplemental Report—Exploring Approaches to Setting English Language Proficiency Performance Criteria and Monitoring English Learner Progress.* Available: https://www2.ed.gov/rschstat/eval/title-iii/implementation-supplemental-report.pdf [August 2018].

Council of Chief State School Officers. (2012). *Framework for English Language Proficiency Development Standards Corresponding to the Common Core State Standards and the Next Generation Science Standards.* Washington, DC: Author.

Cuban, L., and Usdan, M. (Eds.). (2003). *Powerful Reforms with Shallow Roots: Improving America's Urban Schools.* New York: Teachers College Press.

Dabach, D.B. (2015). Teacher placement into immigrant English learner classrooms: Limiting access in comprehensive high schools. *American Educational Research Journal, 52*(2), 243–274.

Darling-Hammond, L. (1993). Reframing the school reform agenda: Developing capacity for school transformation. *Phi Delta Kappan, 74*(10), 752–761.

Davison, C. (2006). Collaboration between ESL and content teachers: How do we know when we are doing it right? *International Journal of Bilingual Education and Bilingualism, 9*(4), 454–475.

Dee, T.S., and Jacob, B.A. (2010). The impact of No Child Left Behind on students, teachers, and schools. *Brookings Papers on Economic Activity,* 149–194. Available: https://www.brookings.edu/wp-content/uploads/2010/09/2010b_bpea_dee.pdf [May 2018].

Dove, M., and Honigsfeld, A. (2010). ESL co-teaching and collaboration: Opportunities to develop teacher leadership and enhance student learning. *TESOL Journal, 1*(1), 3–22.

Education Trust-West. (2018). *Unlocking Learning II: Math as a Lever for English Learner Equity.* Available: https://west.edtrust.org/resource/unlocking-learning-ii-using-math-lever-english-learner-equity [May 2018].

Elfers, A.M., and Stritikus, T. (2014). How school and district leaders support classroom teachers' work with English language learners. *Educational Administration Quarterly, 50*(2), 305–344.

Elfers, A.M., Lucero, A., Stritikus, T., and Knapp, M.S. (2013). Building systems of support for classroom teachers working with English language learners. *International Multilingual Research Journal, 7*(2), 155–174.

Elmore, R.F. (2004). *School Reform from the Inside Out: Policy, Practice, and Performance.* Cambridge, MA: Harvard Education Press.

Erbstein, N. (2016). Placing math reform: Locating Latino English learners in math classrooms and communities. *International Journal of Qualitative Studies in Education, 28*(8), 906–931.

Feldman, S., and Malagon, V.F. (2017). *Unlocking Learning: Science as a Lever for English Learner Equity.* Oakland, CA: Education Trust-West. Available: https://west.edtrust.org/resource/unlocking-learning-science-lever-english-learner-equity [June 2018].

Finnigan, K.S., Daly, A.J., and Che, J. (2013). Systemwide reform in districts under pressure: The role of social networks in defining, acquiring, using, and diffusing research evidence. *Journal of Educational Administration, 51*(4), 476–497.

Frattura, E.M., and Capper, C. (2007). *Leading for Social Justice: Transforming Schools for All Learners.* Thousand Oaks, CA: Corwin.

Futernick, K. (2010). Incompetent teachers of dysfunctional systems? *Phi Delta Kappan, 92*(2), 59–64.

Gándara, P., and Baca, G. (2008). NCLB and California's English language learners: The perfect storm. *Language Policy, 7,* 201–216. Available: http://cmmr.usc.edu/FullText/GandaraNCLB_ELLs.pdf [June 2018].

Gándara, P., and Hopkins, M. (Eds.). (2010). *Forbidden Language: English Learners and Restrictive Language Policies.* New York: Teachers College Press.

Gándara, P., Maxwell-Jolly, J., and Driscoll, A. (2005). *Listening to Teachers of English Language Learners: A Survey of California Teachers' Challenges, Experiences, and Professional Development Needs.* Santa Cruz, CA: The Center for the Future of Teaching and Learning.

Garcia, A. (2017). *Educating California's English Learners: Chula Vista's Expansion of Dual Language Programs in an Era of English-Only Policies.* Washington, DC: New America.

Garcia, A., and Carnock, J.T. (2016). *A Critical Mass: Creating Comprehensive Services for Dual Language Learners in Harrisonburg.* Washington, DC: New America.

Gibbons, P. (2009). *English Learners, Academic Literacy, and Thinking: Learning in the Challenge Zone.* Portsmouth, NH: Heinemann.

Gibbons, P. (2015). *Scaffolding Language, Scaffolding Learning: Teaching English Language Learners in the Mainstream Classroom* (2nd ed.). Portsmouth, NH: Heinemann.

Goldenberg, C., and Rutherford-Quach, S. (2010). Instructing English language learners: Assessing the state of our knowledge. *ERS Spectrum, 28*(1), 1–15.

Greenberg Motamedi, J., and Jaffery, Z. (2014). *Credit for Proficiency: The Impact of the Road Map World Language Credit Program on Student Attitudes Toward Bilingualism and School.* Portland, OR: Education Northwest.

Hansen-Thomas, H., and Richins, L.G. (2015). ESL Mentoring for secondary rural educators: Math and science teachers become second language specialists through collaboration. *TESOL Journal, 6*(4), 766–776.

Hargreaves, A., and Fullan, M. (2012). *Professional Capital: Transforming Teaching in Every School.* New York: Teachers College Press.

Heritage, M., Walqui, A., and Linquanti, L. (2015). *English Language Learners and the New Standards: Developing Language, Content Knowledge, and Analytical Practices in the Classroom.* Cambridge, MA: Harvard Education Press.

Hill, L.E., Weston, M., and Hayes, J. (2014). *Reclassification of English Learner Students in California.* San Francisco, CA: Public Policy Institute of California. Available: http://www.ppic.org/content/pubs/report/R_114LHR.pdf [May 2018].

Honig, M.I. (2006). *New Directions in Education Policy Implementation: Confronting Complexity.* Albany: State University of New York Press.

Hopkins, M. (2016). Beliefs in context: Understanding language policy implementation at a systems level. *Educational Policy, 30*(4), 573–605.

Hopkins, M., and Spillane, J.P. (2015). Conceptualizing relations between instructional guidance infrastructure (IGI) and teachers' beliefs: Regulative, normative, and cultural-cognitive considerations. *Journal of Educational Change, 16*(4), 421–450.

Hopkins, M., Lowenhaupt, R., and Sweet, T. (2015). Organizing English learner instruction in new immigrant destinations: District infrastructure and subject-specific school practice. *American Educational Research Journal, 52*(3), 408–439.

Hopkins, M., Thompson, K., Linquanti, R., Hakuta, K., and August, D. (2013). Fully accounting for English learner performance: A key issue in ESEA reauthorization. *Educational Researcher, 42*(2), 101–108.

Horwitz, A.R., Uro, G., Price-Baugh, R., Simon, C., Uzzell, R., Lewis, S., and Casserly, M. (2009). *Succeeding with English Language Learners: Lesson Learned from the Great City Schools*. Washington, DC: Council of Great City Schools.

Johnson, C.C., Bolshakova, V.L.J., and Waldron, T. (2016). When good intentions and reality meet: Large-scale reform of science teaching in urban schools with predominantly Latino ELL students. *Urban Education, 51*(5), 476–513.

Kanno, Y., and Kangas, S.E.N. (2014). "I'm not going to be, like, for the AP": English language learners' limited access to advanced college-preparatory courses in high school. *American Educational Research Journal, 51*(5), 848–878.

Kelly, L.B. (2016). Supporting academic language. *Science and Children, 54*(3), 52–57.

Koedel, C., and Polikoff, M. (2017). *Big Bang for Just a Few Bucks: The Impact of Math Textbooks in California*. Washington, DC: The Brookings Institution.

Ladd, H.F. (2017). No Child Left Behind: A deeply flawed federal policy. *Journal of Policy Analysis and Management, 36*(2), 461–469.

Lagunoff, R., Spycher, P., Linquanti, R., Carroll, C., and DiRanna, K. (2015). *Integrating the CA ELD Standards into K–12 Mathematics and Science Teaching and Learning*. San Francisco, CA: WestEd. Available: https://www.husdschools.org/site/handlers/file download.ashx?moduleinstanceid=25&dataid=47&FileName=Integrating-the-CA-ELD-Standards-into-K-12-Mathmatics-and-Science-Teaching-and-Learning.pdf [June 2018].

Lee, O., and Luykx, A. (2005). Dilemmas in scaling up innovations in elementary science instruction with nonmainstream students. *American Educational Research Journal, 42*(3), 411–428.

Lewis, L., and Gray, L. (2016). *Programs and Services for High School English Learners in Public School Districts: 2015–16* (NCES 2016-150). Washington, DC: U.S. Department of Education, National Center for Education Statistics.

Linquanti, R. (2001). *The Redesignation Dilemma: Challenges and Choices in Fostering Meaningful Accountability for English Learners* (Policy Report 2001-1). Santa Barbara: University of California, Linguistic Minority Research Institute.

López, F., Scanlan, M., and Gundrum, B. (2013). Preparing teachers of English language learners: Empirical evidence and policy implications. *Education Policy Analysis Archives, 21*(20), 1–35. Available: http://epaa.asu.edu/ojs/article/view/1132 [June 2018].

López, F., McEneaney, E., and Nieswandt, M. (2015). Language instruction educational programs and academic achievement of Latino English learners: Considerations for states with changing demographics. *American Journal of Education, 121*(3), 417–450.

Lowenhaupt, R. (2014). School access and participation: Family engagement practices in the new Latino diaspora. *Education and Urban Society, 46*(5), 522–547.

Martiniello, M. (2008). Language and the performance of English-language learners in math word problems. *Harvard Educational Review, 78*(2), 333–368.

McClure, G., and Cahnmann-Taylor, M. (2010). Pushing back against push-in: ESOL teacher resistance and the complexities of coteaching. *TESOL Journal, 1*(1), 101–129.

McEneaney, E.H., López, F., and Nieswandt, M. (2014). Instructional models for the acquisition of English as bridges into school science: Effects on the science achievement of U.S. Hispanic English language learners. *Learning Environments Research, 17*(3), 305–318.

Menken, K., and Solorza, C. (2014). No child left bilingual: Accountability and the elimination of bilingual education programs in New York City schools. *Educational Policy, 28*(1), 96–125.

Met, M. (1994). Teaching content through a second language. In F. Genesee (Ed.), *Educating Second Language Children: The Whole Child, the Whole Curriculum, the Whole Community* (pp. 159–182). Oakleigh, UK: Cambridge University Press.

Minicucci, C., and Olsen, L. (1992). *Programs for Secondary Limited English Proficient Students: A California Study.* Washington, DC: National Clearinghouse for Bilingual Education.

Mintrop, R. (2016). *Design-Based School Improvement.* Cambridge, MA: Harvard Education Press.

Molle, D., Linquanti, R., MacDonald, R., and Cook, H.G. (2016). *Discerning—and Fostering—What English Learners Can Do with Language: Guidance on Gathering and Interpreting Complementary Evidence of Classroom Language Uses for Reclassification Decisions.* Washington, DC: Council of Chief State School Officers. Available: https://ccsso.org/sites/default/files/2017-11/CCSSOELLUseGuidance20160829_0.pdf [August 2018].

National Academies of Sciences, Engineering, and Medicine. (2017). *Promoting the Educational Success of Children and Youth Learning English: Promising Futures.* Washington, DC: The National Academies Press.

Parker, C.E., O'Dwyer, L.M., and Irwin, C.W. (2014). *The Correlates of Academic Performance for English Language Learner Students in a New England District* (REL 2014–020). Washington, DC: U.S. Department of Education, Institute of Education Sciences, National Center for Education Evaluation and Regional Assistance, Regional Educational Laboratory Northeast and Islands. Available: https://files.eric.ed.gov/fulltext/ED560731.pdf [June 2018].

Parrish, T., Perez, M., Merickel, A., and Linquanti, R. (2006). *Effects of the Implementation of Proposition 227 on the Education of English Learners, K–12: Findings from a Five-Year Evaluation.* Palo Alto, CA: American Institutes for Research.

Penfield, R.D., and Lee, O. (2010). Test-based accountability: Potential benefits and pitfalls of science assessment with student diversity. *Journal of Research in Science Teaching, 47*(1), 6–24.

Penuel, W.R., Fishman, B.J., Cheng, B.H., and Sabelli, N. (2011). Organizing research and development at the intersection of learning, implementation, and design. *Educational Researcher, 40*(7), 331–337.

Petersen, G.J. (1999). Demonstrated actions of instructional leaders: An examination of five California superintendents. *Education Policy Analysis Archives, 7*(18), 1–23.

Remold, J., Rosier, S., Sauerteig, D., Podkul, T., Bhanot, R., and Michalchik, V. (2014). *BaySci: A Partnership for Bay Area Science Education, August 2014 Evaluation Report.* Menlo Park, CA: SRI Education.

Robinson, J.P. (2011). Evaluating criteria for English learner reclassification: A causal-effects approach using a binding-score regression discontinuity design with instrumental variables. *Educational Evaluation and Policy Analysis, 33*(3), 267–292.

Robinson-Cimpian, J.P., and Thompson, K.D. (2016). The effects of changing test-based policies for reclassifying English learners. *Journal of Policy Analysis and Management, 35*(2), 279–305.

Robinson-Cimpian, J.P., Thompson, K.D., and Umansky, I.M. (2016). Research and policy considerations for English learner equity. *Policy Insights from the Behavioral and Brain Sciences, 3*(1), 129–137.

Santos, M., Darling-Hammond, L., and Cheuk, T. (2012). *Teacher Development to Support English Language Learners in the Context of Common Core State Standards.* Stanford, CA: Stanford University.

Santos, M., Castellón, M., Cheuk, T., Greene, R., Mercado-Garcia, D., Zerkel, L., Hakuta, H., and Skarin, R. (2018). *Preparing English Learners for College and Career: Lessons from Successful High Schools.* New York: Teachers College Press

Schleppegrell, M.J. (2004). *The Language of Schooling: A Functional Linguistics Perspective.* Mahwah, NJ: Lawrence Erlbaum Associates.

Scott, B. (2001). Coming of age. *IDRA Newsletter*, March. Available: http://www.idra.org/Newslttr/2001/Mar/Bradley.htm [June 2018].

Skrla, L., Scheurich, J.J., Garcia, J., and Nolly, G. (2004). Equity audits: A practical leadership tool for developing equitable and excellent schools. *Educational Administration Quarterly, 40*(1), 133–161.

Spillane, J.P. (1996). School districts matter: Local educational authorities and state instructional policy. *Educational Policy, 10*(1), 63–87.

Spillane, J.P., and Thompson, C.L. (1997). Reconstructing conceptions of local capacity: The local education agency's capacity for ambitious instructional reform. *Educational Evaluation and Policy Analysis, 19*(2), 185–203.

Spillane, J.P., Hopkins, M., and Sweet, T. (2017). School district educational infrastructure and change at scale: Teacher peer interactions and their beliefs about mathematics instruction. *American Educational Research Journal, 55*(3). Available: http://journals.sagepub.com/doi/abs/10.3102/0002831217743928 [June 2018].

Steele, J.L., Slater, R.O., Zamarro, G., Miller, T., Li, J., Burkhauser, S., and Bacon, M. (2017). Effects of dual-language immersion programs on student achievement: Evidence from lottery data. *American Educational Research Journal, 54*(15), 282S–306S.

Sugarman, J. (2016). *Funding an Equitable Education for English Learners in the United States.* Washington, DC: Migration Policy Institute.

Tanenbaum, C., Boyle, A., Soga, K., Le Floch, K.C., Golden, L., Petroccia, M., Toplitz, M., Taylor, J., and O'Day, J. (2012). *National Evaluation of Title III Implementation: Report on State and Local Implementation.* Washington, DC: American Institutes for Research. Available: https://www2.ed.gov/rschstat/eval/title-iii/state-local-implementation-report.pdf [August 2018].

Theoharis, G., and O'Toole, J. (2011). Leading inclusive ELL: Social justice leadership for English language learners. *Educational Administration Quarterly, 47*(4), 646–688.

Thompson, K.D. (2013). Is separate always unequal? A philosophical examination of ideas of equality in key cases regarding racial and linguistic minorities in education. *American Educational Research Journal, 50*(6), 1249–1278.

Thompson, K.D. (2017). What blocks the gate? Exploring current and former English learners' math course-taking in secondary school. *American Educational Research Journal, 54*(4), 757–798.

Thompson, K.D., Martinez, M.I., Clinton, C., and Díaz, G. (2017). Considering interest and action: Analyzing types of questions explored by researcher-practitioner partnerships. *Educational Research, 46*(8), 464–473.

Umansky, I.M. (2013). *Peeling Back the Label: Do Classifications and Specialized Services Help or Hurt Language Minority Students?* Paper presented at the Segregation, Immigration, and Educational Inequality Conference, Ghent, Belgium.

Umansky, I.M. (2016). To be or not to be EL: An examination of the impact of classifying students as English Learners. *Educational Evaluation and Policy Analysis, 38*(4), 714–737.

Umanksy, I.M., and Reardon, S.F. (2014). Reclassification patterns among Latino English learner students in bilingual, dual immersion, and English immersion classrooms. *American Educational Research Journal, 51*(5), 879–912.

Umansky, I., Hopkins, M., Dabach, D.B., Porter, L., Thompson, K., and Pompa, D. (2018). *Understanding and Supporting the Educational Needs of Recently Arrived Immigrant English Learner Students: Lessons for State and Local Education Agencies.* Washington, DC: Council of Chief State School Officers.

Umekubo, L.A., Chrispeels, J.H., and Daly, A.J. (2015). The cohort model: Lesson learned when principals collaborate. *Journal of Educational Change, 16*(4), 451–482.

United Nations Development Programme. (2009). *Capacity Development: A UNDP Primer.* New York: Author.

Valdés, G., Kibler, A., and Walqui, A. (2014). *Changes in the Expertise of ESL Professionals: Knowledge and Action in an Era of New Standards.* Alexandria, VA: TESOL International Association.

Valentino, R.A., and Reardon, S.F. (2015). Effectiveness of four instructional programs designed to serve English language learners: Variation by ethnicity and initial English proficiency. *Educational Evaluation and Policy Analysis, 37*(4), 612–637.

Warren, M., Hoong, S., Leung Rubin, C., and Sychitkokhong Uy, P. (2009). Beyond the bake sale: A community-based relational approach to parent engagement in schools. *Teachers College Record, 111*(9), 2209–2254.

Wixom, M. (2015). *State-Level English Language Learner Policies.* Denver, CO: Education Commission of the States.

Working Group on ELL Policy. (2015). *Selected Recommendations on ESEA Reauthorization Regarding English Language Learners.* Available: http://ellpolicy.org/wp-content/uploads/ESEA_Updated.pdf [August 2018].

# 9

# Conclusions, Recommendations, and Research Agenda

As established across this report, English learners (ELs) bring a wealth of resources to science, technology, engineering, and mathematics (STEM) learning, including their knowledge and interest in STEM-related content that is born out of their experiences in their homes and communities, home languages, variation in argumentation practices, and, in some cases, experiences with schooling in other countries. There are complex forces (e.g., teachers, families, administrators) including policies (e.g., state policy) and how they are interpreted and enacted that have the potential to shape ELs' opportunities in STEM learning. This chapter presents the committee's conclusions and recommendations for policy, practice, and research and data collection drawn as a synthesis across the full report. They are followed by a research agenda that identifies the gaps in current knowledge with respect to ELs and their success in STEM learning.

## CONCLUSIONS

The committee organized its conclusions by first articulating issues surrounding ELs in the broader educational landscape, including estimations of academic achievement, access, and barriers to inclusion in STEM learning, and the use of ELs' first language during STEM instruction. In the next set of conclusions, we more explicitly emphasized the interaction between STEM learning and language development; the instructional strategies that have been identified as potentially beneficial for serving ELs in STEM learning; the interaction between families, communities, and schools; and the preparation of and professional development for preservice and in-service teachers. The committee then focused on other factors that may affect ELs participation in STEM to include large-scale and classroom-level assessment. All of these culminate into the approaches that actors at different levels of the system need to consider in building capacity to support ELs in STEM learning.

## ELs and the Education System

The *Promising Futures* report (National Academies of Sciences, Engineering, and Medicine, 2017) set the overall context for this report by highlighting the diversity of ELs to include the heterogeneity in cultures, language, and experiences that may have an impact on their education (including the contexts that expose them to a number of risk factors that may have negative impacts). There are nearly 5 million students classified as ELs in U.S. public schools who combined speak more than 350 languages, with the most frequently used language being Spanish (Chapter 2). Like the previous committee, the current committee observed heterogeneity from multiple sources that have impacts on academic achievement including ELs' English proficiency, the home languages they speak, their proficiency in their home language(s), the extent of formal schooling in their home language(s), their previous instruction in their home language(s) in STEM subjects, their STEM-related out-of-school experiences, their experience with U.S. school systems and the quality of that experience, their socioeconomic status, and other factors. Moreover, the *Promising Futures* report concluded that the evidence suggests that "many schools are not providing adequate instruction to ELs in acquiring English proficiency while also ensuring access to academic subjects at grade level from the time they first enter school until they reach the secondary grades" (p. 5). In addition, "many secondary schools are not able to meet the diverse needs of long-term ELs, including their linguistic, academic, and socioemotional needs" (p. 5).

Building from this report and a review of the evidence more specific to ELs and STEM learning, the committee acknowledges the important role that classification plays in helping to identify and track the progress of ELs with respect to developing English proficiency, as well as content area achievement, and to gauge the overall effectiveness of educational systems in serving ELs (see Chapters 2, 7, and 8). What was illuminating were the potential impacts that issues related to classification might have on ELs' opportunities to engage in STEM learning and the consequent implications for academic achievement in STEM subjects. That is, ELs may have limited access to programs of language development and content learning that would be most beneficial to them. Moreover, ELs are often tracked through less rigorous STEM courses (Chapter 2). Inconsistencies in the processes for identifying ELs and failure to account for the dynamic and developmental nature of the EL designation complicate comparisons involving ELs and reduce the coherence in designing, carrying out, or summarizing the research literature.

The evidence on different programs models (see Chapters 2 and 8), particularly in elementary contexts, shows that when bilingual education is done well, it can be beneficial. When bilingual instruction is well designed and implemented, with qualified teachers highly proficient in the languages of instruction, students, on average, develop linguistic and academic competence in English that is superior to students in English-only instruction; develop linguistic and academic competence in their first language; and experience cognitive, social, and economic benefits from being proficient bilinguals. However, simply providing instruction in their home language in addition to English is not sufficient to achieve the benefits of bilingual instruction; program quality and the focus on rigorous academic content and high levels of home language and English proficiency are essential. It would be unwise to assume that simply using students' first language in instruction is sufficient to provide high-quality instruction. At the same time, it goes without saying that such high-quality bilingual instruction is currently not possible in *all* contexts. The diversity of first languages spoken in the United States, the low density of many languages in most communities, the limited availability of teachers of STEM content who are proficient in those home languages and in English, and the limited availability of STEM instructional materials in many languages reduces the chances of effective first language instruction for *all* ELs.

Efforts geared toward developing capacity to effectively educate ELs, including newcomers, through instruction in English and building upon ELs' full range of meaning-making resources are crucial across all program models (see Chapters 2 and 8). Recognition that students' home language and culture is a resource for cognition, for making sense of academic content, and for communication even when instruction is in English enables students to make use of all of their cognitive, linguistic, and meaning-making resources during instruction and reduces barriers to students' understanding as they develop English proficiency (Chapter 3). Teachers providing instruction in English can facilitate their students' access to content and classroom participation when they employ minimally restrictive language policies in instruction, thereby freeing students up to use all of their cognitive and linguistic resources in their route to developing understanding of STEM content and proficiency in English (Chapter 4).

However, too often schools operate under the incorrect assumption that proficiency in English is a prerequisite to meaningful engagement with STEM learning and fail to leverage ELs' meaningful engagement with content and disciplinary practices as a route to language proficiency (see issues related to access in Chapters 2 and 8). Students, including newcomers, do not need to be proficient in English to benefit from and participate in disciplinary learning. Recognition of the assets that ELs bring to the classroom, and that some deficits in student performance arise from lack of access rather than limited ability or language proficiency, or from cultural differences, will enable educators to address the particular needs of students who are learning the language of instruction while simultaneously providing students opportunities to engage meaningfully in STEM instruction. Based on these findings, the committee identified three key conclusions that apply broadly to all ELs.

CONCLUSION 1: The designation of a group of students as English learners (ELs) is important to the U.S. educational system. However, clear and consistent designations of EL and English-proficiency status are needed to reduce misperceptions of ELs' proficiency in science, technology, engineering, and mathematics academic achievement, including misestimation of achievement gaps. Consistent identification, including the ability to report on educational attainment of ELs after they have become proficient in English, would enable a deeper understanding of academic achievement of students who begin school as ELs, as well as what program models and instructional strategies work best, and to determine whether specific approaches work best for particular EL subpopulations under specific conditions.

CONCLUSION 2: Frequently, English learners (ELs) lack full access to school-based science, technology, engineering, and mathematics (STEM) learning opportunities. More specifically:

- For both science and mathematics, ELs lack opportunities to engage with challenging, grade-appropriate content and disciplinary practices. Lack of opportunity arises due to barriers to full participation in classroom activities and exclusion from science and mathematics instruction with never-EL peers.
- In high school, barriers to STEM learning may also involve exclusion from rigorous science or mathematics courses, placement in remedial courses, and poor advising regarding course selection that ultimately limits access to advanced STEM subjects and STEM careers.
- There is little information about inclusion of ELs in technology- and engineering-based instruction.

CONCLUSION 3: When English learners (ELs) have the opportunity to use all of their linguistic and non-linguistic meaning-making resources during science, technology, engineering, and mathematics instruction, these resources can be helpful for communication and learning.

## STEM Learning and Language Development

As described in Chapter 3, the STEM disciplines are unique in that students engage in practices, procedures, and experimentation in developing STEM knowledge. Thus, not all access to meaning in STEM is directly through language, even when understanding is later communicated through language. Because STEM knowledge is gained through meaningful engagement with STEM content and practices, including observation and experimentation, the language used to describe and communicate in these disciplines can be grounded in students' personal experiences with content that is distinct from the way that content is experienced in history, social studies, and reading/language arts. For example, in the science classroom, as students are making sense of phenomena, they engage in science practices, develop shared experience, and use multimodalities to communicate their ideas. Conducting an experiment on gravity, growing cells in a Petri dish, and solving word problems based on real-life experiences of fair shares that ground work with fractions are experiences that convey meaning to the student beyond the language encountered during the experience. In fact, students' knowledge of and memory for the experiences help to give meaning to the language that students encountered in the experiences and will later use to convey their understanding of what was learned.

There is no language-free content—language use always presents some content—and most representations of content require some language, even with multimodal resources for meaning-making (Chapter 3). Students can and do understand concepts encountered in experiments without necessarily having the language for those concepts. Through this process of experience, their language develops and becomes refined. STEM subjects afford more opportunities for alternate routes to knowledge acquisition (e.g., experimentation, demonstration of phenomena, demonstration of practices, etc.) through which students can gain a sense of something without resorting predominantly to language to access meaning. It is through this experience that language is also learned.

As students engage with content early in their educations, they will develop rudimentary understanding of phenomena that increase in sophistication and depth. These deeper understandings are also associated with increasingly sophisticated language registers—as the language and concepts become increasingly sophisticated, support for the increasingly sophisticated language is needed. Despite the recognized developmental nature of both language and content, there is little research on learning progressions/trajectories in the STEM disciplines for ELs. The extent to which

ELs follow the same progressions/trajectories as students whose primary language is English is unknown and under-researched at this time. Homogeneity of learning progressions across students or student groups cannot be assumed. Taken together, two key conclusions from the committee's position grounded in evidence were identified (Chapter 3).

**CONCLUSION 4: Science, technology, engineering, and mathematics (STEM) disciplines offer unique learning opportunities for English learners (ELs). Not only do the disciplinary practices allow for ELs to develop disciplinary knowledge, but also they engage ELs in meaningful language use. Provided that teachers utilize promising instructional strategies, engagement in the disciplinary practices of STEM contributes to both STEM learning and language learning.**

**CONCLUSION 5: Each of the science, technology, engineering, and mathematics (STEM) disciplines are developmental in nature, leading to more and more sophisticated understandings and capabilities within any given discipline. In addition, the acquisition of language proficiency in service of academic success takes time and focused effort on the parts of students and teachers. The developmental nature of STEM learning and language proficiency have substantial implications for structuring and implementing STEM instruction for English learners from the early grades.**

## Instructional Strategies

In reviewing the evidence on instructional strategies (see Chapter 4), although the link with specific students' outcomes is still needed, the committee determined that there are several instructional strategies that show the greatest promise for simultaneously building disciplinary content knowledge, access to practices, and language proficiency; however, less effective instructional strategies are still used.

Teachers of ELs who are more successful understand that ELs learn language through meaningful and active engagement with language in the context of authentic STEM activities and practices (see Chapter 4 and extensions in Chapters 5 and 6). They focus on supporting student understanding of STEM content, participation in disciplinary practices, and grade-level topics, instead of emphasizing remedial work or memorization of STEM facts. These teachers plan lessons—sometimes in collaboration with ESL teachers—that include ELs producing language, draw their students' attention to language during instruction, and judiciously plan and employ explicit vocabulary instruction that allows ELs to use word meanings in the context of disciplinary practices. Moreover, these teachers know that paying attention to language is more than teaching vocabulary.

Teachers of ELs not only strive to integrate an explicit focus on language into the teaching of STEM concepts and practices, but also intentionally encourage ELs to draw on their full range of linguistic and communicative competencies and resources through the use of different modalities (talk, read, write, listen, draw, etc.) and representations (symbols, texts, charts, tables, graphs, etc.) to represent and communicate their thinking, solutions, or arguments in STEM subjects. STEM curriculum that is developed considering ELs from the inception of the design process shows greater sensitivity to the role of language in STEM instruction and will integrate tools into the material that complement the language to convey meaning to learners in multiple ways. As such, these tools facilitate both the development of language in context and the acquisition of content knowledge and practices.

Furthermore, effective teachers of ELs engage in experiences that foster self-reflection about their assumptions regarding diverse students' and families' engagement with STEM and STEM education and consider the positioning of ELs in the classroom. These experiences facilitate teachers' adoption of empowering attitudes and expectations for students. What follows are the six conclusions the committee has identified based upon the review of the evidence as beneficial for ELs in STEM classrooms.

CONCLUSION 6: Teachers play a critical role in positioning English learners (ELs) as competent community members in science, technology, engineering, and mathematics (STEM) classrooms when they recognize that ELs, like all students, are members of social and academic communities. Teachers' positioning of ELs can influence their learning in STEM classrooms.

CONCLUSION 7: Teachers' attitudes, beliefs, and expectations about English learners' (ELs') capacity for grade-appropriate science, technology, engineering, and mathematics (STEM) learning influence teachers' approaches to and engagement of ELs in STEM instruction. When teachers have positive expectations for and beliefs about ELs in STEM, they are more likely to provide meaningful STEM learning opportunities for ELs.

CONCLUSION 8: There are better outcomes for English learners (ELs) in science, technology, engineering, and mathematics when teachers consistently support and actively incorporate ELs in classroom activities and disciplinary discussions. To do so requires that teachers support positive social interactions among peers and incorporate explicit talk about language in disciplinary learning.

CONCLUSION 9: Science, technology, engineering, and mathematics (STEM) curriculum materials are more effective when English learners (ELs) are considered at the beginning of and throughout the design process, rather than being developed as supplemental accommodations. Existing exemplary STEM curricula can be annotated, revised, and expanded to promote STEM learning with ELs.

CONCLUSION 10: Teachers of English learners (ELs) that engage with families in science, technology, engineering, and mathematics (STEM)-based experiences are more likely to be sensitive to and have an appreciation for the cultural and linguistic differences of their EL students and work to improve communication and understanding. Engaging in these experiences can increase teachers' comfort working with diverse families around STEM content area learning.

CONCLUSION 11: The integration of science, technology, engineering, and mathematics (STEM) content and language learning can be achieved in various ways but is facilitated when teachers of STEM content work in concert with English as a second language teachers who recognize the functional use of language in STEM instruction.

## Family-Community-School Interactions

Children do not attend schools in isolation; they are members of families and larger social communities that have helped to shape their knowledge and interest in school and STEM. These affiliations with family and community can be viewed as resources. Effective family and community engagement models for ELs in STEM recognize and make connections to families' and communities' cultural and linguistic practices as they relate to STEM topics. Such models can help teachers and schools shift to an asset orientation toward ELs' STEM learning, can increase the engagement of families of ELs in other school-based activities, and can improve EL students' motivation in their STEM learning. Deficit notions about caregivers of ELs are inaccurate, ethically indefensible, and deleterious to schools' efforts to positively engage and educate ELs. Teacher-caregiver interactions specifically related to success for ELs in STEM education help teachers and schools move to an asset-based perspective on students and their families and communities, which ultimately benefit student learning and school success (see Chapter 5).

CONCLUSION 12: In science and mathematics, caregivers of English learners (ELs) enjoy learning disciplinary content and engaging in discussions about content and teaching. They want their voices and experiences to be heard and validated by their children's teachers and schools.

**CONCLUSION 13:** There is little research on the connections between English learners' (ELs') science, technology, engineering, and mathematics (STEM) learning outcomes and STEM-specific family-school interactions. Although findings generally support that such efforts yield positive benefits for students, families, and schools, there is limited understanding of the full potential for STEM-specific family-school interactions to influence EL STEM learning outcomes or of the specific strategies that might be most or least effective in a given context.

### Teacher Education

When examining the evidence with respect to teacher education, including preservice preparation and in-service professional development (Chapter 6), it is clear that teachers of STEM content generally are not adequately prepared to provide learning opportunities to ELs in their classrooms. Secondary STEM teachers in schools with large EL populations lack adequate preparation in STEM disciplines, strategies for teaching STEM in general, or strategies for teaching STEM to ELs in particular. Some states have initiated course requirements and teacher certification policies focused on EL instruction for content teachers. Moreover, whereas all states offer ESL certificates, only 21 states require specialized certification to teach ELs (Chapter 8).

When teachers and teacher candidates of STEM subjects are provided with ongoing field-based or community-based experiences that allow them to work with ELs in out-of-classroom settings, they are more likely to develop an asset-based orientation to teaching ELs. Opportunities for professional development and collaboration with teachers of ELs in STEM contexts and ESL teachers who are experts at integrating STEM subjects with ELs during their planning and delivery of STEM instruction may be beneficial. The committee identified four conclusions that are specific for teachers of STEM subjects and teacher educators to work with ELs.

**CONCLUSION 14:** Most teachers of science, technology, engineering, and mathematics (STEM) subjects have not received adequate preparation to provide appropriate STEM-related learning opportunities to English learners (ELs) in their classrooms. There are few opportunities for teachers to learn how to integrate language into STEM learning or how to enhance curricula into the teaching of STEM concepts and practices with ELs.

CONCLUSION 15: Teachers and administrators of science, technology, engineering, and mathematics (STEM) often bring biases and beliefs, reflected from bias in the wider society, to their work with English learners (ELs) that negatively affect learning outcomes with ELs. These biases can be effectively addressed through targeted teacher preparation and professional development. Specifically, when teachers and teacher candidates are provided with opportunities to examine their own cultural and linguistic backgrounds and self-perceptions in relation to their work with ELs in STEM, they are more likely to take an asset-based orientation in their classrooms, which leads to increased opportunities for ELs to engage in STEM learning opportunities and to improved STEM outcomes.

CONCLUSION 16: When teachers of science, technology, engineering, and mathematics (STEM) subjects and English as a second language teachers come together for shared professional development about how to advance English learners (ELs') STEM learning and how to collaborate and share their expertise with each other, both groups of teachers are more likely to learn knowledge and competencies that benefit ELs.

CONCLUSION 17: Currently, there are few opportunities for teacher educators to learn how to equip preservice teachers who will teach science, technology, engineering, and mathematics (STEM) to English learners (ELs). Despite the lack of research on the intersection of STEM and ELs in preparing teacher educators, the research on preparing teacher educators to support teachers of ELs more generally suggests that they require

- extended professional development from other teacher educators with expertise in supporting preservice teachers who are learning to work with ELs;
- collaboration with teachers who are successfully teaching ELs in their classrooms; and
- professional development that focuses on student thinking in STEM, disciplinary practices and discourse, and curriculum materials that the teachers will actually be using in their teaching.

## Assessment

The inclusion of ELs in high-stakes assessment (see Chapter 7) for accountability and the alignment of language proficiency objectives with the language demands of content area achievement create significant social responsibility to provide assessments that provide fair, valid, and reliable inferences about what ELs know and can do. Efforts to fulfill this responsibility have been insufficient, and, in some instances, have led to solutions that can be detrimental to student performance when applied indiscriminately. For example, while allowed by recent federal legislation, testing ELs in their first language does not give students an opportunity to exhibit their STEM knowledge when students have not received content instruction in their first language. Even when ELs have received their content instruction in their first language, testing in their first language can result in invalid inferences when sufficient time and resources are not allocated to properly translate and adapt standards-based assessments from English to other languages. Similarly, one cannot assume that students are literate in their first language, even if they are proficient speakers in that language; in such situations, translating an assessment into the child's first language will not improve assessment of the student's knowledge. The policies to include ELs in accountability assessments and to disaggregate results for ELs are generally viewed as positive developments in education because they have drawn attention to the education of ELs and the responsibilities of students, parents, teachers, administrators, and policy makers in bringing about desired educational outcomes for ELs. Nevertheless, much work remains to be done to ensure that the assessments used with ELs yield inferences that are fair, valid, and reliable.

Moreover, critical to promoting fair and valid STEM assessment for ELs is the design of tasks and the features intended to support ELs' access to the content of items. Static visuals (e.g., pictures) and dynamic visuals (e.g., videos) are examples of accommodations that have the potential to support ELs in gaining access to content of items, provided that they are carefully developed. An important consideration in interpreting ELs performance on STEM tasks is the fact that, when they are effective, assessment accommodations tend to benefit all students, not only the EL students for which they are originally created. Moreover, ELs with higher levels of English proficiency are more likely to benefit from effective accommodations than ELs with lower levels of English proficiency, because the former have better linguistic resources than the latter to benefit from those accommodations. An important consequence of this fact is that there is a limit to the extent to which accommodations can eliminate English proficiency as a factor that affects the validity of interpretations of ELs' performance on STEM tasks. As such, these limitations of assessments and accommodations necessitate using multiple pieces of information to ensure that the best decision can be made.

Findings that effective classroom summative assessments use visuals to make content accessible to ELs are comparable to findings in the large-scale summative assessment literature that have found visuals to be an effective test accommodation. Unfortunately, classroom summative assessment approaches still have important challenges to address, particularly how best to assess the STEM learning of students with lower levels of English proficiency, because those ELs who were more likely to demonstrate STEM knowledge in studies of effective classroom summative assessment were predominantly students at higher levels of English proficiency. The role of feedback while learning is taking place is a key aspect of formative assessment.

Based upon the review of the existing evidence in Chapter 7, the committee identified the following four key conclusions.

CONCLUSION 18: Because of the linguistic heterogeneity of ELs, obtaining accurate measures of academic achievement for ELs is more difficult than for never-EL students. More accurate decisions concerning ELs' STEM academic achievement are possible when those decisions are based on multiple sources of information, multiple test scores, and/or qualitative forms of assessment.

CONCLUSION 19: Large-scale STEM assessments yield better-informed decisions about ELs' STEM achievement when accommodations are selected to meet the individual needs of students and when test scores are used in combination with other information about STEM performance.

CONCLUSION 20: Classroom summative assessment of science, technology, engineering, and mathematics (STEM) subjects was found to produce fairer and more valid interpretations of English learner performance when keeping the following task design considerations in mind: incorporating static visuals (e.g., graphics, pictures), incorporating dynamic visuals (e.g., video), dividing tasks into multiple parts, and engaging students in collaborative tasks.

CONCLUSION 21: The incorporation of formative assessment practices in the classroom can lead to a richer language environment for all learners and English learners (ELs) specifically. Although the use of formative assessment has led to documented positive outcomes that are not science, technology, engineering, and mathematics (STEM) specific (i.e., literacy), the outcomes from the use of formative assessments in STEM and, relatedly, learning progressions to inform assessment interpretation, is presently under study and has not generated sufficient evidence to definitively conclude that these positive outcomes generalize to STEM subjects with ELs; there are no theoretical reasons or empirical evidence to suggest that formative assessment does not also work for STEM disciplines and ELs' learning.

## Building Capacity

Policies at the federal, state, and local levels can either facilitate ELs' opportunities in STEM or constrain teaching and learning in ways that are detrimental to ELs' access to and success in STEM learning. School districts demonstrating success with teaching ELs in STEM have leaders who attend to system coherence and do so by designing and implementing organizational structures that enable the integration of language and content within and between levels (i.e., state, district, school) and components of the system (e.g., instruction, curriculum, assessment, professional development, policies for categorization of ELs).

For data to be maximally informative about the performance of ELs, achievement data need to be disaggregated based on ELs' level of English proficiency in order to minimize the confounding influence of language proficiency on achievement. A second data practice that leads to better inferences about EL STEM performance is the inclusion of students who began school as ELs but are now no longer categorized as ELs. Including a category such as "Ever EL" and disaggregating achievement results by English language proficiency allow data users to better understand how well individual schools, districts, and entire states are serving ELs. That is, they have a clearer picture of the academic achievement outcomes of ELs at each grade, including ELs who are not yet proficient in English and students who are recently proficient in English and need access to STEM courses and instruction.

The following set of conclusions reflects the state of evidence on issues around building capacity to support ELs in STEM learning. Overall, the research suggests that integration of STEM learning and English language learning is possible and, in some instances, may require adjustment to the allocation of fiscal and human resources. Some systems that have succeeded in supporting ELs in STEM have demonstrated flexibility in allocating and aligning fiscal and human resources in service of their desired objectives.

**CONCLUSION 22: When system leaders within schools, districts, and states look at data pertaining to English learner (EL) access to science, technology, engineering, and mathematics (STEM) coursework and content, they are better equipped to make data-driven decisions related to teaching ELs in STEM.**

**CONCLUSION 23: There are a few states that have systemic policies or programs in place that attend to the professional development of teachers of science, technology, engineering, and mathematics who work with English learners (ELs). Careful consideration of the types and quality of experiences as well as specialized certifications to teach ELs is necessary.**

CONCLUSION 24: School systems that cohere around an asset-orientation that articulates high expectations for English learners (ELs) in science, technology, engineering, and mathematics (STEM) have been successful in teaching ELs in STEM. School district leadership is critical in facilitating this coherence.

## RECOMMENDATIONS

A prevailing issue acknowledged by this committee and by previous efforts is the lack of a consistent definition of "English learner" both within and across states. This lack of consistency has pervasive impacts at all levels of the education system and for understanding the true potential of ELs broadly and more specifically in STEM. Having a consistent definition at least across districts within a state, as well as consistent accounting practices that include ELs who have gained proficiency in English and been reclassified, would enable states, districts, and schools to adopt methods of collecting and analyzing data in ways that would allow for a clear understanding of ELs' long-term outcomes writ large and with respect to STEM, their time to achieve proficiency in English, and their academic performance in STEM throughout their time in the school system, not just during their time developing proficiency in English. Informative methods of examining STEM data will also enable schools, districts, states, and caregivers to determine how each aspect of the system is serving students in STEM at different levels of English proficiency, as well as how the system is performing in advancing students' proficiency in English.

Overall, it is imperative that ELs have the same quality of STEM-related learning opportunities as their never-EL peers. Based upon the committee's conclusions and the vision that ELs should be afforded the same learning opportunities in STEM, the following set of recommendations are intended to be steps to meeting this objective.

RECOMMENDATION 1: Evaluate current policies, approaches, and resources that have the potential to negatively affect English learners' (ELs') access to science, technology, engineering, and mathematics (STEM) learning opportunities, including classification and reclassification, course-taking, classroom instruction, program models offered, professional development, staffing, and fiscal resources, etc.

- Federal agencies should evaluate the ways in which funds are allocated for research and development that would enhance teaching and learning in STEM for ELs, including efforts that foster pipeline and training programs to increase the number of teachers qualified to teach STEM to ELs.

- States should evaluate their definition of EL, including proper specification of entrance and exit procedures and criteria for districts. Districts should examine the policies and procedures that are in place for consistently implementing these state procedures/criteria for classifying/reclassifying ELs.
- States should evaluate policies associated with the timing of large-scale state assessments and waivers for assessment (i.e., waivers for science assessment), frameworks for teacher certification, and the distribution of financial and human resources.
- District leaders and school personnel should examine (a) the program models and placement of ELs in STEM courses with particular attention to grade bands as well as issues associated with overrepresentation of ELs in remedial courses, (b) preparation of STEM teachers with attention to schools with large EL populations, (c) the opportunities for teacher collaboration and professional development, and (d) the distribution of financial and human resources.
- Schools should evaluate ELs' success in STEM classes, the quality of STEM classroom instruction and the positioning of ELs in the classroom, the qualifications of teachers hired, the professional development opportunities offered to teachers, and the resources (e.g., time and space) allocated to STEM learning.

RECOMMENDATION 2: Develop a high-quality framework to identify and remove barriers to English learners' (ELs) participation in rigorous science, technology, engineering, and mathematics (STEM) learning opportunities.

- District and school leaders should identify and enact norms of shared responsibility for success of ELs in STEM both within the district central office and within schools, developed by teams of district and school leaders associated with STEM and English language development/English as a second language education.
- States should take an active role in collecting and sharing resources across schools and districts.
- Leaders in states, districts, and schools should continuously evaluate, monitor, and refine policies to ensure that ELs' STEM learning outcomes are comparable to their never-EL peers.

RECOMMENDATION 3: Equip teachers and teacher candidates with the requisite tools and preparation to effectively engage and positively position English learners (ELs) in science, technology, engineering, and mathematics (STEM) content learning.

- Preservice teacher education programs should require courses that include learning research-based practices on how to best support ELs in learning STEM subjects.
- Preservice teacher education programs and providers of in-service professional development should provide opportunities to engage in field experiences that include ELs in both classroom settings and informal learning environments.
- English as a second language teacher education programs and providers of in-service professional development should design programs that include collaboration with teachers of STEM content to support ELs' grade-appropriate content and language learning in STEM.
- Teacher educators and professionals involved in pre- and in-service teacher learning should develop resources for teachers, teacher educators, and school and district leaders that illustrate productive, research-based instructional practices for supporting ELs in STEM learning.
- Preservice teacher education and teacher credentialing programs should take account of teacher knowledge of large-scale STEM assessment interpretation, classroom summative task design, and formative assessment practices with ELs.

RECOMMENDATION 4: Develop high-quality science, technology, engineering, and mathematics (STEM) curricular materials and integrate formative assessment into classroom practice to both facilitate and assess English learners' (ELs') progress through the curriculum.

- Curriculum developers, educators, and EL researchers should work together to develop curricular materials and resources that consider the diversity of ELs' needs as the materials are being developed and throughout the design process.
- EL researchers, curriculum developers, assessment professionals, teacher educators, professional learning providers, and teachers should work collaboratively to strengthen teachers' formative assessment skills to improve STEM instruction and promote ELs' learning.

RECOMMENDATION 5: Encourage and facilitate engagement with stakeholders in English learners' (ELs') local environment to support science, technology, engineering, and mathematics (STEM) learning.

- Schools and districts should reach out to families and caregivers to help them understand the available instructional programs in STEM and the different academic and occupational opportunities related to STEM, including what resources might be available in the community.

- Schools and districts should collaborate with community organizations and form external partnerships with organizations that focus on informal STEM learning to make an active effort to directly engage ELs and their caregivers in STEM-related learning activities in an effort to understand their EL families' and communities' assets and needs.

RECOMMENDATION 6: Design comprehensive and cohesive science, technology, engineering, and mathematics (STEM) assessment systems that consider English learners (ELs) and the impact of those assessments on STEM academic achievement for all students.

- Developers of large-scale STEM assessments need to develop and use population sampling frameworks that better reflect the heterogeneity of EL populations to ensure the proper inclusion of statistically representative samples of ELs in the process of test development according to sociodemographic variables including language proficiency, first language, geographical distribution, and socioeconomic status.
- Decision makers, researchers, funding agencies, and professionals in the relevant fields need to develop standards on the numbers and characteristics of students that need to be documented and reported in projects and contracts involving EL STEM assessment.

RECOMMENDATION 7: Review existing assessment accommodation policies and develop accessibility resources.

- States, districts, and schools need to review their existing policies regarding the use of accommodations during accountability assessments to ensure that English learners (ELs) are afforded access to those linguistic accommodations that best meet their needs during instruction as well as during assessment.
- States, districts, and schools should also examine their implementation of accommodations to ensure that accommodations are implemented with high fidelity for all ELs, take steps to improve implementation when high fidelity is not realized, and improve poor implementation when it is present.
- States and districts involved in developing new computer-administered assessments or revising existing computer-administered assessments, should develop those assessments to incorporate accessibility resources rather than rely on accommodations.

- States involved in the development of new science, technology, engineering, and mathematics assessments should apply universal design principles in the initial development and consider ELs from the beginning.

## RESEARCH AGENDA

As described in previous reports by the National Academies (National Research Council, 1992) on bilingual education, the field needs research that utilizes proper statistical designs and that rely on empirically supported theory. That is, the field needs to continue to build from promising practices to more robust models of how instructional practices operate in the complex policy, resource, institutional, and community contexts of schools. To achieve this goal, the field must undertake extensive longitudinal and retrospective research, coupled with qualitative research of various kinds (e.g., ethnographic, discourse analytic) that will elucidate similarities and differences in the trajectories of students learning STEM and the experiences for ELs and never-ELs. This research is needed to describe successful pathways for ELs into STEM careers and postsecondary training, including when and how they can succeed. That is, longitudinal research is needed that identifies early practices that lead to success from elementary to middle school to high school, including influences (e.g., reform curricula, teacher preparation, teacher professional development, frequency of classroom discussions, access to disciplinary practices, etc.) that take place in the early grades that lead to success in the later grades for ELs in STEM. This research must be sensitive to the classification of ELs and especially to the reclassification of ELs to ensure that ELs who have become proficient in English are not excluded from such research, or have their data aggregated into the data for English-only students. The following are a set of broader questions that remain unanswered.

### Research Area 1: ELs and the Educational Context

- What program models and instructional strategies in STEM work for particular EL groups and under what conditions?
- How does the social organization of different settings (e.g., classrooms, laboratories, schools, districts), structure of the school day, and different forms of mediation support, facilitate, or interfere with ELs developing understanding of STEM concepts and engagement in STEM practices?
- What does the performance of ELs look like across different grade bands and what scaffolding is needed across critical transition points?

- How is learning in the areas of engineering, technology, and computational thinking similar to and different from mathematics and science, and to what extent do these differences generalize to ELs and never-ELs? Do these disciplines offer specific advantages to ELs as areas of STEM learning? In what ways can informal technology-based learning settings after school increase our understanding?
- What does a STEM agenda that privileges and centers the culture, language, and experiences of ELs look like? What is afforded for ELs when they are centered in a STEM agenda in more holistic ways? How does the nature of STEM change?

### Research Area 2: STEM Learning and Language Development

- How do different proficiencies in a first language (oral, reading, writing) and previous STEM instruction in a first language affect students' learning of STEM subjects in English?
- How effective are interventions designed to promote asset-based views of ELs and communities in changing ELs' STEM achievement outcomes?
- What are the language learning opportunities and challenges for ELs through engagement in disciplinary practices? What are the barriers to providing high-value language-learning experiences to ELs at different levels of English proficiency within STEM learning contexts, and how do these vary across developmental periods throughout schooling?
- What is the role of the use of the first language and translanguaging in concept formation for ELs in STEM, and how does this role vary across students' academic and linguistic development and across STEM fields?

### Research Area 3: Instructional Strategies

- What do learning progressions in science or trajectories in mathematics look like for ELs and to what extent do they differ from the learning professions of never-ELs?
- What forms of metatalk develop ELs language and communication skills while also building scientific and mathematical understanding? What are effective teaching strategies that can help amplify the successful use of metatalk in classrooms so ELs build robust STEM understanding and language?
- How do differences in student participation and positioning affect how students see themselves as more or less competent in STEM subjects?

- How do teachers provide interaction, scaffolding, and other supports for learning STEM language?
- What are the best strategies for implementing team-teaching and collaboration in STEM classrooms?
- How does including ELs during the design and testing phases of curriculum development lead to high-quality materials that serve linguistically diverse students?

### Research Area 4: School-Home-Community Interactions

- In what ways can research-practice partnerships and other collaborative research models be leveraged to identify elements of the school-home-community system that are working well and elements that are not?
- Under what conditions are schools successful at building deep and lasting partnerships with families of communities of EL students that have positive impacts on those students' STEM learning? For example, how can shared STEM learning experiences both in and out of school contexts support EL students and their families in gaining knowledge about and motivation toward STEM academic and occupational pathways?

### Research Area 5: Teacher Education

- How can preparation of teachers of STEM who work with ELs support teachers' developing knowledge of STEM talk, language, and discourse? How can this be translated to developing knowledge of how to draw on ELs' full range of linguistic competencies and resources, using different modalities and language registers?
- How can preparation of teachers of STEM who work with ELs support teachers' developing knowledge of culturally sustaining pedagogies and strategies for enhancing family and community engagement? How can this work assess and challenge beliefs about ELs?
- What are the best ways to prepare ESL teachers to understand the role of language in content area learning, to structure language development opportunities in content area settings, to collaborate with content area teachers?

### Research Area 6: Assessment

- What properties of large-scale STEM assessments for use with ELs, and the various sources of heterogeneity in the EL population, might affect the psychometric properties of STEM assessments for use with ELs?

- What is the effectiveness of classroom summative and formative assessment of STEM (and learning progressions) with EL students? Are bilingually constructed assessments beneficial?
- What are the implications of allowing students to use any language resources at their disposal in judging student learning, progress, and in predicting student success in STEM courses and/or performance on assessments of STEM content?

### Research Area 7: Building Systemic Capacity

- How does the adoption of policies and the use of data-based decision making for ELs lead to improved student outcomes in STEM learning? Can the potential findings be replicated across other districts and states?
- What are the precise conditions needed to obtain positive effects through aligning policies to open opportunities for ELs? How does improving data-based decision making through more nuanced categories affect opportunities? In what ways does providing systematic professional development for STEM teachers and increasing collaboration between ESL and STEM teachers lead to positive effects?

### REFERENCES

National Academies of Sciences, Engineering, and Medicine. (2017). *Promoting the Educational Success of Children and Youth Learning English: Promising Futures.* Washington, DC: The National Academies Press.

National Research Council. (1992). *Assessing Evaluation Studies: The Case of Bilingual Education Strategies.* Washington, DC: National Academy Press.

# Appendix

# Committee and Staff Biographies

**David Francis** (*Chair*) is the Hugh Roy and Lillie Cranz Cullen Distinguished University Chair of Quantitative Methods and former chairman of the Department of Psychology (2002–2014) at the University of Houston, where he also serves as director of the Texas Institute for Measurement, Evaluation, and Statistics (TIMES) and co-director of the Center for Advanced Computing and Data Systems (CACDS). He is a fellow of Division 5 (Measurement, Evaluation, and Statistics) of the American Psychological Association, an inaugural fellow of the American Educational Research Association, and a fellow of the Association for Psychological Science. He was the chair of the Board on Testing and Assessment at the National Academies of Sciences, Engineering, and Medicine and has served on several consensus studies, including the Committee on Developmental Outcomes and Assessment of Young Children and most recently on the Committee on the Evaluation of NAEP Achievement Levels. Since early 2000, his research has focused on English language learners, including directing a National Research and Development Center funded by the Institute of Education Sciences (IES) along with several large, federally funded individual and program projects. He was a recipient of the 2006 Albert J. Harris Award from the International Reading Association, and received the University of Houston's Teaching Excellence Award, Excellence in Research and Scholarship Award, and Esther Farfel Award. He received his Ph.D. in clinical-neuropsychology from the University of Houston with a specialization in quantitative methods.

**Alison Bailey** is professor of human development and psychology at the University of California, Los Angeles, working on issues germane to children's linguistic, social, and educational development. Her areas of research include first and second language acquisition, early literacy development, and academic language pedagogy and assessment. She has most recently published in *Annual Review of Applied Linguistics, Teachers College Record, Educational Researcher, Journal of Mathematical Behavior*, and *Review of Research in Education*. She is principal investigator of the Dynamic Language Learning Progressions project supported by the Wisconsin Center for Education Research. Her co-authored recent books include *Children's Multilingual Development and Education: Fostering Linguistic Resources in Home and School Contexts; Language, Literacy, and Learning in the STEM Disciplines: How Language Counts for English Learners; Self-Regulation in Learning: The Role of Language and Formative Assessment*; and *Progressing Student Language Day by Day*. She is a faculty research partner at the National Center for Research on Evaluation, Standards, and Student Testing (CRESST) and is a member of the NAEP Standing Committee on Reading and the National Council on Measurement in Education Task Force on Classroom Assessment. She received her Ed.D. in human development and psychology at Harvard University.

**Hyman Bass (NAS)** is the Samuel Eilenberg Distinguished University Professor of Mathematics and Mathematics Education at the University of Michigan. He previously taught in the Columbia University mathematics department, which he once chaired. His mathematical work is mainly in commutative homological algebra, algebraic K-theory, and geometric group theory. He has held visiting appointments in many countries and extensively in India and France, where he collaborated with N. Bourbaki. In the 1990s he was enlisted by Deborah Ball to study the mathematics in elementary classrooms, in part to develop a practice-based theory of the mathematical knowledge demanded by the work of teaching. Currently he is interested in mathematical practices (and their relation to science practices), specifically in how mathematicians' problem-solving/theory-building duality could have a meaningful expression in school mathematics. He is also exploring ways to make mathematics instruction more equitable and inclusive. He is a member of the National Academy of Sciences, American Academy of Arts and Sciences, Third World Academy of Sciences, and National Academy of Education. He is past president of the American Mathematical Society and of the International Commission on Mathematical Instruction. He received the U.S. National Medal of Science in 2007. He received his Ph.D. in mathematics from the University of Chicago.

**Cory Buxton** is a professor in the College of Education at Oregon State University. Before moving to OSU, he was the University of Georgia (UGA) Athletic Association Professor of Education in the Department of Educational Theory and Practice (Middle Grades Education) at UGA. He also held faculty appointments at the University of New Orleans and the University of Miami. Before becoming a teacher educator and educational researcher, he was a Peace Corps volunteer in Guatemala and a middle school and high school science and ESOL teacher in New Orleans and Colorado. His research promotes more equitable science learning opportunities for all students and especially for emergent bilingual learners. His most recent work focuses on creating spaces where students, parents, teachers, and researchers can engage together as co-learners while strengthening their academic relationships, knowledge of science and engineering practices, and ownership of the language of science. His research has been funded by the National Science Foundation, the U.S. Department of Education, and several private foundations. He received his Ph.D. in science education at the University of Colorado Boulder.

**Kathryn Chval** is the Joanne H. Hook Dean's Chair in Educational Renewal, dean of the College of Education, and professor of mathematics education at the University of Missouri. Prior to joining the University of Missouri in 2003, she was the acting section head for the Teacher Professional Continuum Program in the Division of Elementary, Secondary and Informal Science at the National Science Foundation (NSF). She worked at the University of Illinois at Chicago from 1989–2001 after leaving her position as a 3rd-grade teacher. She has directed or co-directed research teams that received nearly $21 million in funding and was funded continuously by the NSF from 1995 to 2016. Additionally, she is the recipient of the NSF Early Career Award and the Association of Mathematics Teacher Educators (AMTE) Early Career Award. Her research focuses on effective preparation models and support structures for teachers, effective elementary mathematics teaching for English language learners, and curriculum standards and policies. She earned her Ph.D. at the University of Illinois at Chicago.

**Marta Civil** is a professor of mathematics education and the Roy F. Graesser Endowed Chair in the Department of Mathematics at the University of Arizona. Her research focuses on cultural, social, and language aspects in the teaching and learning of mathematics, linking in-school and out-of-school mathematics, and parental engagement in mathematics. She led several NSF-funded initiatives involving children, teachers, and parents, including Girls in the SYSTEM (Sustaining Youth in Science, Technology, Engineering and Mathematics), MAPPS (Math and Parent Partnerships in the Southwest), and CEMELA (Center for the Mathematics Education of

Latinos/as). She primarily teaches mathematics and mathematics education courses for preservice and practicing teachers and graduate courses on research in mathematics education. She received her Ph.D. in mathematics education from the University of Illinois at Urbana–Champaign.

**Christine Cunningham** is a vice president at the Museum of Science in Boston where she works to make engineering and science more relevant, accessible, and understandable, especially for underserved and underrepresented populations. As the founding director of Engineering is Elementary (EiE), she has developed engineering curricula for preschool through middle school students and professional development for their teachers. She previously served as director of the Tufts University Center for Engineering Educational Outreach, where her work focused on integrating engineering with science, technology, and math in professional development for K–12 teachers. She also directed the Women's Experiences in College Engineering (WECE) project, the first national, longitudinal, large-scale study of the factors that support young women pursuing engineering degrees. She is a fellow of the American Society for Engineering Education and has been recognized with the K–12 and Pre-College Division Lifetime Achievement Award. She also was awarded the 2014 International Society for Design and Development in Education Prize and the 2015 IEEE Pre-University Educator Award. She received her Ph.D. in science education, curriculum, and instruction from Cornell University.

**Kenne Dibner** is a program officer with the Board on Science Education. Prior to this position, she worked as a research associate at Policy Studies Associates, Inc., where she conducted evaluations of education policies and programs for government agencies, foundations, and school districts. Most recently, she concluded an evaluation of a partnership with the U.S. Department of Education, National Park Service, and Bureau of Indian Education to provide citizen science programming to tribal youth. Previously, she worked as a research consultant with the Center on Education Policy and served as a legal intern for the U.S. House of Representatives' Committee on Education and the Workforce. She has a Ph.D. in education policy from Michigan State University.

**Leslie Herrenkohl** is a professor of educational studies as the University of Michigan. Before moving to Michigan, she was the co-director of the 3DL Partnership and professor in the College of Education at the University of Washington. Her research seeks to understand the contextual and social features of learning environments and their impact on participants' learning and development. She has conducted research on children's school science learning in diverse urban settings across the United States, with many racial, ethnic, and linguistic groups represented. Her work investigates the pedagogical dilemmas that teachers face when engaging elementary and middle school students in scientific inquiry and the practices that the teachers developed to support students' learning around the most challenging aspects of inquiry. Through the 3DL Partnership, collaborations among researchers, local PreK–12 schools, youth organizations, and families provide innovative, community-based solutions to help young learners acquire skills, competencies, and resilience. She received her Ph.D. in developmental psychology from Clark University.

**Megan Hopkins** is an assistant professor of education studies at the University of California, San Diego (UCSD). Before joining UCSD, she held faculty appointments at The Pennsylvania State University and University of Illinois at Chicago. Her research explores how to organize schools and school systems for equity, particularly for English learners and immigrant students. Her current work uses mixed methods, including social network analysis, to examine how organizational structures, norms, and beliefs, influence policy implementation and teachers' professional learning in bi/multilingual contexts. Her research has been funded by the U.S. Department of Education's Office of English Language Acquisition, Spencer Foundation, and W.T. Grant Foundation. Her scholarship has appeared in journals that include *American Educational Research Journal, Educational Policy, Educational Researcher*, and *Journal of Teacher Education*. She is co-editor of *Forbidden Language: English Learners and Restrictive Language Policies* and *School Integration Matters: Research-Based Strategies to Advance Equity*. In 2012, she received the Dissertation of the Year Award from the Bilingual Education Research Special Interest Group of the American Educational Research Association. In 2016, she was selected as a National Academy of Education/Spencer Foundation Postdoctoral Fellow. She is also a member and fellow of the Working Group on ELL Policy. She received her Ph.D. in education at the University of California, Los Angeles.

**Margaret Kelly** is a senior program assistant for the Board on Children, Youth, and Families and the Board on Science Education at the National Academies of Science, Engineering, and Medicine. She has more than 20 years of experience working in the administrative field. She has worked for the private sector, federal government, and nonprofit organizations to include American University, Catholic University, the Census Bureau, International Franchise Association, the Department of Defense, and the University of the District of Columbia. She has received numerous professional honors and awards throughout her career.

**Okhee Lee** is a professor of childhood education at New York University Steinhardt and previously taught in the School of Education at the University of Miami. Her research areas include science education, language and culture, and teacher education. She is currently leading collaborate research to develop instructional materials aligned with the Next Generation Science Standards (NGSS) to support the language development of elementary students, including English learners. She is also leading collaborative research with MIT and Vanderbilt University to integrate computational thinking and modeling in NGSS-aligned instructional materials. She was a member of the writing team to develop the NGSS and leader for the NGSS Diversity and Equity Team through Achieve Inc. She was also a member of the Steering Committee for the Understanding Language Initiative at Stanford University. She was a 2009 fellow of the American Educational Research Association (AERA), received the Distinguished Career Award from the AERA Scholars of Color in Education in 2003, and was awarded a 1993–1995 National Academy of Education Spencer postdoctoral fellowship. She received her Ph.D. in educational psychology from Michigan State University.

**Suzanne Le Menestrel** is a senior program officer with the Board on Children, Youth, and Families at the National Academies of Sciences, Engineering, and Medicine, where her responsibilities have included directing three consensus studies focused on children and adolescents birth to age 18. Prior to her tenure with the National Academies, she was founding national program leader for youth development research at 4-H National Headquarters. Before that, she served as research director in the Academy for Educational Development's Center for Youth Development and Policy Research and was a research associate at Child Trends. She was a founder of the *Journal of Youth Development: Bridging Research and Practice* and chaired its publications committee. She has published in numerous refereed journals, sits on the editorial board of *Applied Developmental Science*, and is an invited member of a research advisory group for the American Camp Association. She received the 2012 Outstanding Leadership and Service to the Extension Evaluation Profession award from the American Evaluation Association. She holds a Ph.D. in human development and family studies from The Pennsylvania State University.

**Judit Moschkovich** is professor of mathematics education at the University of California at Santa Cruz. Her research uses sociocultural approaches to study mathematical thinking and learning, mathematical discourse, and language issues in mathematics education. Her research has focused on the transition from arithmetic to algebraic thinking, mathematical discourse, and learning/teaching mathematics in classrooms with students who are bilingual, Latino/a, and/or learning English. She was co-principal investigator for the Center for the Mathematics Education of Latinos/as (CEMELA) and is a founding partner of the Understanding Language initiative. She has served on the editorial panel for the *Journal for Research in Mathematics Education*, review board for the *Journal for the Learning Sciences*, and chair for the AERA SIG-Research in Mathematics Education. She served as co-editor of the *Canadian Journal for Science, Mathematics, and Technology Education* special issue "Equitable access to participation in mathematical discussions: Looking at students' discourse, experiences, and perspectives" and as member of the editorial panel for a special issue on equity of the *Journal for Research in Mathematics Education*. She currently serves on the editorial boards for the *Journal of the Learning Sciences, Cognition and Instruction*, and the *Journal of Mathematical Behavior*. She is a fellow of the American Education Research Association (AERA) and received a NAED/Spencer postdoctoral fellowship. She received her Ph.D. from the Department of Education in Mathematics, Science, and Technology (EMST) at the University of California, Berkeley.

**K. Renae Pullen** is a member of the National Academies Teacher Advisory Council. She has been an educator in Caddo Parish Public Schools, Louisiana, for more than 17 years. Currently, she is the K–6 science curriculum instructional specialist for Caddo Parish. She previously taught 3rd and 4th grades at Herndon Magnet and Riverside Elementary in Shreveport, and she has been an adjunct professor at Louisiana Technical University (teacher leadership) and Louisiana State University-Shreveport (elementary science methods). She has received numerous awards and honors including Walmart Local Teacher of the Year, Caddo Parish Elementary Teacher of the Year, a Fund for Teachers fellowship to study in Spain, a National Endowment for the Humanities fellowship to study the American skyscraper in Chicago, numerous grants to support science, technology, engineering, and mathematics (STEM) instruction, and the Presidential Award for Excellence in Science and Mathematics Teaching. She has served on local, state, and national committees and presented at numerous district, state, and national workshops and conferences. In 2011, she participated in the White House Champions of Change Event: Women & Girls in STEM. She has an M.Ed. in educational leadership from Louisiana State University in Shreveport, and she is certified as a Teacher Leader by the State of Louisiana.

**María Santos** is the co-chair and senior advisor for leadership at Understanding Language and director for school and district services in the Comprehensive School Assistance Program at WestEd. From 2010–2014, she served as deputy superintendent for instruction, leadership, and equity-in-action at the Oakland Unified School District and was named a 2014

"Leaders To Learn From" leader by *Education Week*. Until 2010, she was the senior instructional manager and superintendent for the Office of English Language Learners in the New York City Department of Education. Before going to New York City, she spent 20 years in the San Francisco Unified School District (SFUSD). As an associate superintendent, she supervised the development of major instructional improvement initiatives, such as SFUSD's Professional Development Initiative and gained SFUSD the recognition of an Exemplary Site by the U.S. Department of Education's National Award for Professional Development. She received her M.S. in educational administration from San Francisco State University.

**Mary Schleppegrell** is professor of education at the University of Michigan. A linguist, she uses systemic functional linguistics to explore meaning in language in ways that illuminate issues in education, with a focus on students for whom English is a second or additional language. Her recent Institute of Education Sciences-funded research with Annemarie Palincsar explored ways of supporting English learners in elementary school through use of metalanguage that brings a focus on meaning to discussion about language in the texts students read and write. She has investigated the linguistic challenges of learning in science, engineering, and mathematics classrooms for 20 years, with publications in *Environmental Education Research, Research in the Teaching of English, Reading and Writing Quarterly,* and *For the Learning of Mathematics,* as well as in numerous book chapters for researchers and teachers. Her books include *The Language of Schooling, Developing Advanced Literacy in First and Second Languages* (co-edited with Cecilia Colombi), *Reading in Secondary Content Areas* (with Zhihui Fang), and *Focus on Grammar and Meaning* (with Luciana de Oliveira). She received her Ph.D. in linguistics from Georgetown University.

**Guillermo Solano-Flores** is professor of education in the Stanford University Graduate School of Education. He specializes in educational assessment and the linguistic and cultural issues that are relevant to both international test comparisons and the testing of cultural and linguistic minorities. His research is based on the use of multidisciplinary approaches that use psychometrics, sociolinguistics, semiotics, and cognitive science in combination. He has conducted research on the development, translation, localization, and review of science and mathematics tests. He has been principal investigator in several NSF-funded projects that have examined the intersection of psychometrics, semiotics, and linguistics in testing. He is the author of the theory of test translation error, which addresses testing across cultures and languages. He has investigated the use of generalizability theory—a psychometric theory of measurement error—in the testing of English language learners and indigenous populations. Current research projects examine academic language and testing, formative assessment practices for culturally diverse science classrooms, and the design and use of illustrations in international test comparisons and in the testing of English language learners. He received his Ph.D. in education with an emphasis in methodology and measurement form the University of California, Santa Barbara.

**Amy Stephens** (*Study Director*) is a program officer for the Board on Science Education of the National Academies of Sciences, Engineering, and Medicine. She is also an adjunct professor for the Southern New Hampshire University Psychology Department, teaching graduate-level online courses in cognitive psychology and statistics. She was the study director for the workshop on *Graduate Training in the Social and Behavioral Sciences*. She has an extensive background in behavioral and functional neuroimaging techniques and has examined a variety of different populations spanning childhood through adulthood. She has worked at the Center for Talented Youth (CTY) on producing cognitive profiles of academically talented youth in an effort to develop alternative methods for identifying such students from underresourced populations. Additionally, she has explored the effects of spatial skill training on performance in math and science classes as well as overall retention rates within science, technology, engineering, and mathematics (STEM)-related fields for students entering the engineering program at Johns Hopkins University. She holds a Ph.D. in cognitive neuroscience from Johns Hopkins University.

**Heidi Schweingruber** is the director of the Board on Science Education at the National Academies of Science, Engineering, and Medicine. She has served as study director or co-study director for a wide range of studies, including those on revising national standards for K–12 science education, learning and teaching science in grades K–8, and mathematics learning in early childhood. She also co-authored two award-winning books for practitioners that translate findings of National Academies' reports for a broader audience, on using research in K–8 science classrooms and on information science education. Prior to joining the National Academies, she worked as a senior research associate at the Institute of Education Sciences in the U.S. Department of Education. She also previously served on the faculty of Rice University and as the director of research for the Rice University School Mathematics Project, an outreach program in K–12 mathematics education. She has a Ph.D. in psychology (developmental) and anthropology and a certificate in culture and cognition, both from the University of Michigan.

**Tiffany Taylor** is a research associate for the Board on Science Education at the National Academies of Sciences, Engineering, and Medicine. Prior to this position, she was a Christine Mirzayan Science and Technology Policy

Fellow at the National Academies. As a Mirzayan Fellow, she also worked with the Board on Science Education providing research support across various projects. In addition to her commitment to academic research, she is concerned about the legacy of science education and its inclusion of persons of diverse backgrounds. Throughout her graduate tenure, she tutored and mentored underserved youths to encourage their pursuit of studies and careers in STEM. As a member of the Graduate Student Association Lobby Corps, she advocated for state support to accommodate recruitment and retention of renowned faculty, and support for building infrastructure and maintenance. She received a doctorate degree in biomedical sciences from the University of California, San Diego.